Procopius on Soldiers and Military Institutions in the Sixth-Century Roman Empire

History of Warfare

Editors

Kelly DeVries (*Loyola University Maryland*)
John France (*University of Wales, Swansea*)
Paul Johstono (*The Citadel, South Carolina*)
Michael S. Neiberg (*United States Army War College, Pennsylvania*)
Frederick Schneid (*High Point University, North Carolina*)

VOLUME 134

The titles published in this series are listed at *brill.com/hw*

Procopius on Soldiers and Military Institutions in the Sixth-Century Roman Empire

By

Conor Whately

BRILL

LEIDEN | BOSTON

SSHRC IDG (Social Sciences and Humanities Research Council of Canada Insight Development Grant), 2016–2019.

Cover illustration: The Roman fort at Da'ajaniya in Jordan. © Photograph by Conor Whately.

Library of Congress Cataloging-in-Publication Data

Names: Whately, Conor, author.
Title: Procopius on soldiers and military institutions in the sixth-century Roman Empire / by Conor Whately.
Description: Leiden ; Boston : Brill, [2021] | Series: History of warfare, 1385–7827 ; 134 | Includes bibliographical references and index.
Identifiers: LCCN 2021011060 (print) | LCCN 2021011061 (ebook) | ISBN 9789004380448 (hardback) | ISBN 9789004461611 (ebook)
Subjects: LCSH: Procopius. | Byzantine Empire—History, Military—527–1081. | Byzantine Empire—History, Military—Historiography.
Classification: LCC DF543 .W43 2021 (print) | LCC DF543 (ebook) | DDC 355.009495/09021—dc23
LC record available at https://lccn.loc.gov/2021011060
LC ebook record available at https://lccn.loc.gov/2021011061

Typeface for the Latin, Greek, and Cyrillic scripts: "Brill". See and download: brill.com/brill-typeface.

ISSN 1385-7827
ISBN 978-90-04-38044-8 (hardback)
ISBN 978-90-04-46161-1 (e-book)

Copyright 2021 by Koninklijke Brill NV, Leiden, The Netherlands.
Koninklijke Brill NV incorporates the imprints Brill, Brill Nijhoff, Brill Hotei, Brill Schöningh, Brill Fink, Brill mentis, Vandenhoeck & Ruprecht, Böhlau Verlag and V&R Unipress.
All rights reserved. No part of this publication may be reproduced, translated, stored in a retrieval system, or transmitted in any form or by any means, electronic, mechanical, photocopying, recording or otherwise, without prior written permission from the publisher. Requests for re-use and/or translations must be addressed to Koninklijke Brill NV via brill.com or copyright.com.

This book is printed on acid-free paper and produced in a sustainable manner.

Contents

Preface IX
List of Tables and Maps XII

Introduction: Writing about War in the Sixth Century 1
  1 Procopius and War in the Sixth Century   1
  2 From Generals to Soldiers   3
  3 The Classicizing Straitjacket   4
  4 Methodology   8
  5 Book Organization   9

1 Generals and Soldiers   11
  1 Introduction   11
  2 Generals vs. Soldiers   11
    2.1 *Soldiers: Numbers*   11
    2.2 *Generals vs. Soldiers: Names*   18
  3 Conclusion   20
  4 Tables   20

2 Tracking Sixth-Century Soldiers   31
  1 Introduction   31
  2 Procopius' Authority   31
    2.1 *Procopius' Credentials*   31
    2.2 *Procopius' Use of Autopsy*   32
  3 Procopius' Sources   39
    3.1 *Oral Sources*   42
    3.2 *Documentary Evidence*   45
  4 Case Study: Looking for Documents at Dara   52
  5 Conclusion   56

3 Catalogues and Legions   58
  1 Introduction   58
  2 Terminology   60
    2.1 *The End of the Legion*   60
    2.2 *Arithmos*   61
  3 Procopius' Regiments   64
    3.1 Katalogos *in Procopius*   64
    3.2 Katalogos *in Antiquity*   65

      3.3   *Field Armies*   71
      3.4   *Count Marcellinus, Jordanes, John Malalas, and Agathias*   73
      3.5   *John Lydus and the Anastasius Edicts*   76
   4   Why Catalogues? The Wars of Generals   82
   5   Conclusion   84

4 Soldiers in the Field   95
   1   Introduction   95
   2   *Comitatenses*   95
      2.1   Katalogoi *and* stratiwtai   95
   3   *Foederati, symmachoi,* and *bucellarii*   108
   4   Horse Archers   117
      4.1   *Infantry vs. Cavalry*   117
      4.2   Hippotoxotai   120
      4.3   *Horse Archers: The Procopian Ideal and the Reality*   125
   5   Conclusion   131

5 *Limitanei* in the Age of Justinian   141
   1   Introduction   141
   2   Procopius on the End of the *limitanei* in the *Secret History*   141
      2.1   *Rome's Frontier Soldiers*   141
      2.2   *Procopius*   143
      2.3   Limitanei *in the* Wars *and* Buildings   145
      2.4   *Ambiguous Garrisons in the* Buildings   150
      2.5   Limitanei *in the* Wars   154
   3   Rome's Frontier Soldiers across the Empire in the Sixth Century   161
   4   Case Study: The *limitanei* in the Southeast   167
      4.1   *Frontier Soldiers in Action: Checking Barbarians*   173
   5   Conclusion   179

6 Recruitment   186
   1   Introduction   186
   2   Procopius on Recruitment   187
      2.1   *The Mechanics of Recruitment*   187
      2.2   *Volunteers and Conscripts*   194
      2.3   *Character Traits*   196
      2.4   *Origins of Recruits*   198
      2.5   *Recruitment Gaps*   203

3 Demographics 208
    3.1 *Recruitment and the Plague* 209
    3.2 *Recruitment and Corruption* 214
4 Conclusion 222

Conclusion 225

Appendix: Soldiers in Procopius' *Wars*, *Buildings*, **and** *Secret History* 231
Bibliography 259
Index Locorum 279
General Index 292

Preface

This book came to life through a long and torturous process, or so it seems. It began as the resurrection of my first book on Procopius, when it was on the verge of collapse. I had been convinced that the earlier book was mostly drivel, and in order to get something people might read out there, I decided I would have to shift to more traditional aspects of military history. Then, Elodie Turquois invited me to Oxford in January of 2014 for a conference she was co-organizing with Chris Lillington-Martin and Miranda Williams on Procopius: it was a godsend, and the collected presentations and assorted chitchat convinced me the initial project was worth saving. It later appeared as *Battles and Generals* (Brill 2016). This left the revised version in limbo. I planned to work on this beast—initially it was to be a complete study of Procopius the military historian—gradually, and I presented much of the chapter on Procopius' sources to some unwitting colleagues at the Universities of Manitoba and Winnipeg not long after. Then, a year or so later, the unthinkable happened: on the day Britain voted to leave the EU, SSHRC, the Social Sciences and Humanities Research Council of Canada, awarded me a two-year Insight Development Grant based on the revised Procopius project. And this came when my enthusiasm for all of my current research was at a spectacularly low ebb, perhaps not coincidentally after I had finally got the notice that I had received tenure. Given how much failure I had had, so much so that just days before I had lamented that I would never get a grant because of my interests (and had just been denied an institutional one), this was a complete and utter shock. That grant has now spawned a handful of publications, two of which have already appeared, my chapter on combat motivation in the sixth century and my chapter on the siege of Rome, while two other outputs are forthcoming, a journal article in the *Journal of Ancient History* on the late antique military revolution and a chapter on war and society in late Roman Arabia. Two more might not be far off, one on unit cohesion in late antiquity, the other on unit sizes in Procopius, though the latter is still up in the air.

The first draft of the manuscript was submitted to Brill at the end of 2019 when nobody, or almost nobody, had any idea what lurked around the corner. In mid-March, when Covid-19 was ramping up and I had received a host of rejections for other things (2020 was the year that keeps on giving), I received my first round of reviewer feedback for this book. It helped enormously, and I went off and revised the manuscript. Initially, I had thought it would take forever (months? years?), as the transition to distance education while my two young daughters were home proved difficult, to say the least. But when

Manitoba's esteemed provincial government started ramping up their rhetoric about budget cuts and the prospect of crushing financial hardship seemed inevitable, one of my primary means of "escape" turned out to be working ruthlessly and relentlessly on getting this book into better shape. Not surprisingly, given the devastating impact Covid has had on everyone, not least those who have lost their lives, in rejigging this book I incorporated some of the fantastic new research on the Justinianic plague in my wider discussion of military demographics. But I made other changes too, which I think have made the whole better, and I hope those one or two people who will read this book appreciate the effort I have put into it. After resubmission, I received another round of invaluable feedback, and I was, again, in debt to their efforts. Indeed, I cannot thank enough the two (possibly four?) anonymous reviewers who read this manuscript. I accepted just about all of your suggestions—just about. Obviously, there were a few places where I disagreed and stuck to my guns. I can honestly say, however, that the feedback I got throughout this process has been extremely useful, and as some past experiences have taught me this often is not the case. Thanks to my inability to say no and my foolhardy decision to undertake a wide and dizzying array of research projects, this has not been the smoothest of writing processes. If this book is any good, or at least not awful, a big reason is those reviewers.

I should add too that this book is something like book two in what has become a four-book enterprise. The first, *Battles and Generals*, focused on descriptions of battles in Procopius' *Wars* and the cultural framework that underpinned them. This, the second, as I alluded to above, focuses more on traditional aspects, like unit types and recruitment, though the central item of focus that serves as the core of the book is the rank-and-file soldier of the sixth century. While the *Wars* plays an important role in this book too, so too do the *Buildings* and *Secret History*, as well as much of the other varied and wonderful kinds of evidence, like sixth-century inscriptions, papyri, and law codes. The other two books that will round out this four-book collection are not yet finished (though they were supposed to be): one will look at the broader practice of describing battle in sixth-century historiography and beyond (and it might see the light of day in the next couple of years), while the other will focus more squarely on the *limitanei* that feature so much in this book. That books is some years off. When those four books are all done, they should put me in good stead to look at the wider impact of war on the Roman world at the end of antiquity.

Besides the four (two?) reviewers noted above, there are, undoubtedly, others I should thank for this book. Obviously, Hannah, Ella, Penny, and Don are, as always, wonderful. This awful pandemic would have been much worse without them. In fact, much more exciting than this book are the two books

Hannah was commissioned to write on math puzzles for kids in kindergarten and grade one, which will be read by far more people than this one. I am superexcited to see those in print in 2021. If you are reading this preface, you have small children, and you want some extra help with math, check out Hannah's amazing array of resources. Ella (6) and Penny (3) are a constant and consistent source of joy and happiness. They are truly wonderful, and I hope that the late nights for months on end as Hannah and I divided our time between our respective projects and the family mean that, in years to come, this pandemic will only be a relatively small part of their lives. As for Don, he is a legend, and has been such a good dog, those times he does a poo in the house aside. He is gentle, smart, and funny, and I could not imagine going on long walks without him. He and I spent a lot of time on weekly walks in Manitoba's fantastic provincial parks (hidden gems to those outside of Manitoba) while I was on leave in the fall of 2019. They were wonderful.

I should give a big shout out to colleagues in my university, province, and further afield who contributed in big and small ways to this book. Matt Gibbs deserves thanks for listening to me moan about how the book was going. Fraser and Darryl deserve thanks for indulging my cidery fantasies when things were bleak. Thanks to SSHRC for the money, which allowed me to do so much. Thanks to Mustafa, who served as my driver and guide on two trips to Jordan (an invaluable influence on this book). Indeed, Jordan is a magical place, and I am tempted to say that everyone should go visit, but I like the relative solitude you find on the fortifications of the *limes Arabicus* and so maybe not quite everyone. Only some of you. Thanks to my mom and dad for being wonderful companions on those two trips. I should also give thanks to the University of Winnipeg for granting me research leave in fall of 2019, and for continuing to employ from the summer of 2009 to today (December 9, 2020). I want to thank Marcella Mulder at Brill and the editorial board of the *History of Warfare* series for their support of this project, as well as all those at Brill who worked on this in some capacity or other. If I have missed anyone, I apologize.

I have had a few students (miraculously) express some interest in Procopius and military things. In fact, in one, glorious term I taught a fourth-year honours seminar on Procopius. Even though my students might only occasionally be exposed to Procopius, given how much time I spend in the classroom, even if the classroom these past several months has been a chair and table at home, I want to thank all of them for their contributions, big and small.

Tables and Maps

Tables

1.1	Roman soldiers (not officers)	20
1.2	Non-Roman soldiers (not officers) in Procopius	21
1.3	Bodyguards (Roman and non-Roman) in Procopius	21
1.4	Roman commanders and officers in Procopius	23
3.1	John Lydus' use of the term *katalogos*	78
3.2	*Katalogos* in the *Secret History*	85
3.3	*Katalogos* in the *Buildings*	85
3.4	*Katalogos* in the *Wars*	86
3.5	Roman troop numbers in Procopius' *Wars*	90
4.1	*Magistri Militum* in Procopius' works	132
4.2	Roman infantry in Procopius' *Wars*	135
4.3	Roman cavalry in Procopius' *Wars*	137
5.1	The garrison of the *Dux Arabiae* from the *Notitia Dignitatum*	146
5.2	Select southeastern frontier fortifications	171
5.3	Garrisons/guards (φρούριον or φρουρός) in Procopius' *Buildings*	181
5.4	Garrisons (φυλακή or φυλακτήριον) in Procopius' *Secret History and Buildings*	185

Map

1.1	Map of the Limes Arabicus Southeast of the Dead Sea	140

INTRODUCTION

Writing about War in the Sixth Century

1 Procopius and War in the Sixth Century

It is pretty hard to escape the pull of Procopius when it comes to the sixth-century East Roman Empire if the focus is military and political issues. That is part of the reason why scholars like Roger Scott have devoted so much attention to the other historians and sources like Malalas.[1] Scott's four pillars of the age of Justinian are: the construction of Hagia Sophia, the codification of Roman law, the closing of Plato's Academy in Athens, and Justinian's reconquest of the west. Three of those subjects are covered by Procopius' three works in some capacity or other, with Procopius devoting considerable attention to Hagia Sophia in the *Buildings*, aspects of the law in the *Secret History*, and the reconquest in all three, the *Wars*, *Buildings*, and *Secret History*. There is no doubt that Procopius' world, to follow Cameron, is a skewed one.[2] In this book, however, I would like to flip things around. To what degree do Procopius' interests in only a few facets of war, like battles and generals, obscure other pertinent military matters, the military's institutional features, and in turn cause us to overlook other important pieces of evidence?

To address this question, this book will focus on Procopius' treatment of the rank-and-file soldiers. In that light, while Kaegi's article on Procopius as a military historian has influenced my approach, so too has Foss' wide-ranging article on Theodora, in which he highlights what other sources have to say about the empress, and Cameron's pioneering book, in which she stressed the importance of considering all three of Procopius' works to get as balanced and complete a picture as possible.[3] Those studies that have highlighted the limitations of Procopius' war-writing, like Sarantis' definitive study of war in the Balkans or Rance's insightful paper on Procopius and Busta Gallorum, have also had an impact, as have those works that have tried to incorporate a wide variety of diverse material in their discussions, like Koehn's book on Justinian's war policy.[4] In many ways, then, this book will follow the tenor of much recent scholarship on Procopius and the military in the sixth century more generally.

---

1 Scott 2012.
2 Cameron 1985.
3 Kaegi 1990, Foss 2002, Cameron 1985.
4 Sarantis 2016, Rance 2005, Koehn 2018.

Indeed, the study of war and historiography in late antique and early Byzantine history, and the age of Justinian in particular, has come to the fore in recent years, especially with the publication of important works on regions like the Balkans,[5] broader topics like early Byzantine historiography,[6] detailed treatments of specific conflicts,[7] larger studies of war in the age of Justinian,[8] and papers on select aspects of Procopius' war writing.[9] The various categories of evidence are still often used in isolation, however, and the question of the relationship between Procopius, our most important source for war in the sixth century, and the reality, especially as we find it in the epigraphic, legal, material, and papyrological evidence remains unclear.[10] Some scholars of history and war in late antiquity have argued that research should concentrate on the literary evidence to the exclusion of other categories of evidence.[11] On the one hand, some scholarship on war and material culture has sought to uncover the inaccuracies and biases in that literary evidence,[12] and has shown how a focus on different kinds of evidence, like sword design, can ask different sorts of questions from those posed by our literary sources.[13]

For the sixth century, the most important single source is Procopius, and without an adequate analysis of Procopius' treatment of war and warfare in all three of his works (*Wars*, *Buildings*, *Secret History*) that evaluates his literary account in light of major categories of evidence, we undervalue Procopius' value as a military historian and overlook larger changes in the waging of war, which ultimately leads to a one-sided understanding of the impact of war at the end of antiquity.[14] This book will examine, and utilize, a broad range of evidence, including the textual, papyrological, documentary, and material. At its core, however, will be the three texts written by Procopius: *Wars*, *Buildings*, and *Secret History*. Procopius' works offer our most detailed set of evidence for the practice of war in the sixth century, and regardless of the quality of that information it deserves to be given due attention, and to be the focal point of any such study. The relationship between Procopius' three texts remains an item of

---

5   Sarantis 2016.
6   Treadgold 2007, Greatrex 2014a, 2014b, Stewart 2016.
7   Howard-Johnston 2010, Hoyland 2015.
8   Syvänne 2004, Parnell 2017, Heather 2018, Koehn 2018.
9   Rance 2005, Lillington and Turquois 2017), Greatrex and Janniard 2018.
10 Sarantis and Christie 2013: xvii.
11 Howard-Johnston 2013, Kouroumali 2013, Whitby 2013.
12 Colvin 2013, Lillington-Martin 2013, Sarantis 2016.
13 James 2011.
14 For an excellent, recent overview of the scholarship concerning many of the literary aspects of Procopius' oeuvre, see Stewart (2020: 31–67), and his wonderful nod (I believe) to Eminem.

scholarly debate, and despite some positive assessments, Procopius' status as a leading military historian of the pre-modern world requires further analysis. Whereas much research on the subject focuses on either Procopius' *Wars* or *Buildings*,[15] this book will consider those two texts and the *Secret History*, the historicity of which is still a subject of debate.[16]

The primary issue of this book is Procopius' historicity, at least with respect to the soldier. Although in many respects this book will be a study of military historiography in the sixth century, it will straddle the middle ground between historiography and history. In order to reach a satisfactory verdict, I will situate his accounts in their proper historical and evidential context.[17]

2   From Generals to Soldiers

Battles and Generals was a top-down account of the battles fought by the sixth-century Roman state, the commanders and generals who dominated the narrative of Procopius' *Wars*, Belisarius in particular, and their impact in shaping Procopius' writing. I argued that the *Wars* was carefully constructed, didactic in focus, and geared towards an audience comprising commanders and other members of the elite. In this book, I have decided to turn the tables and look at all three of Procopius' works, the *Wars*, *Secret History*, and *Buildings*, from the bottom-up, focusing on that large group of individuals who arguably played just as big a role in the outcome of the wars the Romans waged in the sixth century CE as the generals: the soldiers. Although they do not often the get same degree of attention as the generals in Procopius' oeuvre, they are there, and if you dig deep and pull back the classicizing rhetoric in Procopius' works, you can find valuable information about them. This book looks at what Procopius' three texts can tell us about the largest group within the sixth century military, a seemingly faceless horde to the elites like Procopius, whom recent scholars have been increasingly drawn towards. One of the first scholars to do so was Giorgio Ravegnani, who devoted an entire book to the Justinianic soldier.[18] More recently, Syvänne looked at the tactics and structure of the armies of the age of Justinian, and not without recourse to the role of individual soldiers; though ranging across late antiquity, Stewart examined the masculinity of Rome's military men; Parnell looked closely at the relationships between

15   Kaegi 1990, Sarantis 2013, Whitby 1986a, 1986b.
16   Brubaker 2004, Signes Codoñer 2000: 95–105.
17   Greatrex 2014a: 105; Sarantis 2016: 10.
18   Ravegnani 1998.

officers in the sixth-century Roman world, including those between commanders and their men; and Koehn has gone further, even arguing that Procopius' *Wars* betrays some of the hallmarks of Keegan's "face of battle" approach to narrative, which emphasizes a focus on the perspective of the rank and file soldiers.[19]

That reference to Keegan brings up the question of historiography. There has been quite a lot of research on the soldier's perspective in past research, including some work on the ancient Mediterranean, as I noted above. Keegan's pioneering approach on the experiences of rank and file soldiers ushered in a wave of works on the lower ranking soldiery. As he noted, most previous work had emphasized the collective images of soldiers, which led to misleading impressions and understandings of combat.[20] A decade later, its impact started to be felt in ancient Mediterranean history, with, first, work on classical Greece and then classical Rome.[21] Koehn's aforementioned study of Justinianic war policy is one of two treatments to give this issue any consideration for the sixth century, the other being Lenski's paper on Amida.[22] To some degree, in this book I will be touching on the soldiers' experiences, though also their role in sixth century military affairs more broadly as filtered through Procopius.

3 The Classicizing Straitjacket

As I have said and as we know, Procopius' interest was primarily on those in leadership positions, which poses significant challenges to this undertaking.[23] Although Procopius provides a wealth of detail on war, warfare, and military affairs in the sixth century, his classicizing approach means Procopius uses archaic vocabulary better suited to the military of Thucydides' day than his own. This applies to military matters too, and we get hints of this in the words he uses for divisions within the military. Decades ago, Cameron noted that his classicizing literary form produced a narrowing of approach.[24] She also argued

---

19 Syvänne 2004; Stewart 2016, Parnell 2016, Koehn 2018.
20 Keegan 1976: 35–37, 61.
21 Hanson 2000 (Greece—first edition in 1989); Goldsworthy 1996 (Rome). See too Gilliver (1999), Sabin (2000), and Daly (2002) for Rome. Lee's (2007) book on the soldiers of Xenophon's *Anabasis* ranges much more widely than battle. The same is true for many of the chapters in the section entitled "the Face of Battle in the Classical World" in Campbell and Tritle (2013). Kagan's (2006a) book on Ammianus and Caesar also deserves special consideration.
22 Koehn 2018; Lenski 2007.
23 Evans 1972: 75; Whately 2016a.
24 Cameron 1985: 17.

that the relative continuity in ancient warfare made it easier for him to apply this classicizing framework.[25] In keeping with this outlook, much of his terminology is vague: the men with general X, the infantry, the horsemen, etc. In other cases, his diction has occluded more than it has illuminated. He likes to use the word *katalogos*, for instance, a word rarely used by classical or even classicizing historians, when describing groups of soldiers (units or even regiments). Quite a few have taken this to mean that the term had a more technical meaning, and more specifically that it denoted the army's field units. It is not an unreasonable assumption if we assume that Procopius is mostly concerned with the field unit soldiers (at the expense of frontier soldiers) in his works. That the term *katalogos* features in virtually no other military source for the sixth century should give us pause, however, and as A H M Jones has noted, he is one of the only ones to have done so. If we did not have Procopius' *Wars'* narrative where he used words like *katalogos*, we would probably devote more attention to the words we do occasionally find in the inscriptions and papyri. The newly published inscription from Perge would receive more attention, and scholars would likely be much more interested in how we get from the regiments of the eastern section of the *Notitia Dignitatum* to the units of Maurice, with no unnecessary—even unhelpful—pauses to consider Procopius.[26] Indeed, it is interesting that Theophylact Simocatta can talk of legions on the eastern frontier around the same time that we find the word "legion" in Egyptian papyri, and just a few decades after the Anastasian inscription from Perge detailing the structure (it seems) of a legion.

Using Procopius to detail select minutiae of the sixth-century Roman military is no straightforward process. His language is often imprecise and overly general. It is fair to ask, however, whether this practice is peculiar to Procopius and his three texts, or whether it is in keeping with what we find elsewhere. The papyrological and epigraphic evidence frequently identifies regiments using the term *arithmos*, or unit/number, as we will see in chapter three below. On the other hand, that same material provides plenty of evidence for the ranks within the military. To give but a few examples, a *campidoctor* (drill master) is identified on an inscription from Lycaonia.[27] The Anastasius edict from Qasr el-Hallabat lists a handful of different ranks including *dux*, *primicerius*, and *draconarius*.[28] In an inscription from Rome dated to 547, we find a *primicerius*

---

25 Cameron 1985: 39.
26 Onur 2017.
27 *MAMA* 1.168.
28 *SEG* 31.1554, 3 (dux), 19 (primicerius), 36 (draconarius).

primi Th(e)odosianorum numeri.[29] And from Sardinia we find an *optio draconarius numero draconariorum Sardorum*.[30] There is none of this variety of rank nomenclature in Procopius.

Turning to combat, Maurice's *Strategikon*, taken on its own, might give the impression that cavalry played a major role in combat at the end of the sixth century. But it does not, on its own, explain how we got there from the infantry/cavalry divisions apparent in the *Notitia Dignitatum*. Our material evidence is limited—we do not have much in the way of combat equipment from for the sixth-century Roman military,[31] and whatever other evidence we have is ambiguous. If we had to rely on Pseudo-Joshua, we would not get far, his emphasis being much more on the impact of the war on its participants, both active and passive. Corippus' *Iohannis*, though quite detailed, is a panegyrical epic, and his combat scenes are vaguely Homeric and/or Vergilian: they involve single combats, and the dashing to and fro of soldiers into and out of battle. Agathias, on the other hand, does go to some lengths to describe the experience of combat even if he spends only a little time on the finer details. Indeed, for Koehn Agathias describes the transition between Procopius and Maurice.[32] In Agathias' most detailed battle, the Battle of Casilinum, there is little in his account that betrays a clear emphasis on either cavalry or infantry. That might help provide context for the anonymous treatise of political science which includes that fictional debate between Menas and Thomas on the relative merits of these two solitudes, infantry and cavalry, to borrow a Canadian literary-cum-historical phrase.[33] But whether cavalry had supplanted infantry would not yet be clear.

Another dominant feature of Procopius' account of sixth-century war and warfare is his emphasis on Belisarius, which has served to boost that general's reputation at the expense of many other notable commanders. Indeed, it is no great stretch to state that Belisarius' reputation rests solely on the literary efforts of Procopius. If we ignore Procopius, however, no mean feat, and look instead at the other material, like the epigraphic evidence, other figures feature much more prominently like Solomon, who published his successes in North Africa quite widely. Belisarius features in maybe a dozen Latin inscriptions, and a handful of Greek ones. Solomon, however, features in nearly three times as many Latin inscriptions from North Africa. On this limited evidence—and

---

29 *CIL* 11.1693.
30 AE 1990, 446 = AE 2002, 624.
31 Sarantis 2013: 172–174.
32 Koehn 2018: 132.
33 This is also the title of Hugh MacLennan's famous novel of the same name, *Two Solitudes* (1945).

if we had no Procopius—the impression might be that Solomon was the great general of the age, or at least the campaign.[34] Thanks to Agathias, Narses' reputation might rise too, and though the historian is not unflattering towards Belisarius, his account gives only the vaguest impression of the man's military accomplishments. Indeed, if all we had to go on were the many later references to Procopius' works, we would be left wondering what the scope of Belisarius' accomplishment truly was, and perhaps a little baffled by the comments of authors like the one who wrote the entry on Procopius in the *Suda*, or the later Byzantine historian Manasses.

In the *Secret History*, Procopius emphasizes the suffering of most of the empire's inhabitants, and the soldiers are no exception. One particular group that Procopius complains suffered a great deal were the border troops, who got into such a sorry state that they effectively stopped being soldiers. But if we forget about Procopius' comments here and in the other two texts, in which frontier troops feature hardly at all, and instead look at the surviving evidence we get quite a different picture. We have plenty of documentary evidence for frontier soldiers in Egypt and Israel/Palestine, and to a lesser degree Jordan. That material points to thriving frontier communities full of soldiers. Most seem fully integrated into local life, and if anything, the abundance of property documents, not to mention marriage certificates, point to some degree of wealth and prosperity amongst those very soldiers. So where are they getting their money? Have they managed to supplement their income through other means, as some has suggested was the case with the soldier from Aphrodito, Flavius Patermouthis, who also served as a boatman?[35] Or is their income derived primarily if not entirely from their state income?[36] If we did not have Procopius' comments, I suspect the argument would be that the frontier soldiers were flourishing, at least in the sixth-century southeast. The legal evidence, which is full of material concerned specifically with soldiers, would reinforce these sorts of arguments.

All this is to suggest that the survival of Procopius' long works has not only obfuscated our understanding of the wider world of sixth-century Byzantium, but also more specifically Byzantine military affairs. While his work has undoubtedly shed a great deal of light on matters like combat, in other instances, such as the careers of "lesser" generals like Solomon or the hardships of the frontier soldiers, what he has provided has obscured other important aspects of the empire's military history. A greater focus on these other kinds

---

34   On Solomon's high reputation in the sixth century, see Stewart (2020: 133–137).
35   See Whately 2015b: 296–297.
36   On soldier's pay in late antiquity, see Whately (2013a: 209–211), with references.

of evidence for sixth-century military affairs will bring much more about this period to light.

4 Methodology

How do we uncover more on the empire's rank and file soldiers when Procopius' works, such as they are, provide some significant challenges? One option is to look at what has been done for other authors. A particularly useful approach is focused on Xenophon's *Anabasis*, which is a history of Greek mercenaries in the employ of the would-be Persian king Cyrus the Younger. After making the long journey to Mesopotamia, they witness the utter failure of their employer, and are then forced to escape through some difficult country to make it back to Greece.[37] A key figure in the text is the aforementioned author, Xenophon, who plays a leading role in the Greeks' getaway. The tale is an exciting one, told in fairly straightforward Attic Greek.[38] With that said, the text is not without its problems. In chapter three of his insightful study of Xenophon's *Anabasis*, Flower explores the factual and fictional character of ancient historiography, and in particular the interplay between literary considerations and total accuracy.[39] One of the items of discussion is how Xenophon went about achieving balance between these seemingly incompatible concerns, for Xenophon's account, like those of other ancient historians, presented a rather complex problem: "what is the relationship between what actually took place, the context of remembering what took place, the motive for recording what one remembers, and the literary choices that shape that recording?"[40] Part of the discussion is focused on what Flower calls the truth status of the *Anabasis*, and in his estimation there are a number of ways of judging factual accuracy: "in terms of probability (does the story make sense?) and internal consistency (does the narrative contain contradictions within itself?) and by comparison with other extant accounts of the same events".[41] Procopius' three works pose similar challenges. Although Procopius, was no commander, he was in the service of another famous general, Belisarius, and like Xenophon was a participant in—or at least a witness to—much of the action that he described. That action involved Persians, squabbling generals, and an exciting journey across much of the Mediterranean, not to mention a good part of Mesopotamia. Thus,

---

37   See Rop (2019) on Greek mercenaries in the fourth century BCE.
38   On the use of the *Anabasis* to uncover details of the experience of the Cyreans, Xenophon and his fellow mercenary soldiers, see Lee (2007).
39   Flower 2012: 60–61.
40   Flower 2012: 62.
41   Flower 2012: 68.

it stands to reason that some of the ways we evaluate what actually happened in a text like Xenophon's *Anabasis* hold for Procopius.

This book will take Flower's points and apply them to Procopius, with a special focus on how they apply to the regular soldiers, the rank and file. This means considering what took place. As we will see, there were lots of rank and file soldiers who played a big role in sixth century combat, but he hardly mentions them. It is also a question of examining the context of remembering what took place, which in this instance means looking into how Procopius could get information about the soldiers, and what sort of record they would have left behind. Along those lines, I will also consider what his motive for recording them might have been. Afterall, and as I have already noted in *Battles and Generals*, the *Wars* in particular is all about generals, and as Parnell observed, Procopius has little to say on those rank and file soldiers.

5 Book Organization

In chapter one, I start off by examining the place of generals and soldiers in Procopius' three works. I begin by looking at generals and soldiers in terms of relative numbers. Procopius refers to soldiers several hundred times, but usually in the most general of ways. His naming practice echoes this, for generals are named while rank and file soldiers are not. This will allow me to outline the nature of the problem, how little he focuses specifically on rank and file soldiers.

Chapter two examines Procopius' experiences, authority, and research methods with a view to uncovering what Procopius could have known about the rank and file soldiers and how he could have known it. This means taking into consideration what sort of information existed about these rank and file soldiers in the sixth century, including that material which we no longer have. In this chapter, I examine Procopius' use of autopsy, and his use of both oral and documentary sources. Procopius travelled across the Mediterranean while Rome was at war, which meant he was able to witness some combat firsthand, and meet those who had themselves fought. Oral sources would have been an important tool in Procopius' repertoire, but so too would documentary sources. Documentary sources can be difficult to recreate—or, as I argue, produce in the first place, as what we know about the aftermath of combat indicates. I finish the chapter by using Dara as a case study to examine whether we can really find evidence of Procopius' varied sources in the narrative. Ultimately, I conclude that the results are mixed.

The third chapter focuses on the different ways that Procopius characterizes the sixth-century Roman military's regiments, with a particular focus on *katalogos*, in contrast to the Greek work *arithmos* (Latin *numerus*), the official word for unit/regiment. It turns out that *katalogos* does not mean what most people think it does. At the same time, Procopius' use of the word reflects his experiences and his subconscious or conscious minimizing of the role of the empires' rank and file soldiers. This close look at unit and regiment terminology brings Procopius' emphasis on the collective into even greater focus.

With the specific challenges that Procopius offers us set out in chapters one to three, in the second half I turn to the specifics, to determine what about the rank and file soldiers we can glean from Procopius' three works. In chapter four, I start with the particular group most often associated with them, the field army soldiers (*comitatenses*), as well as the *foederati* and *bucellarii*. In addition, I look at the outsized role of the horse archer in warfare, including its long history with the Roman military, and its limited use in Justinian's wars.

The penultimate chapter focuses on *limitanei*, who make a well-known appearance in the *Secret History*, but who also feature in the other two works. This particular component of the sixth-century military is usually left out of discussions of Procopius on war. Here I examine all the evidence he provides about them. The frontier soldiers are difficult to track down, but they are there, and they do seem to have played a role, despite Procopius' attempts to downplay their effectiveness. A closer look at the *limitanei* in one region, the empire's southeast, reveals that their role in sixth century military affairs was much more significant than Procopius lets on.

The final chapter turns to recruitment, where we can best see evidence of rank and file soldiers in action in Procopius' works. Their experiences come out of Procopius' references to recruitment campaigns across parts of the empire, especially in the context of the campaigns in Africa and Italy. Through careful reading, we can uncover in a little more than outline form the mechanics of recruitment. After this, I look at how Procopius' discussions of recruitment fit into larger issues, like the demographic challenges that arose in the context of the plague and which are reflected in some of Justinian's legislation.

CHAPTER 1

Generals and Soldiers

1   Introduction

This chapter lays the foundation of the rest of the book by highlight the dominant role of the generals in Procopius' works and the limited role of the rank-and-file soldiers. This might seem obvious: Procopius was an elite author who wrote for an elite audience. The *Wars* is a text about war, and the ones who made the big decisions in those wars were the empire's commanders. In fact, in *Battles and Generals* I argued that one of the *Wars*' primary aims was to provide instructional material for would-be generals.[1] But it is worth setting out just how prominent a place the commanders play in this narrative, for it will show how stark the contrast is between them and all those soldiers who did most of the work, the low-ranking grunts, the ones for whom John Keegan wrote his *Face of Battle*.[2] It is here that we must face the facts about the place of the rank and file soldiers in Procopius' works. In this short chapter, I look at the absolute numbers: I set out how many commanders (and officers in general) Procopius identifies, and how this contrasts with the rank and file soldiers.

2   Generals vs. Soldiers

2.1   *Soldiers: Numbers*

Let me start with the numbers. First, I will take a closer look at Procopius' approach to the common soldiery, as reflected in the many places that he identifies soldiers, in some capacity or other. In the course of this analysis, I will also set out some of the patterns that emerge when we look at all those places where Procopius uses the term "soldier", and what it means for how we evaluate Procopius as a military historian.

The appendix contains a list of each time that Procopius used the word soldier in his three works. At the most basic of levels, the starting point for ancient combat was the soldier, and on my reckoning there are 475 places in Procopius' three works where he refers to soldiers (στρατιώτης), in one way or another, mostly in the *Wars*. In most cases, Procopius uses soldier to indicate

---
1   Whately 2016a: 224–231.
2   Keegan 1976.

who is participating in a given battle, siege, or operation. The soldier, of course, is the most basic of participants. In other words, we expect them to be there. In a number of those cases, soldier is used to modify some other noun. For example, sometimes Procopius says something like "garrison of soldiers", in which Procopius uses soldier to specify what kind of garrison he is talking about, as he does at 1.24.44. But in nearly every instance Procopius refers to soldiers in the plural, as a collective. Of the 475, only 13 uses are in the singular.[3] Even then, of those thirteen uses, only three had to do with individual soldiers, only one of whom was named, a soldier named Burcentius.[4] This practice effectively eliminates their individuality.

And yet a soldier was not a soldier was not a soldier. True, some pieces of legislation indicate a major legal distinction was between soldiers and civilians, with soldiers usually tried in military courts, and civilians in civil ones, unless one of the parties involved was a soldier in which case the trial would take place in a military court.[5] In fact, even the law stipulated that there were different classes of soldier, who fought in different regiment types. There existed a legal definition of a soldier, found in the *Codex Justinianus*, which reads, "Therefore We order that all those who serve under arms, whether of greater or lesser rank—We call soldiers both those who are known to tolerate service under the high Master of Soldiers and those who are counted in the eleven most elevated corps (*scholae*), as well as those who have been decorated as allies under diverse officials (*optiones*)—in the future to refrain completely from every lease of property belonging to another".[6] By this definition, on the surface the *limitanei* would seem to be excluded, though as we will see in chapter five below, this is misleading.[7] Indeed, the many Justinianic-era laws on military affairs indicate that not all soldiers were treated the same, a detail that underscores the variety of different classes of soldier. One law, for example, makes a distinction between military police (*stationarii*) and urban soldiers (*urbanis militaribus*).[8] The point is, in the eyes of the law there was considerable variety.

---

3 Procop. *Wars* 1.13.30, 4.11.32, 4.17.32, 4.20.27, 5.18.4, 6.10.10, 6.26.5, 7.1.8, 8.12.17, 8.32.34, *SH* 5.30, 10.9, 24.29.
4 Procop. *Wars* 6.26.5.
5 *Cod. Iust.* 9.41.8pr.
6 *Cod. Iust.* 4.65.35, trans. Kehoe.
7 This is, in fact, what Kohen (2018: 44–47) argued. Given that *limitanei* were led by dukes (*duces*) and they in turn were led by *magistri militum*. So, though they are not named, *limitanei* are implied by this piece of legislation (I owe the clarification on this point to one of the anonymous referees).
8 *Cod. Iust.* 4.61.5.

So how do we figure out which kind of soldier Procopius is referring to? To distinguish between different types in Procopius' texts requires some careful reading, though even then certainty can be illusive. Procopius does often distinguish between infantry and cavalry soldiers, which helps, at least a little. If we can identify the commander of a group of soldiers, and know something about his position, we can then infer something of the kind of troops under his command. That Procopius regularly identifies commanders, which we will discuss further below, makes this easier. While Procopius might often name commanders, he usually does not give their rank, a tendency which complicates matters. Several entries in the *PLRE* do give the rank of commanders, but quite often their information is based solely on the information found in Procopius. Sinnion, the Hun leader, and Buzes, the Thracian commander, are two such examples.[9] Cases like Areobindus, Artabanes, and Conon, whose positions as *magistri militum* are given in other sources besides Procopius, are not as ubiquitous as we would like them to be.[10] On the other hand, a simple measure would be to identify all those soldiers attached to frontier fortresses as *limitanei*. The trouble is, our most detailed source for late antique regiments, the *Notitia Dignitatum*, does not give the garrison for the field army troops, and it dates to the early fifth century CE (broadly speaking). This means, in a lot of cases, we do not know where field army regiments were based. So, while it is tempting to see the garrisons of forts like these as frontier soldiers, it is possible they were field army soldiers.

If most of the soldiers identified by Procopius in the *Wars* are of one particular kind, then it would seem fair to consider all unclear soldiers as of that same type. If we look closer at the army that Procopius describes at the start of the Vandal expedition (*Wars* 3.11.1–21), there is no evidence for the presence of *limitanei* amongst the army's regiments. What we find, instead, is that the expeditionary army, composed of 10,000 infantry and 5,000 cavalry "from the soldiers" and the *foederati*, was composed of the following: Belisarius had 1,500 στρατιῶται with the commanders Rufinus, Aigan, Barbatus, and Pappus; 3,500 *foederati* under the command of Dorotheus, Solomon, Cyprian, Valerian, Martin, Althias, John, Marcellus; Cyril had 400 men; 1,000 allies (*symmachoi*) with 400 Heruls under Pharas and 600 Huns under Sinnion and Balas; over 2,000 *bucellarii* with 300 under John the Armenian and 800 under Uliaris, Boriades, Diogenes, and others unnamed. The subtotals that Procopius provides do not match the grant total; on the other hand, the specific details he provides (names of commanders and some numbers) do not allow for greater

---

9   *PLRE* Sinnion, p. 1156; Buzes, p. 254–255.
10 *PLRE* Areobindus 2, p. 108; Artabanes 2, p. 127–129; Conon 1, p. 331.

certainty on the army's composition. If this army comprises solely soldiers from the field armies and *foederati*, should we consider all references to soldiers in the *Vandal Wars* as of this type, unless otherwise specified? Procopius' language is unhelpful.

A better solution might be to come up with a Procopian definition of a soldier. The abundance of examples from the appendix gives us a lot of material to work with; but I will start with those cases that bring us closer to fully comprehending a "Procopian soldier". The first has to do with Andreas, the Roman bath attendant who gets involved in back-to-back single combats at the start of the Battle of Dara. After the first Persian warrior comes up face the Romans, Procopius says that the only one who came out to meet him was Andreas, who was "not a soldier nor one who ever practises war" (*Wars* 1.13.30). This could mean that a soldier need not be associated explicitly with war and combat, or that one need not be a soldier to practise war. The next case provides a bit of clarity. At 1.24.51, Procopius says, "when they saw the armoured soldiers" (στρατιώτας ... τεθωρακισμένους). This statement implies that not all soldiers involved in a battle like this were armoured.[11] In this case as in most others, it is not easy to pin down who Procopius means when he refers to these soldiers, though they could be the soldiers of Belisarius and Mundo, who had fought against Persia, some of whom were spearmen and shield bearers—more on those below. By this line of reasoning, the "armoured soldiers" would be more likely to be the spearmen or shield bearers of the two commanders, who often were better supported.[12] His comment at 2.19.13 that "some of our soldiers who are good fighters" (μαχίμων) is even more suggestive. But would this mean all the other soldiers would or at least could be poorly armoured, and maybe even mediocre fighters? A few books later, Procopius says "the garments that Roman soldiers are accustomed to wear" (4.23.23), which reveals that the soldiers were not always expected to be clad in armour—or at least certain ones were not.[13] In Totila's last battle, Procopius says he dressed "in the fashion of a simple soldier" (*Wars* 8.32.34). A Procopian soldier could either be an armoured bodyguard (maybe) or a more simply armoured, nondescript soldier of indeterminate type.

---

11 One of the issues I do not get into in this book is the specifics of the armour of Rome's soldiers, beyond some comments like those here. Beyond what Procopius has to say in the preface of the *Wars*, there are few other specific details in the rest of the text. Nevertheless, I intend to investigate the matter in greater depth in a future journal article.

12 See Breccia (2004: 73–77) and Rance (2007: 356).

13 This is what the limited evidence we have for the equipment of soldiers in the sixth century shows. Note, for instance, D'Amato's (2018) illuminating discussion, as well as Sarantis' (2013) overview.

Though non-combatants like Andreas could fight, Procopius also hints at the overall professionalism of the soldiers in his works. At 4.15.34, we read the following, which comes in a speech, "as soldiers you will be required to spend all your lives in the dangers of war". Later still we find, "began to fight in the front ranks like a soldier" (5.18.4). The training implied in those comments points to the long term process of becoming a soldier, which in part was designed to overcome some of the potential reticence of recruits, which we read about in the *Secret History*: "no one, either commander or soldier, cared to face the perils of war" (*SH* 5.30). Procopian soldiers were professionals.[14] This point aside (professionalism), a clear definition of a Procopian soldier remains elusive.

Another approach might be to look into those places where Procopius discusses the origins of soldiers. At 4.14.10 he says that the Roman Empire allowed some men to "both become and be called soldiers". Later we read about the Arborychi, who "had become soldiers of the Romans" (*Wars* 5.12.13). Later still, Procopius digresses to note that some of the Heruls had also become Roman soldiers (*Wars* 7.33.13). Soldiers could be Roman in origin, or they could be from somewhere else. But many of them came from specific places, and Procopius implies that recruitment was a matter of Roman commanders travelling through regions like Thrace and Illyricum and rounding up new recruits (*Wars* 7.12.4).[15]

Speaking of origins, we might get answers if we look more closely at Procopius' commanders. One issue of relevance for the third chapter, on catalogues and legions, is all those places where Procopius refers to a commander who leads soldiers in a certain geographic region. There are several examples: provinces/regions, "soldiers in Lebanon" (*Wars* 1.13.5, 2.8.2, 2.16.17), "soldiers in Mesopotamia" (*Wars* 1.17.39, 1.22.3, 2.24.12), "Soldiers in Palestine" (*Wars* 2.1.9), "among the soldiers in Libya" (*Wars* 4.14.7); cities/fortifications, "soldiers in Dara" (*Wars* 1.22.16), "the soldiers in Carthage" (*Wars* 4.16.9), "soldiers in Byzacium" (*Wars* 4.23.14), "the soldiers at Rome" (*Wars* 7.6.18), "soldiers in Byzantium" (*Wars* 1.8.2, 7.31.10); palace, "soldiers of the palace garrison" (*Wars* 1.24.47, 2.23.6), "soldiers of the court" (*Wars* 3.7.19); and "there", "soldiers who had been stationed there" (Beroia, *Wars* 2.7.7), "all the soldiers who were there" (Chalkis, *Wars* 2.12.1, 2.12.2), "the soldiers holding all the fortresses there" (Salones/Dalmatia, *Wars* 5.16.4), "the soldiers keeping guard there" (Toperus,

---

14   He does try to undermine this with respect to *limitanei* in the *Secret History*, a point to which I will return.

15   Koehn (2018: 96) argues that when Belisarius engages in his recruitment trips, he is mostly interested in barbarian federates.

Wars 7.38.11). And those are just the examples from the *Wars*. There are plenty more like this in the *Buildings*. In many ways, phrases like this epitomize Procopius' cavalier and opaque attitude to technical terminology. Are the soldiers frontier soldiers? Are they part of a detachment of field army soldiers based in the region? Without additional information, in most cases we are in the dark. Ultimately, a Procopian definition that includes the distinctions which existed escapes us.[16]

There is another central tenet of the "Procopian soldier" that lay behind the surface of all those entries in the appendix. With few exceptions, a soldier in Procopius' work was a Roman, not a Goth or a Vandal, Rome's two principal enemies in six of the eight books of the *Wars*. The Persians are the principal concession, and it seems to be that it comes down to where they fall in the Roman-barbarian spectrum, i.e., they were not barbarians, while the others most certainly were.[17] It is a different story for Goths and Vandals. When Totila takes over as king of the Goths, a pivotal point in the story in more ways than one, as others, like Stewart, have recognized, Gothic combatants start to be called soldiers.[18] In this part of the *Gothic Wars*, the Goths are more like Romans and less like barbarians, and it would seem that this is reflected in their soldiers.[19] When Gothic or Vandalic soldiers fight for Rome, they too earn this distinction, as some Vandals do at one point.[20] The only other cases are rare, and often involve speeches.[21]

Some have argued the στρατιῶται that Procopius regularly mentions were *comitatenses*, the field army soldiers.[22] Based on what I have discussed so far the answer seems to be no, but we can and should look deeper. The first time Procopius provides any clarification regarding the different categories of evidence, it comes early and has to do with soldiers in Constantinople (*Wars* 1.8.2). Given what we know about the kinds of soldiers based in the capital, it seems likely that the soldiers he has in mind were bodyguards. Besides those in the capital, there were also the private bodyguards, the spearmen and shield bearers who accompanied most of the generals and played a significant role in much of the combat. Were they soldiers? The armoured soldiers that Procopius

---

16 I owe part of this to one of the anonymous reviewers.
17 Procop. *Wars* 1.6.18, 1.14.1, 1.14.25, 1.18.52. 1.18.53, 1.23.25, 2.8.19, 2.8.33, 2.10.23, 2.18.8, 2.18.13, 2.21.20, 2.28.32, 8.12.17.
18 Procop. *Wars* 7.8.20, 7.21.4, 8.31.8, 8.32.2.
19 See Stewart 2016: 296–309.
20 Procop. *Wars* 2.21.3, 4.14.18.
21 Procop. *Wars* 4.7.20, 5.12.51, 5.29.16, 6.16.11.
22 Note Teall (1965: 296), Scharf (2001: 89), Evans (2005: 6), Parnell (2017: 16), and Koehn (2018: 20).

refers to 1.24.51 of the *Wars* that I noted above probably included these men. Later, of the 1,200 soldiers at 2.19.15, Procopius says "most of [them] were his spearmen". The only other case is Busta Gallorum at 8.31.3, when Procopius refers to "other soldiers", and here he includes Narses' spearmen and shield bearers. But that is it. Along the same lines, there are few occasions where he says that *foederati* were soldiers. Some of the 10,000 infantry and some of the 5,000 cavalry that go to Africa were *foederati* (*Wars* 3.11.2). In the early stages of the Gothic war, we find something similar, namely that some of the 5,000 soldiers were *foederati* (*Wars* 5.5.2). Later, in his brief discussion of the enlisting of Heruls in the Roman military, Procopius says that they were enrolled amongst the *foederati* (*Wars* 7.33.13). Finally, a book later some Goths are similarly noted as serving in the *foederati* (*Wars* 8.5.13), but they are the last ones so named.

None of the bodyguards or *foederati* are necessarily field army soldiers, *comitatenses*, or explicitly classified as such. A better place to look, then, might be among the soldiers categorized as either infantry or cavalry. Unfortunately, Procopius very rarely specifies whether a soldier is infantry. There are only four places where an infantry soldier or soldiers is/are implied, and they are vague enough as to provide no clear evidence for field army soldiers.[23] As for the cavalry, the situation is only a little better, for there are seven places.[24] As before, they too are vague. Thus, it is hard to discern where and when Procopius is referring specifically to field army soldiers, which are often seen to be one of the most common types of soldier in the conflict that Procopius describes.[25] Given that of the two common types, *comitatenses* and *limitanei*, it is only the latter that gets referred to in any of Procopius' works, we cannot say that Procopius means "field army soldier" when he uses a form of the word στρατιῶται, soldiers.

The takeaway from this section is that, despite some hints at what a soldier could and could not be in his texts, where Procopius does provide certainty, it is not in the fields where we would expect to find them. A soldier could be just about anyone under arms—or not. That said, a soldier was almost certainly Roman, and so not Goth or Vandal, save in exceptional circumstances. But it is also the case that any kind of individual fighting for Rome, a bodyguard, field army soldier, frontier soldier, or otherwise could be classified as such— with the proviso that στρατιώτης is the most general of ways to classify all these different types. But it is also clear that he very rarely names the rank and file soldiers.

---

23   Procop. *Wars* 1.26.5, 3.11.2, 4.20.12, 7.19.6.
24   Procop. *Wars* 3.11.2, 3.11.7, 5.17.17, 5.27.1, 6.5.1, 7.19.6, 7.19.25.
25   See Parnell (2017: 16), for example.

2.2 *Generals vs. Soldiers: Names*

Now that we have seen the numbers, let us turn to the names. How many officers and commanders does Procopius name, and how does this contrast with the rank and file soldiers? The data from the tables, found at the end of this chapter, though drawn ultimately from Procopius, comes from the work of Parnell. As we will see in chapter two, Parnell composed a detailed prosopography of Justinian's soldiers;[26] his names are drawn from the *PLRE* (hence numbers and names), though he also includes references from Procopius. The tables at the end of this chapter include all named soldiers who fought for Rome, whether Roman or non-Roman; this includes the bodyguards. Collectively, there are 227 soldiers identified, most of whom are named. Of those 156 are commanders of some rank or other, which works out to about two-thirds of the total (c. 68%). To be included on this list, an individual had to be in some sort of leadership position as specified by Procopius. In practice this meant they were likely to have been a *dux*, commander of a frontier army, or a *magister*, commander of a field army. As plenty have observed and as is standard practice in the genre, Procopius usually shies away from using technical vocabulary in his work, and he is no different in his treatment of those in charge.[27] As for those individuals in the tables whose rank I have included, it is there because it can be deduced from other material, whether that is a comment of Procopius' or some other evidence.[28]

What about the rank-and-file soldiers? From the list of twelve of what Parnell called Roman soldiers, only five are named. The other seven were not. The proportion of the other group, the non-Roman soldiers, is about the same, with only four of nine named. There are four unnamed Roman soldiers listed at 7.20.4, all Isaurians, who had been tasked with guarding the Asinarian Gate at Rome but who snuck out and made a deal with Totila. Similarly, Burcentius has several lines (6.26.3–26) devoted to him and for similar reasons: he acts treacherously by conveying messages to Vittigis behind the Romans' back. Not all of the soldiers were so identified because of treachery, however, for Ansilas was marked out for his actions in combat (8.29.22–28).

But it is also worth looking more closely at the bodyguards, for on the surface they seem to fall in a group somewhere between the officers and the rank and file soldiers. Scholars have long commented on the attention that Procopius plays to bodyguards, as we will see in chapter two below. Their

---

26   See Parnell (2012).
27   Elton (2007: 271), Turquois 2015.
28   For the most part, those named soldiers are identified in terms of the name used in the *PLRE* (almost always volume 3).

privileged position in relation to Belisarius afforded them a privileged position in the text. But their status above the ordinary soldier is beyond question, as Procopius' account of the exploits of Ansilas and Paul at 8.29.22 makes plain. Though both men performed extraordinary deeds, Paul's exceeded Ansilas'. When Paul's sword was bent from overexertion and so rendered useless, he grabbed the spears at hand and continued to wreak as much havoc on the Goths (8.29.26–27). As a result of these actions, Narses made him a bodyguard (shield bearer, 8.29.28), so elevating him above his comrade. As we will see in the next chapter, one of the other distinctive features of the bodyguards is the terminology that Procopius employs; he either calls them a spearman (*doryphoros*) or a shield bearer (*hypapistes*). While the two terms are used interchangeably in some contexts, we noted above that often the spearmen ranked higher than the shield bearers. Sometimes there are exceptions. At 5.16.1, early in the *Gothic War*, Procopius notes, "When he thought that his preparations were complete, he gave to Constantinus a large number of his own shield bearers together with many spearmen, including the Massagetae Zarter, Chorsomanus, and Aeschmanus, and an army besides, commanding him to go into Tuscany and win over the towns there."[29] In this case, the shield bearer would seem to be the bodyguards, and this is how translators like Dewing and Kaldellis have rendered *hypaspistai*. The spearmen, on the other hand, would seem to be something else—not bodyguards, as the term *doryphoros* is usually understood in other parts of the *Wars*. Indeed, as some have argued, the *doryphoroi* were, in fact, the elite private soldiers employed by generals like Belisarius, the *bucellarii*.[30] Greatrex has said that these troops, the *bucellarii*, were divided into the two groups, *doryphoroi* and *hypaspitai*, with the former group, the spearmen, used as leaders of regiments while the latter group, the shield men, used as bodyguards.[31] Ultimately, the same pattern applies to these types of soldiers, with only six of the fifty identified as individual shield bearers, and the remaining, with one exception whose position is not specified (and who is not named himself—see Table 3.3). This in itself would support the view that spearmen rank higher than shield bearers, and Procopius' tendency to give much more coverage to officers than rank-and-file soldiers.

Procopian soldiers were indeterminate fighters who could belong to any category in Procopius' works. They were many but they were faceless. This

---

29 Procop. *Wars* 5.16.1, trans. Kaldellis (slightly modified).
30 Parnell 2017: 59.
31 Greatrex 1998: 37. On *bucellarii* see Schmitt (1972). On *bucellarii* in Egypt, see Sarris (2006: 162–175).

pattern was replicated in microcosm among the bodyguards, with Procopius giving much more attention to spearmen than shield bearers.

3 Conclusion

In this chapter I have looked at the manifold ways that Procopius privileges commanders, generals particularly, over the course of his works, though the *Wars* especially. Regular, low-ranking, soldiers feature only as somewhat indeterminate masses, who are rarely named, let alone highlighted. The contrast with the generals could not be more marked, and Belisarius in particular shines above the rest. We have seen here plenty of concrete evidence that Procopius minimizes, to a significant degree, the amount of detail that he affords the regular soldiery. The next task is to determine if this was due to deficiencies in his research method, a lack of sources, or something else. In the remaining chapters, I will dig deeper to tease out some details on these rank and file soldiers from Procopius' works. Before I get there, however, I will investigate Procopius' sources.

4 Tables

TABLE 1.1 Roman soldiers (not officers)

Number	Name	Location
1	Burcentius	Wars 6.26.3–26
2	Gezon	Wars 4.20.12
3	Martinianus 1	Wars 7.23.1–7
4	Meligedius	Wars 8.33.10
5	Mindes	Wars 7.36.26
6	Unnamed	Wars 6.1.11
7	Unnamed	Wars 4.20.27
8	Unnamed	Wars 5.9.11
9	Unnamed	Wars 7.20.4
10	Unnamed	Wars 7.20.4
11	Unnamed	Wars 7.20.4
12	Unnamed	Wars 7.20.4

GENERALS AND SOLDIERS

TABLE 1.2 Non-Roman soldiers (not officers) in Procopius

Number	Name	Location
1.	Ansilas	Wars 8.29.22–28
2.	Artabanes	Wars 8.8.21
3.	Coccas	Wars 8.31.11
4.	Theudimund	Wars 7.1.36
5.	Unnamed	Wars 3.12.8
6.	Unnamed	Wars 3.12.8
7.	Unnamed	Wars 3.12.8
8.	Unnamed	Wars 6.23.36
9.	Unnamed	Wars 6.26.20

TABLE 1.3 Bodyguards (Roman and non-Roman) in Procopius

Number	Name	Location	Shield bearer/Spearman
1.	Anzalas	Wars 8.31.13	Spear
2.	Aquilinus	Wars 6.5.18	Shield
3.	Athenodorus	Wars 5.29.20	Spear
4.	Barbation	Wars 7.11.37; Wars 7.28.5	Spear
5.	Boriades	Wars 3.16.9	Spear
6.	Cutilas	Wars 6.2.10	Spear
7.	Diogenes	Wars 2.21.2; 3.23.5; 5.27.11; 6.5.9; 6.9.9; 7.36.1; 7.37.9	Spear
8.	George 2	Wars 5.29.20	Spear
9.	Gudilas	Wars 7.30.6–20	Spear
10.	John 12	Wars 4.5.6	Shield
11.	Maxentiolus	Wars 6.8.3	Shield
12.	Maxentius 1	Wars 5.18.14	Spear
13.	Maximinus 1	Wars 4.18.1, 4.18.18	Spear
14.	Paucaris	Wars 5.9.17	Shield
15.	Paulus 16	Wars 8.29.22–28	Shield
16.	Petrus 7	Wars 4.28.3	Spear
17.	Phocas 2	Wars 7.15.1–8	Spear
18.	Principius	Wars 5.28.23, 5.29.39	Spear
19.	Sabinianus	Wars 7.11.19; 7.11.34	Spear

TABLE 1.3 Bodyguards (Roman and non-Roman) in Procopius (*cont.*)

Number	Name	Location	Shield bearer /Spearman
20.	Senecius	Wars 1.21.27	Spear
21.	Stotzas	Wars 3.11.30; 4.15.1	Spear
22.	Tarmutus	Wars 5.28.23; 5.29.39	Spear
23.	Theodoriscus	Wars 5.29.20	Spear
24.	Trajan 1	Wars 2.19.15; 5.27.4; 6.4.6; 6.5.9; 6.5.24	Spear
25.	Ulimuth	Wars 6.13.14	Spear
26.	Adegis	Wars 6.7.27; 6.11.22	Spear
27.	Aeschmanus	Wars 5.16.1	Spear
28.	Argek	Wars 2.26.26	Spear
29.	Artasires 1	Wars 6.2.10; 7.11.37	Spear
30.	Artasires 2	Wars 4.27.10; 4.28.27–33	Spear
31.	Arzes	Wars 6.2.16	Shield
32.	Bochas	Wars 6.2.10; 6.24.32	Spear
33.	Chalazar	Wars 7.30.6,20	Spear
34.	Chorsamanus	Wars 5.16.1; 6.1.21	Spear
35.	Dagaris	Wars 1.15.6; 1.22.18	Spear
36.	Gouboulgoudou	Wars 6.13.14	Spear
37.	Indulf	Wars 7.35.23; 8.23.1; 8.35, 37	Spear
38.	Mundilas	Wars 5.27.11; 6.4.3; 6.10.19; 6.12.27	Spear
39.	Oilas	Wars 5.27.13	Spear
40.	Ricilas	Wars 7.11.19–25	Spear
41.	Sinthues	Wars 6.4.7	Spear
42.	Siphilas	Wars 5.7.34	Spear
43.	Suntas	Wars 6.7.27	Spear
44.	Thurimuth	Wars 7.11.10–19; 7.37.20; 7.39.5	Spear
45.	Uliaris	Wars 3.19.23; 4.4.15; 6.16.21; 6.21.1–13; 6.22.3	Spear
46.	Ulifus	Wars 7.12.19; 8.33.10	Spear
47.	Ulitheus	Wars 4.25.8; 4.26.33; 4.28.27–33	Spear
48.	Unigastus	Wars 6.27.14	Spear
49.	Unnamed	Wars 8.8.27	Not indicated
50.	Zarter	Wars 5.16.1	Spear

GENERALS AND SOLDIERS

TABLE 1.4 Roman commanders and officers in Procopius

Number	Name	Location	Rank, background
1.	Adolius	Wars 2.21.2, 2.24.13	Commander, Roman, Armenian
2.	Adonachus	Wars 2.12.2	Dux, Roman
3.	Alexander	Wars 6.5.1	Commander, Roman
4.	Althias	Wars 3.11.5–15, 4.13.14	Thracian, commander
5.	Apollinarius	Wars 4.5.7	Commander, Roman, Thracian
6.	Areobindus	Wars 4.24.1, 4.26.33	General, roman
7.	Arsaces	Wars 2.5.11	Commander, Roman, Armenian
8.	Artabazes	Wars 7.3.10, 7.4.29	Commander, Roman, Armenian
9.	Babas	Wars 8.9.5, 8.13.8	General (?), Roman, Thracian
10.	Barbatus	Wars 3.11.5–15, 4.15.50	Commander, Roman, Thracian
11.	Belisarius	Practically all the Wars	Supper general, Roman, Thracian
12.	Bonus	Wars 7.10.14	Roman, commander
13.	Buzes	Wars 1.13.5, 2.3.28, 2.20.20, 7.32.41, 7.34.40, SH 4.4	General, Roman, Thracian
14.	Calonymus	Wars 3.11.5–15, 3.20.24	Admiral, Roman, Alexandrian
15.	Claudian	Wars 7.35.27	General, Roman
16.	Conon	Wars 6.5.1, 7.6.2, 7.17.2, 7.30.7	General, Roman
17.	Constantianus 1	Wars 2.24.3, 2.27.2	General, Roman, Illyrian
18.	Constantianus 2	Wars 5.7.26, 5.16.1, 15, 6.30.2, .2.8, 7.3.4, 7.6.8, 7.32.41, 7.34.40, 7.40.34	General, Roman
19.	Constantinus	Wars 5.53, 5.16.1, 5.19.16, 6.1.4, 6.8.1–18	General, Roman, Thracian
20.	Coutzes	Wars 1.13.5	General, Roman, Thracian

TABLE 1.4 Roman commanders and officers in Procopius (cont.)

Number	Name	Location	Rank, background
21.	Cyril	Wars 1.13.21, 3.11.1, 3.24.19, 4.5.2, 4.15.50, SH 17.32	Commander, Roman, Thracian
22.	Cyrus	Wars 4.21.1, 4.21.16	General, Roman, Mesopotamian
23.	Damianus	Wars 6.7.26, 8.33.2	Officer, Roman, Thracian
24.	Demetrius 1	Wars 5.5.3, 6.23.2, 7.6.13	General, Roman
25.	Domentiolus	Wars 2.24.15, 7.39.3	Commander, Roman, Thracian
26.	Domnicus 2	Wars 4.16.1, 4.19.1, 6.29.1	Commander, Roman
27.	Dorotheus 1	Wars 1.13.21	Commander, Roman
28.	Dorotheus 2	Wars 1.15.3, 3.11.5–15, 3.14.14	General, Roman
29.	Ennes	Wars 5.5.3, 5.10.1, 6.12.27	Commander, Roman, Isaurian
30.	Florentius 1	Wars 1.15.15	Tribune maybe, Roman, Thracian
31.	Germanus 01	Wars 1.13.21	Officer, Roman
32.	Germanus 04 (02)	Wars 2.6.9, 4.15.1, 4.19.1, 7.37.24–26, 7.39.9, 7.40.6, 7.40.9	General, Roman
33.	Gilacius	Wars 7.26.24	General, Roman, Armenian
34.	Herodian	Wars 5.5.3, 5.14.1, 6.16.21, 7.1.1, 7.6.10, 7.12.14, 7.21.15–16	Commander, Roman
35.	Himerius 1	Wars 4.23.3	Dux, Roman, Thracian
36.	Himerius 2	Wars 7.37.20, 7.39.5	Commander, Roman
37.	Ildiger	Wars 4.8.24, 4.15.49, 4.17.6, 6.7.15, 7.1.1, 2.24.13	Commander, Roman, Germanic
38.	Innocentius	Wars 5.5.3, 5.17.17, 7.15.1–17	Commander, Roman
39.	Irenaeus	Wars 1.12.14–15, SH 29.16	General, Roman, Syrian
40.	John 002	Wars 1.17.44	Commander, Roman

GENERALS AND SOLDIERS 25

TABLE 1.4 Roman commanders and officers in Procopius (*cont.*)

Number	Name	Location	Rank, background
41.	John 014	Wars 3.17.1, 4.2.2, 4.4.15	Optio, Roman, Armenian
42.	John 015	Wars 3.11.5–15, 4.3.4	Commander, Roman, Thracian
43.	John 016	Wars 3.11.5–15, 4.3.4	Commander, Roman, Thracian
44.	John 020 Tzibus	Wars 2.15.9, 2.17.4	General, Roman
45.	John 027	Wars 4.19.1, 4.22.3, 4.24.6–14	Commander, Roman
46.	John 032	Wars 1.13.21, 2.19.36, 2.24.15	Commander, Roman
47.	John 036 Troglita	Wars 2.14.12, 4.17.6, 4.28.45, 8.17.20, 8.24.33	General, Roman, Thracian
48.	John 044 Guzes	Wars 2.30.4, 8.8.15, 8.8.38, 8.11.64	Commander, roman, Armenian
49.	John 046 Vitalian	Wars 6.5.1, 6.10.8–10, 6.21.23, 6.30.2, 7.6.8, 7.13.20, 6.26.1–14, 7.39.10, 8.23.7, 8.26.24	General, Roman
50.	John 064 the Glutton	Wars 2.19.15, 2.24.15, 6.23.3, 7.13.23, 7.40.34, 8.26.13, SH 4.4	Commander, Roman
51.	Joseph	Wars 4.15.7	Chartularius of excubitors, Roman
52.	Justinian 3	Wars 7.40.10, 8.25.1–11	General, Roman
53.	Justinus 02	Wars 6.13.17, 6.21.16, 6.23.2, 7.5.1–4, 7.13.19, 8.28.4	General, Roman
54.	Justinus 04	Wars 7.32.14–15, 7.40.34, 8.25.1–11	General, Roman, Thracian
55.	Justus 1	Wars 1.24.53. 2.20.20, 2.24.15, 2.28.1	Commander, Roman
56.	Lazarus 2	Wars 7.35.22	Commander, Roman
57.	Leonianus	Wars 8.27.13	General, Roman, Thracian
58.	Libelarius of Thrace	Wars 1.12.23	General, Roman

TABLE 1.4 Roman commanders and officers in Procopius (*cont.*)

Number	Name	Location	Rank, background
59.	Liberius	Wars 7.36.6, 7.37.26. 7.39.6, SH 27.17	Commander, Roman
60.	Longinus 1	Wars 1.18.7; 6.10.19	Commander, Isaurian
61.	Magnus	Wars 5.5.3, 5.10.1, 6.4.7, 6.28.1, 7.11.19	Commander, Roman
62.	Marcellus 1	Wars 1.13.21, 3.11.5–15, 4.15.50	Comes excubitorum, Roman
63.	Marcellus 2	Wars 1.25.24, 7.32.22, 7.23.48–51	General, Roman
64.	Marcellus 3	Wars 2.28.2	Dux, Roman
65.	Marcentius	Wars 4.27.5, 6.5.1	Commander, Roman, Thracian
66.	Marcian 1	Wars 3.11.5–15	General, roman, Thracian
67.	Martinus 2	Wars 1.21.27, 2.13.16, 2.24.13, 3.11.5–15, 4.14.39, 5.24.18, 6.21.13, 7.1.1, 8.17.12, SH 4.13	Commander, Roman, Illyrian
68.	Nazares	Wars 7.11.18, 7.40.34	Commander, Roman
69.	Odonachus	Wars 8.9.5, 8.13.8	Commander, Roman
70.	Palladius 2	Wars 8.24.24	Commander, Roman, Thracian
71.	Pappus	Wars 3.11.5–15, 4.3.4	Commander, Roman
72.	Paulus 01	Wars 5.5.3, 5.23.2	General, Roman
73.	Paulus 02	War 6.5.1, 6.7.16	Commander, Roman
74.	Paulus 07	Wars 6.12.27	Officer, Roman, Cilician
75.	Paulus 13	Wars 7.36.16	Commander, Roman
76.	Petrus 02	Wars 1.18.6	Dux, Roman, Thracian
77.	Rhecithancus	Wars 2.16.17, 2.30.29, 8.27.13	Commander, Roman, Thracian
78.	Rufinus 1	Wars 3.11.5–15, 4.10.3–11	Commander, Roman, Egyptian
79.	Sarapis	Wars 3.11.5–15, 4.15.50	General, Roman
80.	Scholasticus 1	Wars 7.40.34	General, Roman, Mesopotamian

GENERALS AND SOLDIERS

TABLE 1.4   Roman commanders and officers in Procopius (*cont.*)

Number	Name	Location	Rank, background
81.	Sergius 04	Wars 4.21.1, 4.22.1, 4.24.16, 7.27.2, SH 5.28–33	Commander, Roman, Phoenician
82.	Severianus	Wars 4.23.6	General, Roman, Mesopotamian
83.	Solomon 1	Wars 3.11.5–15, 3.24.19, 4.8.23, 4.11.47, 4.19.1, 4.21.28	Commander, Roman, Mesopotamian
84.	Solomon 2	Wars 4.21.19, 4.22.12ff, SH 5.33–38	Commander, Roman, Isaurian
85.	Stephanicus	Wars 1.18.7	Dux, Roman, Palestine
86.	Summus	Wars 2.1.9	Commander, Roman, Thracian
87.	Terentius	Wars 3.11.5–15, 4.15.50	General, Roman
88.	Theoctistus 1	Wars 2.8.2, 2.24.13	Commander, Roman, Thracian
89.	Theodorus 006 Cteanus	Wars 3.11.5–15	Commander, Roman, Cappadocian
90.	Theodorus 008 the Cappadocian	Wars 4.8.24, 4.14.32, 4.15.6, 4.15.49, 4.17.6	Comes excubitorum, Roman
91.	Theodorus 009	Wars 4.12.17, 4.14.35	General, Roman, Armenian
92.	Thomas 2 Guzes	Wars 2.30.4–5	Dux, Roman
93.	Timostratus	Wars 1.17.44	Commander, Roman
94.	Ursicinus	Wars 5.5.3, 5.23.3	Commander, Roman
95.	Valentinus 1	Wars 5.53, 5.28.16, 7.10.6, 7.15.8	General, roman, Thracian
96.	Valerian 1	Wars 2.14.8, 3.11.5–15, 4.14.40, 5.24.18, 7.1.1, 8.23.4, 7.27.3, 8.33.2	Commander, Roman, Thracian
97.	Venilus	Wars 8.9.5	General, Roman
98.	Vitalius 1	Wars 6.22.7, 6.28.2, 7.1.34, 7.10.2, 7.11.11	Commander, Roman
99.	Zeno 2	Wars 6.5.2, 6.7.13	Phylarch, Arab, Ghassanid
100.	Abocharabus	Wars 1.19.8–13	Commander, Massagetae

TABLE 1.4 Roman commanders and officers in Procopius (*cont.*)

Number	Name	Location	Rank, background
101.	Aigan	Wars 1.13.20, 3.11.5–15, 4.3.4, 4.10.3–11	Commander, Herulian
102.	Aluith	Wars 6.13.18, 6.22.8	General, Gothic
103.	Amalafridas	Wars 8.25.11–15	Officer, Germanic
104.	Anonymous 69	Wars 2.29.40	General, Persarmenian
105.	Aratius	Wars 1.12.21, 6.1317, 7.34.40, 7.40.34, 8.19.3, 8.25.11, 8.27.13	Phylarch, Arab, Ghassanid
106.	Arethas 2	Wars 1.17.47, 1.18.7, 2.16.5, 8.11.10, SH 2.23.28	Commander, Germanic
107.	Arimuth	Wars 8.27.13	Commander, Herulian
108.	Artabanes 2	Wars 4.24.2, 4.27.9, 4.28.27–33, 7.31.10, 7.39.8, 8.24.1, 8.25.24	Commander, Herulian
109.	Arufus	Wars 7.26.24	Commander, Germanic
110.	Aruth	Wars 8.26.13	Commander, Gepid
111.	Asbadus 1	Wars 7.38.4–6	Commander, Massagetae
112.	Asbadus 2	Wars 8.26.13, 8.32.22	Commander, Massagetae
113.	Ascan	Wars 1.13.21, 1.18.38	General, Herulian
114.	Balas	Wars 3.11.5–15	General, goth, Thracian
115.	Beros/Verus	Wars 2.24.14, 7.27.3, 7.37.28	Officer, Persian
116.	Bessas	Wars 1.8.3,	Commander, Persian
117.	Bleschames	Wars 7.3.11	Phylarch, Arab, Kindite
118.	Cabades	Wars 1.23.12–14, 8.26.13	General, barbarian
119.	Caisus	Wars 1.20.10	General, moor
120.	Chilbudius	Wars 7.14.2	General, Germanic
121.	Cutzinas	Wars 2.28.50, 8.17.21	Commander, Herulian
122.	Dagisthaeus 2	Wars 2.29.10, 8.8.1–16, 8.9.4, 8.26.13, 8.33.24	General, Germanic
123.	Gontharis 1	Wars 6.4.8	Commander, Persarmenian

GENERALS AND SOLDIERS

TABLE 1.4 Roman commanders and officers in Procopius (*cont.*)

Number	Name	Location	Rank, background
124.	Gontharis 2	Wars 4.19.6–9, 4.25.1, 4.26.33, 4.28.27–33	Commander, Lombard
125.	Gregorius	Wars 4.27.10	Dux, Persarmenian
126.	Ildisgal	Wars 8.27.1–6	Persarmenian
127.	Isaac	Wars 1.15.32, 2.24.14, 7.13.20, 7.19.29–34	Commander, Lazian
128.	John 34	Wars 4.24.2–16	General, Gepid
129.	Leontius 2	Wars 4.19.1. 4.20.19	Dux, barbarian
130.	Mauricius 1	Wars 5.7.2	General, Gepid
131.	Molatzes	Wars 2.8.2	General, Persarmenian
132.	Mundus	Wars 1.24.43, 5.5.2, 5.7.5	Commander, Persarmenian
133.	Narses 1	Wars 1.15.31, 6.13.16, 7.13.21, 8.21.6, 19, 8.26.13, 8.33.1, 8.35.33	Commander, Hun
134.	Narses 2	Wars 1.12.21, 2.24.12, 2.25.23, 6.13.17	Commander, Iberian
135.	Odalgan	Wars 7.23.6–7	General, Iberian
136.	Pacurius	Wars 7.27.2, 8.26.4	General, Persian
137.	Peranius	Wars 2.24.15, 2.28.1, 2.24.15, 5.5.3, 5.23.13, 6.19.1, 2.28.1	Commander, Herulian
138.	Petrus 1	Wars 1.12.9, 2.16.16, 2.24.13, SH 4.4	Officer, Herulian
139.	Phanitheus	Wars 6.13.18, 6.19.20	Commander, Iberian
140.	Pharas	Wars 1.13.20, 3.11.5–15, 4.4.28–31	Commander, Gepid
141.	Phazas	Wars 7.6.10, 7.28.5	General, Herulian
142.	Philegagus	Wars 8.8.15	General, Lazian
143.	Philemouth	Wars 2.24.14, 6.22.8, 7.13.21, 7.34.42, 7.39.10, 8.26.13	Dux, Massagetae
144.	Rufinus 2	Wars 4.19.1, 4.20.19	Commander, Massagetae
145.	Simmas	Wars 1.13.21	Commander, Gothic
146.	Sinnion	Wars 3.11.5–15, 8.19.7	General, Gothic
147.	Sisifridus	Wars 7.12.12	General, Herulian

TABLE 1.4   Roman commanders and officers in Procopius (*cont.*)

Number	Name	Location	Rank, background
148.	Sittas 1	Wars 1.12.20, 1.15.3, 2.3.25–27, B 3.6.6	Commander, Massagetae
149.	Suartuas	Wars 8.25.11	Commander, Germanic
150.	Sunicas	Wars 1.13.20, 1.14.50	Commander, Herulian
151.	Tattimuth	Wars 3.10.23, 4.5.10	Officer, Massagetae
152.	Uligagus	Wars 8.9.5	Commander, Persarmenian
153.	Unnamed	Wars 3.18.13	Commander, Herulian
154.	Varazes 1	War 7.27.3, 8.13.10	Commander, Arab
155.	Visandus	Wars 6.13.18, 7.1.35	Commander, Roman, Armenian
156.	Zaidus	Wars 3.11.5–15	Dux, Roman

CHAPTER 2

Tracking Sixth-Century Soldiers

1   Introduction

The purpose of this second chapter is to set out whether Procopius was in a position to learn about rank-and-file soldiers, and what role the sources might have played in his attention to these men. Although some scholars have expressed their reservations, if indirectly, about the value of an emphasis on Procopius' sources, the subject's very prevalence in Procopian scholarship demands attention.[1] Indeed, you could make a case that an important part of the process of examining the usefulness of Procopius for understanding sixth century military history is assessing his reliability, especially vis-à-vis his sources, a point raised by Flower.[2] In this chapter, I tackle Procopius' sources and their relationship to "what actually happened" in the *Wars*, though the *Secret History* and *Buildings* too, especially when it comes to his writing on soldiers. Topics that I will cover include literary concerns like Procopius' authority, and historical concerns, like his use of oral sources and documentary sources.

2   Procopius' Authority[3]

2.1 *Procopius' Credentials*

I begin with Procopius' authority as an historian, and the criteria by which he and the majority of his peers might have judged him, at least in terms of his reliability.[4] Following tradition, Procopius crafted a preface to his *Wars* with a character that would be familiar to Herodotus, Thucydides, and most other classical and classicizing historians. Therein he states his name, where he is from, and he identifies the subject of his text. Procopius then gives his credentials for engaging in such an enterprise, noting that he became an assessor, effectively Belisarius' secretary, and that he was present for nearly everything that he described.[5] This is followed by his truth claim: truth is the most

---

1 Kaldellis 2014: ix.
2 Flower 2012.
3 The standard treatment on authority in classical historiography is Marincola (1997).
4 Not the comments of Kaldellis (2017).
5 Procop. *Wars* 1.1.3, σχεδόν τι ἅπασι παραγενέσθαι τοῖς πεπραγμένοις ξυνέπεσε.

important part of history in his eyes,[6] which is the sort of attitude we find in the prefaces to other works in the classical tradition.[7]

One of the problems Procopius faced, however, was that he lived in what was, in many respects, an unfree society.[8] For Marincola, this left historians like Procopius with three choices, two of which are pertinent here: he could claim a close relationship with the main character of his history while indicating to the audience that he had privileged access, something which left him liable to charges of bias or favouritism; and he could compose an account of military campaigns in which he had served.[9] Procopius did both: he wrote a history of the wars of Justinian, and he served as assessor of Belisarius, the age's most famous general. At the same time Procopius seems to have been well aware of the potential charges of bias, and countered them by noting: "In accordance with this principle he has not concealed the failures of even his most intimate acquaintances, but has written down with complete accuracy everything which befell those concerned, whether it happened to be done well or ill by them".[10] If we still doubted his truthfulness, he returned to the issue shortly thereafter.[11] In his own eyes then, and likely those of many of his readers, Procopius met his potential critics face on and argued forcefully for his authority as historian. We are, then, meant to expect some factual reporting on Procopius' part, and as an historian he is to be trusted.

2.2 *Procopius' Use of Autopsy*[12]

While Procopius includes many of the stock phrases that are part of an historian's attempts at establishing his authority,[13] what Procopius does not do is

---

6   Procop. *Wars* 1.1.4.
7   On prefaces in ancient historiography, see Earl (1972).
8   On this issue and late antique historiography, see Kaldellis (2017).
9   Marincola 1997: 89.
10 Procop. *Wars* 1.1.5: ταὐτά τοι οὐδέ του τῶν οἱ ἐς ἄγαν ἐπιτηδείων τὰ μοχθηρὰ ἀπεκρύψατο, ἀλλὰ τὰ πᾶσι ξυνενεχθέντα ἕκαστα ἀκριβολογούμενος ξυνεγράψατο, εἴτε εὖ εἴτε πῃ ἄλλῃ αὐτοῖς εἰργάσθαι ξυνέβη.
11 Procop. *Wars* 1.1.6.
12 On this topic, note especially, the insight discussion of Ross (2018). In this chapter, I will focus specifically on autopsy and authority as it pertains to military affairs (admittedly, a central component of classical and classicizing historiography).
13 These include statements about the importance of the subject matter, their value to later generations (and the contemporary audience), explicit statements about the competency of the author, and, among other things, what qualified the historian to write such a work. Historians also make methodological statements or allude to their practices. Procopius says he would not conceal the failures of those he knew best, and he wrote down accurately everything that happened to them—it is, after all, a character-driven text (*Wars*).

provide us with anything like Thucydides' famed methodological statements.[14] Instead, to get at the same kinds of materials, we need to dig deeper. The familiar, classicizing form of his preface and the rest of the text imply that we can expect Procopius' writing practices to have been a lot like other writers operating in the classical tradition. For many an ancient historian autopsy was the most important item in his toolkit, and, as we have just seen, Procopius claims to have seen much of what he describes.[15] Still, it is worth asking: how much did Procopius actually see and are there any hints in the *Wars* about Procopius' expertise for the task at hand, writing a military history?

Beginning with his documented movements, Procopius enters history in 527 CE when he was appointed assessor, or secretary, of Belisarius.[16] Thereafter, Procopius seems to have accompanied Belisarius on his campaigns in the east against the Persians between 527 and 531, before ending up in the capital, presumably, along with the general in 532.[17] Our historian was off on campaign against the Vandals in 533 as part of the mission to reclaim North Africa. In 535 Procopius went to Italy as part of the expeditionary force charged with unseating the ruling Ostrogoths.[18] He would remain there for a few years, before returning to Constantinople, possibly in 538, and then, perhaps, back to the east to face the Persians with Belisarius in 541 and 542. After that, most scholars now assume that Procopius spent the rest of his days in the capital.[19]

Besides being present at much of the action he describes, can we find of any evidence of his direct involvement in military matters? Before we take a look at specific episodes in which Procopius featured, a disclaimer. We are, for better or worse, at the whim of the predilections of our historian and his constructed persona, for we have virtually nothing in the way of independent evidence for Procopius' activities.

Some of Procopius' interventions betray little evidence of expertise in military matters. For example, Procopius' digressions on siege machines are suspect and betray little familiarity with how they worked, as Turquois has shown us.[20] On the other hand, there are various points where Procopius the narrator intervenes to indicate that he had visited a particular place. In the midst of a digression on Orestes he claims that he had seen parts of Armenia

---

14 Thuc. 1.22.1.
15 See Ross (2018: 77). cf. Börm 2007: 53.
16 Procop. *Wars* 1.12.24. This discussion is drawn from Whately (2016a), which in turn follows the generally accepted adventures in Procopius' life.
17 Procop. *Wars* 1.24.1–58.
18 Procop. *Wars* 5.11.3; 6.23.23–28; 6.29.32.
19 Note the comments of Cameron (1985: 13), for example, and Treadgold (2007: 184).
20 Turquois 2015. See too Kelso (2003).

and Cappadocia.[21] Other episodes reveal more about his mindset regarding significant military operations. For example, with the African campaign looming, our historian intervenes to let us know how he was feeling about the whole enterprise, claiming that he was terrified to go until a dream allayed some of his fears.[22] There are less dramatic incidents too, such as Procopius' alleged witnessing of a baby suckled by a goat with the appropriate name of Aigisthus.[23] Procopius' expertise also seems to have been extended to the sensible interpreting of omens.[24]

Yet, there are places where Procopius plays a significant role in military affairs. With the African invasion in full swing, Belisarius sends Procopius to Sicily to collect information.[25] While there, Procopius runs into an old friend in Syracuse involved in the shipping business, and finds out some useful information, namely that the Vandals were not planning an ambush, because they were occupied elsewhere.[26] There are other places where Procopius ends up collecting intelligence for the Roman military in Africa,[27] and Belisarius even praises him, at times, for his actions.[28] The last couple of references to Procopius' movements have to do with his movements, both with and without Belisarius.[29] Shifting to Italy, we find Procopius taking on something of a leadership role, a fact which might suggest that Belisarius had decided to increase Procopius' purview. Belisarius sends him to Naples to investigate rumours that Justinian had sent along an army and possibly some supplies, including grain. In addition, he is to organize the collection of men and materials and get them to Ostia, so that they could be sent on to Rome.[30] Although the episode lacks the drama and excitement of Ammianus' escape from Amida, Procopius does go into considerable detail about his exploits and experiences.[31]

One of Procopius' most detailed interventions, and the last noteworthy one, in the *Wars*, centres on some communication problems that the Roman forces experienced at Auximum, modern Osimo, in the course of the war. It

---

21 Procop. *Wars* 1.17.17.
22 Procop. *Wars* 3.12.3.
23 Procop. *Wars* 6.17.10.
24 Procop. *Wars* 3.15.35.
25 Procop. *Wars* 3.14.3–6.
26 Procop. *Wars* 3.14.7.
27 Procop. *Wars* 3.14.11–13.
28 Procop. *Wars* 3.14.15.
29 Procop. *Wars* 4.14.39, 4.14.41.
30 Procop. *Wars* 6.4.1–2.
31 Procop. *Wars* 6.4.3–4, 6.4.19. On Ammianus and Amida, note the comments of Ross (2017: 163–164). On the trouble with an historian's authority, especially as it relates to Ammianus, see Kelly (2008: 31–158).

turns out that the Romans were having trouble communicating over the vast distances that served as the location for the operation: there was quite a lot of shouting, but barbarian (i.e. Gothic) counter-yelling and banging of equipment was drowning it out.[32] The Romans' saviour manifested itself in the form of Procopius, who piped up in the midst of a meeting and offered a solution, presented in the form of a dialogue with Belisarius, which draws on Procopius' knowledge of the past—he refers, for instance, to "the Roman army in ancient times".[33] He argues in favour of trumpets that emit different tunes for different commands: one that urged soldiers on and out into battle, and another that summoned them back.[34] Procopius also refers to different trumpets for different divisions within the military, cavalry and infantry.[35] We cannot be certain where Procopius' knowledge comes from, though there are a number of late antique, even sixth century, texts which cover similar material.[36]

Just as we can see some of Procopius' interests and movements over the long term, we can also chart them over the short term, which can give us a better sense of how his experiences impacted his writing. One particularly detailed scene that allows us to see what impact Procopius' physical presence had in influencing what he wrote is the siege of Rome in 537/538 CE. In the chapter from which this discussion hails, I looked at aspects of Procopius' account that stood out, and argued that Procopius was able to blend an accurate account of aspects of siege warfare with the attendant literary considerations incumbent upon a classicizing historian.[37] The two facets I examined were his use of numbers and his graphic wounding and death scenes.[38] Although we may not have much of the materiel of the siege, we know something of the city's

---

32 Procop. *Wars* 6.23.23ff.
33 Procop. *Wars* 6.23.23.
34 Procop. *Wars* 6.23.23.
35 Procop. *Wars* 6.23.24–28.
36 Vegetius, for instance, who spends a good amount of time in his mid-fifth century *Epitoma Rei Militaris* on some vague ancient legion (Veg. *Mil.* 2.4.1ff—"*legiones antiqui*"), does get into the use of trumpets, bugles, and the like (Veg. *Mil.* 3.5.6–8). Maurice too, in his late sixth century *Strategikon*, refers to the use of trumpets (Maur. *Strat.* 2.13), though from the perspective of Procopius his text is hardly ancient. There is one other text worth noting, the anonymous *Dialogue on Political Science*, where we find another reference to the value of the trumpet in warfare (4.12). It could be that the anonymous author and Procopius were drawing on the same text or at least the same tradition. Given the author's focus on infantry versus cavalry and Procopius' philosophical leanings, is there any chance that the anonymous author of the dialogue and Procopius were one and the same? Perhaps not, but it would be interesting to find out.
37 Whately 2019: 275–278.
38 Whately 2019: 266–274.

fortifications, such as they were, in the sixth century.[39] The siege is also sufficiently detailed to allow us to deduce where Procopius, the person, was, generally speaking, for part of the siege. By considering the state of the walls and Procopius' movements, we then glean some idea whether Procopius was able to see what happened through personal observation or through interaction with those in the vicinity.

As I said above, for a number of years Procopius served as the famous commander Belisarius' assessor, and played an active role in many of the wars that he describes.[40] In that capacity, Procopius was with Belisarius in Rome in the months leading up to the siege and throughout most of its course. According to the *Liber Pontificalis* (147–148), Belisarius arrived in Rome around the 10th of December, 536, and Witigis arrived outside the city with his army on the 21st of February, 537. By most accounts, the siege lasted the better part of a year,[41] only breaking up in the spring of 538.[42] At some point in the fall of 537, Procopius was sent off to Naples to gather the men and supplies that had arrived from the emperor.[43] Procopius does not say when he returned, though he notes that once his reinforcements and some others had been collected in Campania, they set off immediately for Rome.[44] It is quite possible that Procopius was among those who returned to the city with Antonina and a host of provisions around the winter solstice in 537.[45]

We know roughly when Procopius was in Rome. We also have a good idea where he spent most of his time while in the city. When Procopius set out the defensive allocations of the Romans' forces along the city walls, the historian said that Belisarius took the Pinciana Gate and the Salarian Gate.[46] Given that Procopius worked for Belisarius, it seems likely he spent much of his time with the commander, or at least in the general vicinity. Over the course of the narrative, a significant proportion of the action takes place round those two gates. Indeed, the first detailed account of a gruesome death comes at the Salarian

---

39 By materiel, I mean weapons we can date conclusively to the conflict, whether larger items like swords or small ones like arrowheads, or any other small finds usually associated with conflict. We also lack bodies and physical evidence of destruction. On the connection between small finds and conflict in the ancient Mediterranean world, see Ball (2016).
40 See Howard-Johnston (2000: 23) and Ross (2017).
41 Jord. *Rom.* 373–374, *Get.* 60.312, *Liber Pontificalis* 148.
42 Procop. *Wars* 6.2.38.
43 Procop. *Wars* 6.4.1. He was later joined by Antonina, Belisarius' wife (6.4.20).
44 Procop. *Wars* 6.5.2.
45 Procop. *Wars* 6.7.12–15.
46 Procop. *Wars* 5.19.14.

Gate.[47] A chapter later we get our next such death, and it too takes place in the neighbourhood of that gate.[48] According to Procopius, one of the most significant raids also takes place at the Salarian Gate, the one which led to around 30,000 dead Goths.[49] In fact, many of the most detailed encounters take place in the vicinity of said gate, including a later charge led by the spearman Trajan.[50] One odd such case is the incident of the Roman Peranius and the Goth, who fell and got trapped down the same hole. This too took place near the Salarian Gate.[51] Many of the detailed accounts that do not take place round the Salarian Gate, take place round the Pinciana Gate, the other part of Rome's walls under Belisarius' command.[52] There is the miraculous tale of Chorsamantis, who was wounded in his left leg, was rendered unfit for battle, got drunk, sought revenge for his leg, snuck out the Pinciana Gate, and was eventually killed, though not before killing some Goths.[53] Not much later we read of Belisarius' dispatch of 600 from the gate, who get involved in a skirmish while employing steppe-style pursuit and withdraw tactics, after which a more general engagement breaks out.[54] In this battle, Koutilas is struck in the head with a javelin, and Arzes between the nose and right eye.[55] When Procopius returns to the action of the siege, after a pause for discussion of the impact of disease and some medical treatment, he returns to the Pinciana Gate. Trajan and Diogenes are sent through this gate. In the skirmish that ensues is the incident with the visually striking Goth, whom Mundilas kills.[56] During this engagement, one of Belisarius' guardsman, Aquilinus, charged into the enemy camp before joining his comrades round the Pinciana Gate.[57] There is little doubt that much of the most detailed episodes involved action around or leading from the Salarian and Pincian gates.

Procopius was in Rome and close to most of the action, but was it ever possible for him to see the action? The landscape might have muddled his view; Lillington-Martin argues that "Belisarius' view, towards the bridge from the Pincian-Salarian Gate section of the wall, was obstructed by the hilly landscape, as was his view to the Salarian Bridge (which crosses the Anio, where

---

47   Procop. *Wars* 5.22.4–5.
48   Procop. *Wars* 5.23.9–12.
49   Procop. *Wars* 5.23.24–27.
50   Procop. *Wars* 5.27.6.
51   Procop. *Wars* 6.1.11–19.
52   Procop. *Wars* 6.1.20.
53   Procop. *Wars* 6.1.26–34.
54   Procop. *Wars* 6.2.9–13. On these tactics, see, for instance, Janniard (2015).
55   Procop. *Wars* 6.2.14–15.
56   Procop. *Wars* 6.5.14–16.
57   Procop. *Wars* 6.5.18–20.

it is approximately 30 m wide)".[58] As for Rome itself, nineteen kilometres of walls surrounded the city, and there was a covered walkway through some of the walls,[59] with an average height of about eight metres and were closed off by a metre-high crenellated parapet.[60] The initial Aurelianic height of the walls was extended, possibly during the reign of Honorius, in some cases upwards of twenty metres high.[61] Every thirty metres there was a tower. The towers usually had five windows, with two at the front and one on each side (including the back), which would have been large enough to use artillery.[62] According to the ninth-century anonymous *Einsiedlensis*, a travelogue for pilgrims, at that time Rome had 383 towers. If we assume that total is not far off the sixth-century total, even if the Romans only manned half of the wall, that makes for close to 190 towers that could be manned by artillery.[63]

While Procopius describes the machines, he does not give any indication how many were employed; he was more interested in their operations and specifics.[64] Petersen maintains that the Romans kept military engineers in the sixth century, some of whom were used in the Gothic War.[65] Indeed, in his account Procopius says that men—he does not specify how many—would stand on each side of a ballista,[66] though he does not specify how many would stand round the onagers.[67] We know that military engineers were active in the siege; we just do not know how many.[68] They might well have clogged all possible vantage points from the walls during the siege, and it is unlikely Procopius could have shared space during the action with the military engineers even if he had permission to do so. Nevertheless, the comparatively low numbers of the Roman defenders suggest they did not have artillery for every vantage point. Given the height of the walls was not prohibitive, it is possible Procopius might have had many opportunities to see the action firsthand.

Even if Procopius did not see everything, his personal access to Belisarius means he likely had access to those closest to the commander.[69] Procopius

---

58 Lillington-Martin 2013: 620.
59 Carafa 2017: 86.
60 Carafa 2017: 86.
61 Dey 2011: 13; Carafa 2017: 87.
62 Dey 2011: 27–28; Carafa 2017: 86.
63 If there were towers every 30m, along 19000m of wall that would make for between 500 and 600 towers. That makes the 190 tower-estimate a low one.
64 Procop. *Wars.* 5.21.14–22. Cf. Petersen (2013: 273).
65 Petersen 2013: 116–119.
66 Procop. *Wars.* 5.21.17.
67 Procop. *Wars.* 5.21.18.
68 Procop. *Wars* 5.27.6.
69 Note the comments of Rance (2005: 452).

was also personally involved in a number of matters during the war including, potentially, communications with the emperor, and the collection and organization of reinforcements and supplies, at least in some instances. If the historian spent much of his time around Belisarius, which seems likely in the course of the nearly year-long siege, it would make sense for him to have been in the vicinity of the Salarian and Pincian gates. This would seem to be reflected in the focus of much of the narrative. What we have, then, is an account that tends to focus on those details about which Procopius would have been able to learn a great deal. He does not provide nearly as detailed accounts of actions around the other gates of the city, and he keeps his Gothic numbers to a minimum. In other words, Procopius was in a good position to know certain things, and those are the things that he describes, at least when it comes to the 537/538 siege of Rome.

So ends our survey of the character of Procopius' experiences in the *Wars*. What, if anything, does this tell us about Procopius' expertise, and the value of his own autopsy? On the surface not a lot. At one of a number of sieges, and not an important one, he suggested, as noted above, the use of trumpets.[70] On the other hand, Procopius seems to have witnessed a great deal of the action, and though he was not a soldier, per se, he did have a hand in adjacent activities like logistics, particularly during the reconquest. What is more, I have left out all those activities that he did not write about, and I have not covered Procopius' direct and indirect interventions—those spots in the text where, as narrator, he intervenes to comment on military matters. Ultimately, Procopius provides only modest evidence in support of the quality of his autopsy, but not in insufficient quantities for him to be dismissed outright. Autopsy goes a long way towards understanding and evaluating Procopius' writing. But as we well know, there were events for which Procopius could not get firsthand access, or even others for which his experiences were limited. How did Procopius overcome these limitations?

3   Procopius' Sources

Moving beyond Procopius' own credentials for writing history we turn to his sources, the oral and the documentary, to try to uncover what they tell us about his accuracy. Unfortunately, classicizing historians usually do not identify their sources, which is in stark contrast to many of Procopius' late antique peers,

---

70   Cf. Petersen 2013: 514–515.

like Malalas and Evagrius.[71] This makes an evaluation of their value a difficult task. The frequency with which his sources are mentioned in studies that rely on Procopius necessitates some sort of discussion, however.[72]

To focus on just one of his three works, there are plenty of anecdotes in the *Wars* that give us some idea of what sources he used. On a few occasions there are hints at his use of reports of some kind or other, especially in book seven, which is after Belisarius' return to Italy.[73] For instance, there are a number of references to military rosters or rolls, though more on this in chapter three.[74] In other places Procopius alludes to what he knew about the past, as at 1.18.3 when he says that this was the first time anyone had invaded Roman territory from Commagene (in 531 CE). In another place, Procopius describes al-Harith's account of the *strata Diocletiana* and Roman ownership of that tract of land. In this instance, al-Harith even says that he relied on the testimony of the most ancient men.[75] But there are also plenty of references to writing itself and the use of documents in the *Wars*. At 2.3.14, while in the midst of Roman relations with the Armenians, Sittas, the chief Roman representative, is described as being asked to put into writing his claim that a particular branch of the Armenians would be safe from persecution if they went over to the Roman side. Sittas agrees, writes his promises down, seals the document, then sends it off. Two books later, while describing the commander Germanus' arrival in Carthage, Procopius says the following: "When they sailed into Carthage, Germanus counted the soldiers whom they had and, upon looking over the books of the secretaries where the names of all the soldiers were registered, he found that a third of the army was in Carthage and the other cities while all the rest were arrayed with the tyrant against the Romans."[76] Procopius even provides clues in the text, on occasion, that he has evaluated, carefully, disparate or conflicting accounts of particular events before taking his own position, as he does with a story about Theodohad's lack of preparations for the war in Italy.[77] Even more noticeable in this regard is his geographical digression on

---

71 Evagrius, for instance, used Procopius as a source (*HE* 5.25). Note Malalas' (18.8–10) comments on the use of rescripts and more besides.
72 Note the comments of Treadgold (2007: 215–217).
73 Procop. *Wars* 7.13.19, 7.14.21, 7.19.23.
74 Procop. *SH* 24.1ff.
75 Procop. *Wars* 2.1.7.
76 Procop. *Wars* 4.16.3, trans. Kaldellis. ἐπειδή τε ἐς Καρχηδόνα κατέπλευσαν, τούς τε παρόντας σφίσι στρατιώτας ὁ Γερμανὸς ἠρίθμει καὶ τῶν γραμματέων ἀναλεγόμενος τὰ βιβλία οὗ πάντα ἀναγέγραπται τῶν στρατιωτῶν τὰ ὀνόματα, εὕρισκε τὸ μὲν τριτημόριον τοῦ στρατοῦ ἔν τε Καρχηδόνι καὶ ταῖς ἄλλαις πόλεσιν ἄν, τοὺς δὲ ἄλλους ἅπαντας τῷ τυράννῳ ἐπὶ Ῥωμαίους ξυντεταγμένους.
77 Procop. *Wars* 5.9.2.

the relationship between the Black Sea and the Sea of Azov, which is found in the most Herodotean part of the work, book eight.[78]

Perhaps the most obvious clues that Procopius provides about his research methods is his use of the phrase "they say". This very phrase, "they say", had a well-established classical pedigree—it is not specific to Procopius.[79] In this case, when describing the siege of Amida, Procopius includes the following comment, "they say that no one escaped from there, although Patricius and Hypatius had succeeded in getting away at the beginning of the charge."[80] The phrase "they say" could be understood as evidence that Procopius is referring to his sources. It would be tempting to understand it as Procopius using oral sources, though it could just as easily refer to documentary ones too. Procopius uses the phrase at least 88 times in the *Wars*.[81] Of those 88 instances, many of the cases are unlikely to involve discussion with oral informants, given the location and timing.[82] For example, when Procopius says "they say" at 1.17.11 when he refers to the sanctuary of Artemis-in-Tauris, he is almost certainly referring to Euripides.[83] Some cases might refer to conversations that Procopius had with relevant individuals.[84] Some of them are ambiguous, and could be the

---

78 Procop. *Wars* 8.6.16–31. This part of the passage is the most suggestive of Procopius' entire digression: "At this point I will also mention the fact that some experts in these matters think that the Sea of Azov creates the Black Sea, and that the latter flows out from the former partly to the right and partly to the left, this being the reason why the Sea of Azov is called the mother of the Black Sea. [17] They make this statement on the basis of the observation that from the place called Hieron the outlet of the Black Sea flows down toward Byzantium just as if it were a river, and consequently they consider this to be the limit of that sea. [18] But those who oppose this view explain that the entire sea is, of course, one, coming from the Ocean and, without any other ending, extends to the land of the Lazi, unless, they say, anyone considers the mere change of name to constitute a real difference, seeing as it is simply called the Black Sea after a certain point. [19] But if the current does flow down from the place called Hieron to Byzantium, this is irrelevant. Phenomena exhibited in all straits appear to be inexplicable, nor has anyone ever been able to account for them." (trans. Kaldellis).

79 Note the comments of Woodman (1988: 16–17) and Marincola (1997: 121).

80 Procop. *Wars* 1.18.9. trans. Kaldellis (slightly revised).

81 The 88 uses often involve a form of λέγω. The first instance (1.4.14), for example, uses the masculine, nominative, plural participle form, λέγοντες. But they also involve a form of φημί, with the second case (1.4.16) using φασι, the third plural, present, indicative, active.

82 Procop. *Wars* 1.4.14, 1.4.16, 1.4.20, 1.4.21, 1.4.22, 1.4.39, 1.8.4, 1.8.19, 1.17.11, 1.17.13, 1.17.19, 2.12.26, 3.2.25, 3.2.26, 3.2.27, 3.3.32, 3.4.5, 3.4.30, 3.4.30, 3.4.35, 3.5.5, 3.5.24, 3.6.1, 3.6.2, 3.6.4, 3.6.14, 3.7.10, 3.7.10, 3.8.18, 5.1.25, 5.11.2, 5.12.2, 5.24.30, 6.4.28, 6.25.18, 7.18.19, 7.27.17, 8.2.2, 8.2.16, 8.3.5, 8.3.10, 8.5.7, 8.5.23, 8.6.2, 8.6.3, 8.6.18, 8.6.24, 8.29.4.

83 Procop. *Wars* 1.17.11. Kaldellis 2014 (translation of Procopius' *Wars*): 42, n. 83.

84 Procop. *Wars* 1.25.25, 2.8.35, 2.9.10, 2.12.32, 2.12.33, 3.21.21, 4.24.13, 5.9.2, 5.9.6, 5.9.7, 5.16.20, 5.16.20, 5.16.21, 6.20.30, 7.12.16, 8.11.8, 8.15.25, 8.20.9, 8.32.32, 8.32.34.

result of conversations Procopius had with those involved with the events, or they might be based on his reading of any available documentary materials.[85] Then there are those that are something else entirely—they might be included as a *topos* to lend weight to the claims of a character, as seems to have been the case when al-Mundhir gives a long speech to Kavadh.[86]

Although Procopius tends to hold the traditional line by not divulging too much about his sources, there are plenty of places where he provides clues about his research methods. And so, after looking at those Procopian anecdotes, let us look closer at one of the principal bodies of sources, the oral sources.[87]

3.1 Oral Sources

In the ancient historiography hierarchy, the second most important element after autopsy is the oral source. For many scholars, oral sources are considered the bedrock of Procopius' writing.[88] Because of his relatively diverse experiences scholars have put a lot of stock in Procopius' access to well-positioned informants, whom he could speak to about the events that he describes.[89] Confidence in the value and accuracy of Procopius' writing often rests on his presumed reliance on this particular group of evidence—and it is worth remembering the complete absence of any methodological statements. The thinking goes: because Procopius had an important position beside Belisarius, he could speak to those people who knew what happened in the wars, people who were in a position to make some of the important decisions, ones who had a variety of perspectives, and ones who might have had access to the research materials Procopius needed. To evaluate their worth, it would help if we knew something about his informants, no mean feat given that all we have to work with is the texts themselves.

In this discussion, I will focus on the *Wars*. To begin, some scholars have suggested that Procopius sought to repay the debt he owed to those he spoke to by naming them and highlighting their actions in the text. The particular individuals that most scholars have turned their attention towards are the spearmen, the *doryphoroi*, and shield bearers, the *hypaspistai*, that fill the pages of the

---

85 Procop. *Wars* 3.15.8, 3.15.10, 3.15.15, 3.15.24, 4.21.4, 5.14.3, 5.14.9, 6.4.27, 7.36.15, 8.14.44, 8.14.44, 8.19.2, 8.20.48, 8.20.49, 8.20.56, 8.25.14.
86 Procop. *Wars* 1.17.36, 4.6.22, 8.19.10, 8.21.17.
87 For a thorough discussion of the hierarchy of sources in ancient historiography, see Marincola (1997: 63–127). For two late antique methodological statements see Ammianus (Amm. Marc. 15.1.1) and Eunapius (Eunap. *Hist.* 1.1.6–94). See too Whately (2016a: 9–10).
88 Kalli 2004: 2.
89 Cameron 1985: 136; Börm 2007: 53–54. Cf. Treadgold 2007: 218.

Wars.[90] And it is true that spearmen and shield bearers abound. Parnell's 2010 thesis on Justinian's officers includes a detailed prosopography of all known soldiers from that era, and his excellent work makes tracking down spearmen and shield bearers straightforward.[91]

Parnell lists 870 soldiers fighting for Rome. That includes both those called Romans and non-Romans, such as Armenians, Arabs, and so forth. The majority of the known soldiers are officers.[92] Of the 870 in total, 239 come from the pages of the *Wars*, and nearly a fifth, 52, are bodyguards (the *bucellarii*), the spearmen and shield bearers. For interest's sake, the evidence for the soldiers not found in Procopius comes from other literary sources as well as the surviving inscriptions, papyri, and seals. Thirty-two of the bodyguards in Procopius are assigned to Belisarius, more than half of the total.[93] It is also worth noting the numbers for non-officers in Procopius. There are only 13 Roman non-officer soldiers in Procopius, and 10 non-Roman soldiers, and 7 of each, Roman and non-Roman, that is 14 total, are unnamed. If we look at the figures for bodyguards, we find comparable numbers, for a case has been made that the spearmen ranked higher than the shield bearers—they were the officers of this group.[94] Only six of the named bodyguards were *hypaspistai*. Procopius favours the higher-ranking soldiers—indeed, this is the foundation of this book. As a point of comparison, regarding Procopius' usage of forms of the words δορυφόροι and ὑπασπισταί, he uses the former much more than the latter, 120 times to 47. High-ranking soldiers, then, reign supreme.

What should we make of these figures, and do they go any way towards illuminating us about the value of Procopius' sources and his accuracy as an historian? Given his position as assessor to Belisarius we should expect Procopius to have been much more familiar with officers than rank and file soldiers. And we might expect officers to have been much more aware of all that went on in a war than those at the front. So, those officers might very well have provided Procopius with a good deal of his information, he might have felt some need to thank them, and he might have done so by naming them in the text. And yet, it is not as simple as that, for, as Lucian reminds us, historians were not to spend too much time describing the actions of rank and file soldiers. Rather, the historian was to draw his attention to the commanders.[95] Procopius' interest in

---

90 Note Rance (2005: 451–452).
91 Republished in slightly modified form in Parnell (2012).
92 The prosopography can be found on pages 225–311 of his thesis (Parnell 2010).
93 More on this in chapter five below.
94 Petersen 2013: 57.
95 Lucian *Hist. Conscr.* 49. This is the thrust of Whately (2016a).

officers might have more to do with historiographical convention than the historical reality.

Still, the relative preponderance of references to bodyguards may yet point towards their role as important sources. Procopius' interest in bodyguards far surpasses that of any other Justinianic era source, even considering that we have much more of Procopius than most other writers. For instance, Agathias and Theophylact spend little time on bodyguards. If we go back to the total known soldiers from Parnell's prosopography, bodyguards make up only 7% of the total, a figure that includes Procopius' references. Interestingly, if we leave out Procopius' evidence, they make up only 3% of the total. Bodyguards do apparently make up a disproportionate proportion of the total number of known soldiers in Procopius. That would seem to support the suggestion that bodyguards were important sources for Procopius.

Even then, however, their role is far from certain, for there are other explanations for the prevalence of bodyguards. There might have been more bodyguards in Procopius because Belisarius, the dominant figure in the *Wars*, chose to hire a great deal more of them than his peers.[96] He was one of the wealthiest men of his day, and he spent a great deal of his money on the raising of private armies to supplement the public force supplied by Justinian and the state. In other words, they might have played a more important and active role in these particular expeditions led by Belisarius than in any other military encounters of the sixth century. Indeed, Procopius uses cognates of δορυφόροι and ὑπασπισταί much more often in the *Vandal Wars* and the *Gothic Wars* than he does in the *Persian Wars*. The fact is that Justinian was not always forthright in his allocation of troops for the wars of reconquest, and Belisarius was frequently left to his own devices to make up any manpower shortfalls.[97] Plus, unlike the wars against Persia, there were no ready collections of soldiers in the employ of the state in Africa and Italy upon which Belisarius could draw if needed.

But this does not mean we can or should rule out oral sources entirely. In a judiciously argued article that sought to contradict some of the arguments in favour of Procopius' use of documents, Brodka looked at the potential role of six men who received limited attention, Peter from Thrace (one of Solomon's spearmen),[98] Marcellus (a *comes excubitorum*), George (one of Belisarius' confidants), Paul of Cilicia (a cavalry officer), Sinnion (a leader of the Kutrigurs),

---

96   As noted, we return to this in chapter five.
97   This is the central thrust of Procopius' *Secret History* section on soldiers. Agathias makes similar claims—and the *Wars* backs this up.
98   Brodka 2016.

and Ortaias (a ruler of the Moors).[99] In the course of his examination, Brodka argued that Procopius provides circumstantial evidence that implies that these individuals provided him with information about some curious episodes. This led Brodka to downplay the role of documentary evidence and instead emphasized Procopius' use of a wide range of sources, though he noted finding evidence for individual sources was made worse by Procopius' relative silence.[100] In the end, Brodka reached a number of important conclusions: that Procopius was in contact with many of Belisarius' staff members; that oral information was used for the most important events within a narrative episode; and that Procopius supplemented his source material with typical or probable things, as the rules of rhetoric dictated.[101]

Brodka's paper shows that regardless of the role of bodyguards as a source for Procopius, we should not discount the possibility that Procopius used oral sources altogether. Rather, we should not put much stock in estimating the value of a source solely on the basis of their position within the Roman military. What is more, as Brodka himself argued, while oral sources are important, we should not place too much confidence in Procopius' accuracy on the basis of his use of oral sources alone.

3.2 *Documentary Evidence*

Oral sources are only part of the story. So, from oral sources we shift to that other major body of evidence, documentary sources. The Roman military is well known for its record keeping throughout the imperial era. The particular documents I want to focus on in this book on soldiers are the campaign reports and dispatches that occasionally surface in our sources. Some have argued that, when Procopius' position with Belisarius came to an end, and he no longer followed the military on its many campaigns, he was forced to turn to documentary material alone, material which might have supplemented the oral sources that made up such a significant part of the earlier sections of the work.[102] Most scholars have questioned how far Procopius' use of documentary sources should be taken, though there have been some thought-provoking attempts to challenge what might be called the orthodoxy.[103] Can we find traces of documentary sources in Procopius' narrative, and if we can what does this mean for our interest in his accuracy?

---

99   Brodka 2016: 110.
100 Brodka 2016: 109–110.
101 Brodka 2016: 122.
102 Cameron 1985: 12.
103 Colvin 2013.

Before we get to Procopius, what exactly do we mean when we are talking about military dispatches, bulletins, or reports? Well, the topic has attracted some attention,[104] and this despite the fact that we have little in the way of concrete examples of this documentary material beyond a few scattered inscriptions, papyri, and the odd document from the legal record. As for battle reports, which have attracted the most attention among those interested in Procopius' sources, late antique and Byzantine writers do not have a single term for such a document, with versions of *apokriseis*, *sakrai*, *epinikia*, and *gramma* used.[105] With that said, Sinclair has collected all of the evidence for dispatches in the Byzantine era, and he has made a strong case for their employment.[106] These reports could take many shapes and sizes, with some written for private consumption by the powers that be, and others written for public consumption by the residents of Constantinople.

Malalas, who was the author of a chronograph that detailed the history of the world from creation to his own day, operated in a tradition that permitted the identification of sources. One of the battles that both he and Procopius describe took place at Calllinicum.[107] Although their accounts are broadly similar, they differ on some matters of interpretation. After Malalas finishes his account, one of the most detailed of all his descriptions of combat, he alludes to a report (the phrase he uses is συμβολῆς τοῦ πολέμου), that took the form of a letter, that implied the creation of an inquiry to investigate the defeat that the Romans suffered there to the Persians.[108] A few sections later we find a reference to another report, in this case he uses the term τῆς συμβολῆς, concerned with a battle between Romans and Persians near the city of Martyropolis.[109] More evidence for military dispatches in the sixth century might be found in Marcellinus Comes' *Chronicle*, a man whose career was quite similar to Procopius'.[110] For instance, Marcellinus describes an operation with the Bulgars involving the Master of Illyrian Soldiers, Aristus, who campaigned in Thrace with 15000 men and 520 wagons.[111] His account provides us with the location

---

104 The most notable piece of research on the subject is Sinclair's (2013) excellent thesis.
105 Sinclair 2013: 158.
106 Note his comments at Sinclair 2013: 174.
107 See Whately (2016a: ix-xi).
108 Malalas 18.60.
109 Malalas 18.65. Procopius alludes to this battle as well, though he does not have much to contribute. Cf. Procop. *Wars* 1.21.1ff.
110 Cf. Colvin 2013: 592–592.
111 Marc. Com. 499.1; 530.

of the encounter, gives us some idea of the numbers involved, and highlights the actions of a few individuals.[112]

The reports referred to by Malalas and Marcellinus Comes were likely private ones, however, that is they were designed for the eyes and ears of the powers that be alone—and those who could access them. An excellent illustration of the form the public versions of these reports might have taken comes from the HBO drama *Rome*, and episode seven, entitled "Pharsalus". There the character "Newsreader" or "Senate Crier", reads from a scroll a few details about the famed Battle of Pharsalus. Interestingly enough, the best-known late antique military dispatch was a public one, and can be found in the pages of the *Chronicon Paschale*. Scholars generally agree that the report found in that chronicle is presented verbatim.[113] That dispatch was delivered in May of 628 in the ambo of Hagia Sophia, and it celebrated Heraclius' victory over Persia in the last great war of antiquity.[114] Indeed, it seems that the emperor Heraclius was keen on keeping the Constantinopolitan public apprised of his long, brutal war with Persia, for we have evidence of a number of dispatches from the front, which are found in the pages of Theophanes' *Chronograph*. Getting back to the 628 dispatch, for all its apparent value, it does not seem to be typical in any sense, in part because it was given by an emperor, one particularly keen on promoting his military exploits, for quite often these reports seem to have been composed by leading commanders.

Of course, as the survey implies, we do not really know what a typical dispatch might have looked like, and if anything, variety might be the distinguishing feature. This makes attempts at finding clues to their use by Procopius in the *Wars* particularly challenging, even if we assume Procopius would have been in a position to access them.[115] For all the discussion of the abundance of clichés in ancient battle writing, a close reading of Procopian combats reveals a dizzying array of details and a considerable variety of combat types.[116] In fact, there is good reason to believe that the discrepancies we see in his descriptions of combat have more to do with the skill of Procopius the writer than with the sources he had at his disposal. For instance, we might well expect military

---

112 On Marcellinus' probable career as a soldier and his treatment of this event see Croke (2001: 48–77) for his career as a soldier and Illyricum in general; 69–72 for Bulgars in the chronicle). Stein (1949: 89) only refers to this war in passing. Cf. Bury 1923: 435–436.
113 *Chron. Pasch.* 727. On the chronicles use of documents, see Howard-Johnston (2010: 44–54).
114 On the war cf. Howard-Johnston (2010), Wood (2013: 176–220), and Hoyland (2015).
115 In fact, his responsibilities as Belisarius' assessor might have entailed the writing of these reports on behalf of his employer, though we do not know.
116 Whately 2016a.

dispatches and reports of combat to include some sense of the numbers involved, who won and who lost, who was involved, and where it happened. If Procopius was to rely on this sort of documentary evidence, when describing those battles for which he was absent, then we should expect those sorts of details to appear. But closer looks at just such events reveal something else. In his account of the aforementioned battle round Martyropolis described by Malalas, Procopius refers to a raid, but claims that the Persians, whom Malalas says were defeated thanks to the actions of Roman forces, withdrew because of political upheaval. No numbers are given, and we are not even told which commanders or what types of soldiers on the Roman side were involved in the encounter.[117] Plus, this battle came at a time when Procopius was well connected. In other words, even though he was not at the battle, he should have had access to the report alluded to by Malalas.

Battle reports are only part of the story, for we also need to consider the vast array of organizational documents produced by and for the military, the military registers, permission certificates (*probatoria*), morning reports, and more. We have one surviving permission from for a new recruit, which comes from Egypt and dates to the sixth century CE. We will return to it in chapter six. We also have the odd document that might provide part of a roster, including one of the three slabs (Slab C) from an edict from Perge, and a papyrus from Nessana.[118] Scattered pieces of legislation in the *Code* of Justinian provide the subtlest of hints about the character of military reports and otherwise, and how Procopius' experiences as assessor might have impacted this. At least two laws, both from the *Codex Justinianus*, stress the importance of quarterly reports, which were compiled for several branches of the Roman state.

The legislation at 1.31.5 provides lots of interesting material on record-keeping for the empire's regiments, though its specific emphasis is on bodyguards. This law stresses the importance of official permission when recruits are enrolling, and documents, *probatoria*, in particular. Additionally, it reads "we desire that quarterly lists [*quadrimenstruos breves*] of the aforesaid *Scholares* be compiled at the direction of Your Sublimity and of every acting *vir excellentissimus* Master of Offices, and that they be presented to the Sacred Bureau of the Register for archiving [*scrinio laterculi*], so that the record of the aforesaid *Scholares* shall always be accurate and no loss shall be inflicted on the State".[119] But there were also quarterly reports for the civil and

---

117   Procop. *Wars* 1.21.21–28.
118   Onur 2017, P. Ness. 3.37.
119   *Cod. Iust.* 1.31.5.2, trans. Dillon. *Ad haec quadrimenstruos breves eorundem scholarium cura tuae sublimitatis et pro tempore viri excellentissimi magistri officiorum conscribi volumus et*

military service in general, which were to be truthful.[120] Even those in charge of the frontier armies were to provide reports to the emperor, albeit annual ones.[121] Admittedly, we do not know what was in these reports, but the earlier imperial *pridiana*, of which we have a few, might be what the legislators had in mind.[122] Surviving *pridiana* include a variety of information. Hunt's details the activities of the soldiers of a unit called the *cohors I Hispanorum veterana*, some members of whom were in Gaul to get clothing, some were in Dardania at the mines,[123] some were across the Danube on an expedition, some were at the grain-ships (*ad naves frumentarias*), and some were guarding draft animals, among other things. One of the most important things these documents do is provide a record of who was in a particular unit. Yet another edict of Anastasius, this time from Cyrenaica, stresses just this.[124] These different classes of document are the sort of material that Procopius is likely to have had access to when he researched and wrote his three texts. In fact, his engagement with these documents manifested itself especially in how Procopius described military units, a point to which I will return in chapter three below.

The Roman state went to some lengths to keep track of its soldiers, on some level or other. Indeed, one of the chief concerns was keeping track of those who lived and those who died. Ammianus Marcellinus notes that 243 Romans died in the Battle of Strasbourg, waged in 357, and he names four of the Roman fallen, Bainobaudes, a tribune of the Cornuti, Laipso, and Innocentius, commanders of cataphracts, and "one unattached tribune, whose name was not available to me." Importantly, he also says that "... of the Alamanni ... [they] counted six thousand corpses lying on the field, and heaps of dead, impossible to reckon".[125] Theophylact Simocatta recounts the story of an unknown soldier whom some scouts stumbled upon: "they observed a Roman soldier

---

eos sacro scrinio laterculi praestari ibi deponendos, ut semper notitia eorundem scholarium certa sit neque publico damnum aliquod infligatur.

120   *Cod. Iust.* 1.42.
121   *Cod. Iust.* 1.31.4.
122   Phang 2007: 295, RMR 63.
123   Fink (RMR 63) notes that the Erar river has not yet been identified.
124   "In regard to the inspection of assembled troops: the first names on the roll of each detachment or camp shall not be subject to review as ill or unfit for service, that is, the first five, if there are 100 names, or the first ten, if there are 200. The same proportion shall be maintained, whether there are more or less." SEG 9.356.7, trans. Johnson.

ὥστε ἰνσπεσίμου συνοδιακοῦ μὴ καταζητῖσθαι ὡς ἀσθενεῖς {ι} ἢ ἀ[χ]ρείους τοὺς πρώτους ἑκάστου ἀριθμοῦ καὶ κάστρου, τουτέστιν, εἰ μὲν [ἑ]κατὸν εἶεν ἄνδρες, τοὺς πρώτους πένται, εἰ δὲ διακόσιο[ι τ]οὺ(ς) {εἰ δ[ὲ δ]ιακόσιοι, τ[οὺς} πρώτου]ς δέκα· τὴν δὲ αὐτὴ[ν ἀ]ναλ[ο]γείαν καὶ ἐ[πὶ τ]οῖ[ς] πλίοσιν καὶ ἐπὶ τοῖς ἐλάττοσιν ἀνδράσιν φυλάττεσθαι..

125   Amm. Marc. 16.12.63 Trans. Rolfe.

in the throes of death, his body adorned by four wounds … (9) they say that the hero was on the roll of the Quartoparthoi, which is the appellation borne by the men stationed in the city of Beroea in Syria".[126] Vegetius, the author of one of the two most important military manuals from late antiquity (the other being Maurice's *Strategikon*), says that the Romans used to paint different signs for different cohorts on the shields of soldiers, *digmata*, and the name of the soldiers on the shields with a note for cohort or century (2.18).

There is other evidence that the Roman command kept records of their soldiers in the sixth century. One early piece of legislation in the *Code* states that quarterly military reports were to be kept—though we do not know what they entailed (1.42). Another piece of legislation, dating to the reign of Anastasius, notes that "names [were] inscribed on the military rolls [*nomina eorum matriculis militaribus referri videantur*]" (6.21.16).[127] Yet one further piece of legislation from the *Code*, which comes many books later, discusses the *probatoria*, a certificate of appointment for a soldier, the ultimate granting of which comes down to the emperor.[128] What is relevant for us is that masters of soldiers and dukes were tasked with sending reports to the emperor if they lost men through death, after which the emperor would make an investigation and determine whether a request for new troops was approved or not.[129]

At this point, it should suffice to say that the state attempted to keep track of who lived and who died. One of Agathias' signature accounts is of the Battle of Casilinum between the Romans and Franks in Italy. At its conclusion, he says that the Romans buried their dead according to their rites and customs, without specifying what that entailed.[130] In a later encounter with the Dolomites, Agathias claims the Romans "killed in action … were given an honourable burial and won universal admiration for the valour with which they acquitted themselves".[131] Maurice, the author of the *Strategikon*, argues that after battle the general should give prompt attention to the wounded and see to burying the dead; not only is it a religious duty but it greatly helps the morale of the living.[132] As for what the burying of the dead might involve, Procopius

---

126 Trans. Whitby and Whitby.
127 Trans. Frier, Kehoe, and McGinn.
128 A sixth century (578 CE) papyrus (P. Muench 1.2) from Syene refers to a recruitment certificate of a Flavius Patermouthis, son of Dios. For recruitment in the sixth century, see Jones (1964: 614–623, 668–670), Whitby (1995), and chapter six below. Cf. Teall (1965) and Fotiou (1988).
129 *Cod. Iust.* 12.35.17.
130 Agathias 2.10.7.
131 Agathias 3.28.4, trans. Frendo.
132 Maur. *Strat.* 7B.6.

gives us a vague idea. When discussing the challenging funerary practices in his detailed account of the plague, Procopius notes that there was often a procession with the dead to the grave which included some ritual chanting.[133] In his account of the 537/538 siege of Rome, he notes that an officer named Ennes had been covered with wounds, but had made it back to the Pinciana Gate. His Roman compatriots had thought he was dead, however, so they lifted him on a shield and carried him back to the Roman garrison, a possible portrait of a funerary practice used, at least, when the deceased were higher ranking officers.[134]

These few accounts reveal something of the procedures involved with death in battle and imply that efforts were made to carry out proper burials, at least for the higher-ranking soldiers. When it comes to keeping track of who survived combat or service more broadly, we have to look beyond Procopius for evidence of how this took place.

As I suggested above, we do have evidence that the Romans kept track of who lived and who died. Some of the documents that include this kind of information are earlier, like Hunt's *Pridianum*.[135] Based on the comments of a handful of authors, the Romans seem to have used a pretty basic system, with thetas marked beside those who died on the registers of units.[136] Rufinus, in his treatise, *Against Jerome*, includes the following passage:

> This was no more than what is done in the army when a list is made out containing the names of the soldiers. If the captain wishes to see how many of them have survived after an action, he sends a man to make inquiry; and he makes his own mark, a (θ) (theta), for instance, as is commonly done, against the name of each soldier who has fallen, and puts some other mark of his own to designate the survivors. Do you suppose that he who makes one mark against the name of a dead man and another of his own against that of a survivor, will be thought to have done anything which causes the one to be dead and the other to be alive? He has only, as is well understood, marked the names of those who have been killed by others, so as to call attention to the fact.[137]

---

133 Procop. *Wars* 2.23.12–13. On mass burials in late antiquity, see McCormick (2015, 2016).
134 Procop. *Wars* 5.29.43. There has been a good deal of research on burial customs in late antiquity, the west especially, some of which has discussed the difficulty in identifying interred individuals. Effros (2003: 71–118) provides a good overview of the practices in the Merovingian world.
135 RMR 34. See too ChLA 43.1242.
136 For more on the registers themselves, see the discussion in chapter three below.
137 Rufinus, *Against Jerome* 2.36, trans. Schaff and Wace. See too Isid., *Etym*. 1.24.1–2.

As it happens, we have independent evidence for the application of thetas to Roman military records that include details about deaths.[138]

There is some comparative evidence from combat. The most famous case of a Roman battle where the dead were left abandoned for some time after is Kalkriese in Germany. The bones recovered there had been weathered by the elements, and had Germanicus not returned to bury them, they likely would have been lost entirely.[139] One other case is the mid-third century siege of Dura. Whether the bodies in tunnel 19 were moved or not, that they were left for eternity, so to speak, seems likely.[140] In a much better documented later case, the Battle of Towton from the War of the Roses, one suggestion is that a large grave was made to fit in as many bodies as possible.[141] A century earlier at Visby in Sweden, a number of mass graves included the remains of the losing side in that battle. Many of those buried were still wearing their armour, which has been taken to mean that little care was taken to dispose of the dead. This might have been hampered by a shortage of citizens available to carry out the rites, and the time between their deaths and inhumation.[142] The remains of a medieval battle in Portugal produced comparable evidence, for the bones of nearly 400 bodies seem to have been deposited in a mass grave perhaps several years after the battle itself.[143]

In these few cases where we have human remains, the evidence reveals some of the challenges that came with affording the dead proper burials after battle. At the same time, the basic pattern of the evidence supports the literary accounts: it was not always possible to bury everyone the usual way, and this would make the possibility of keeping track of who died and then passing on the news of a loved one's death difficult, if not impossible, particularly if details regarding who died was hard to come by. Indeed, if it was this difficult to keep track of who died on the field of battle, it was likely just as difficult if not more so to make a record of it.

4   Case Study: Looking for Documents at Dara

The thrust of this chapter has been on Procopius' background and the sources he used. I have also set out some of the many detailed records the Romans used

---

138   Bellucci and Bortolussi (2016).
139   Smith 2017: 160.
140   James 2004; James 2011.
141   Sutherland 2000; Curry and Foard 2016: 70.
142   Smith 2017: 210.
143   Cunha and Silva 1997; Woosman-Savage & DeVries 2015: 42.

in the sixth century and earlier. If we look closer at one detailed episode in one of his works, would we be able to find traces of the sources he used and what impact they had on his writing? I would argue that while some documents are visible just below the surface, like the rosters that I will return to in chapter three, others, like battle reports, are more difficult to identify. In this last section of the chapter I take a closer look at aspects of Procopius' description of the Battle of Dara, which will reveal more about the difficulty in tracking down evidence of Procopius' use of both documentary and oral sources. There are clues scattered amidst Procopius' account that give us some insight, though, as we will see, some are more obvious than others.

I start with the Roman deployment at Dara, rather than the Persian.[144] Procopius gives a pretty lengthy account of the Roman deployment at the battle, including details about a number of commanders and officers. At the head of the Roman forces was Belisarius, in Procopius' words, general of the East (στρατηγὸν τῆς ἕω), that is *magister militum per Orientem*.[145] Alongside Belisarius at the head of the Roman army was Hermogenes, whom Procopius calls magister (τοῦ μαγίστρου), and who was likely *magister officiourum*.[146] Other leading Roman commanders include Buzes (1.13.19),[147] Pharas the Herul (1.13.19),[148] Sunicas the Massageta (1.13.20),[149] Aigan the Massageta (1.13.20),[150] John (1.13.21),[151] Cyril (1.13.21),[152] Marcellus (1.13.21),[153] Germanus (1.13.21),[154] Dorotheus (1.13.21),[155] Simmas the Massageta (1.13.21),[156] and Ascan the Massageta (1.13.21).[157] Procopius also provides some general comments about the size and character of the army (ὁ δὲ στρατιὰν λόγου πολλοῦ ἀξίαν ἀγείρας). On the left was Buzes with many cavalry (ξὺν ἱππεῦσι πολλοῖς) (1.13.19); right of Buzes was Pharas with 300 countrymen (Heruls) (1.13.19) (ξὺν ὁμογενέσι

---

144 On Procopius' understanding of the Persians see Börm (2007).
145 Procop. *Wars* 1.13.9. His first stint as *magister militum per Orientem* came in 529–531, then again 533–542, and then in 549–551 (*PLRE* Fl. Belisarius I, p. 181).
146 Procop. *Wars* 1.13.10. According to the *PLRE* (p. 590), Hermogenes 1, he was *magister officiorum* from May 12, 529 to Nov 17, 533.
147 *PLRE* Buzes, (p. 255), was *dux phoenices libanensis* at Palmyra in 528, based in part on 1.13.5, where they argue that he was based in Lebanon.
148 *PLRE* Pharas, (p. 1015) Herul leader, who led armies in 530 and in 533 in north Africa.
149 *PLRE* Sunicas, p. 1207.
150 *PLRE* Aigan, p. 32.
151 *PLRE* Ioannes 32, p. 642.
152 *PLRE* Cyrillus 2, p. 372.
153 *PLRE* Marcellus 2, p. 814.
154 *PLRE* Germanus 1, p. 527.
155 *PLRE* Dorotheus 1, p 420.
156 *PLRE* Simmas, p. 1153.
157 *PLRE* Ascan, p. 133.

τριακοσίοις); right of Pharas and Buzes were Sunicas and Aigan with 600 (Hun) cavalry (1.13.20) (ξὺν ἱππεῦσιν ἑξακοσίοις); and on the far right were many horsemen.[158] Left of all them were the 600 horsemen (Huns) under Simmas and Ascan.[159] Belisarius and Hermogenes were positioned in the middle, with the entire army numbering 25,000 soldiers.[160] Additionally, Procopius notes that there were both infantry and cavalry, though he does not provide specific totals or details.[161]

The overall course of the battle is clear enough, and Procopius even gives us some idea of why it turned out the way it did, at least in his eyes. We also know something about the numbers involved, but only a little. There is little on the experience of the combatants, beyond a few general, generic, points. Even the identity of the majority of the participants is missing besides a few officers. We know the identities of some of the different kinds of soldiers, but not how they were deployed. For example, what did the infantry do, to whom Procopius alludes at the start? It could be that they worked to hold Belisarius' and Hermogenes' position, but Procopius does not mention them by name (or type) at any other point in the battle.

Procopius presents the battle as a series of manoeuvres and countermanoeuvres employed by those in charge of the two sides. While it is hard to imagine Procopius getting his hands on any reports compiled by the Persian side, it could be that Procopius read (if he did not also compose) some of Belisarius' battle notes, *commentarii*.[162] As we saw above, however, it is hard to know what was in one of the battle reports. It is easy to imagine that a report about Dara would contain the basics: who participated, how many soldiers there were, where it happened, and a basic outline of the battle itself. Dara has all this, and more besides. A report might also list the names of soldiers whose actions were particularly noteworthy, whether grunt or commander. Much later, in his pseudo-eulogy for Belisarius following the general's departure

---

158 ἱππεῖς πολλοί. Procop. *Wars* 1.13.21.
159 Procop. *Wars* 1.13.21. ἱππεῖς ... ἑξακόσιοι.
160 Procop. *Wars* 1.13.23.
161 πανταχῇ δὲ τῆς τάφρου οἵ τε τῶν ἱππέων κατάλογοι καὶ ὁ πεζὸς στρατός. Greatrex (1998: 174–175) says the forces of Belisarius and Hermogenes were likely *bucellarii* (mostly), ready to intervene at any time, and they are part of the 25,000. Pharas' men likely served as *foederati* rather than *symmachoi*. Whitby (1995: 108 (n. 217)) argued that the Heruls served as both *foederati* and *symmachoi*. Additionally, Greatrex (1998: 174–175) says of the four Hunnic commanders named, only Ascan is heard of again at Callinicum. Greatrex also says that the Huns (the *symmachoi*) were probably entirely horse archers.
162 I imagine the Persians kept detailed records too. Indeed, his comments at *Wars* 1.18.52–53 after the Battle of Callinicum about counting the arrows of returning soldiers suggests to me that they had a sophisticated record-keeping procedure of their own.

from Italy, Procopius says that he would give bracelets and necklaces to those soldiers who distinguished themselves in battle.[163] Would these soldiers find their names recorded on a report? That all depends on when the awards were distributed. If it happened in the immediate aftermath of a battle, there is no good reason to record this information for later purposes, especially given we have no evidence that such awards played any role in promotion.[164] Indeed, so far as we know, what little evidence we have for the service records of the empire's soldiers implies that it was limited to the most basic of details.[165] The quarterly military reports sent to Constantinople were sent to the Sacred Bureau of the Register, though it is difficult to know what kind of information they would contain about individuals.[166]

When it comes to casualties, Procopius' presentation is uneven. Early on, Procopius gives the number of Persian dead in one of the opening skirmishes involving Buzes and Pharas. In that case, seven Persians died, and Procopius says he knew because the Romans gained possession of their bodies, so explaining how they knew exactly how many were killed. Later in the battle, Procopius provides brief accounts of the deaths of select Persians, like Sunicas' charge against Baresmanas, which led to his death. Procopius tells us about the 3,000 Persian casualties in one stage of the battle and the 5,000 total casualties reported at the end. What Procopius does not tell us is how many Romans died, even though we know that the Romans kept records of who lived and who died in a battle, and usually this information was recorded on the rosters of each of the participating units.

Procopius' breakdown of the Roman army is inconsistent: he gives a total of 25,000, and then smaller groupings of 300 (Heruls with Pharas), 600 (Huns with Sunicas and Aigan), and 600 (Huns with Simmas and Ascan). Those three smaller groups fall far short of 25,000, when added up, but we never learn the breakdown of the remaining 23,500 men. If Procopius knew the details about the groups of Huns and Heruls, he probably knew about the others belonging to Buzes, John, Cyril, Marcellus, Germanus, and Dorotheus, none of whom are given regiments. But then, none of them featured later in the battle, and so extra details, like the size of the units under their control, were superfluous. The regiments, and in some cases the commanders, that he does give numbers

---

163   Procop. *Wars* 7.1.8.
164   On promotion, see Jones (1964: 633–636—admittedly concerned with the fourth century military), Ravegnani (1998: 120–121), and more recently Parnell (2017: 28–31).
165   See the comments of Phang (2007: 289), even if she is focused on a much earlier period. See too *Cod. Theod.* 7.20.4.1, which, though not found in the later *Codex Justinianus*, implies that some record was kept, at least up until a soldier retired.
166   *Cod. Iust.* 1.31.5.2.

for often feature later in the action, like the aforementioned Sunicas who slew Baresmanas. Procopius also tells us about a charge of Sunicas and Aigan's Hun cavalry. Thus, while the figures, the 300 and 600, might well come from some sort of register or document, the participation and identification of select officers would seem to come from different kinds of evidence, like discussion with participants like Pharas or Sunicas, or even battle reports that highlighted the actions of these individuals.

In sum, it is difficult, if not impossible, to find definitive evidence for the use of sources in Procopius' *Wars*, largely because he rarely includes the kind of information we find in these documents.[167] It is particularly striking that we see this in the most detailed of battle accounts here at Dara. So, to hold them up as a mark of the accuracy of his account is unwarranted. I should add too that this is to say nothing of the accuracy of those very battle reports and more. Close consideration of the disparate accounts of the Battle of Callinicum, which took place in 531 and involved a Roman defeat at the hands of the Persians, have revealed that the most official of versions, that of Malalas, leaves much to be desired.[168] Documentary evidence is interesting in and of itself, but holds little value when it comes to evaluating Procopius' accuracy.

5 Conclusion

At the end of this chapter, it is worth taking stock. Procopius did many of the kinds of things that classical and classicizing historians do to stress their authority. What is more, Procopius did make a perfectly reasonable case for his accurate reporting in his preface, and he does by some measures seem to have been engaged in autopsy, something to be applauded. Plus, Procopius seems to have had some real experience in the waging of war in the sixth century. But if we dig a bit deeper and try to get at the sources for his narrative we run into some dead ends, despite their initial promise. Procopius' naming of high-ranking officials might be suggestive of the identity of his sources; but it is also sound historiographical practice. Moreover, the abundance of spearmen and shield bearers likely has more to do with the exigencies of the wars of conquest than any gratitude Procopius felt because of their value as sources of information. The hunt for documentary sources has also revealed little. In short,

---

167 This too is well established. Keegan, (1976, esp. 35–65), for instance, noted the confusion inherent in battle. On the perils of ancient historians and their sources, see Pitcher (2009: 47–91). See too Fornara (1984: 47–90) and Marincola (1997: 66–79).
168 Whately 2016a: ix–xi.

Procopius had access to the kinds of sources that would inform him about these soldiers. There were plenty of firsthand opportunities for Procopius to see low-ranking soldiers. He likely knew officers who had information about these men, and we have every indication that documents existed that documented their lives. What we have also seen, however, is there are a few scattered traces of these sources in Procopius' works, at least based on what we have seen so far. In the end, this does not cast doubt on our ability to judge the accuracy of Procopius' military history. But it does mean that a careful consideration of Procopius' sources offers little in our attempt to uncover the rank and file soldiers in Procopius' oeuvre.[169] To do this, we need to broaden the scope. In the next chapter, I will look closer at the terminology Procopius uses to identify the Roman military's regiments.

169   And so, in this, I am very much in agreement with Pitcher (2009: 79–91).

CHAPTER 3

Catalogues and Legions

1 Introduction

In the midst of his long and detailed account of the siege of Rome in 537/538 CE, Procopius includes the following detail about one of the Roman units used in the city's defence: "The Reges [Regii], an infantry unit, were on guard there along with Ursicinus, who led them."[1] This passage represents one of the few points in any of Procopius' texts where he makes an attempt to identify a specific regiment fighting for Rome. This unit appears in the *Notitia Dignitatum* as one of the *auxilia palatina* serving under the *magister militum praesentalis*.[2] That this is such an oddity deserves special notice, and indeed its very rarity stands out. While other late antique historians like Ammianus Marcellinus do, on occasion, refer to specific units in the Roman military, this is not something Procopius does.[3] Instead, more often than not, his language is vague and general. The point of this chapter is to highlight the extent of the lack of technical specificity when it came to organizational matters in Procopius' oeuvre.

Two terms used regularly in scholarship on sixth-century (CE) military organization to denote regiments are *arithmos* and *katalogos*. The two are often used interchangeably. As I will argue in this chapter, however, the equation of the two terms rests on a faulty understanding of Procopius' use of the latter, *katalogos*. *Arithmos* alone is the official Greek term for a sixth-century military regiment, an assertion borne out by close analysis of the epigraphic, legal, and papyrological evidence. Procopius, on the other hand, uses *katalogos* to refer to a military roll or register, or soldiers, and not a regiment. This has a bearing on a principal focus of this book: Procopius' tunnel-vision approach to military narrative, and his systematic downplaying if not downright exclusion of Rome's frontier forces.

Although the subject of the term *katalogos* has received a good deal of attention, much of the organization of the sixth-century Roman military remains elusive, or at least unclear. The main culprit is the manifold forms the evidence

---

1 Procop. *Wars* 5.23.3. οἱ Ῥῆγες ἐνταῦθα πεζικὸν τέλος ἐφύλασσον καὶ Οὐρσικῖνος, ὃς αὐτῶν ἦρχε.
2 *Not. Dign. or.* 6.49.
3 Note, for example, Ammianus' account of the garrison at Amida at 18.9.3, which he said comprised the *Magnentiaci*, the *Decentiaci*, the *Tricensimani*, *Decimani Fortenses*, the *Superventores*, and the *Praeventores*.

often takes: classicizing histories, military manuals, inscriptions, legal texts, and papyri. The countless terms for organizational structures have bedeviled attempts at determining whether a term might pertain to one kind of regiment, or any number of different regiments, even if authoritative studies have implied otherwise.[4] While a full-scale examination of all sixth-century military terminology would be far beyond the scope of this chapter, a close consideration of these two terms and some attendant phraseology rewards closer study.

Both ἀριθμός and κατάλογος are terms which continue to be used interchangeably by late antique scholars, with the latter often dismissed as mere literary affectation. The principal cause of this confusion is Jones' nearly sixty-year-old study of the sixth-century army, which includes the following misleading statements: "*comitatenses* ... regiments are ... the *numeri* (in Procopius' Greek κατάλογοι)", "regiments are spoken of under the colourless style of numerus (ἀριθμός, or in literary Greek κατάλογος or τάγμα)", and "to close, in virtually no official sixth-century documents do we find *katalogos* as a regiment or unit, or even detachment. [...] Procopius' choice, then, must be understood as mere literary affectation."[5] While it might seem that Jones' pronouncements would have settled the matter, for many scholars recognize *arithmos* as the standard term for a regiment or unit in the sixth century,[6] only a few highlight *katalogos'* literary character.[7] Indeed, for many the term *katalogos* refers either to a unit distinct from an *arithmos*,[8] or a regiment in the sixth-century field army.[9]

In this chapter, I will revisit the evidence for these two terms, *arithmos* and *katalogos*, the usage of which was widespread in the sixth century.[10] A significant portion of the analysis will focus on Procopius' use of the term *katalogos*, the source of much of the confusion. I will highlight Procopius' practice in

---

4   Jones 1964: 654–668.
5   Jones 1964: 655.
6   To give but two fairly recent examples, Decker (2013: 77) and Petersen (2013: 107) both recognize this.
7   Ravegnani (1998: 30).
8   Haldon 1993: 51, n. 13; Whitby 2000: 301; Schmitt 2001: 98; Petersen 2013: 117; Laniado 2015: 95.
9   Teall 1965: 296; Elton 2007: 282; Sabin et al. 2007: 480; Koehn 2018: 20. Note that I use the terms unit/regiment interchangeably to refer to any large organized body within the military, like the Roman legion.
10 See Grosse (1920: 273) on the abundance of these two terms in the sixth century. One word that Procopius hardly ever uses is *lochos*, which he only uses ten times. In the two uses in the *Buildings* (3.4.16) it means something like "detachment" or unit—it is used in reference to the legion at Melitene. In the *Wars*, it is used to refer to a unit of the Immortals (1.14.31, 1.14.49), Vandal and Alan units (3.5.18, 4.3.8), an infantry unit (4.5.5), a large unit of Romans under Germanus (4.17.5) in Africa; as a unit of Scholae (8.27.2); and once as a synonym for *katalogos* (8.35.18). I return to this issue, his use of this term (*lochos*), below.

his eight-book *Wars*, contextualize it in terms of Procopius' wider oeuvre, the *Buildings* and *Secret History*, and situate his custom in the broader, evidential, sixth-century context. Upon closer inspection, I argue that *katalogos* was not merely a Greek literary version of *arithmos* (or *numerus*), a generalization which ignores some of Procopius' idiosyncrasies: *katalogos* never means *arithmos* in the sixth century. Rather, Procopius' employment of the term reflects his experiences and duties as Belisarius' assessor, and in this capacity matches the use of the term by his contemporary, John the Lydian, and the slightly earlier Anastasius Edict from Perge.

2 Terminology

2.1 *The End of the Legion*

Early in his *Historiae*, Theophylact Simocatta discusses the garrison of Circesium and identifies it as the "roll of the Quartoparthoi" (καταλόγου ... τῶν Κουαρτοπάρθων).[11] This is the only place in his work where Theophylact includes this level of detail regarding the garrison of any site. The unit in question, the IV *Parthia*, did have a long history, one which illustrates the changing character of the Roman legion. The *Notitia Dignitatum* gives the garrison of Circesium as the *Legio IV Parthica*.[12] The unit in question was created by Diocletian, who also transformed Circesium into a major, fortified settlement.[13] But there are other legions that had much longer histories.

After the *Notitia* and 400 CE, there is a lot of uncertainty. Frankly, we do not know what happened to all those units over the course of the fifth century, which lacks evidence for military organization outside of Egypt; moreover, there is nothing like the *Notitia* for the sixth century.[14] What we do have are the *Justinianic Code* and the attendant novels, the Egyptian (Aphrodito, Oxyrhynchus) and Israeli papyri (Nessana), the epigraphic evidence from the Balkans and the Levant, and a range of useful texts, from Procopius and his historiographical successors Agathias and Theophylact Simocatta, to the *Strategikon* of Maurice. Outside of bodyguards and those soldiers based in the capital—Procopius generally avoided affairs in Constantinople—there were four or five main groups of soldiers. The *comitatenses*, field troops, and *limitanei*, frontier soldiers, still existed in some capacity or other, though the

---

11 Theophyl. Sim. 2.6.9, trans. Whitby.
12 Not. Dign. or. 35.24.
13 Pollard 2000: 292.
14 Note the comments of Jones (1964: 654).

distinction between them might have blurred by now.[15] Two other groups of soldiers are the federates, *foederati*, and the "biscuit men," the *bucellarii*.[16] We should also add the generic allies, usually identified by the Greek *symmachoi*.[17]

2.2 Arithmos

All these broad groups of soldiers appear in the evidence in some form or other, though tracking major changes at the macro and micro levels is difficult. While the *Notitia* is useful up to a point, the absence of sufficient evidence for continuity or quantifiable change in nomenclature from the fifth century complicates matters to no end. The default title for a generic unit accepted by most scholars is the Latin *numerus*, and the Greek *arithmos*.[18] Maurice, one of our two most important literary sources for military matters, the other being Procopius, serves as the foundation for most studies of organization, with many scholars skipping Procopius entirely and focusing on Maurice.[19] Maurice mentions *arithmos* on a number of occasions, and while in some instances his use is vague,[20] in other cases *arithmos* seems to refer to a unit or regiment of a particular size,[21] perhaps 300 men.[22] Another major sixth-century source is Malalas' *Chronographia*, which some have seen as a work that toed the imperial line.[23] Malalas made unabashed use of all sorts of sources. He too uses a form of *arithmos* on a few occasions to mean a unit or regiment.[24]

Arithmos appears very rarely in the extant epigraphy, though this has more to do with the content of the surviving inscriptions than anything else. We have, for instance, three large edicts of the emperor Anastasius that provide tremendous insight into military affairs in the early sixth century. One of

---

15   Le Bohec (2007: 672) argues we should see the late antique military as divided in three or four between a Gallic army, an Illyrian army, a Thracian army, and an eastern army. See too Brennan (2015: 1051), but note Parnell's (2017: 16) comments.
16   On the *foederati* see Laniado (2015), and the *bucellarii* Schmitt (1994).
17   For an overview see Ravegnani (2004: 23–36), who also breaks down his discussion into corpora, as I have done here, and individual units, which I do below. See too Maspero (1912: 45–46) and Laniado (2015: 104–109).
18   See Jones (1964: 655), Keenan (1990: 141), Ravegnani (2004: 36), and Brennan (2015: 1050) for instance.
19   Treadgold 1995: 93–98; Syvänne 2004: 31–42. Note the caution of Janniard (2011: 238–239).
20   Maur. *Strat.* 2.5.6, 8.2.31.
21   Maur. *Strat.* 1.3.8, 12.B.4.
22   At 12.B.4, Maurice effectively likens an *arithmos* to a *tagma*, while at 1.3.8 he likens it to a *bandon* in addition to a *tagma*. Admittedly, the former deals with infantry soldiers, the latter with cavalry.
23   Note Treadgold's (2007: 235–256) comments on Malalas. On the relationship between Malalas and Procopius, see Greatrex (2016).
24   Mal. *Chron.* 18.2, 18.5, 18.10, 18.129.

them, from Umm el-Jimal and Qasr el-Hallabat in Jordan, ranges from taxes and regulations concerning the frontier soldiers in the east to protecting soldiers against extortion.[25] A final edition is awaiting publication; suffice to say, in the published fragments there are no hints of *arithmos*, though a form of *limitanei* appears,[26] a designation that also appears on the Beersheba tax edict.[27] Another edict, only recently published and originating from Perge in Turkey, details complaints made by a praesental army and matters pertaining to promotion, and it sets out aspects of the army's supplies.[28] It does include the term *arithmos*, and it means regiment or unit.[29] This edict is full of technical, and official-sounding, terminology, which lends support to the view that *arithmos* was in some sense an official term. The last of those three edicts, though the first one published, from *Cyrenaica*, refers to an *arithmos*, and the sense seems to be something akin to regiment or unit.[30]

Before we turn to the papyri, it is worth highlighting the uses of *arithmos* in Justinian's *Novels*, part of the *Corpus Iuris Civilis*. The term appears in the *Codex*, including 12.37, which includes decrees of Anastasius not unlike the aforementioned inscriptions. In 12.37.19.2, Anastasius addresses the secretaries of the most stalwart units (ἀριθμῶν). More than a few of the novels deal with military affairs too and some of those use the term *arithmos*. For instance, Novel 85, concerning arms, uses *arithmos* to mean unit or regiment. The law too, then, provides evidence of *arithmos*' official meaning.

Though sixth-century inscriptions detailing military affairs may be few in number, the same certainly cannot be said about the papyri, for, of the many thousands published, many hundreds identify soldiers and/or military units. Some papyri survive from Nessana in Israel, and while none of them name the regiment based in that Negev village, one names the unit based up the road in Rhinocorura, the *Arithmos* of the Most Loyal Theodosians.[31] If we turn to Egypt, we find an array of terms used for regiment or unit.[32] The

---

25   SEG 32.1554; Arce, Feissel, and Weber 2014.
26   SEG 32.1554.45.
27   Di Segni 2004: 136.
28   Onur 2014, 2017.
29   A, 43, 45; B, 44, 68. Incidentally, it also uses the term legion on a couple of occasions (B, 10, 12), including one instance where it specifies "military legions" (B, 30). The use of this term (legion) implies that the references to legion in the Egyptian papyri, which we turn to below, were unlikely instances of antiquarianism.
30   SEG 9.356.26.
31   P. Ness. 3.15; Whately 2016b: 122.
32   On the army in Byzantine Egypt, see Maspero (1912), Keegan (1990) and Dijkstra (2008: 23–36).

soldiers at Syene who served as witnesses to all sorts of documents are regularly listed as members of the legion, λεγεών, of Syene.[33] With two exceptions, an ostrakon from Thebes,[34] and a papyrus from Syene which refers to a legion of Philae,[35] these soldiers at Syene are from the only sixth-century unit so styled.[36] A form of *tagma* is occasionally used to mean regiment in the sixth century, as is the case with the *Tagma* of the Numidians of Justinian.[37] Far more common, however, is a form of *arithmos*. The aforementioned unit at Syene is also styled as an *arithmos*, and the relevant papyri tend to be later in date than those that list it as a legion.[38] We also find an *arithmos* of Moors,[39] an *arithmos* of Leontoclibanarii,[40] an *arithmos* of Transtigritani,[41] an *arithomos* of Hermonthis,[42] an *arithmos* of Antaiopolis,[43] an *arithmos* of Scythians,[44] and an *arithmos* of Sextodalmaticae.[45] One papyrus even lists a vexillation of the *arithmos* of Ombos.[46] Given that most of these papyri are in some sense official—plenty list soldiers as witnesses to official documents—we clearly have more evidence here of *arithmos*' place as an official term for unit or regiment in the sixth century.[47]

[33] P. Lond. 5.1734: στρ(ατιώτης) λεγ(εῶνος) Συήνης μαρτυρῶ. Grosse (1920: 272–273) argued that the *codex* (*Cod. Iust.* 12.35.14, 12.37.8, 12.42.1) demonstrated that *cohors*, *legio*, and *vexillatio* were still official terms in the sixth century. Note too Keegan (1990: 141–142) and Dijkstra (2008: 30–31).

[34] SB 18.13321.

[35] P. Muench 1.16.

[36] P. Lond. 5.1722, 1724, 1728, 1734, 1855; P. Muench 1.4+5v, 8, 9, 11, 15, 16. P.Lond. 5.1722 uses both legion and *arithmos* to refer to the unit at Syene, and there is no indication that there was more than one unit based in the town.

[37] SB 5.8028. A mid-fifth century papyrus names the *tagma* soldiers of the frontier of Thebes (P. Ross. Georg. 5.30). See too SB 20.14704.

[38] See P. Lond. 5.1723, for instance.

[39] BGU 19.2804.

[40] P. Worp 33.

[41] CHLA 10.407. Though it dates nearly eighty years too soon, SB 22.15801, from 419 CE in the Arsinoite nome, identifies the legion of Memphis (λεγεῶνος Μέμφεως) and the Transtigritani *arithmos* or *numerus* (νουμέρου τῶν γενναιοτάτων Τρανστιγριτανῶν and τοῦ αὐτ]οῦ ἀριθμοῦ). On this papyrus, see Hoogendijk (1995: 110), who identifies the unit with the *legio V Madeconica* of the *Notitia Dignitatum*, without getting into the particularities of the *arithmoi* so named. On the *legio V Macedonica*, see Zuckerman (1988).

[42] BGU 2.673.

[43] CHLA 41.1193.

[44] P. Cair. Masp. 1.67009.

[45] P. Cair. Masp. 2.67126.

[46] P. Laur. 3.111.

[47] Petersen 2013: 107.

Procopius does use the word *arithmos* and its forms in places, but never to mean unit or regiment.[48] Given that *arithmos*' designation as an official term seems undeniable, Procopius' silence is remarkable; as noted at the beginning of the chapter, a few scholars have lumped the terms *arithmos* and *katalogos* together.[49] It is for this reason that discussing the two terms in tandem makes sense.

3   Procopius' Regiments

3.1   Katalogos *in Procopius*

I turn now to *katalogos*, and I will begin with Procopius' own usage. Procopius uses a form of *katalogos* throughout his oeuvre. He uses a form of *katalogos* eight times in the *Secret History* and eleven times in the *Buildings*. In nearly each of the eight instances in the *Secret History* where Procopius uses *katalogos*, it means a register or list, or something to that effect, and the contexts are military matters (Table 3.2).[50] The majority come in Procopius' discussion of the suffering of soldiers in book 24. For instance, some of his uses even have to do with phantom soldiers being enrolled on military rosters to enrich corrupt commanders.

The uses in the *Buildings* are just as straightforward. Several have nothing to do with military matters, though they do mean something like a catalogue or list.[51] The other uses in the *Buildings* are a bit more problematic, though by this point quite familiar. Six of them are usually understood as referring either to a detachment of soldiers, or regular soldiers. In each case, however, they are accompanied either with the adjective στρατιωτικός or a form of στρατιώτης. The standard English translation (Loeb) translates the phrase in a variety of ways, with no clear reason why *katalogos* might be "troops" in one case, and "detachments" in another.[52] The translations offered would seem to be conditional on the presence of that now distinctive adjective. Given the vaguely official air of the *Buildings*, this is perhaps unsurprising, for it is in keeping with the practices of the very select novels and papyri that use the term in a comparable context.

Procopius uses the term *katalogos* even more often in the *Wars*: forty-seven times, to be exact (see Table 3.3). Unlike those uses in the *Buildings*, Procopius

---

48 See Procop. *Wars* 2.19.41, 2.22.14, 4.19.3, 4.23.13, 5.25.11, 6.3.30, 6.29.34, 7.8.20, 7.38.23, 7.40.38.
49 Jones 1964: 655, Haldon 1993: 51, n. 13, and Laniado's 2015: 95.
50 Procop. *SH*. 6.3.5, 11.2.4, 24.3.1, 24.5.2, 24.5.5, 24.19.2, 24.30.2.
51 Procop. *Build*. 1.2.19.2, 4.3.15.3, 4.4.1.4, 4.4.3.1.
52 Whitby (1995: 82, n. 81) draws the attention to the ambiguity of the translation of the same term in Evagrius (*HE* 6.1).

never uses *stratiwtikos* with *katalogos*. In fact, he never employs *stratiwtikos* at all. What we often find instead, at least with *katalogos*, is either a form of *hippikos*, or more rarely a form of *pezikos*. There are places where, matching one of the Menander Protector examples noted below, Procopius uses a form of τῶν ἐν (people or place) καταλόγων. In these instances, we should understand *katalogos* as referring to a muster-roll. So, they would mean something like "those on the rolls among people X/in place I". This is, as it happens, what his first usage looks like. Even those cases where he uses an adjective like *hippikos*, it could be read or understood as meaning "roll/register/list". On the other hand, perhaps we should bear the official examples in mind, where the phrase στρατιωτικοῖς καταλόγοις and its forms is best understood as meaning "men", i.e., "soldiers", so "cavalry soldiers" for *hippikos stratiwtikos* and "infantry soldiers" for *pezos stratiwtikos*. There are other examples, however, where it makes most sense to understand *katalogos* to mean something like regiment or even detachment, as his modern English translators sometimes have.[53] The very last usage of the term, at 8.35.18, οὐ κατὰ ἄρχοντας ἢ λόχους ἢ καταλόγους τὴν τάξιν καταστησάμενοι, is one such example, and in many respects a very classicizing phrase at that. Even then, it is obvious this is not a specific kind of unit for a specific group of soldiers. When he mentions Trajan's garrisoning of Colchis with Roman troops he uses *katalogoi*, for instance.[54] For the most part, however, *katalogos* meant something akin to men or soldiers, or list or roll.

Müller effectively catalogues Procopius' uses of the *katalogos* without delving deeply into its significance.[55] Given that Jones classified *katalogos* as literary affectation, and Procopius' wider classicizing tendencies, it behooves us to look closer at how the term has been used. The criticism usually lodged at classicizing writers is that they tend to seek anachronistic terms at the expense of something contemporary and more relevant.[56] If we follow Jones' logic, *katalogos* would seem to be just such a term. But is this how the term has been used?

3.2 Katalogos *in Antiquity*

In classical Athens, *katalogos* was a register or army list of citizens liable for military service.[57] Thucydides himself only uses a form of the word seven

---

53 Whitby (1995: 82) says that Procopius regularly uses a form of the term *katalogos* to designate a regiment.
54 Procop. *Wars* 8.2.16.
55 Müller 1912: 101–107.
56 See, especially, Mango (1980: 8).
57 Thuc. 6.43, Aristoph. Eq. 1369, Lys. 25.16, Xen. Mem. 3.4.1; Xen. Hel. 2.4.9; (variations) Demost. 13.4, Demost. 18.105, Thuc. 6.26.1, Demosth. 50.6, Thuc. 6.31.3, Luc. Nav. 33, Polyaen. 3.3.

times.[58] A *katalogos* was an important part of the recruitment process. In fifth century BCE Athens, generals would put together conscription lists of would-be recruits, *katalogoi*, drawn from each tribe (ten total).[59] These lists would be compiled whenever the Athenian assembly voted in favour of war. At the level of the tribe, the taxiarchs, of which there was one for each tribe, *phyle*, was responsible for putting these lists together. Although there were volunteers in classical Athens, these conscription lists played an important role as well.

Jumping ahead several centuries, Cassius Dio, writing in the third century CE, uses the term to mean levies[60] and legions,[61] and a few decades later Dexippus, in one of the fragments of his *Histories*, uses it to mean something like a list.[62] What it does not mean is a regiment or unit. In classical Greece, the preferred terms for different sizes of regiment or unit were *lochos* and *taxis*.[63] Both are used regularly by Thucydides and Xenophon, two of our most important writers for classical-era warfare, and two who had a significant impact on Procopius.[64] If Procopius had been truly interested in using the most appropriate classical Greek terms for military organization, words like these would have been better choices. His choices are telling, though more on this later.

Katalogos' usage picks up in the fourth century CE, with several authors from the fourth and fifth centuries using it in conjunction with *stratiwths* to mean military rolls/registers such as Basil and Libanius,[65] Julian,[66] and Theodoret,[67] among others. Hesychius' definition of *katalogos* is as a register of those obliged to campaign/serve in the army.[68] We have an even later definition from the *Suda*, which echoes this: it defines *katalogos* as a list or roster, "the listing of those obligated to serve in the military, and their enumeration",[69] and mentions *katalogoi* in reference to quotations from Aristophanes and Aelian, and with regard to Trajan.[70]

---

58 Thuc. 1.10.4, 6.26.2, 6.31.3, 6.43.1, 7.16.2, 7.20.2, 8.24.3.
59 For detailed discussion of the Athenian *katalogos* (and the source of this discussion), see Burckhardt (1999), Christ (2001), and Crowley (2012: 27–30).
60 Cass. Dio 40.65.1.
61 Cass. Dio 40.65.2.
62 Dex. frag. 24.21.
63 Hunt 2007: 130. See too Lee (2007: 80–96).
64 Pazdernik 2000, 2006.
65 Basil, letter to Libanius 351.
66 Or. 1.18B, Or. 1.29B, Or. 1.34C, Or. 1.48C.
67 EH, 2.11.
68 Hesych. *Lex.* 1249: ἡ ἀναγραφὴ τῶν ὀφειλόντων στρατεύεσθαι Σ, καὶ ₁ἐξαρίθμησις g.
69 Sud. Kappa 630, 1.
70 Sud. Kappa 630, 2–4.

Katalogos appears in several relevant sixth-century texts, whether legal, epigraphic, or literary. Agathias, Procopius' historiographical successor, uses the word a handful of times, and in each instance, it means something like list;[71] moreover, in only one of those cases is the context specifically military matters. In that case the explicit sense is list, or roll: οὗτοι δὲ στρατιῶται μὲν ὀνομάζονται καὶ ἐγγεγράφαται τοῖς τῶν καταλόγων βιβλίοις, "Though they are called soldiers and have their names entered on the books of rolls".[72] Theophylact Simocatta's usage is a lot like Agathias'; for there are only a handful of examples, only one of those pertains to the military, and each time it means list or roll.[73] As we saw at the start of the chapter at 2.6.9, Theophylact discusses the garrison of Circesium, and calls them the "roll of the Quartoparthoi"; καταλόγου ... τῶν Κουαρτοπάρθων.[74] Menander Protector, whose history survives only in fragments, uses *katalogos* to mean list in most extant cases.[75] There are a few exceptions, however, where his use of *katalogos* might mean something like regiment or unit.[76] In one case, Menander includes the adjective στρατιωτικῶν to specify that all the *katalogoi* in question are military in nature: πάντων τῶν στρατιωτικῶν καταλόγων.[77]

I have found no inscriptions that used *katalogos* to mean regiment or unit. As for the papyri, there are very few that use a form of *katalogos*; in some of those the word means a list or catalogue.[78] In others, some sort of military connection is implied, though some qualifications are usually included.[79] Three papyri,[80] orders for military supplies dated to between 533 and 550 involving the aforementioned *arithmos* of Numidians of Justinian and the praeses of the Thebaid, include a form of *katalogos*, but qualify it by means of the adjective στρατιωτικοῖς (ὅπλοις καὶ **στρατιωτικοῖς καταλόγοις** εἰς παράταξιν παρεσκευασμένοις τῇ τῶν τακτικῶν [ἐ]μπειρίᾳ). This passage appears in all three papyri, and has been translated, "is fortifying them with arms and military troops trained for battle by tactical experience", but which perhaps should read something like "preparing them with arms and units for battle by means of experience of tactics".[81] In these cases *katalogos* means something akin to regiment or

---

71 Aga. *Hist.* 2.27.7, 4.30.2, 5.6.7, 5.14.2, 5.15.2.
72 Aga. *Hist.* 5.14.2.
73 Theophyl. Sim. 2.6.9, 2.16.6, 3.10.1, 3.11.7, 4.2.9, 8.9.3.
74 trans. Whitby.
75 Men. Prot. 3.232, 243, 245; 13.43, 23.18.
76 Men. Prot. 1.4, 3.285, 5.9, 31.15.
77 Men. Prot. 31.15.
78 CPR 9.56; P. Cair. Masp 2.67151; P. Cair. Masp. 2.67200.
79 P. Cair. 2, 67321; P. Lond. 5, 1663; SB 5.8028.
80 P. Cair. Masp. 3.67321, P. Lond. 5.1663, SB 5.8028.
81 Trans. Hunt and Edgar (Loeb 282).

unit, though the inclusion of the adjective *stratiwtikos* is, to my mind, telling; it implies that in its absence *katalogos* cannot mean a regiment or unit on its own, despite the translation offered in the Loeb volume.

In fact, this form, *stratiwtikos katalogos*, also appears in the last set of official documents for us to discuss, Justinian's *Novels*. As with the papyri, *kataologos* appears rarely (twelve times), and only occasionally, twice as it happens, is used in any military sense. Novels 102 and 148 use the now familiar phrase, γενναιοτάτου στρατιωτικοῦ καταλόγου in *Novel* 102, and τῶν ἐπὶ Μυσίας καὶ Σκυθίας στρατιωτικῶν καταλόγων in *Novel* 148. While it seems perfectly reasonable to translate the former as "the noblest soldiers", in the latter it is a bit more problematic. In that same novel, and just a line or so later, we find τάς τε στρατιωτικὰς καὶ φοιδερατικάς, and a little after that τοῖς στρατιωτικοῖς τάγμασιν ἢ φοιδερατικοῖς. In these few legal examples, it is clear that *katalogos*' association with military affairs is the inclusion of the adjective *stratiwtikos*, and there is no apparent reason why it should be associated with field troops and not just soldiers in general, i.e. the men on the military rolls.

Perhaps the most contentious papyrus to this discussion of *katalogos* is a late sixth century CE papyrus from Antinoopolis discussed by Bouvier and Wherli, and Mitthof.[82] Bouvier and Wherli translate *katalogos*, which appears twice, as unit. But the fragmentary papyrus also includes *arithmos* in four places. It is not impossible that the author of the document might have chosen to vary his or her vocabulary by using two different words for unit in this papyrus that pertains to the *annona militaris*, which is Bouvier and Wherli's suggestion, a view shared by Mitthof.[83] This is not common practice, however, particularly on official documents, at least of those that survive from the sixth century. Rather they are, with one sixth-century exception discussed above (P.Lond. 5.1722), consistent in their word choice, as the papyri discussed in this document suggests. Is it possible that *katalogos* has a different meaning in either of its two usages? In the first we read: γὰρ δεδιδάγμεθα παρὰ τῶν ἀποκρισιαρίων [το]ῦ αὐτοῦ καταλόγ[ου τ]ὴν τοῦ ὀπτίονος [ἀ]δικοῦντος χρείαν. In the second, we read: εἰ γὰρ ὑπερθῶνται, μέλλουσιν αὐτοί τε καὶ ὅλος ὁ αὐτῶν γενναῖος κατάλογος τὰ μέγιστα βλαβῆναι. In the same document, *arithmos* is used four times. Minus the fragmentary opening, the entire document reads as follows, using *katalogos* and *arithmos* as synonyms:

> ... for we were instructed about the business of the guilty *optio* from the *apokrisiarii* of the same **unit** [*katalogos*]; if the *optiones* themselves think

---

82 SB 18.13884; Bouvier and Wherli 1985; Mitthof 2001: 561–562.
83 Bouvier and Wherli 1985: 73, n. 4; Mitthof 2001: 561, n. 1192.

it necessary to be accompanied to Antinoopolis by a few other men from the **unit** [*arithmos*], they must be ordered to go there with them to avoid any other grievances to be added to the bread *annona* for this year. On receipt of this letter Your Excellency will take steps to have the aforesaid Theodore and John with the other men from the **unit** [*arithmos*] whom they think should be brought before us. For if they are different, they and their entire noble **unit** [*katalogos*] risk suffering the greatest harm. We have just written to the superiors of their **unit** [*arithmos*], so that they send them here immediately and do not expose themselves to the danger which threatens them personally in case they neglect our injunctions on this point. Take the necessary measures to send under our escort the junior officers named above, so that because of their wrongdoing the State does not discover the damage inflicted and that as a result of this their **unit** [*arithmos*] suffers harm.[84]

An alternative reading is possible, however. First, there are several lines missing from the beginning, at least ten, and then the next three are fragmentary. Second, there is no doubt that the *arithmoi* should be translated as they are, unit or regiment. One word that poses problems, however, is *apokrisiarios*. In late antiquity an *apokrisiarios* was usually a messenger representing a bishop or some high ecclesiastical office who might convey messages to the emperor.[85] They feature in Justinian's Novel 6 on the ordaining and appointing of major religious officials and in Novel 25 on the ecclesiastical matters.[86] All the papyri that use the term are late: the earliest ones, like this, date to at least 500 CE.[87]

---

84 ... δεδιδάγμεθα παρὰ τῶν ἀποκρισιαρίων [το]ῦ αὐτοῦ **καταλόγ**[ου τ]ὴν τοῦ ὀπτίονος [ἀ]δικοῦντος χρείαν· εἰ δὲ καὶ αὐτοὶ οἱ [ὀπ]τίονες νομίζουσιν χρείαν εἶναι[ι] τῆς κατὰ τὴν Ἀντινοέων παρουσίας ἄλλ[ων] τινῶν προ[σώπων τοῦ] ἀρ[ι]θμοῦ, δεήσει κἀκείνους σὺν αὐτοῖς πεμφθῆναι ἐνταῦθα τοῦ μὴ αἰτίας ἑτέρας ἐπιτεθῆναι τῷ πράγματι τῶν ἀφωρισμένων αὐτοῖς ἀννωνικῶν ἄρτων. ἅμα οὖν τῇ τῶν γραμμάτων λήμ[ψ]ε[ι] αὐτίκα ἡ σὴ λ[α]μπρότης παρασκευάσῃ τοὺς μνημονευθέντας Θεόδωρον καὶ Ἰωάννην μετὰ καὶ ὧν νομίζουσιν χρείαν ἔχειν ἄλλων προσώπων ἐκ τοῦ κατ' αὐτοὺς **ἀριθμοῦ** γενέσθαι πρὸς ἡμᾶς· εἰ γὰρ ὑπερθῶνται, μέλλουσιν αὐτοί τε καὶ ὅλος ὁ αὐτῶν γενναῖος **κατάλογος** τὰ μέγιστα βλαβῆναι. ἰδοὺ δὲ καὶ πρὸς τοὺς πρίορας τοῦ αὐτῶν **ἀριθμοῦ** γεγραφήκαμεν ἵνα παραχρῆμα αὐτοὺς \ἐκ/πέμψωσιν ἐνταῦθα καὶ μὴ ἐπιδ[έξωνται] κίνδυνον καθ' ἑαυτῶν ἐκ τοῦ παραμελεῖν τῶν ἡμετέρων ἐπὶ τ[οῦτο] κελεύσεων, τοὺς δὲ προονομασθέντας ὀπτίονας ὑπὸ ἐγγύας ἀσφαλεῖς ἐνταῦθα παραπεμφθῆναι παρασκεύασον, [ἵνα μὴ] διὰ τὴν αὐτῶν πρόφασιν εὑρεθῇ τὸ δημόσιον βλαπτόμενον καὶ ἐκ τούτου οὗτος ὁ **ἀριθμὸς** αὐτῶν εἰς πράγματα περιπέσῃ.

85 Kazhdan 1991.

86 *Iust. Nov.* 6.2–3; 123.25.

87 CPR 22.58; P. Apoll. 37; P. Apoll. 87; P. Cair. Masp. 2.67168; P. Horak 32; P. Lond. 4.1360; P. Lond. 4.1379; P. Lond. 4.1401; P. Lond. 4.1406; P. Lond. 4.1436; P. Oxy. 1.144; P. Oxy. 8.1108; P. Oxy. 16.1913; P. Ross. Georg. 4.4; PSI 3.196; SB 18.13884 (this papyrus).

Leaving aside the papyrus being discussed here, they uniformly deal with church matters. Thus, we need to consider the possibility that the *apokrisarii* referred to in this papyrus are not your bog-standard messengers, and instead classify them as the religious messengers that feature in various late antique documents. Indeed, at least one use of *katalogos* in the papyri comes in a text dealing with religious matters.[88] The inclusion of αὐτοῦ in the attributive position, between the definite article and the noun (καταλόγ[ου) is also suggestive, for it usually means "same", which is how I translated it above. It also presupposes that the *katalogos* in question was referred to earlier, and so probably in the missing lines above. To my mind, then, all of this is enough to cast the equation of *katalogos* with *arithmos* in the first usage into doubt. Instead, we should go with list or register, "*apokrisiarii* of the same list".

This still leaves the second usage. In that case, there is one significant word, γενναῖος, which modifies κατάλογος, and again in the attributive position. The word γενναῖος appears in this form (nominative singular) in late antique papyri only in this one instance. There is only one other case, and it is from the first century CE,[89] and a few more in the accusative singular (none in the dative or genitive singular).[90] We do find several examples that use the superlative (*gennaiotatos*) however, and many of those refer to soldiers or units/regiments like BGU 12.2141, which includes γενναιοτάτων Μαύρων, "the noblest of the Moors". Sometimes the word modifies soldiers as in CHLA 41.1193, which includes the phrase τῶν γ[ε]νναιοτάτων στρα[τ]ιωτῶν τῶν ἀπὸ το(ῦ) ἀριθμο(ῦ) Ἀνταίο(υ), "the noblest of the soldiers from this *arithmos* of Antinoopolis". In not one of those cases, however, do we find a form like γενναιοτάτου ἀριθμοῦ, or "noblest unit/regiment". So, if the γενναῖος κατάλογος which we find in this papyrus really does mean "noble unit/regiment", it is the only one of its kind (among 136 papyri that date from 200 CE on) to use this specific language. The closest we get is something like τὸν ἀριθμὸν τῶν [γενναιοτάτων καὶ] καθοσιωμένων Λεοντοκλ[ιβαναρίων, or "the unit of the noblest and best known Leontoklibanarii".[91] While this is not definitive proof—we may no longer have the others that used to say this or the author of the document might not have been familiar with the standard terminology—it is very suggestive. Again, while *katalogos* could mean unit/regiment in this second case, I would argue that we should read it as list/register or even roster, "their entire noble roster". In non-literary evidence, *katalogos*, when it appears, means something like list,

---

88   CPR 9.56.
89   P. Oxy. 9.1184.
90   TM 63877 is the only one of eight with the accusative century that is not BCE in date.
91   P. Oxy. 72.4920.

CATALOGUES AND LEGIONS

register, or catalogue. When it is included with στρατιωτικός it takes on a military meaning, and means "military rolls", or, even better, "soldiers", i.e. the ones on the military rolls (where the words are used substantively).

3.3 Field Armies

As I suggested in the introduction to this chapter, Procopius' use of *katalogos* is more than literary affectation, for it has a bearing on how he structures his work, especially when it came to deciding which regiments to emphasize. The armies of conquest were comprised largely of soldiers from the field armies, the *comitatenses*, though also the elite *bucellarii* and *foederati*. Procopius regular refers to the bodyguards, as we saw in chapter two above. Some have highlighted the blurring of boundaries between the *comitatenses* and *limitanei* in the sixth century, which we can see even in the composition of some campaign armies.[92] The evidence of Procopius, particularly his account of the expeditionary army sent to Africa at the start of the Vandal War, shows that they played no part in the African campaign, as Pringle confirmed.[93] The only case where we seem to have evidence of frontier soldiers off campaigning in the field come in the *Persian Wars*, when the very campaigns take place on or near the eastern frontier.[94]

I noted above that Procopius makes little use of classical Greek terms for detachment (regiment, or unit) like λόχος and τάξεις, despite their regular, contemporary usage by historians like Thucydides and Xenophon.[95] There are two in the *Buildings*, both from the same section, where he notes the garrison of Melitene, which he also calls a legion.[96] The other instances come in the *Wars*. Procopius uses it twice to refer to the Persian Immortals in the context of Callinicum.[97] In the *Vandal War* they are used to refer to regiments of Vandal forces deployed by Gaiseric,[98] and those led by Gelimer at Tricamarum.[99] There are two instances in the *Vandal War* where it refers to Roman detachments, the latter of which comes in the Battle of Scalae Veteres.[100] The final two cases come in book eight, with the first referring to a detachment of the

---

92   See Haldon (1999: 67), and Koehn (2018: 108), for example.
93   Procop. *Wars* 3.11.1–19; Pringle 2001: 51.
94   More on this in the next chapter, five, below.
95   Of many examples, for λόχος, note, for instance, Thucydides at 4.43.4 and 5.67.1, and Xenophon, in the *Anabasis*, at 1.2.25 and 3.4.22; for τάξεις, note Thucydides at 2.79.6 and 3.87.3, and Xenophon, in the *Anabasis*, at 1.8.8 and 2.2.14.
96   Procop. *Build.* 3.4.16.
97   Procop. *Wars* 1.14.31, 49.
98   Procop. *Wars* 3.5.18.
99   Procop. *Wars* 4.3.8.
100 Procop. *Wars* 4.5.5., 4.17.5.

Scholae, the latter in the Battle of Mons Lactarius, where they refer to a Roman detachment.[101] As for τάξεις, the larger grouping of the two terms—perhaps unit rather than detachment—Procopius uses a form of the term twenty-two times. In many of these cases it means something like order, a far cry from its classical Greek usage.[102] There are military uses in Procopius, like rank.[103] In several places we find it with ἐν, as in ἐν τάξει, and in these cases it means "in order", which often, though not always,[104] is associated with the order of the battle line.[105] These are also the cases at 4.14.29 and 8.32.7, even if ἐν is not used. There is but one instance where it refers to something like the formation of a battle line.[106] As a point of comparison, Procopius' classicizing successors make little use of these terms as well.[107] A more common term used by Procopius' classicizing predecessors is a form of *tagma*, which also found its way into Maurice's *Strategikon*.[108] Both Agathias and Theophylact use it a number of times, while Menander just a handful—and Procopius only twice.[109] All of this is to say that Procopius' choice to use *katalogos* when referring to groups of soldiers must be seen not as part of the wider classicizing historiographical genre, but as a choice specific to him. Why *katalogos*, and what, if anything, does it tell us about him?

While *katalogos* seems to have had this wider meaning of a list that harkens back to the classical age, there is no denying it has an official meaning. In fact, the set of three matching papyri might give some indication of just what a military *katalogos* might be: namely a list of all soldiers in an individual regiment, of which we have a few, particularly from Dura Europos, and which are conspicuously absent for most of late antiquity.[110] While we may not have

---

101 Procop. *Wars* 8.27.2, 8. 35.18.
102 Procop. *SH* 7.31.2.
103 Procop. *SH* 24.25.1, 24.30.7.
104 Procop. *Build*.1.11.19.
105 Procop. *Wars* 1.13.29, 1.24.51, 4.11.49, 5.22.10, 5.23.9, 5.23.12, 5.23.21, 5.28.22, 5.28.29, 6.9.14, 6.16.4, 8.9.21, 8.32.4. There is the odd instance where Dewing has interpreted uses of this phrase as "in their proper divisions", as is the case at 2.25.14, though "in order" conveys the sense better. On battle order in Procopius see Whately (2016a: 89–96).
106 Procop. *Wars* 4.3.8.
107 Agathias does not use the term, while in the surviving fragments Menander uses it only once (13.72). Theophylact uses the term to refer to units on a few occasions. Note 1p.14.1 and 5.10.5, for example. As with λόχος, Agathias does not use a form τάξεις, Menander uses it only twice, and Theophylact several times.
108 Book three of Maurice's *Strategikon* is devoted solely to the tagma.
109 Procopius: *Wars* 1.8.2; *SH* 15.29. Menander: 3.6, 3.240, 8.87, 8.91. There are nearly a dozen examples in Agathias and Theophylact.
110 *RMR* 1.

any, we know of their existence. They are implied, for instance, in the edict of Anastasius found in Cyrenaica.[111] Indeed, we might well imagine a *katalogos* used in the transfer of the *arithmos* of Numidians to Hermopolis named in those papyri. A *stratiwtikos katalogos* naming a particular regiment might, in official circles, have come to be associated with that regiment. Procopius himself was likely very familiar with them, as some of his comments in the *Secret History* make plain and as some of his experiences with Belisarius, discussed in chapter two above, demonstrate. When you consider the phrase's classical pedigree, it is easy to imagine Procopius coming to liken these registers to particular units over time. It is worth stressing too that the particular and extensive use of *katalogos* in military contexts is unique to Procopius: no other late antique author that I am aware of used the phrase as often as he has, which to my mind reinforces the idea that his experiences influenced his diction in this regard.

3.4 Count Marcellinus, Jordanes, John Malalas, and Agathias

To this point, it should be clear that Procopius' decision to use *katalogos* as frequently as he did—more on the why in the final section of this chapter—was a practice few people shared. To emphasize the point, it is worth taking a look at the practices of some contemporary (and near contemporary) sources, Count Marcellinus, Jordanes, John Malalas, and Agathias, the first two of whom wrote in Latin while the other two wrote in Greek.

Marcellinus' accounts of combat tend to be brief and his references to armies and regiments very general.[112] In fact, with his emphasis on the commanders to the exclusion of the rank and file soldiers, his accounts read as summary versions of Procopius'. For example, while describing some of the unrest in North Africa, all he says is "In Africa, John, making an attack on the usurper Stotzas, killed him and was himself killed by his armour-bearer. In that usurpation a certain John was elected and called Stotzas the younger."[113] That summary excludes the efforts of most of the participants. To give another example, when noting the Roman preparations for war against Persia and the west, he calls the Roman military an army, *exercitus*, a term he uses elsewhere.[114]

Jordanes is not much better. His references to armies and regiments are as sparing as Marcellinus'. All discussions of contemporary events are brief. His

---

111   *SEG* 9.356.7.
112   On Marcellinus see Croke (2001).
113   Marc. Com. 545.2, trans. Croke.
114   Marc. Com. 529. See too, for example, Marc. Com. 535.1.

longest description of any military encounter, the Battle of the Catalaunian Plains, generally ignores regiments and instead focuses on commanders and the main military groupings.[115] When setting out the Roman deployment for battle, for example, Jordanes notes "Now Theodorid with the Visigoths held the right wing and Aëtius with the Romans the left. They placed in the centre Sangiban (who, as said before, was in command of the Alani), thus contriving with military caution to surround by a host of faithful troops the man in whose loyalty they had little confidence."[116] Earlier, he had said:

> On the side of the Romans stood the Patrician Aëtius, on whom at that time the whole empire of the west depended; a man of such wisdom that he had assembled warriors from everywhere to meet them on equal terms. Now these were his auxiliaries: Franks, Sarmatians, Armoricians, Liticians, Burgundians, Saxons, Riparians, Olibriones (once Romans soldiers and now the flower of the allied forces), and some other Celtic or German tribes.[117]

It is tempting to read the list of peoples as not unlike those references to peoples, *symmachoi* and others, we find in Procopius, but there is no indication that Jordanes here means regiments and not people. In earlier parts of the *Getica*, Jordanes only occasionally uses language that could be considered technical, for he refers to *foederati*.[118] That said, these are not the *foederati* of the sixth-century military.[119] There are no references to legions or *numeri*; however, he does, on a few occasions, name legions in his *Romana*, though they are historical legions (i.e., not contemporary, and all before events in the second century CE).[120]

---

115 Jordanes' description of the Catalaunian Plains is based on Priscus' fifth century version, which is now lost. We have no idea what details he may or may not have included, at least for material like this (warfare).
116 Jord. Get. 38.197, trans. Mierow.
117 Jord. Get. 36.191, trans. Mierow (slightly adapted). *A parte vero Romanorum tanta patricii Aetii providentia fuit, cui tunc innitebatur res publica Hesperiae plagae, ut undique bellatoribus congregatis adversus ferocem et infinitam multitudinem non impar occurreret. Hi enim adfuerunt auxiliares: Franci, Sarmatae, Armoriciani, Liticiani, Burgundiones, Saxones, Ripari, Olibriones, quondam milites Romani, tunc vero iam in numero auxiliarium exquisiti, aliaeque nonnulli Celticae vel Germanie nationes.*
118 Jord. Get. 16.89, 21.112, 28.145.
119 On these earlier federates, see Heather (1997).
120 Jord. Rom. 155, 217, 236, 239, 261.

CATALOGUES AND LEGIONS 75

Shifting to the Greek, Malalas' *Chronographia*, like Marcellinus', is short on detail, though as we saw above, Malalas does refer to *arithmoi*.[121] He includes two references to *limitanei*, one of which concerns events in the sixth century.[122] More often than not, however, as is the tendency amongst sixth-century historians, he prefers to describe battles in terms of the commanders as he does in his description of the Battle of Dara.[123] In one of his most detailed accounts, the Battle of Callinicum, Malalas prefers to list the Roman combatants not in terms of regiments but in terms of men. So, Belisarius arrives with 8,000 men, and Sunicas with 4,000.[124] Another term he sometimes uses is *tagma*, though most of these are all in earlier books (no later than book 13).[125] The two exceptions do deal with sixth-century events. Malalas uses it to refer to armies in his account of the siege of Amida,[126] and again to mean something like "ranks" or "regiments" during another conflict near Amida.[127]

Our final author in this section, Agathias, was writing closer to the end of the sixth century. His *Histories* describes a few of the years that followed Procopius' *Wars*; his discussion is detailed and lengthy.[128] Like Procopius, Agathias is a classicizing historian. Agathias is much more verbose, however, and keener on using archaic vocabulary like "phalanx". To give one example, early in his account of the Battle of Casilinum, while the armies are drawing up, he simply says, "As soon as Narses reached the battlefield he made the regular tactical arrangements and dispositions of the troops".[129] This is just one of several instances where Agathias uses a form of "phalanx", where it usually means something like "army" or "rank/s".[130] Another term he regularly uses was *tagma*, one with, as we saw above, a little better pedigree. For Agathias, *tagma* sometimes means army just like *phalanx*.[131] In other places, it means something

---

121 Mal. *Chron*. 18.2, 18.5, 18.10, 18.129.
122 Mal. *Chron*. 18.2. The other comes at 12.40.
123 Mal. *Chron*. 18.50.
124 Mal. *Chron*. 18.60: μετὰ χιλιάδων τεσσάρων (Belisarius), and μετὰ χιλιάδων τεσσάρων (Sunicas).
125 Mal. *Chron*. 2.11, 2.16, 5.2, 12.10, 13.27.
126 Mal. *Chron*. 16.9.
127 Mal. *Chron*. 18.65.
128 Estimations of Agathias vary. Kaldellis (1997, 1999, 2003) is more positive while Cameron (1970) is more circumspect. See too Whitby (1992: 31–38).
129 Agathias 2.8.1, trans Frendo. Ναρσῆς δὲ ἐπεὶ ἐν τῷ χώρῳ ἐγεγόνει, οὗ δὴ συμπλέκεσθαι ἔμελλεν, αὐτίκα ἐς φάλαγγα καθίστη τὸν στρατὸν καὶ διέταττεν.
130 Agathias 1.14.3, 1.21.6, 1.22.2, 2.3.8, etc.
131 Agathias 1.4.4.

like unit.[132] One last point: like Procopius, Agathias sometimes refers to groups of soldiers as either some number of infantrymen or cavalrymen.[133]

3.5 John Lydus and the Anastasius Edicts

There are two other important pieces of evidence relevant to this story, John the Lydian and the edicts of Anastasius. John the Lydian, of course, was a contemporary of Procopius, and possibly even a friend.[134] He wrote a few texts, but the most relevant to us is his *On the Magistrates*. It contains all sorts of useful details on the military; moreover, John, a writer with antiquarian interests, includes lots of historical military terminology. On the surface, John the Lydian might not seem the most obvious comparator with Procopius, but his emphasis on appropriate vocabulary makes him well worth paying attention to. His position as an administrator likely meant he had ready access to detailed administrative records, and his career as a professor of Latin put him in a position to understand Latin military documents.[135] Plus, John intended to write (and possibly did write) a military history of Justinian's Persian wars, and by all accounts was well read.[136]

John filled his *On the Magistrates* with Latin words, often (though not always) Hellenized, even if questions about the accuracy of his Latinity abound.[137] For instance, in a discussion of expense payments for soldiers that originated during the early fourth century BCE during war with Veii, he gets into the component parts of the Roman military and refers to a wide range of different regiments and soldier types. He identifies the auxiliary troops, the *alae* and *cohortes*, but also other divisions and regiments like *vexillationes*, *turmae*, and then the legions themselves, in each case giving the size of the unit or subunit.[138] Then he gives a long list of what he considered to be the component parts of the legion, which includes subdivisions like *turmae* and different kinds of soldiers like *signiferi* (standard-bearers) and *lanciarii* (lancers).[139]

---

132 Agathias 5.14.3, 5.15.4.
133 For example, at 4.13.1, Agathias describes a mixed force under Buzes and Justin numbering 4000.
134 Kaldellis 2004c, Dmitriev 2010.
135 Maas 1992: 29.
136 Maas 1992.
137 On his Latinity, see Kelly (2006) and Dmitriev (2018). For a detailed discussion of the text, see Dubuisson and Schamp (2006: xiii–dcclxxi). For an example where John Lydus uses Latin when referring to military matters, see Joh. Lyd. *De Mag.* 3.3.1: *et <coll>ocare eum in legione prima adiutrice nostra* (and station him in the first legion which helps us, trans. Bandy).
138 Joh. Lyd. *De Mag.* 1.46.3–7.
139 Joh. Lyd. *De Mag.* 1.46.

CATALOGUES AND LEGIONS 77

Indeed, John uses the word legion on a few occasions including the long list of ranks just discussed.[140] His usage implies that, at least in his eyes, the legion was a thing of the past.[141]

Besides the historical ranks, in other places he uses what could be called contemporary terms for assorted divisions. The term that John Lydus regularly uses to mean regiment or unit is *tagma*.[142] The very first usage in the table of contents reads "On units under arms, their names and ranks, and the so-called *tirones*".[143] In the second, it is found in a quote from the now lost *Tactics* of Paternus, a work also referenced by Vegetius, where it also means unit or regiment.[144] As noted, it also sometimes means ranks, as it does at 1.48.2. John also often uses it to mean something akin to "body" as in collection or group—and usually in reference to the Augustales.[145] Forms of phalanx appear too on occasion as a substitute for *tagma*.[146] *Arithmos*, which has been established as the standard Greek term for a unit or regiment, is used only once in this way in the *On the Magistrates*. At 1.47.2, John says, "the so-called *tirones* give themselves for service to those who are truly soldiers or to have been stationed at all up to this point in any unit, manifestly on account of the beggarliness of their station in life and inexperience in fighting".[147]

John's lone usage of *arithmos* in a military sense serves as a fitting segue for a discussion of the last term to discuss from John the Lydian' *On the Magistrates*, *katalogos*, which he uses seventeen times. They are all listed in the following table.

In every instance, John Lydus uses *katalogos* to mean register. In most cases, the register in question has something to do with the imperial civil service, with a few exceptions. Sometimes John specifies what kind of register is under discussion, and in two cases he means military registers. At 2.11.1, John is discussing the division of civil and military powers, and uses στρατιωτικοὺς καταλόγους to indicate all the soldiers. He uses a different phrase entirely for the members of the civil service. The second use at 3.41.1 uses identical language and has the same meaning. A careful, thorough investigation of John

---

140 Joh. Lyd. *De Mag.* 1.16.3; 3.3.6, 3.34.1.
141 Note his comments at Joh. Lyd. *De Mag.* 3.34.1, for instance: "before Marius had organized the so-called *legiones*."
142 See Joh. Lyd. *De Mag.* 3.3.2: καὶ τάξειας αὐτὸν ἐν τῷ πρώτῳ τάγματι τῷ βοηθοῦντι ἡμῖν.
143 Joh. Ldy. *De Mag.* 1.12, trans. Bandy.
144 Joh. Ldy. *De Mag.* 1.9.5; Veg. Mil. 1.8.
145 Joh. Ldy. *De Mag.* 3.9.1–2.
146 Joh. Ldy. *De Mag.* 1.48.2.
147 οἱ λεγόμενοι τείρωνες εἰς ὑπηρεσίαν τῶν ἀληθῶς στρατευομένων, οὐ μὴν ἄξιοι τέως στρατιῶται καλεῖσθαι ἢ ὅλως ἐν ἀριθμῷ τέως τετάχθαι διὰ δὴ τὸ πτωχὸν τῆς τύχης καὶ ἄπειρον τῆς μάχης.

TABLE 3.1   John Lydus' use of the term *katalogos*

Passage number	Greek terms	English translation (trans. Bandy)
Table of contents 7	περὶ τῆς τάξεως τῶν ἐπάρχων καὶ τῶν ἐν αὐτῇ **καταλόγων**	"on the staff of the prefects and the registers on it"
2.11.1	τοὺς μὲν στρατιωτικοὺς **καταλόγους** ἔταξεν ἡ βασιλεία ὑπὸ τοῖς τότε καλουμένοις κόμισιν καὶ στρατηγοῖς,	"the emperor placed the military registers under the authority of those who were called at that time *comites*"
2.18.1	πόσοις τε καὶ ποίοις συμπληροῦται **καταλόγοις**	"and of what sort of registers it is composed"
2.22.1	περί τε τῶν ἐν αὐτῇ **καταλόγῳ**,	"and about the registers in it"
2.24.3	τὸ γὰρ μάγιστρος ὀφφικίων ὄνομα οὐδὲν ἢ τὸν ἡγούμενον τῶν αὐλικῶν **καταλόγων** σημαίνει, ὡς προέφαμεν, ἐν οἷς ἥ τε ἱππικὴ καὶ ἡ πεζομάχος δύναμις τῆς βασιλείας θεωρεῖται εἰς μυρίους συναγομένη πολεμιστάς.	"As for the name *magister officiorum*, it signifies, as I already said, nothing but 'head of the court registers', in which both the equestrian and the infantry forces of the emperor are observed amounting to ten thousand warriors."
2.27.2	οὐκ ἄν τις ἐν ἀρχόντων ἀριθμήσειέ ποτε **καταλόγῳ**	"not, in fact, ever reckon in a list of magistrates"
3.2.2–3	ἀντὶ τοῦ ἀπογραφαὶ τῶν **καταλόγων**	"master list of the registers"
3.3.1	Κοινῇ μὲν οὖν ἅπασι τοῖς **καταλόγοις** ἐκ τῆς βασιλέως ὑποσημειώσεως ἀδιούτωρες	"now then all the registers dependent on the emperor's signature commonly had *adiutores*"
3.3.2	ὅθεν ὁ πρωτεύων τοῦ παντὸς **καταλόγου** ἔτι καὶ νῦν κορνικουλάριος ἀναφέρεται	"the one who heads the entire register still even to this day is referred to as *cornicularius*"
3.4.1	ὁ ὕπαρχος δι' οἰκείας ὑποσημειώσεως δίδωσι τῷ πρὸς τὴν στρατείαν ἐρχομένῳ εἰς ὃν αὐτὸς ἕλοιτο ταχθῆναι **κατάλογον**.	"the prefect through his personal signature gave to him who came to the service permission to be stationed into the register into which the former chose."
3.4.2	αἱ δὲ προσηγορίαι τῶν πάντων **καταλόγων** τῆς τάξεως αὗται·	"the designations in all the registers are these"

TABLE 3.1 John Lydus' use of the term *katalogos* (*cont.*)

Passage number	Greek terms	English translation (trans. Bandy)
3.8.1	Τοιαῦται μὲν καὶ τοσαῦται τομαὶ τῶν **καταλόγων** τῆς ἀρχῆς.	"Such, indeed, and so many are the classifications of the magistracy's registers"
3.12.4	ὡς ἔφην, τοῦ **καταλόγου**, ἐν ᾧ τελεῖ τυχὸν ὁ τὰς ψήφους ἐγχειριζόμενος	"as I said, of the register in which the one entrusted with the decisions"
3.22.1	Πάντων, οἶμαι, τῶν **καταλόγω**, εἰ μή τι σφάλλομαι,	"Now that all the registers, I believe, if I am not mistaken"
3.38.1	καὶ τούτων συνέβη ἀποτελεσθῆναι τὸν **κατάλογον**	"it came about that the service roster consisted of these, too"
3.41.1	τοὺς μὲν στρατιωτικοὺς **καταλόγους** ἔταξεν ἡ βασιλεία ὑπὸ τοῖς τότε καλουμένοις κόμισιν καὶ στρατηγοῖς	"the emperor placed the military registers under the authority of those who were called at that time *comites*, that is, generals"
3.66.4	ἀντὶ τοῦ τῶν **καταλόγων** φύλακι	"namely, 'custodian of the registers'"

Lydus' uses of *katalogos* reveals that they are all unambiguous, and that he uses it the same way as Procopius, namely to mean list/register/catalogue/roster.

Also of interest is John Lydus' *On the Months*, in which he touches on relevant subject matter. John Lydus gives the number of soldiers under Diocletian, which was very specific.[148] In the next section, he includes more relevant information:

> [What is called] a "baked brick" among the Greeks is called *laterculus* by the Romans.[149] There was a "public brick-work" which had the names of the senators and those of the armies written on it, and the 'brick' was inscribed as a sort of linear figure on a wall, in the shape of a square. Some too name it a *titlus*, not knowing that *titlus* properly is used of the written ascription of ranks, not indeed of the square figure. The names of the other armies were inscribed on a (wooden) tablet; and among the

---

148   Joh. Lyd. Mens. 1.27.
149   Lews and Short identify two words, *laterculus* and *laterculum*.

Romans, the flat, thick plank is called a *matricium*. For the ancients used pieces of wood and bark and lime-wood for writing.[150]

This passage betrays John's familiarity with lists of this sort, the possible source—at the most basic of levels—for his notice on the number of soldiers.

From a reader of catalogues[151] we move to one such catalogue itself, found on the Anastasius edict from Perge.[152] The inscription has three parts, three slabs, with the first slab, A, one of Anastasius' speeches, the second, B, the precept of the *magister militum*, and the third, C, the list itself. A form of *katalogos* appears twice, one where Onur translates it as "unit", and another where he translates it as "catalogue".[153] The second case makes sense—it could not mean unit—for the phrase includes a form of *arithmos*: "on the register of each *arithmos*", ἐν τῷ τοῦ παντὸς ἀριθμο(ῦ) καταλό[γ]ῳ.[154] The first case is more ambiguous, for it reads, "ὅπερ μάλιστα [ἐν τῷ ὑμε]τέρῳ καταλόγῳ συνβένι", which, as noted, Onur translated as "which occurs particularly in your unit".[155] On the surface this seems reasonable, except that the line that immediately follows this phrase reads, "... since it is clear that your promotions, ranks and terminations of service". In other words, these are the very items that appear in slab C, the list (catalogue or register) at the end of the three-part inscription. Thus, a case could be made that what the author of the speech means when he (or she) uses *katalogos* in the first instance is a list or register.

There are other edicts from Anastasius including a near complete one from Ptolemais in Libya and another being painstakingly put back together (by Feissel) from Qasr el-Hallabat in Jordan. Both detail some of the rights and responsibilities of the frontier soldiers in their respective regions, and both make explicit reference to military registers, only their language differs significantly from Procopius' and John's. In the case of the edict from

---

150   Joh. Lyd. Mens. 1.28, trans. Hooker. Ἡ παρ' Ἕλλησιν ὀπτὴ πλίνθος λατέρκουλον παρὰ Ῥωμαίοις λέγεται. ἦν δὲ πλίνθος δημοσία, ἐφ'οὗ τά τε τῶν βουλευτῶν καὶ τὰ τῶν στρατευμάτων ὀνόματα ἀπεγράφετο, καὶ ἐγράφετο ἐπὶ τείχους εἰς τετράγωνον σχῆμα τύπος τις καὶ γραμμὴ πλίνθος. τίτλον καὶ αὐτὴν τινες ὀνομάζουσιν οὐκ εἰδότες, ὡς τίτλος κυρίως ἡ προσγραφὴ τῶν ἀξιωμάτων λέγεται, οὐ μὴν ἡ τετράγωνος γραμμή. τὰ τῶν ἄλλων στρατευμάτων ὀνόματα ἐπὶ σανίδος ἀπεγράφετο· λέγεται δὲ παρὰ Ῥωμαίοις ματρίκιον τὸ πλατὺ καὶ παχὺ ξύλον·
151   Note the comments of Kelly (2004: 43).
152   Onur 2017. For a more detailed treatment in Turkish (though the reading has been improved in the more recent publication), see Onur 2014.
153   Onur 2017: 164–165. The Greek can be found at Onur 2017: A.7, B.45.
154   Onur 2017: B.45.
155   Onur 2017: 163.

Cyrenaica, in section one it reads: "those who have completed their term of imperial service or those who are completing it, shall not receive the personal subsistence allowances of soldiers nor shall they be enrolled on the military registers."[156] About the same section of the edict from Qasr el-Hallabat we find: "that each of the dukes, the *scriniarii*, and the *officiales* shall serve according to their order in the personnel register, and not person, either now or hereafter, shall alter his rank except according to the established order of the register".[157]

These three edicts use different words for unit or regiment, and each one varies, at least somewhat, depending on the subject of the decree. In the edict from Cyrenaica, it uses a form of *arithmos* to indicate five regiments of soldiers, τῶν στρατιωτῶν τῶν πέντε ἀριθμῶν.[158] It uses the same term in other sections. Later we read, τοὺς πρώτους ἑκάστου ἀριθμοῦ καὶ κάστρου, "the first names in each unit or camp".[159] Then, further down the inscription we find, [τῶν] γε[νν]αιωτάτων στρατιωτῶν ἐκ πάντων τῶν ἀριθμῶν, "the noblest soldiers from all the units".[160] In this inscription, particularly concerned with frontier soldiers, *arithmos* is the word of choice for a regiment. The edict from Qasr el-Hallabat does not use the term *arithmos*, though that might be due to the current state of the inscription (i.e. fragmentary and problematic).[161] It does make regular reference to the *limitanei*, which are listed a few times in the dative plural, λ[ιμι]ταναίοις, however, along with a host of assorted ranks like duke (δουκικῶν—genitive plural, for example) and *primicerius* (πριμισκρινίους—accusative plural).[162]

The edict from Perge, which dates to the very end of the fifth century CE and is roughly (if not almost exactly) contemporary with the Cyrenaica and Jordan edicts, deals with a very different sort of unit. It is longer than any of the other Anastasian edicts, and provides a wealth of detail on not just the make-up of the regiment in question but also its provisioning and the internal struggles it

---

156   SEG 9.356, trans. In Ancient Roman Statutes, #321, pp 253–255. The Greek reads: τοὺς ταύτην ἀ[πο] πλ[ηρ]ώσα[ντ]ας]ἢ πληροῦντας τὴν στρατίαν μήτε στρατιωτικὰ κομί[ζε]σθαι σιτηρέσια μήτε εἰς μάτ⟨ρ⟩ικας στρατιωτι[κ]ὰς ἀ⟨ν⟩αφέρεσθαι.

157   SEG 32.1554. ὥ[σ]τε ἕκαστον [τ]ῶν δουκ[ικῶν καὶ σκρινιαρίων καὶ] ὀφφικιαλίων καὶ ⟨τὴν⟩ ἐν ταῖς μάτριξειν ὀρδ[ιν]ατίονα φ[υλα]ττειν κ[αὶ μηδένα] βαθμὸν ἢ νῦν ⟨ἢ⟩ μετὰ ταῦτα ἐναλλάττει[ν] παρὰ τὴν τάξιν τῆς [μάτρικος]. The translation is based on Kelly (2004: 43), slightly revised.

158   SEG 9.356.5.
159   SEG 9.356.7.
160   SEG 9.356.14.
161   SEG 32.1554.
162   We will return to this inscription in chapter six below.

faced. That unit was a legion, (λεγεόνων—genitive plural, for example), which is the term it often uses.[163] As we saw above, legions had not disappeared entirely in the sixth century, even if they appear only sparingly. They were also much smaller.[164] That said, it uses *arithmos* (ἀριθμὸν—accusative singular) too.[165]

To close, in virtually no official sixth-century documents do we find *katalogos* as a regiment or unit, or even detachment. This word should not be used to refer to the units of a field army.[166] Before we get to the why, there is one phrase that Procopius uses to describe units or regiments that is worth looking at.

4   Why Catalogues? The Wars of Generals

It comes as little surprise to see the regularity with which Procopius uses the vaguest of phrases when referring to military units. In his survey of late antique historians, Treadgold emphasized Procopius' access to official rolls.[167] It is this comment that, to my mind, best explains Procopius' regular use of forms of *katalogoi* when discussing soldiers. Procopius spent a good part of his career analysing the rolls, and perhaps came to think of military regiments as "the men on the rolls".[168] Though we have little in the way of concrete evidence, we do have some circumstantial material that supports such a claim. Given his position as Belisarius' assessor, Procopius knew the official terms for regiments and units in the sixth century military.[169] Nevertheless, in most cases he shows no desire to describe things in anything that could be considered a technical way, a practice which extends to his discussion of tactics, for instance.[170] Procopius himself might even have been intimately involved in managing troop totals. But for his largely literary and popular audience,[171] a word with good pedigree, the right amount of obscurity, and without much in the way of technicality would have been preferable, like

---

163   Onur 2017: 147.
164   On the size of late Roman legions, see Duncan-Jones (1990: 105–118) and Coello (1996: 12–17, 32–42). Cf. Salway 2015: 381, who says they numbered about 500. This edict from Perge reveals that they could be much bigger, at least 1,200 strong.
165   Onur 2017: 146.
166   Sabin et al. 2007: 480.
167   Treadgold 2007: 218.
168   Cameron (1985: 136) made a similar observation in her landmark book without taking the matter further.
169   See the discussion of Lillington-Martin 2017.
170   Whately 2016a: 93–96.
171   Whately 2016a: 219–224.

katalogos, which has vague classical connotations, to *arithmos*, which does not. Indeed, the very phrase *stratiwtikos katalogos* might well have originated in the hyper-classicizing and rhetorical fourth century, and been one of the archaizing words or phrases of choice for soldiers amongst the literati, for we find skilled rhetoricians like Basil the Great and Libanius using the phrase in such a way.[172]

What were the catalogues to which Procopius and John Lydus refer? Two of the Anastasius edicts refer to registers, but the word they use is not *katalogos*, but *matrix*, the same word used in the edict from Perge in most cases when referring to a list or register.[173] According to Onur, a *matrix* (also found as μάτριξ, or *matricula*) was the master list of a regiment that contained all the necessary information about the regiment's soldiers.[174] John Lydus defines the word in his *On Magistrates*, where he says, "the so-called *matrices*, namely, 'master-lists of the registers'".[175] For John, these lists give the ranks within a particular regiment. On the basis of the Perge edict's own language, Onur argues that a matrix should include information on the number and pay of the men.[176] We find the word *matrix* in some sixth-century CE documents. At least two papyri use the term.[177] One is the *probatoria* for the enrolment of Flavius Patermouthis, son of Dios, into the regiment at Elephantine, where it reads: "the most excellent Commander and all-praiseworthy Prefect of the Justinians, with (the grace of) God *dux* and *Augustalis* of the Thebaid, orders us to enter your name onto our roster".[178] Those papyri go along with the Anastasius edicts just noted.[179] The one from Cyrenaica refers explicitly near the beginning to "the military registers".[180] To get back to the edict from Perge, the inscribers imply that the matrix was compiled, or at least authorized, by the highest authority, which would have been a *magister militum*.[181] These *matrices*

---

172 Basil *Epist.* 351, *Ennaratio in prophetam Isaiam* 3.101, *Homilia exhortatoria ad sanctum baptisma* 31.440, *In ebriosus* 31.457, etc.; Lib. *Epist.* 17.1. See too Hephaestion *Apotelesmatica* 143.6, John. Chyrsos. *Catecheses ad illuminandos* 7.30. That said, Josephus uses such a phrase in his *Jewish Antiquities* (12.47) at least once, and it means "soldiers".
173 Onur 2017: 167.
174 Onur 2017: 176.
175 Joh. Ldy. *De Mag.* 3.2.2, trans. Bandy.
176 Onur 2017: 177.
177 P. Muench 1.2; P. Pommersf 1.
178 P. Muench 1.2 = D31, trans. Porten.
179 IGLSyr 13,1 9046; SEG 32,1554; SEG 9.356.
180 SEG 9.356.1. εἰς μάτ⟨ρ⟩ικας στρατιωτι[κ]άς.
181 Onur 2017: 164.

might have been connected to the quarterly military reports referred to in the *Codex Justinianus*.[182]

In chapter two in the discussion of Procopius' experiences, I noted that he had been personally involved in organizing men and supplies from Ostia (Procop. *Wars* 6.4.1–2). It was these experiences, shared by John Lydus, which comes across in his own use of the term *katalogos* that impelled Procopius to use *katalogos* in this way. Procopius was intimately familiar with these lists, or registers, *matrices*, and might well have come to think of regiments as men on a list. But I think this is only part of the explanation. As I emphasized in *Battles and Generals* and as I have been arguing throughout this book, Procopius was keen on focusing on the role of commanders in his work to the detriment of the lower ranking soldiers. By characterizing these soldiers as little more than men on lists he was not only echoing his own experiences with making these lists, but actively downplaying their role in the outcomes of the many wars that he described. And yet, in some respects *katalogos* reads much better than those "with a commander". In the case of the latter, those soldiers only exist vis-à-vis their relationship to their commander; without him, they would be erased from the record.

5 Conclusion

In this chapter we have seen that *arithmos* is the correct term for a generic unit, while *katalogos* is not. Nor does it denote particular units, like regiments of *comitatenses*. Procopius' use of *katalogos* was likely due both to his experiences organizing men in the army using official matrices, and his desire to give a nod to a truly classical structure, the Athenian *katalogos*, or conscription list. But it also allowed him to minimize the soldiers, whom he glosses over regularly, in a new way. This examination of Procopius' terminology for regiments has, to some degree, served to explain some of Procopius' authorial practices, and to understand what we found in chapters one and two. Procopius' plentiful experiences with the military arranging troop supplies (often with Antonina's help) conditioned how he saw groups of soldiers. It also provided a means for him to minimize the common soldier's role in the narrative. In the next chapters, however, I will look into how we can glean something about the soldiers in Procopius' three works, starting with field army soldiers.

---

182 *Cod. Iust.* 1.42.

TABLE 3.2   *Katalogos* in the *Secret History*

Passage number	Greek	English
6.3.5	ταχθέντας τε ἐν τοῖς στρατιωτικοῖς καταλόγοις	"enrolled them in the ranks of the soldiers"
11.2.4	τῶν στρατιωτῶν τοὺς καταλόγους	"the rosters of soldiers"
24.3.1	μέσοις που ἤδη καταλόγου	"at about the middle of the muster-roll"
24.5.2	ἀλλ' οἱ λογοθέται καλούμενοι οὐκ εἴων ἐκ τῶν καταλόγων ἀφαιρεῖσθαι τὰ τῶν τετελευτηκότων ὀνόματα	"but the *logothetes* would not allow the names of the deceased to be removed from the rolls"
24.5.5	οὐ μὴν οὐδὲ τοὺς καταλόγους ἔτι ἐπλήρουν,	"they would no longer fill out the muster-rolls"
24.8.3	ἐν τοῖς καταλόγοις	"on the rosters"
24.19.2	τούτοις τοῖς καταλόγοις	"in those rosters"
24.30.5	ἐν τοῖς καταλόγοις	"on the rosters"

TABLE 3.3   *Katalogos* in the *Buildings*

Passage number	Greek	English
1.2.19	κατάλογον πεποιημένοις	"make a catalogue"
2.6.9	στρατιωτικῶν δὲ καταλόγων	"military rosters"
2.8.11	στρατιωτικῶν καταλόγων	"military rosters"
3.1.16	στρατιωτικῶν καταλόγων	"military rosters"
3.1.16	στρατιωτικῶν τε καταλόγων	"military rosters"
3.1.29	Ῥωμαίων στρατιωτῶν καταλόγους	"rosters of Roman soldiers"
3.3.14	στρατιωτικοὺς καταλόγους	"military rosters"
4.3.15	τοῖς ἐν Μακεδονίᾳ τετειχισμένοις ἐν καταλόγῳ	"in the list [of towns] in Macedonia which have been provided with walls"

TABLE 3.3   *Katalogos* in the *Buildings* (cont.)

Passage number	Greek	English
4.4.1	τὸν κατάλογον ἐποιούμεθα τῶν τῇδε φρουρίων	"making this catalogue of the forts"
4.4.3	ὡς ἐν καταλόγῳ ἐπελθεῖν ἅπαντα	"set them all down together in catalogue form"
4.10.17	στρατιωτῶν καταλόγους	"military rosters"

TABLE 3.4   *Katalogos* in the *Wars*

Passage number	Greek	English
1.12.24	ἄρχοντα καταλόγων τῶν ἐν Δάρας	"commander of those on the rolls in Dara"[a]
1.13.22	οἵ τε τῶν ἱππέων κατάλογοι καὶ ὁ πεζὸς στρατός	"the rolls of cavalry and the infantry army"
1.15.15	καταλόγου ἱππικοῦ ἄρχων	"leading a cavalry-unit/register"
1.15.25	ἐς καταλόγους αὐτοὺς Ῥωμαϊκοὺς ἐσεγράψαντο	"having registered on the Roman rolls themselves"
1.26.5	ἐν καταλόγῳ τεταγμένος πεζῶν	"deployed in a roll of infantry"
2.14.8	τῶν ἐν Ἀρμενίοις καταλόγων	"the ones on the rolls among the Armenians"
2.18.16	τῶν ἐν Μεσοποταμίᾳ καταλόγων	"those on the rolls in Mesopotamia"[b]
2.19.33	τῶν ἐν Λιβάνῳ καταλόγων ἄρχοντες	"the commanders of those on the rolls in Libya"
2.24.12	ξὺν τοῖς ἀμφ' αὐτὸν καταλόγοις	"with those on the rolls with him"
2.24.14	τῶν ταύτῃ καταλόγων	"those on the rolls there"

a   Whitby (1995: 82, n. 82) translates *katalogos* here as regiments, though I think roll is more correct.
b   Here too Whitby (1995: 82, n. 82) prefers regiment.

TABLE 3.4 *Katalogos* in the *Wars* (*cont.*)

Passage number	Greek	English
3.11.5	ὁ τῶν ἐν Ἀρμενίοις **καταλόγων** στρατηγός	"the general of those on the rolls among the Armenians"
3.11.18	τῶν ἑῴων αὖθις **καταλόγων** ἦρχε	"led those on the rolls of the east again"
3.14.14	ὁ τῶν ἐν Ἀρμενίοις **καταλόγων** στρατηγός	"the general of those on the rolls among the Armenians"
4.3.4	ὅσοι τῶν ἱππικῶν **καταλόγων**	"as many cavalry soldiers"
4.10.5	τούτω τὼ ἄνδρε ἱππικῶν **καταλόγων** ἡγουμένω ἐν Βυζακίῳ	"these two men leading the cavalry soldiers in Byzacium"
4.14.17	ἐς **καταλόγους** ἱππικοὺς πέντε	"in five cavalry units"
4.14.18	τοὺς **καταλόγους** πληροῦντες	"and filled up the lists"
4.15.50	**καταλόγου** δὲ ἱππικοῦ μὲν Βαρβᾶτος	"of the cavalry unit/register Barbatos"
4.20.12	τοῦ **καταλόγου** ὀπτίων, εἰς ὃν αὐτὸς ἀνεγέγραπτο	"*optio* of the unit/register, in which he himself belonged"
4.23.3	τῶν ἐν Βυζακίῳ **καταλόγων** ἄρχων	"leading those on the rolls in Byzacium"
4.23.6	**καταλόγου** ἱππικοῦ ἄρχων	"leading the cavalry unit/register"
4.24.4	τῶν στρατιωτῶν τοὺς **καταλόγους**	"the lists/units of soldiers"
4.25.1	αὐτὸς τῶν ἐν Νουμίδαις **καταλόγων** ἡγούμενος	"he himself commanding the rolls among the Numidians"
4.27.5	Μαρκέντιον, ὃς τῶν ἐν Βυζακίῳ **καταλόγων** ἦρχεν	"Markentios, who led those on the rolls in Byzacium"
5.5.2	Βελισάριον δὲ ναυσὶν ἔστελλε, στρατιώτας ἐκ μὲν **καταλόγων** καὶ φοιδεράτων τετρακισχιλίους	"he sent Belisarius by sea 4000 soldiers from the military registers and the *foederati*"
5.5.3	**καταλόγων** δὲ ἱππικῶν	"cavalry soldiers"
5.10.1	ὃς ἱππικοῦ **καταλόγου** ἡγεῖτο	"who led a cavalry unit/register"
5.14.1	ἀπολέξας οὖν ἄνδρας ἐκ **καταλόγου** πεζικοῦ τριακοσίους	"thus selected 300 men from an infantry unit/register"

TABLE 3.4 *Katalogos* in the *Wars* (cont.)

Passage number	Greek	English
5.17.17	ἐκ καταλόγου ἱππικοῦ, οὗπερ Ἰννοκέντιος ἦρχεν	"from the cavalry unit/register which Innocentius led"
5.19.18	τὰς δὲ λειπομένας τῶν πεζικῶν καταλόγων τοὺς ἄρχοντας διαφυλάσσειν ἐκέλευε	"ordered the remaining commanders of infantry soldiers to stand guard"
5.23.2	ξὺν καταλόγῳ πεζικῷ, οὗ αὐτὸς ἦρχεν	"with an infantry unit/roster, which he himself led"[a]
5.28.16	καταλόγου ἱππικοῦ ἄρχοντα	"who led a cavalry unit/roster"
6.5.1	ξὺν αὐτοῖς ἕτεροι στρατιῶται ἐκ καταλόγου ἱππικοῦ χίλιοι·	"1000 other soldiers with these from the cavalry unit/roster"
6.23.2	πεντακοσίους πεζοὺς ἐκ καταλόγου, οὗ Δημήτριος ἦρχεν	"500 infantry soldiers from the unit/roster, which Demetrius led"
7.6.14	ὃς δὴ τὰ πρότερα ξὺν Βελισαρίῳ ἐστράτευε καταλόγου πεζικοῦ ἄρχων	"who campaigned previously with Belisarius while leading an infantry unit"
7.36.16	ὕστερον δὲ καταλόγου ἱππικοῦ ἄρχων	"later leading a cavalry unit"
7.38.5	τῶν δὲ ἱππικῶν καταλόγων ἦρχεν, οἳ ἐν Τζουρουλῷ τῷ ἐν Θράκῃ φρουρίῳ ἐκ παλαιοῦ ἵδρυνται	"who led the cavalry soldiers, who were stationed in Tzouroulos as the garrison in Thrace in the past"
7.39.6	στόλον τε ἀγείρας νηῶν καὶ στράτευμα λόγου ἄξιον ἐκ καταλόγων πεζῶν ἐν τῷ στόλῳ τούτῳ ἐνθέμενος	"having gathered a fleet of ships and put an army worthy of note from the infantry rolls in this fleet"
7.39.8	στρατηγὸν καταλόγων τῶν ἐπὶ Θράκης καταστησάμενος	"having made him [Artabanes] general of the units in Thrace"
7.39.10	στρατηγὸς γὰρ ὢν τῶν ἐν Ἰλλυριοῖς καταλόγων	"for being general of those on the rolls among the Illyrians"

a B's letter to J came at 5.24ish.

TABLE 3.4 *Katalogos* in the *Wars* (cont.)

Passage number	Greek	English
7.39.18	τινὰς δὲ καὶ ἐκ **καταλόγων** ἱππικῶν, οἳ ἐπὶ τῆς Θράκης ἵδρυντο	"having also chosen some of those from the cavalry rolls encamped in Thrace"
8.2.16	λέγουσι μὲν οὖν ὡς κατὰ τοὺς Τραϊανοῦ τοῦ Ῥωμαίων αὐτοκράτορος χρόνους **κατάλογοι** Ῥωμαίων στρατιωτῶν ἐνταῦθά τε καὶ μέχρι ἐς Λαζοὺς καὶ Σαγίνας ἵδρυντο	"Thus they say that in the time when Trajan was the emperor of the Romans units of Roman soldiers were based there and as far as among the Lazi and the Sagani"
8.4.5	τὰ μὲν γὰρ πρότερα **κατάλογοι** Ῥωμαίων στρατιωτῶν	"for in the past the units of Roman soldiers"
8.25.11	Ῥωμαίοις **στρατηγὸς** τῶν ἐν Βυζαντίῳ καταλόγων	"[Suratas] Roman general of those on the rolls in Byzantium"
8.29.13	Ναρσῆς πεντήκοντα ἐκ **καταλόγου** πεζοὺς ἀπολέξας	"Narses, having chosen 50 infantry from a roll"
8.31.5	πεζοὺς μέντοι τοξότας ἐκ τῶν **καταλόγου** στρατιωτῶν ὀκτακισχιλίους μάλιστα ἔστησαν ἐς ἄμφω τὰ κέρα	"however, he placed on both wings about 8000 foot archers from the register of soldiers"
8.35.18	οὐ κατὰ ἄρχοντας ἢ λόχους ἢ **καταλόγους** τὴν τάξιν καταστησάμενοι	"not arranging the line by commanders (*archontas*) or *lochoi* or *katalogoi*"

TABLE 3.5 Roman troop numbers in Procopius' *Wars*

Number	Passage	Figure	Troop type
1.	1.13.19	300	Heruls
2.	1.13.20	600	Horsemen (Huns)
3.	1.13.21	600	Horsemen (Huns)
4.	1.13.23	25,000	Romans
5.	1.15.1	3,000	Huns
6.	1.15.10	1,000	Men
7.	1.15.11	15,000 (half 30,000)	Men
8.	1.18.5	20,000	Roman army
9.	1.18.5	2,000	Isaurians
10.	1.25.7	1,000	Spearmen
11.	2.6.9	300	Followers
12.	2.8.2	6,000	Men
13.	2.8.13	300	Men
14.	2.19.15	1,200	Soldiers
15.	2.21.2	6,000	Men
16.	2.21.2	1,000	Horsemen
17.	2.21.18	100,000	Men
18.	2.21.18	1,000	Horsemen
19.	2.24.16	30,000	Men
20.	2.29.10	7,000	Men
21.	2.29.10	7,000	Tzani
22.	2.29.34	100	Men
23.	2.30.8	100	Garrison of Romans
24.	2.30.22	2,000	Romans
25.	2.30.30	3,000	Garrison
26.	2.30.40	14,000	Whole army
27.	3.6.1	100,000	Army
28.	3.11.1	400	Soldiers
29.	3.11.2	10,000	Foot soldiers
30.	3.11.2	5,000	Horsemen
31.	3.11.11	400	Heruls
32.	3.11.11	600	Massagetae
33.	3.11.14	30,000	Sailors
34.	3.11.16	2,000	Men of Byzantium
35.	3.17.1	300	Shield bearers

CATALOGUES AND LEGIONS 91

TABLE 3.5 Roman troop numbers in Procopius' *Wars* (*cont.*)

Number	Passage	Figure	Troop type
36.	3.19.23	800	Shield bearers
37.	3.21.9	500	Roman soldiers
38.	4.2.1	500	Horsemen
39.	4.2.2	500	Horsemen
40.	4.3.6	500	Horsemen
41.	4.4.9	200	Men
42.	4.7.20	5,000	Men
43.	4.11.51	500	Men
44.	4.12.17	1,000	Foot soldiers
45.	4.14.12	1,000	Soldiers of Arian
46.	4.15.2	8,000	Men
47.	4.15.4	1,000	Men
48.	4.15.9	100	Spearmen and shield bearers
49.	4.15.11	2,000	Army
50.	4.25.10	1,500	Roman soldiers
51.	4.27.7	1,000	Soldiers of Stotzas
52.	4.27.8	500	Romans
53.	4.27.8	80	Huns
54.	5.5.2	4,000	Catalogues and foederati
55.	5.5.2	3,000	Isaurians
56.	5.5.4	200	Huns
57.	5.5.4	300	Moors
58.	5.10.1	400	Men
59.	5.10.3	400	Men
60.	5.10.8	200	Men
61.	5.14.1	300	Infantry rolls
62.	5.18.2	1,000	Horsemen
63.	5.22.17	5,000	Men
64.	5.24.2	5,000	Men
65.	5.26.19	300	Men
66.	5.27.1	1,600	Horsemen (Huns, Slavae, Antae)
67.	5.27.4	200	Horsemen of the shield bearers
68.	5.27.6	200	Men
69.	5.27.11	300	Shield bearers
70.	5.27.13	300	Horsemen
71.	5.27.18	1,000	Men

TABLE 3.5   Roman troop numbers in Procopius' *Wars* (*cont.*)

Number	Passage	Figure	Troop type
72.	5.27.22	1,500	Men
73.	6.2.3	100	Shield bearers
74.	6.2.9	600	Horsemen
75.	6.4.6	1,000	Men
76.	6.4.7	500	Men
77.	6.4.19	500	Soldiers
78.	6.5.1	800	Thracian horsemen
79.	6.5.1	3,000	Isaurians
80.	6.5.1	1,000	Soldiers from the cavalry rolls
81.	6.5.2	300	Horsemen
82.	6.5.2	500	Men
83.	6.5.9	1,000	Horsemen
84.	6.7.3	100	Horsemen
85.	6.7.25	800	Horsemen
86.	6.7.26	400	Men
87.	6.7.26	800	Shield bearers
88.	6.10.1	2,000	Horsemen
89.	6.11.4	1,000	Horsemen
90.	6.11.7	2,000	Horsemen
91.	6.11.22	400	Men
92.	6.12.26	1,000	Men (Isaurians and Thracians)
93.	6.12.40	300	Men
94.	6.13.17	5,000	Soldiers
95.	6.13.18	2,000	Heruls
96.	6.16.18	1,000	Men
97.	6.18.6	10,000	Men
98.	6.23.2	500	Foot soldiers
99.	6.23.5	11,000	Men
100.	7.1.20	7,000	Horsemen
101.	7.3.4	12,000	Men (Roman army)
102.	7.3.12	100	Men
103.	7.6.2	1,000	Romans and Isaurians
104.	7.10.3	4,000	Men
105.	7.11.19	1,000	Soldiers
106.	7.11.27	1,000	Men
107.	7.15.3	3,000	Soldiers
108.	7.15.3	500	Men

CATALOGUES AND LEGIONS 93

TABLE 3.5   Roman troop numbers in Procopius' *Wars* (*cont.*)

Number	Passage	Figure	Troop type
109.	7.18.29	300	Guards
110.	7.19.25	100	Horsemen
111.	7.21.4	7,000	Greeklings
112.	7.21.5	20,000	Enemy (Romans)
113.	7.22.3	300	Antae
114.	7.22.21	300	Antae
115.	7.23.8	1,000	Soldiers
116.	7.26.10	70	Soldiers
117.	7.26.16	1,000	Men
118.	7.27.3	300	Heruls
119.	7.27.3	800	Armenians
120.	7.27.3	1000	Spearmen and shield bearers
121.	7.27.15	500	Men
122.	7.27.16	900	Men distinguished for valour
123.	7.27.16	700	Horsemen
124.	7.27.16	200	Foot soldiers
125.	7.29.3	15,000	Men
126.	7.30.1	2,000	Foot soldiers
127.	7.30.6	300	Illyrian horsemen
128.	7.30.6	100	Infantry
129.	7.30.17	1,000	Men
130.	7.34.40	10,000	Horsemen
131.	7.34.42	1,500	Heruls
132.	7.36.1	3,000	Men noted for valour
133.	7.36.17	400	Horsemen
134.	7.36.20	400	Men
135.	8.10.7	1,000	Romans
136.	8.11.32	40	groups of no less than 40
137.	8.11.42	6,000	Romans
138.	8.13.8	12,000	Roman army
139.	8.13.8	3,000	Garrison
140.	8.13.10	800	Tzani
141.	8.26.12	2,500	Followers
142.	8.26.13	3,000	Heruls
143.	8.26.13	3,000	Fighting men
144.	8.29.13	50	Men from the infantry rolls
145.	8.31.5	8,000	Foot archers from the rolls of soldiers

TABLE 3.5 Roman troop numbers in Procopius' *Wars* (*cont.*)

Number	Passage	Figure	Troop type
146.	8.31.6	1,500	Horsemen
147.	8.31.7	500	Men
148.	8.31.7	1,000	Men
149.	8.32.5	4,000	Foot archers
150.	8.32.5	4,000	Foot archers
151.	8.32.9	8,000	Foot soldiers

CHAPTER 4

Soldiers in the Field

1 Introduction

It is time to turn to some of the principal groups of soldiers, those in the field, the *comitatenses*, the prevalence of horse archers, and the *foederati*. One of the principal arguments from previous research has been that *katalogos* is usually used as a synonym for field army unit. Along those lines, *stratiwths* is usually claimed to have been the standard word not for a generic soldier, but a field army soldier (*comitatensis*). In other words, *stratiwths* had become synonymous with the field army soldier. In this chapter I will test these claims, and investigate the degree to which we can tease out one group of soldier, like the *comitatensis*, from another, like the *foederati*.

The next part of this discussion will centre on the *foederati*, one of the most important classes of soldier in the sixth century, and ones to which Procopius devotes due attention, and a related group of soldiers, the *symmachoi*, some of whom were allied, non-Roman soldiers, under their own commanders.

In the third and final part of this chapter, I turn to the horse archer, one of the most iconic components of Procopius' Roman armies. This subject has been touched on in the preface, but further discussion serves the purpose of this book: to uncover valuable details about the empire's rank-and-file soldiers in Procopius' works. By focusing on them at the beginning in the preface, Procopius makes them front and centre, even if the ensuing narrative reveals that their impact was a little more restricted. In this discussion we will situate Procopius' coverage into broader discussions of the Eurasian milieu, which will highlight the degree to which Procopius' emphasis is overblown. Before I get to horse archery and cavalry more generally, I want to highlight the role of infantry in Procopian combat, at least in terms of sheer numbers.

2 Comitatenses

2.1 Katalogoi *and* stratiwtai

In the previous chapters I talked at length about the field army soldiers, first with respect to the likening of Procopius' *stratiwths* with the *comitatensis*, field army soldier, second to the likening of *katalogos* to the field army unit. Given all that time spent laying out what was not a field army soldier and unit, are there places where we can truly find them? One broader class of soldier that Procopius spends a great deal of time describing is the barbarian or ethnic soldier. Rance argued that Procopius' emphasis on these soldiers led to a concomitant silence regarding the regular Roman units.[1] At the same time, literary sources like Procopius tended to prefer discussing the field army soldiers at the expense of the others soldiers at Rome's disposal, like the *limitanei* discussed in the next chapter.[2] That said, in most overviews of the *comitatenses* in late antiquity, discussions tend to pass over their presence in the sixth century, or at least give them only limited attention.[3] Some have argued for a blurring between the units of *comitatenses* and those of *limitanei*.[4] Furthermore, Carrié suggests that the primary distinction between the members of the armed forces under Justinian was between the palatine troops and the provincial troops.[5] That said, for others, the *comitatenses* were a substantial part of invasion armies of North Africa and Italy, a point to which we will return below.[6]

Le Bohec has raised questions about the term *comitatenses* in a careful study that revisits a much earlier paper by Mommsen.[7] Indeed, for Brennan *comitatensis* and the related term *pseudocomitatensis* were status terms that first appeared in 365, though a law in the *Codex Justinianus* dates to 347, implying that they first came into being some time earlier.[8] Our specific evidence for *comitatenses* in the sixth century is limited, but it does exist. A few select pieces of legislation in Justinian's legal corpus identify *comitatenses*.[9] The law on newly conquered Vandal North Africa refers to *comitatenses*.[10] The aforementioned law from 347, on inheritances, refers to *comitatenses*, both legionary units as well as cavalry vexillations and wedges.[11] A novel dated to 536,

---

1 Rance 2005: 444.
2 Parnell 2017: 16.
3 Jones 1964: 659; Ravegnani 1998 (passim); Janniard 2015: 265; Parnell 2017: 14–17.
4 Note, for instance, Whitby's (1995: 68–72, 2007: 146) and Haldon's (1999: 67–69) comments.
5 Carrié 1995: 33; Whitby 1995: 70–71. See too Jones (1964: 659).
6 Jones 1964: 660.
7 Mommsen 1889; Le Bohec 2007.
8 Brennan 2015: 1050; *Cod. Theod.* 8.1.10; *Cod. Iust.* 6.62.2.
9 There are more references to *comitatenses* and *pseudocomitatenses* in the Theodosian Code (7.1.18, 7.4.22pr, 7.13.7.3, 7.20.4pr, 7.20.4.2, 7.20.4.3, and 7.22.8 -at least in book seven). See Le Bohec (2007: 670–672).
10 *Cod. Iust.* 1.27.2.8.
11 *Universis tam legionibus quam vexillationibus comitatensibus seu cuneis insinuare debebis.* The editors and translators of book six of the fantastic new edition and translation of the Codex Justinianus mistranslated this passage as, "You will be obliged to communicate to all the legions as well as to all the border detachments and cavalry units" (Frier et al. 2016: 1767). Rather, it should read, "You will be obliged to communicate to all the legions as well as the field army vexillations or the wedges". Field army soldiers, *comitatenses*, could be

addressed to the *quaestor exercitus* Bonus, and concerning appeals from the provinces of Caria, Cyprus, the Cyclades, Moesia, and Scythia, includes the line, "It is also directed how the *annonae* of the troops, both *comitatenses* and *limitatenses*, should be allocated".[12] Cassiodorus uses the term *comitatensis* twice, but for him it does not mean field army soldier, but rather as the adjective of *comitatus*, "of or pertaining to the dignity of the office of courtiers".[13] Two of the usages in the *Codex Iustinianus* use the term in this way, and both can be found in the same legislation.[14]

The basis of its meaning as a field army soldier is the information we find in the *Notitia Dignitatum*: the *Notitita Dignitatum* is full of references to *comitatenses* and *pseudocomitatenses*.[15] It is, then, to some degree, a question of working backwards (though chronologically forwards) with the data from the *Notitia*, a not unproblematic endeavour. Fortunately, recent research on the armies of Egypt found in the eastern list of the *Notitia*, the half of the document most relevant to our discussion (given the dissolution of a pan-Mediterranean empire), has made a good case for the accuracy of the information for unit dispositions found therein.[16]

There is one other potential piece of evidence for the *comitatenses* in the sixth century, the edict of Anastasius from Pamphylia.[17] The long, detailed inscription from Perge includes all sorts of technical detail about the unit so inscribed. What the inscription does not do is include the name of the unit, though we know it was a *legio*, perhaps numbering 1,200.[18] The *Notitia* provides

---

enrolled in *legio* units or *vexillatio* units, while *cuneus* units were something else. All of these unit types are found in the *Notitia Dignitatum*. To give but three examples from the eastern list of the *Notitia Digntiatum*, we find *comitatenses* legions under the *magister militum per Orientem* at *Not. dign. or.* 7.38, *comitatenses* vexillations under the *magister militum per Orientem* at *Not. dign. or.* 7.24, and cunei under the *dux Moesiae secundae* at *Not. dign. or.* 40.11–17.

12 *Iust. Nov.* 41. Trans. Miller. Novel 50, dated to a year later, is much more substantial. Indeed, Sarantis (2016: 143), dubs 41 a novella, and 50 a novel. For a detailed discussion of these novels and their role in Balkan military supply during the reign of Justinian, see Sarantis (2016: 143–149).
13 Lewis and Short, "comitatensis". Cass. Var. 6.10, 12.22. See too Amm. Marc. 18.4.2.
14 *Cod. Iust.* 12.23.7pr, 12.23.7.18.
15 On the units in the *Notitia Dignitatum*, see Brennan 2015.
16 Pollard 2013; Kaizer 2015.
17 Although Jones (1964: 661), following Maspero (1912: 23–25), argued that the five units named in the edict in Libya Pentapolis were *comitatenses*, I am unconvinced. Though Procopius discusses the region in outline, he has nothing to say about its troop complement besides his comment that Justinian established two strongholds with garrisons. See Procop. *Build.* 6.2.1–8.
18 Onur 2017: 186.

no clues about its nature, for there were no legions based in the region when that list was compiled at the end of the fourth century, aside from the units serving under the *magister militum praesentalis* (II), the locations of whose bases are unknown, but which likely were partially or wholly near the capital far to the north, Constantinople.[19] By Jones' reckoning, several other field army units continued to operate in the sixth century. At the moment, I will leave out Belisarius' expeditionary forces in Africa and Italy, which I will return to shortly. Others include the *Felices Theodosiani*, the *Primi Theodosiani*, the *Daci*, and the *Armeni*, all found in Italy.[20]

So, what do we find in Procopius?[21] First, as noted, some have argued that the terms *milites* (Latin) and *stratiwtai* (Greek) came to be associated, wherever they are found, with *comitatenses* and, to some degree, *palatini*.[22] Jones also notes that the *comitatenses* were often contrasted either with the federates (*foederati*, on which more in section III) or the *limitanei* (more in chapter five). Jones based his comment in part on the legal texts, though also on his reading of Procopius.[23] To return to some of the material discussed in chapter two, if we were to focus on the *Secret History* alone, there would be no doubt that when Procopius uses the word στρατιώτης he means soldier, and any kind of soldier not a specific one. Indeed, some of his uses make it clear he means all soldiers, as when he says that no soldier would rise up when Theodora sent them all to war.[24] But section 24 is even more explicit about what a soldier could be, and that means everything from the frontier soldiers (the *limitanei*) to the bodyguards (like the *scholarii*).[25] As for the *Buildings*, all the garrisons comprise soldiers (*stratiwtai*) though it is not clear what kind of soldiers they are. While it is tempting to argue that each one of those soldiers were frontier soldiers, the reality is that many units of *comitatenses* were based in frontier locations, as would be the case for the new units based in North Africa referred to above.[26] In this text then too, στρατιῶται is a general term for all soldiers so

---

19   *Not. Dign. or.* 6.
20   Jones 1964: 660.
21   This section, as in chapter one, will draw on the data compiled in the appendix.
22   Jones 1964: 659; Syvänne 2004: 31–32; Ravegnani 2005: 189; Janniard 2015: 265; Parnell 2017: 16.
23   Jones 1964: 1273, n. 119, 1275, n. 133–134. See *Iust. Nov.* 41, 103, 117; Procop. 4.5.2, 5.17.7, 5.27.1–2, 7.33.13.
24   Procop. *SH*. 10.9.
25   Procop. *SH*. 24.12 (*limitanei*), 24.15 (*scholarii*).
26   *Cod. Iust.* 1.27.2.8. See Pringle (2001: 70–74, 79–83).

described, whether he identifies a φρουρά (garrison) of soldiers, or a φυλακτήριον (garrison, again) of soldiers, or a κατάλογος (roll) of soldiers.[27]

Pringle identified several locations where fortresses were garrisoned by *comitatenses*. The starting point for his discussion was Justinian's law on the garrison of the newly conquered province of Africa. That is where we find the three explicit references to *comitatenses* in the legislation. It specifies that the new territory should be garrisoned by frontier troops (*limitanei*) along with field army soldiers (*comitatenses*), and reads:

> For the deployment of frontier soldiers [*limitanei*]—because it seems necessary to Us that in addition to field army soldiers [*comitatenses*] frontier soldiers be stationed in camps, who could defend the camps and cities on the frontier [*limitis*] and work the land, so that other provincials, upon seeing them in areas, shall also move to those places—We have drawn up an example of one unit of frontier soldiers [*unius numeri limitaneorum*], so that by following the example We have sent, Your Greatness may station them in camps and places as you shall see fit in a similar way to Our example ... if some disturbance should arise, the frontier soldiers themselves, without the field army soldiers [*limitanei sine comitatensibus militbus*], together with their dukes, may help the places where they are stationed ... We want these provisions to apply not only to the frontier soldiers [*limitaneos*] but to the field army soldiers [*comitatenses milites*] as well.[28]

This piece of legislation is full of useful details concerning corruption, frontier soldiers, and foreign policy. Here, of course, I am concerned with its value for

---

27   Procop. Build. 3.3.6 (φρουρά), 3.6.22 (φυλακτήριον), 3.1.9 (κατάλογος).
28   *Cod. Iust.* 1.27.2.8, trans. Dillon (slightly modified). *Pro limitaneis vero ordinandis (quia necessarium nobis esse videtur, ut extra comitatenses milites per castra milites limitanei constituantur, qui possint et castra et civitates limitis defendere et terras colere, ut alii provinciales videntes eos per partes ad illa loca se conferant) exemplum fecimus unius numeri limitaneorum, ut secundum exemplum, quod nos misimus, per castra et loca, quae providerit tua magnitudo, eos ad similitudinem nostri exempli ordinet, sic tamen ut, si inveneris de provinciis idonea corpora, aut de illis, quos antea milites habebant, limitaneorum constituas numero in unoquoque limite, ut, si forsitan commotio aliqua fuerit, possint ipsi limitanei sine comitatensibus militibus una cum ducibus suis adiuvare loca, ubi dispositi fuerint, non longe limitem exeuntes nec ipsi limitanei nec duces eorum, ut nullum etiam dispendium a ducibus vel ducianis praedicti limitanei sustineant, nec aliquas sibi consuetudines de eorum stipendiis per fraudes ad suum lucrum convertant. Haec autem non solum in limitaneos volumus observari, sed etiam in comitatenses milites.*

what it reveals about the field army soldiers, though I will return to the value of this passage for the *limitanei* in the next chapter. What it shows is that *comitatenses* units were involved in the garrison of the new province, though their role seems to have been minimized with respect to the *limitanei*, which goes against some widely held views on the value of frontier soldiers. What the law does not do, however, is specify where we might find units of each kind—the kinds of structures, towns, cities, and forts; moreover, the epigraphic evidence is limited.[29] There are some inscriptions from Africa that name soldiers of select units, but they are few in number. We know about a Maximus from the *numerus bis Electorum*, a Buraido from the *numerus Hipponis Regii*, and a Flavius Ziper from a *numerus* of *Primi Felices Iustiniani*.[30] Pringle argues that these three *numeri* were all for *comitatenses* units and that there were no inscriptions which explicitly name a unit of *limitanei*.

To try to determine this, Pringle turned to the much more abundant evidence from Egypt and a framework developed, over a century ago, by Maspero.[31] Maspero, drawing, in part, upon the evidence of *Synecdemus* of Hierocles, argued that each *polis* in Egypt with a garrison was manned by *comitatenses*, while each *castrum* was manned by *limitanei*.[32] Pringle, for the most part, follows Maspero, though also the evidence of Justinian's edict on north Africa, which, as we just saw, states that the field army soldiers along with the frontier soldiers would be stationed in camps (*castra*), who could defend the camps and cities on the frontier (*castra et civitates limitis defendere*).[33] Using all this material, along with the information included in Procopius' *Buildings*, Pringle identified several *poleis* in Africa with garrisons of *comitatenses*.[34] Unfortunately, he noted that garrisons of *comitatenses* could be identified securely with only four of those sites, Hippo Regius, Cululis, Mascula, and Rusguniae.[35] He also notes that the evidence is insufficient to determine the garrison of most locations in Africa, which makes it even more difficult to pin down the existence of *comitatenses*.[36]

---

29 Pringle 2001: 79.
30 Pringle 2001: 332–333, n. 43; Pringle 2001: 333, n. 44; Pringle 2001: 333, n. 45. Conant's (2012: 211–214) discussion of the names of individuals in North Africa is, understandably, focused on the elites, about whom we have a great deal of information. See too Conant's (2012: 227–231) discussion of subordinate officers.
31 Maspero 1912.
32 Maspero 1912: 100.
33 *Cod. Iust.* 1.27.2.8.
34 Pringle 2001: 80–81.
35 Pringle 2001: 82.
36 Pringle 2001: 82.

SOLDIERS IN THE FIELD

If Pringle is right about cities, in general, being garrisoned by *comitatenses* rather than *limitanei*, then we could have traces of the former in those cities identified by Procopius in the *Buildings*.[37] Procopius does not, however, associate a garrison of troops with all those cities he identifies. Carthage, for instance, does not have a garrison.[38] But this is true of many of the other places that he names, like Lepcis Magna, Oea, Girgis, and Tapacae.[39] In fairness to Procopius, his aim in the *Buildings* is to focus on physical defences erected through Justinian's patronage rather than to give precise details about the identity of their garrisons.[40] One of the best examples of this comes in his discussion of Numidia, near the end of the text, where he simply states that he (Justinian) brought safety to the land by means of fortifications and garrisons of soldiers.[41] Therein he names several cities, like Ad Turres, Ammaedara, Badias, Bagai, Calama, Laribus, Milev, Obba, Sicca Veneria, Thamugadi, and Tigisi. None of these cities are explicitly given garrisons, though the fortresses of Dabusis (Thabudeos?) and Gaeana (Diana Veteranorum?) are.[42] Following Pringle's reasoning established above, that would mean that these fortresses had garrisons of *limitanei*, though Procopius uses the same term both for Numidia as a whole and for these forts, φυλακτήριον.[43] Despite all this, we are no closer to finding specific references to field army soldiers in Procopius' works.

There is one other avenue we could try concerning Africa, and that is to look closer at those soldiers we find living with Vandal women and children in the *Vandal War*, many of whom formed a key component of the mutiny that beset the region shortly after the conquest. Some if not many of these could have been *comitatenses*. Is this what Procopius' language implies? The uprising itself comes just as Belisarius is sent to Italy to fight the Goths. After he had left, in the spring of 536 CE, the mutiny arose involving "the soldiers in Libya".[44] When he turns to explain who these soldiers were, he simply states that it was Roman soldiers, which tells us nothing about the kinds of troops they were.[45] Fortunately, as noted earlier, the catalogue of forces given earlier in book three of the *Vandal War* gives us some idea, though it too is not unproblematic

---

37 Pringle (2001: 121–122) neatly lays out these cities in appendix one.
38 Procop. *Build.* 6.5.1–15.
39 Procop. *Build.* 6.4.1, 11, 14.
40 Note Jacobs' (2013: 19–110) detailed discussion of walls in late antique cities.
41 Procop. *Build.* 6.7.1.
42 Procop. *Build.* 6.7.8–11.
43 For more on this terminology, see the discussion below in chapter five.
44 Procop. *Wars* 4.14.7.
45 Procop. *Wars* 4.14.8.

given its varied components. In other words, using that catalogue as the starting point, those soldiers could have been among the 15,000 soldiers and federates who participated. Pringle characterizes the soldiers as a varied group comprising soldiers, federates, and barbarian allies—that is, any of those soldiers so set out in Procopius' catalogue, which included the Arians.[46] This is matched by Kaegi, who notes that the mutiny, which persisted for many years to 546, involved many and varied participants on both sides, without saying too much about the details of the "rank and file" who made up a significant component during its initial stages.[47] As the appendix shows, Procopius uses the term στρατιώτης at several places in his account of the uprising.[48] He also speaks, as he had before and would again, in terms of generalities: both those soldiers serving for and against the emperor are described thus.[49] The Arians who revolted were soldiers, the new recruits enrolled by Solomon became soldiers, and the men fighting with Stotzas were soldiers.[50] Some if not most of these men might have been *comitatenses*, but it is not at all clear that any were.[51]

This unrest takes place in the *Vandal War* and Procopius filled his account with vague and indeterminate references to στρατιῶται. This is significant, for the *Wars*, for all intents and purposes, serves as the foundation for the claims that κατάλογος and στρατιώτης came to apply to *comitatenses* soldiers. And yet, this vagueness is not specific to the African wars, for if we go back to the beginning we find that the very first use of the term in the text applies to Persians, and their military as a whole, in the build-up to the famed battle between Persians and Hephthalites.[52] There are plenty of other cases where στρατιώτης is applied to Persians, as is the case for Dara and in the aftermath of Callinicum.[53] We sometimes find Vandal soldiers, admittedly a much rarer group than the Persians.[54] He also occasionally refers to Gothic soldiers, which is surprising given the amount of text he devotes to the war in Italy.[55]

---

46 Pringle 2001: 24–25.
47 Kaegi 1981: 47–51. See too Kaegi 1965.
48 The description takes up much of the second half of book four of the *Wars*.
49 Procop. *Wars* 4.14.40, 42.
50 Procop. *Wars* 4.14.12, 4.19.3, 4.23.12.
51 As we note in the next chapter, the Arians were, by most accounts, *foederati* (i.e., not *comitatenses*).
52 Procop. *Wars* 1.6.18. On the conflict, see Bonner (2020: 135–137), with references.
53 Procop. Wars 1.14.1, 1.18.52.
54 Procop. Wars 4.7.20, 4.14.18.
55 Procop. Wars 5.12.21, 6.16.11, 7.8.20.

SOLDIERS IN THE FIELD

On at least two occasions, he makes it clear that a soldier could be a Roman or a Goth, as is the case during the siege of Rome.[56]

Procopius' language is ambiguous, as we have seen, and he never explicitly calls a soldier a field army soldier or *comitatensis*. There are other options, however. If we can identify the commanders of field armies in the narrative, the *magistri militum*, masters of soldiers, we should be able to find field army soldiers. Of course, Procopius tends not to use technical Latin vocabulary, so the most obvious Greek equivalent is *strategos*, general, though at one stage Procopius explicitly connects ἀρχηγός (a commander of the palace guard) with the word *magister*.[57] But we can also use additional information—look beyond Procopius—to determine which generals were *magistri militum*, like Parnell's prosopography.[58] In Parnell's appendix, based on Procopius' works, sixty men probably achieved that rank (see Table 5.1).[59] The majority of them, thirty-six, served as *magister militum vacans*, a general in command of an expeditionary army. Of those, five were *vacans* and something else (Bessas, Buzes, Constantianus 2, John 14 of Vitalian, and Valerian). That leaves twenty-four who were in command of *comitatenses*, a general of one of the principal eastern field armies, the Illyrian Field Army (*magister militum per Illyricum*), the Thracian Field Army (*magister militum per Thracias*), the Eastern Field Army (*magister militum per Orientem*), the Armenian Field Army (*magister militum per Armeniam*), or the African Field Army (*magister militum per Africam*). If they appear in the *Wars*, or the other texts for that matter, with an army, it stands to reason that at least some of their men would be field army soldiers, *comitatenses*. While three of those positions dated back to the era of the *Notitia*, two, the master of soldiers for Armenia and the master of soldiers for Africa, were a creation of the age of Justinian.

Even if we know the titles of these men, however, that does not mean we know anything about the soldiers under their command. In most cases, Procopius does not provide enough information to determine their respective armies. To give but one example, when Artabanes (2) is absolved of the conspiracy charges, he is immediately made *magister militum per Thracias* and sent to Italy to help in the fight against Totila. All Procopius says, however, is that he was sent with "an army of no great size".[60] But if we go through the armies reported by Procopius and attached to these men, there is nothing

---

56   Procop. Wars 5.29.16, 8.23.16.
57   Note his comments at 1.8.2.
58   Parnell 2012.
59   The names follow the *PLRE*, which is why they are all Latinized and, in some instances, include numbers.
60   Procop. *Wars* 7.39.8.

explicit about his language that marks them out as leading field army soldiers. The same is true of the others in the list.

Unsurprisingly, the big exceptions to this pattern concern the principal generals of the narrative, like Belisarius; moreover, looking more closely at the size of armies could be used as a means to track down *comitatenses*. On at least two occasions, Procopius includes some significant detail about Belisarius' armies, as noted in chapters two and three above, especially in the build-up to the Battle of Dara and then again during the invasion of Vandal Africa. In the Battle of Dara, Belisarius served as the *magister militum per Orientem*,[61] and according to Procopius he had at his disposal the following:

> Buzes with a large force of horsemen and by Pharas the Herul with 300 of his people ... Sunicas and Aigan, Massagetai by birth, with 600 horsemen ... on the other wing [was] a large force of horsemen, who were commanded by John, the son of Nicetas, and by Cyrillus and Marcellus; with them were Germanus and Dorotheus; while at the angle on the right were stationed 600 horsemen, commanded by Simmas and Ascan, also Massagetai ... all along the trench stood the cavalry rolls and the infantry army. And behind these in the middle stood the forces of Belisarius and Hermogenes. [23] Thus were the Romans arrayed, amounting to twenty-five thousand.[62]

Belisarius is put in charge of the eastern army and dispatched to meet the Persian invaders, and Hermogenes goes with him. Are all these men and units part of the eastern field army, and do any differences between it and what we find in the *Notitia* reflect changes in army organization or something else? Well, the *Notitia* lists ten *vexillationes comitatenses*, two *auxilia palatina*, nine (at least) *legiones comitatenses*, and ten *legiones pseudocomitatenses* for a total of thirty-one units.[63] Of the different divisions that Procopius describes, several

---

61 Procop. *Wars* 1.13.9.
62 Procop. *Wars* 1.13.19–23. Βούζης εἶχε ξὺν ἱππεῦσι πολλοῖς καὶ Φάρας Ἔρουλος ξὺν ὁμογενέσι τριακοσίοις ... Σουνίκας τε ἦν καὶ Αἰγὰν Μασσαγέται γένος, ξὺν ἱππεῦσιν ἑξακοσίοις, τῆς μὲν γὰρ εὐθείας τὰ ἔσχατα ἱππεῖς πολλοὶ εἶχον, ὧν Ἰωάννης τε ὁ Νικήτου ἦρχε καὶ Κύριλλός τε καὶ Μάρκελλος· ξυνῆν δὲ αὐτοῖς καὶ Γερμανὸς καὶ Δωρόθεος· ἐς γωνίαν δὲ τὴν ἐν δεξιᾷ ἱππεῖς ἐτάξαντο ἑξακόσιοι, ὧν Σίμμας τε καὶ Ἀσκὰν Μασσαγέται ἦρχον ... πανταχῇ δὲ τῆς τάφρου οἵ τε τῶν ἱππέων κατάλογοι καὶ ὁ πεζὸς στρατὸς ἵστατο. ὧν δὴ ὄπισθεν οἵ τε ἀμφὶ Βελισάριον καὶ Ἑρμογένην κατὰ μέσους εἱστήκεσαν. ὧδε μὲν Ῥωμαῖοι ἐς πεντακισχιλίους τε καὶ δισμυρίους ξυνιόντες ἐτάξαντο.
63 Not. Dign. or. 7.24 (*vexillationes comitatenses*), 35 (*auxilia palatina*), 38 (*comitatenses*), 48 (*pseudocomitatenses*).

are small, the 300 Heruls, 600 Massagetae, and the 600 horsemen. Neither the Heruls nor the Massagetae appear under the eastern general. There are plenty of cavalry and infantry units, however, and so the remaining soldiers, who number 24,100, could have been dispersed in those units.

A year later, before the Battle of Callinicum, Procopius gives a different figure for the Roman army, nearly 20,000, which included close to 2,000 Isaurians.[64] It is this lower figure, 20,000, that Treadgold estimated was deployed in the east in 395 and 559, a figure also brought up by Kaldellis.[65] The difference between the two figures is hard to reconcile, though the presence of Hermogenes at Dara, and the assorted losses sustained over the intervening months, not to mention the casualties the Romans suffered in 530, could have contributed to the discrepancy. Yet another figure, emphasized by Treadgold, is for the army of Illyricum, which Procopius reportedly gives at 7.29.3. What Procopius actually says, however, is that, "the commanders of Illyria kept following them with an army of fifteen thousand men without, however, having the courage to get close to the enemy." He does not give the names of the commanders, nor does he specify whether these 15,000 men represented the entirety of the Illyrian army, only that this was the number off in pursuit of the Slavs.[66] That said, the difference in size between the two armies, 20,000 at Callinicum and 15,000 in the face of the Slavs, could be due to the difference in size of the two armies in general, the eastern and Illyrian, and at least what was the case when the *Notitia*'s eastern list was compiled. In the Illyrian list we find two *vexillationes comitatenses*, one *legio palatina*, six *auxilia palatina*, eight *legiones comitatenses*, and nine *legiones pseudocomitatenses*, for a total of twenty-six units.[67] It would help, however, if we knew the size of the units in each army; but much of this material is speculation too, as we discussed above in chapter three.

A number of scholars have tried to work out the size of individual units in the late Roman army, a subject fraught with difficulty due to the absence of clear figures.[68] Indeed, in the sixth century before Maurice's *Strategikon*, the closest to an official figure is for the unit at Perge, which numbers at least 1172, and the one for the Numidae Iustiniani at Hermopolis, which numbers

---

64   Procop. Wars 1.18.5.
65   Treadgold 1995: 63. In this, at least for the date of 395, he follows Jones (1964: 680–682). See too Kaldellis (2014: xiii).
66   On these invasions, see Curta (2001: 82–87) and Sarantis (2016: 278–288).
67   Not. Dign. or. 9.18 (*vexillationes comitatenses*), 21 (*legio palatina*), 6 (*auxilia palatina*), 30 (*legiones comitatenses*), 39 (*legiones pseudocomitatenses*).
68   Note Ravegnani's (2005: 186) comments.

508.[69] That Perge unit is a legion, and we do not know how representative the figure is for legions from earlier parts of late antiquity. The other is a unit of *limitanei*. Another major piece of evidence for unit sizes in late antiquity is the collected Panopolis papyri, discussed by Jones, Duncan-Jones, and others.[70] Opinions differ widely regarding what figures the papyri illustrate, with Jones and Duncan-Jones differing significantly, the former preferring a figure just above 1,700 for the Egyptian legionary vexillation and the latter just over 570. Discrepancy aside, another potential issue is the applicability of these figures for late third/early fourth century Egypt to other parts of the empire. It is probably best, then, to stick with the figure of about 1,200 for legions noted above and very much in line with the Perge inscription. As for other units, given what we found at Hermopolis, something in the 500 range also seems reasonable.[71] Using these approximate unit sizes, where *vexillationes comitatenses*, *auxilia palatina*, and *legiones pseudocomitatenses* are 500 strong while *legiones comitatenses* are 1,200 strong, that gives us an eastern army numbering 21,800, and an Illyrian one numbering 19,300. These figures are slightly higher than those given by Jones and Treadgold for the same armies, though they were using legions with 1,000 soldiers, and the evidence of the Perge inscription, not available when those two works were published, shows that the paper strength, at least, was a little higher. Both these numbers are higher than those given by Procopius. On the other hand, though the difference between the two figures is of a much lesser magnitude than it is in Procopius' works, the figures are also not that far off. If the two armies only comprised *comitatensis* units, then that makes for a significant number of *comitatenses* soldiers in those parts of the *Wars*. But we still lack precision, and so the question must be left open.

If we stay with the *Persian War*, there is one other battle where we might consider Procopius' language, but he only uses the word for soldier on two occasions at Callincum.[72] Conversely, at Dara, Procopius uses a form of στρατιώτης several times, and for both Roman and Persian soldiers, and both frontier soldiers in particular and soldiers in general.[73] Although a significant proportion of the soldiers could well have been in the eastern army, as noted above, several hundred seem to have been something else (Heruls and Massagetae). Incidentally, Procopius only uses the word *katalogos* once at Dara, where it

---

69 Onur 2017: 187; *P. Cair. Masp.* 3.67321.
70 Skeat 1964; Jones 1964: 187–189; Duncan-Jones 1978, 1990: 105–117; Zuckerman 1988; Coello 1996: 33–42.
71 See too Jones (1964: 680–682) and Treadgold (1995: 47).
72 Procop. *Wars* 1.18.12, 1.18.24.
73 Procop. *Wars* 1.14.28 (Roman), 1.14.1 (Persian), 1.13.5 (frontier), 1.13.30 (in general).

refers to cavalry soldiers, and not at all at Callinicum, two battles where there is little doubt that *comitatenses* participated on a wide scale.[74] If the two terms, κατάλογος and στρατιώτης, really did apply primarily to *comitatenses* soldiers and their units, I think we would expect them to be used more regularly in detailed descriptions of pitched battles like these.

Before I dismiss the value of emphasizing numbers in tracking down field army soldiers and discard *katalogos* and *stratiwths* as terms specifically for field armies and soldiers, a few comments on the two catalogues of forces Procopius provides, starting with the one for the Vandal expeditionary army. Regarding *katalogos*, the term is used twice, once while introducing Dorotheus, "the general of those on the rolls among the Armenians", and again while noting the role of Belisarius.[75] The word soldier he uses a few times: the 400 soldiers under Cyril, the 10,000 foot soldiers that make up the expeditionary force, the 5,000 horsemen, from among the soldiers and *foederati*, and the commanders of the mounted soldiers (Rufinus, Aigan, Barbatus, and Pappus).[76] In the second and fourth examples, στρατιώτης is used to specify the general tactical characteristic of the soldier, foot or mounted. In the third, it is used to distinguish one category of soldier from the *foederati*, not to distinguish explicitly between *comitatenses* and *foederati*.

Procopius uses similar language, ἐκ μὲν καταλόγων καὶ φοιδεράτων, in his account of the catalogue of forces that comprised the Italian expeditionary force: "he sent Belisarius by sea with 4,000 soldiers from the military registers and the *foederati*, and about 3,000 more Isaurians … There followed also 200 allied Huns and 300 Moors. The general in supreme command over all was Belisarius, and he had many notable men as spearmen and shield bearers."[77] It is tempting to see those from general rosters as soldiers in the field army, *comitatenses*, but the language is vague. That said, in this instance at least, those on the rosters are one of four principal groups of soldiers in the army: regular Roman soldiers, Isaurians, *foederati*, and private soldiers/*bucellarii*.

Very occasionally, we can compare what Procopius has to say about soldiers and compare it with other contemporary material to deduce the identity of field army soldiers in his works. A good potential candidate is the Vandal war in Africa, for which we have both Procopius and the Corippus. Though Procopius provides hardly any detail about John Troglita's army in 546, Corippus provides

---

74 Procop. *Wars* 1.13.22. Note the comments of Greatrex (1998: 200–204).
75 Procop. *Wars* 3.11.5, 3.11.18.
76 Procop. *Wars* 3.11.1, 2, 7.
77 Procop. *Wars* 5.5.2–4.

a bit more detail.[78] Corippus' units are *agmina* (singular *agmen*), nine in total. The catch is, it is not entirely clear that we can or should trust Corippus' vague figures; moreover, Procopius' account of John's activities comes at the very end of the *Vandal War*, when there is no more detail to be found about affairs in Africa.

Arguably the only place in any of Procopius' three works where he uses the term κατάλογος and στρατιώτης to refer to *comitatenses* and their units comes in the *Buildings*, when Procopius refers to Justinian's military reforms in Armenia. Procopius says that the emperor put under the command of the new dukes "a very large number of rosters of Roman soldiers" ('Ρωμαίων στρατιωτῶν καταλόγους παμπληθεῖς).[79] We know that these are almost certainly field army soldiers because the army created was the command of the *magister militum per Armeniam*, and both the *Codex Justinianus* and Malalas confirm that soldiers and units were transferred from the praesental and eastern armies, both field armies themselves, as Greatrex notes.[80] Some of the newly recruited soldiers for this army would be *limitanei*, however.[81] Ultimately, this one instance does not mean that all those other examples then refer to field army soldiers. Rather, these are the exceptions, and in the absence of good, comparative, evidence, cannot be considered otherwise.

Comitatenses are not as prevalent in Procopius' works as previous scholarship has suggested. They are there, though we usually find them as collectives, often under their commander, and so only as extensions of their commanding officers. In the next section, we turn to another significant body of troops in the sixth century military, the *foederati*, *symmachoi*, and *bucellarii*.

3   *Foederati, symmachoi,* and *bucellarii*

In this section, I will turn to the third of the three principal legal groups of soldiers, the *foederati*, as well as a related group found in Procopius, the *symmachoi*. By some estimations, they played a key role in sixth century combat and beyond and have been given plenty of attention in the scholarship; the majority of our evidence for them from this era comes from Procopius. They appear in two inscriptions, one for an Estotzas and his wife Dody, another for

---

78 Procop. *Wars* 4.28.46; Corippus *Ioh.* 1.426, 4.472–563. See Pringle 2001: 34–35.
79 Procop. *Build.* 3.1.29.
80 Mal. *Chron.* 18.10; *Cod. Iust.* 1.29.5; Greatrex 1998: 153–155.
81 Greatrex 1998: 154.

SOLDIERS IN THE FIELD

a Candac.[82] They appear in a few select pieces of legislation.[83] We also find them in a few other sixth century texts, like Malalas' *Chronographia*, where Eusebius, a *comes foederatum*, is named.[84] Jordanes refers to them in his *Getica* in several places, though it usually has to do with *foederati* of earlier eras, and Gothic ones at that (unsurprisingly).[85] For Koehn, the *foederati* were the elite soldiers of the sixth century, whose prominence grew thanks to some of the big reforms Justinian unleashed on the empire.[86] That said, it is worth situating them in the broader context of soldiers in Procopius' works, especially their relationship with the *comitatenses* and in light of the difficulties in generalizing about Procopius' use of the word στρατιώτης. Though there was a clear legal distinction between *comitatenses* and *foederati*, and *limitanei* for that matter, it is worth investigating the degree to which Procopius also follows this legal distinction.

This type of soldier, the *foederatus*, raises an important issue, long observed by scholars from Müller to Jones to Rance, and which I have touched on at various points in this book.[87] Procopius often took great pains to distinguish between Roman and non-Roman soldiers.[88] Indeed, Kaldellis argued that the very horse archers that feature so prominently in the preface to Procopius' *Wars* were not in fact Roman, though as we will see later, some of them most certainly were. In fact, in this section I will demonstrate Procopius' ambiguity regarding *comitatenses* and *foederati*.[89] This brings to mind another point some have made, Kaldellis included, about the barbarization of the military, a process which Procopius' works reflected.[90] Another purpose of this section is to look at the relationship between Roman and non-Roman soldiers in the sixth century military. As I noted in chapter two, in the majority of the cases where Procopius refers to soldiers, he is referring to Roman ones, which is what we would expect in a work focused on war from a Roman perspective. In the first instance, the Roman soldiers absent at

---

82 Regarding the two inscriptions that identify a federate soldier: first, SEG 45.850, the epitaph for Estotzas and his wife Dody (Trombley 2007: 32); and second, SEG 51.921, for Candac, both of which probably date the sixth century, the latter to late in the sixth century.
83 *Cod. Iust.* 1.5.12.17; 4.65.35; *Iust. Nov.* 116, 117.11, 147.2, *Iust. Nov.* 148.2.
84 Mal. *Chron.* 18.141. See too Mal. *Chron.* 14.22.
85 Jord. *Get.* 16.89, 21.112, 28.145, 32.165.
86 Koehn 2018.
87 Müller 1912; Jones 1964: 663; Rance 2005: 444.
88 Jones 1964: 660; Kaegi 1990: 76.
89 Kaldellis 2004b: 195–196.
90 Kaldellis 2004b: 211. See too Liebeschuetz 1996.

Amida could be frontier soldiers, though his language is vague.[91] Sometimes, he makes it clear that a Roman soldier could be many things, as is the case when Procopius describes Belisarius' arrangement of his forces in advance of a meeting with an envoy from Khusro, where we read, "he [Belisarius] arranged the soldiers as follows. On either side ... Thracians and Illyrians, with Goths beyond them, and next to them Heruls, and finally Vandals and Moors".[92] In this passage we return to the nebulous world of Roman and non-Roman: while the Goths and Vandals clearly were not Roman, the Thracians and Illyrians assuredly were, which makes Procopius' choice to refer to these contingents as collective peoples unhelpful.

How should we classify all these non-Roman soldiers, fighting for Rome, mentioned in the *Wars*? Teall argued that the distinction between Roman *stratiwths* and non-Roman *foederatus* became blurred during the reign of Justinian owing to the frequent, long-running, campaigns.[93] Indeed, this takes us to the subject of the *foederati*, the elite soldiers of Justinian's armies, at least as described by Procopius.[94] Nearly a century ago, Maspero had argued that the *foederati* were ethnic units under Roman commanders, which is how they differed from the *comitatenses*, Roman soldiers commanded by Roman officers.[95] Maspero's view was supported more recently by Laniado, but in a much more nuanced way.[96] Thanks to this earlier work, many now argue that the *foederati* could be composed of both Roman and non-Roman soldiers.[97] Scharf, however, argued for a much local character to the *foederati*, claiming that they hailed exclusively from the Balkans, a view which Koehn dismissed.[98] For Koehn, the *foederati* featured prominently enough for him to argue that Procopius adopted a face-of-battle approach when describing their actions, particularly at Rome, though they feature prominently in Africa too.[99] Before the age of Justinian, *foederati* were allied, non-Roman, troops who fought for Rome, what Koehn calls mercenaries, who stopped serving as non-Roman soldiers for hire by Procopius' day.[100] Koehn notes that there are two main issues with understanding the sixth-century *foederati*: they had been

---

91 Procop. *Wars* 1.7.4.
92 Procop. *Wars* 2.21.3.
93 Teall 1965.
94 See too Parnell's (2017: 16) comments.
95 Maspero 1912.
96 Laniado 2015.
97 Haldon 1984: 100; Zuckerman 2004: 167; Lee 2005: 117; Parnell 2017: 17.
98 Scharf 2001; Koehn 2018: 72.
99 Koehn 2018: 189–197. Note Syvänne's (2015: 407) comments.
100 Procop. *Wars* 3.11.3.

non-Roman mercenaries, but by Justinian's reign were regular troops with the same privileges as the others. Ultimately, Koehn concludes that Justinian's military reforms led to the following distinction between *comitatenses* soldiers and *foederati* soldiers: the former were recruited amongst orthodox Romans and non-Romans, the latter among unorthodox Romans and non-Romans.[101]

While Koehn made a good case for a clear distinction between the two types of soldier in the sixth century, what is most relevant for my purposes is whether there was a clear distinction between *comitatenses* and *foederati* in Procopius, since this has a huge impact on understanding the place of the soldiers in Procopius' works. One important issue, raised by Koehn, is the presence of barbarian soldiers among the *comitatenses*, attested, by his reckoning, in the *Gothic* War. During Belisarius' march to Rome, Procopius notes the following: "22 deserters came to them, men who were barbarians by race but Roman soldiers from the cavalry register of Innocentius."[102] This presupposes that *katalogos* refers specifically to *comitatenses* units, perhaps the ones mentioned in Procopius' catalogue of forces earlier in book five. But is this what Procopius means?

Laniado identified two key passages integral to his understanding of *foederati*, especially as we find them in Prococpius' *Wars*.[103] Indeed, the primary places to find evidence of federates in action in Procopius are in the *Vandal War* and the *Gothic War* where, as we will see, they feature in the catalogues of forces. These catalogues allow us to probe the presence of federate commanders and their men in the respective wars. When describing the Vandal expeditionary force, Procopius says that the army was composed, in part, of soldiers from the *foederati*.[104] The language, unsurprisingly, is vague:

> The commanders of the *foederati* were Dorotheus, the general of the armies in Armenia, and Solomon, who was acting as manager for the general Belisarius (such a person the Romans call *domesticus*) ... There were also Cyprian, Valerian, Martin, Althias, John, Marcellus, and ... Cyril ... [11] There followed with them also four hundred Heruls, whom Pharas led, and about six hundred barbarian allies from the nation of the Massagetai, all mounted archers.[105]

---

101   Koehn 2018: 86–94.
102   Procop. *Wars* 5.17.17.
103   Laniado 2015: 53–57.
104   The key passage comes at Procop. *Wars* 3.11.2–12.
105   Procop. *Wars* 3.11.5–6, 11. ἄρχοντες δὲ ἦσαν φοιδεράτων μὲν Δωρόθεός τε, ὁ τῶν ἐν Ἀρμενίοις καταλόγων στρατηγός, καὶ Σολόμων, ὃς τὴν Βελισαρίου ἐπετρόπευε στρατηγίαν· (δομέστικον τοῦτον καλοῦσι Ῥωμαῖοι ... καὶ Κυπριανὸς καὶ Βαλεριανὸς καὶ Μαρτῖνος καὶ Ἀλθίας καὶ Ἰωάννης

Procopius is clear enough about the identity of the federate commanders, but not about the composition and number of federate soldiers, unless these Heruls and Massagetai are to be understood as the sole federate complement. Of course, a few lines earlier he had made it clear that the invasion army was composed of 10,000 infantry and 5,000 cavalry from the field army and the *foederati*, with no clear distinction given between the two.[106] In fact, from Procopius' language it is not even clear which commanders command which forces, at least in some places.[107] Still, if we divide the commanders into different groups, field army commanders and federate commanders, it follows that each time one of those commanders is mentioned with soldiers, they should be one type or the other.

Procopius provides more useful material in his account of the catalogue of forces dispatched to Italy, but this too is problematic, and provides little help in determining the character of Innocentius' soldiers:

> he sent Belisarius by sea with 4,000 soldiers from the military registers and the *foederati*, and about 3,000 more Isaurians. The commanders were distinguished: Constantinus and Bessas from Thrace, and Peranius from Iberia near Media, a man who was by birth a member of the royal family of the Iberians … the leader of the Isaurians was Ennes … There followed also 200 allied Huns and 300 Moors. The general in supreme command over all was Belisarius, and he had many notable men as spearmen and shield bearers.[108]

καὶ Μάρκελλος καὶ Κύριλλος … εἵποντο δὲ αὐτοῖς Ἔρουλοι τετρακόσιοι, ὧν Φάρας ἦρχε, καὶ ξύμμαχοι βάρβαροι ἑξακόσιοι μάλιστα ἐκ τοῦ Μασσαγετῶν ἔθνους, ἱπποτοξόται πάντες·

106 Procop. *Wars* 3.11.2.
107 Procop. *Wars* 3.11.6–9. Procopius adds, "there were also Cyprian, Valerian, Martin, Althias, John, Marcellus, and the Cyril whom I mentioned above. [7] In charge of the cavalry were Rufinus and Aïgan, who were of the household of Belisarius, as well as Barbatus and Pappus, while the infantry was commanded by Theodorus, whom they also called Kteanus, and Terentiou, Zaïdos, Marcian, and Sarapis." From this, it seems likely the first seven commanders were in charge of federate units, and the latter field army units, but the language is vague, especially since he explicitly said the army comprised infantry and cavalry from both groups.
108 Procop. *Wars* 5.5.2–4. Βελισάριον δὲ ναυσὶν ἔστελλε, στρατιώτας ἐκ μὲν καταλόγων καὶ φοιδεράτων τετρακισχιλίους, ἐκ δὲ Ἰσαύρων τρισχιλίους, ἐκ δὲ Ἰσαύρων τρισχιλίους μάλιστα ἔχοντα. ἄρχοντες δὲ ἦσαν λόγιμοι μὲν Κωνσταντῖνός τε καὶ Βέσσας, ἐκ τῶν ἐπὶ Θρᾴκης χωρίων, Περάνιος δὲ ἐξ Ἰβηρίας τῆς ἄγχιστα Μήδων, γενόμενος μὲν τῶν ἐκ βασιλέως Ἰβήρων … ἀρχηγὸς δὲ Ἰσαύρων Ἔννης. εἵποντο δὲ καὶ Οὖννοι ξύμμαχοι διακόσιοι καὶ Μαυρούσιοι τριακόσιοι. στρατηγὸς δὲ αὐτοκράτωρ ἐφ' ἅπασι Βελισάριος ἦν, δορυφόρους τε καὶ ὑπασπιστὰς πολλούς τε καὶ δοκίμους ἔχων.

As with the case in Africa, the infantry and cavalry comprised both federates and field army soldiers, and so it is not clear whether Innocentius' soldiers were the latter, field army soldiers. These deserters might well have been barbarians serving in field army units, and if we accept that στρατιώτης refers to these kinds of soldiers and κατάλογος refers to these kinds of units, this would make sense. But Procopius had made it clear that the Italian army was composed of both kinds of soldiers; moreover, I have argued throughout this book that neither term applied exclusively to field army soldiers. Thus, these deserters might just as likely have been federate soldiers as field army soldiers. This, too, casts doubt on Koehn's conclusions.

In fact, many of the cases that Koehn adduces as evidence of *foederati* in Procopius' works are not so clear cut. Procopius' description of the skirmishes with Heruls during the reign of Anastasius does not explicitly state what role they took once they were defeated.[109] Indeed, Sarantis has made a strong case that the Heruls filled many roles in the Roman military in the course of their service, and not always as allied groups under their own leaders, which is what we sometimes find in the *Wars*, as we have just seen.[110] Koehn does not only draw on Procopius, however, for he refers to two laws, one which stipulates that all those in service must be orthodox.[111] The language is general, and to my mind is more likely to apply to the civil service than military service, though it does not, necessarily, exclude this as a possibility. The other piece of legislation is concerned specifically with unorthodox Goths who are allowed to serve as federates despite their religious proclivities.[112] This evidence is suggestive, though it only deals with one particular group of soldiers, and some caution is required before we can apply it to all possible federates. There is one other key piece of evidence that Koehn includes in his discussion, the soldiers who participated in the Arian uprising.[113] Notably, Procopius calls all of them soldiers, says most of them were barbarian, and some of them Heruls. What he does not do is specify whether they are federates or field army soldiers. Indeed, as noted, the Heruls were described as separate from the main body of the army, which comprised field army soldiers and federates.[114] By Koehn's reckoning, this would make the soldiers recruited by Tiberius II, a few decades later, *foederati* too given the claims made by John of Ephesus that they followed

---

109 Koehn 2018: 87.
110 Sarantis 2016: 254–257. See too Procopius *Wars* 7.33.13.
111 *Cod. Iust.* 1.4.20 (orthodox in service).
112 *Cod. Iust.* 1.5.12.17.
113 Procop. *Wars* 4.14.12–15. On this story, see too Kaegi (1965).
114 Procop. *Wars* 3.11.2–3.

the doctrine of Arius. Evagrius' account does not include these same details, though Theophanes, writing later but using earlier materials, is even more explicit about the types of soldiers they are: *foederati*.[115] In fact, Theophanes puts them under the command of Maurice, a *comes foederatum*.[116]

If we are going to distinguish any federates from field army soldiers in Procopius, we need to track down more of Procopius' federate commanders. In the *Wars*, several can be traced with certainty, while others are much more problematic. Known federate commanders include Althias, Cyprian, Cyril, Dorotheus, John, Marcellus, Martin, Solomon, and Valerian, a comparatively small number of men, all of whom were involved in the invasion of Africa in 533. But as we have seen, Procopius' language is usually ambiguous.

The *symmachoi*, the allies raised in the short term for assorted expeditions and who were often under their own commanders, complicate matters too.[117] As Greatrex notes, in places like Italy and Africa, the employment of these groups often made distinguishing between Roman armies and enemy armies difficult.[118] He also notes that there was some overlap between barbarians and *symmachoi*. Some of those ethnic units discussed in the previous chapter, and which appear in a variety of different kinds of evidence, would fall into this category.

Is there a way to distinguish between these different soldier groups, *comitatenses* and *foederati*, definitively? It could be that the problem lay with us, and this is probably not far from the truth. Procopius did not write with us in mind, but his contemporaries, to whom the distinction might have been obvious.[119] While he made it clear that there was a difference between the two soldiers, he elided many of these in the text, so regularly grouping both field army soldier and federate regularly together in the course of his discussion. Thus, while *foederati* were a distinct and undoubtedly important group of soldiers in Procopius, who deserved at least identifying at the start of major foreign wars (Africa and Italy), when the regular narrative took hold, a soldier was a soldier, was a soldier.

---

115   Joh. Eph. *EH* 3.25–3.26; Evag. *EH*. 5.14.
116   Theophanes AM 6074, p. 251.
117   See McMahon (2014: 58–59).
118   Greatrex 2018: 340. See too Wolfram 1993, Liebeschuetz 1996: 237–238; Amory 1997: 166–167.
119   On his audience, see Whately (2016a: 219–224). On the distinction between two different troop types, *comitatenses* and *limitanei*, in the sources, see the comments of Parnell (2017: 16).

The real exception was the *bucellarii*. Although the spearmen, the *doryphoroi* and higher-ranking of the *bucellarii*, are named far more often than the shield bearers, the *hypaspistai*, they both appear with some regularity in the *Wars*, enough for Koehn to use them as the basis for his face-of-battle approach to Procopius.[120] These terms seem more specific than *stratiwtai*, but they were old terms used long before by classical practitioners of history, with both Herodotus and Xenophon employing the terms regularly.[121]

As noted earlier, the *bucellarii*, the biscuit men, played a big role in Procopian combat, but feature only rarely in Justinian's legislation.[122] Not only do the *bucellarii* seem to have played a growing role in sixth-century military affairs,[123] and serve as a reflection of the increasingly common warlords of the fifth century and beyond, but they feature in quite a number of papyri working in concert with some of the region's leading men, as Sarris and Hickey have argued—albeit while coming to different conclusions.[124]

The primary legal definition for soldiers in the *Corpus Iuris Civilis* involved the distinction between *comitatenses*, *foederati*, and *limitanei*. The *bucellarii* feature only rarely in the legislation. One law, which specifically identifies them, denies permission to all those in the empire from keeping *bucellarii* for their own ends, one of the main issues raised by Sarris.[125] A few refer to bodyguards kept for protection and other means.[126] The novel on soldiers prohibits "soldiers or *foederati*" from private employment, presumably service as *bucellarii*.[127] So far as I know, a *bucellarius* is identified in only one surviving Greek inscription, one which names a Stephanes from Constantinople.[128] A single inscription from Rome, dated to 538, might name another, an Emalac

---

120   Koehn (2018: 189–197).
121   See, for example, Hdt. 3.139, 4. 78, 5.33, and 7.46, and Xen. *Cyr.* 2.2.10, 7.5.84, and 8.3.6. On bodyguards in the ancient Mediterranean, see the collected papers in Hebblewhite and Whately (forthcoming).
122   On *bucellarii* more generally, see Diesner (1972), Gascou (1976), Schmitt (1994), and Lenski (2009).
123   Ravegnani (1998: 93) ranks with *foederati* as some of the most important soldiers.
124   Sarris 2006: 162–175; Hickey 2012: 111–129.
125   *Cod. Iust.* 9.12.10pr, 9.12.10.1. See too 12.35.15.
126   *Iust. Nov.* 28.5.1, 30.5.1. Also, of note, is Justinian's novel on armaments (85), which touches on the prevention of civilians buying and selling weapons. It also specifies that armourers are only to dispense weapons to those soldiers enrolled in units (*milites in numeris*).
127   *Iust. Nov.* 116.1. See Sarris 2006: 169–170.
128   SEG 45.856.

who, admittedly, is called a *spatharius*.[129] They also feature occasionally in other sixth century texts, like Agathias' *Historiae*, where we mostly here about Narses' bodyguards, presumably his *bucellarii*, though also those of other commanders, like Rusticus and Justin.[130] In Agathias they rarely feature in combat and are more often found carrying out their boss' orders, like when the Herul chief Narses orders his bodyguards to execute a "barbarian" for murdering a servant.[131] This is not dissimilar from how we find them in Theophylact Simocatta's *Historiae*, though he at least lumps them in as part of the army receiving the generals' exhortation before battle.[132] These other sources provide no indication of their recruitment, numbers, or fighting capabilities.

There are only a few places where we can identify them definitively, with one being the 7,000 under Belisarius. That figure has garnered a good deal of debate. Some have argued that the number was an exaggeration, and far too large for any one man.[133] Procopius' language implies that this figure was accurate, for in that same passage he notes that, during the siege of Rome (537/538), "one man's [Belisarius'] household was destroying the power of Theoderic".[134] Indeed, it is hard to imagine a much smaller number of *bucellarii* being sufficient in circumstances like this. That said, other commanders had fewer bodyguards, like Narses' 400 and Valerian's 1,000, and this indeed seems to have been the norm.[135]

The spearmen, as noted, are often found leading contingents of shield bearers, and above they surface primarily in books three to eight. Uliaris led 800 of them in the build-up to Ad Decimum.[136] Diogenes, on the other hand, performed feats of bravery with only twenty-two men (shield bearers).[137] They are not above censure, for that same Uliaris, in a bout of drunken debauchery, attempted to shoot a bird in a tree but missed and killed John the Armenian.[138] Much later, Ulifus, a spearman of Cyprian, went over to Totila during the

---

129   *CIL* 6.9898. The core piece of the inscription reads, *Emalac spat(h)arius dom(i)ni / patrici(i) B<e=I>lisarii*.

130   Agathias 1.12.6, 1.15.1, 1.19.4, 2.14.4, 3.4.6, 3.6.1, 3.16.4, 3.27.1, 4.18.1, 4.21.5, 4.21.6.

131   Agathias 2.7.3–4.

132   Theophyl. Sim. 1.15.2: συγκαλεσάμενος τοὺς ταγματάρχας καὶ λοχαγοὺς καὶ ὑπασπιστὰς [presumably the *bucellarii*] καὶ τῆς μαχίμου δυνάμεως, "summoning ... the brigadiers, captains, bodyguards, and the more distinguished of the fighting force". See too 1.14.5, 2.10.11, 5.2.8, 8.8.11.

133   Whitby 1995: 117; Elton 2007: 282. Contra, see Parnell (2017: 18, n. 26).

134   Procop. *Wars* 7.1.21.

135   Procop. *Wars* 7.27.3. For Narses' figure, see Agathias (1.19.4–5).

136   Procop. *Wars* 3.19.23.

137   Procop. *Wars* 3.23.5.

138   Procop. *Wars* 4.4.15–25.

latter stages of the *Gothic War*.[139] So, much like Maximinus, the spearman who went over to Germanus, their loyalties, at least to their commanders, were not unwavering.

4 Horse Archers

4.1 *Infantry vs. Cavalry*

In the next section of the chapter, I will broaden the scope to look at Procopius' treatment of horse archers more generally. Before I get to that important topic, however, I want to take a look at the role of infantry and cavalry in sixth-century combat. Infantry in sixth-century combat is a topic that has not lacked for attention. For obvious reasons, much scholarship emphasizes the changes in the cavalry of the sixth-century Roman military. The survival of Maurice's *Strategikon*, which focuses almost entirely on cavalry to the exclusion of infantry, save for the last book, has had a role in this.[140] Scholars like Rance have shown how Procopius puts most of his attention on the empire's cavalry forces, particular in the Battle of Taginae/Busta Gallorum.[141] Koehn has gone further and argued that Agathias, Procopius' successor who was writing some decades later, shows the transitional period between the more mixed combat found in Procopius and the cavalry-heavy combat in Maurice.[142] Indeed, contemporaries, or at least some of them, were debating the efficacy of the two traditional components of any ancient military, infantry and cavalry. One of the surviving books from the anonymous *Dialogue on Political Science* devotes an entire book to which branch was better.[143]

Procopius uses some form of the word for infantry (πεζός) dozens of times in the *Wars* and the adjectival form (πεζικός) a handful.[144] Many of these have little to do with the relative proportion of infantry to cavalry in any particular engagement, like the use of πεζικόν when discussing the regiment called "*Reges*" or "*Regii*" (5.23.3). Sometimes he uses one of the terms for infantry simply to specify, at least on some level, the kind of forces involved in an operation. Such is the case at 5.14.1, when Belisarius sends ahead 300 infantry soldiers with Herodian. In this case and a few others, Procopius uses the adjectival form to

---

139   Procop. *Wars* 8.33.10.
140   Rance 2004, 2007. I eagerly await the publication of Rance's text, translation, and commentary of the *Strategikon*.
141   Rance 2005.
142   Note Koehn's comments (2018: 132).
143   Bell 2009.
144   Procopius' references to infantry can be found in Table 4.2.

specify the kind of unit or regiment in operation, and sometimes it is a *pezikos katalogos* (7.6.14), sometimes a *pezikos lochos* (4.5.5).

With respect to infantry, the term does figure in plenty of contexts, battles included, but its role is often limited. At Dara, for example, we do not find infantry in the list of different troops deployed to face the Persians, but plenty of cavalry. They first occur just before Procopius tells us how many soldiers the Romans had at their disposal when he says so stood "the rolls [*katalogoi*] of cavalry and the infantry army" (1.13.22). Other than the odd reference to Persian cavalry, that is it.[145] The story is much the same at Callinicum, where the Roman infantry, again, feature briefly. We do not know how many there were: the 20,000 Roman troops were a mixture of cavalry and infantry (1.18.5). When the armies lined up for battle, all the infantry were deployed on the left by the river (1.18.26). A bit later, we discover the Roman infantry fighting against the entirety of the Persian cavalry (1.18.45). In this instance they only seem to be highlighted because Belisarius ends up fighting along with them.

Two of the tables (5.2 and 5.3) focus on those places where Procopius specifically uses a word for infantry and cavalry, and so leaves out those instances where cavalry, of some sort or other, might be implied, as is the case, for example, with Aquilinus, one of Belisarius' shield bearers who is described undertaking bold actions outside Rome, but whose horse succumbs to his assault.[146] Or those cases where Procopius is even more subtle—only using the person and number of a verb to refer to the actions of cavalry soldiers. Such is the case at 6.5.20, where Procopius says, "yet overtaking the pursuing barbarians they killed them, shooting them from behind." The first "they" are the cavalry of Trajan and Diogenes, noted at 6.5.9, but not named in this later sentence, even if they are participants.

There are other quirks of Procopius' mentions of infantry. One archaic term that Procopius uses a few dozen times is phalanx, φάλαγξ, traditionally an infantry formation, comprising hoplites, widely used in Classical Greece, but which continued to be used in some capacity or other in the Hellenistic world and beyond, even by the Romans.[147] There were lots of other terms that the Romans used in later years (i.e. beyond the republican era) for their formations, though the phalanx, or a version of it, continued in use for some

---

145 Procop. *Wars* 1.13.23, 1.14.25, 1.14.52.
146 Procop. *Wars* 6.5.18–19.
147 The scholarship is vast. See, for instance, the discussions of Konijnendijk (2017) and Sears (2019), as well as the papers in Kagan and Viggiano (2013).

SOLDIERS IN THE FIELD

time thereafter.[148] Getting back to Procopius, he uses the term phalanx thirty-one times, all in the *Wars*, which is more often than the even more classicizing Agathias, who uses it sixteen times.[149] Interestingly, as with the lists for infantry and cavalry, some engagements are more likely to provide the context for his use of phalanx than others.

The table with the cavalry (4.3) does reveal some interesting differences between how Procopius describes the two broad types of soldier. The most glaring difference, besides the fact that the table of cavalry includes more entries, is the much more regular inclusion of numerical data. Ten of sixty-two entries in the infantry table give figures for Roman infantry. In contrast, twenty-seven of eighty entries for cavalry include numbers.[150] This could be a question of access: Procopius' contacts might, by and large, have been cavalry commanders who were willing to give him the information he desired. Additionally, nine of them are found in the most detailed account of the *Wars* in its entirety, the 537/538 siege of Rome. This skews things then too, an important point and Procopian tendency that is apparent in some of the other engagements he describes at length. The Battle of Dara, for example, the most detailed of the lot, includes no specific reference of the number of participating infantry soldiers, but refers specifically to cavalry twice—and this excludes those indirect references, like the Heruls with Pharas.[151] The same thing happens at Tricamarum, where Procopius includes no figures for infantry, but three for cavalry. The one exception, Busta Gallorum, skews towards cavalry in other ways, as Rance has demonstrated.[152]

Then there are the infantry and cavalry battles. Procopius uses the term *hippomaxia* four times, and *pezomaxia* twice;[153] I have not included them in my tables, though their existence presupposes the presence infantry and cavalry at the respective encounters. That he uses these terms implies, at least to my mind, that all other battles that he describes would involve both, infantry and

---

148 On Roman phalanxes/phalanges, see Wheeler (1979, 2004a, 2004b).
149 Procop. *Wars*: 1.13.24, 1.13.27, 1.13.38, 1.14.16, 1.14.42, 1.18.26, 1.18.30, 1.18.36, 1.18.42, 3.8.27, 3.23.13, 5.22.10, 5.28.19, 5.28.22, 5.28.24, 5.29.14, 5.29.21, 5.29.38, 6.1.2, 6.13.9, 7.5.13, 8.8.31, 8.8.32, 8.29.15, 8.29.22, 8.31.1, 8.31.5, 8.32.34, 8.35.19, 8.35.23.
150 A note: these two figures, ten for infantry and twenty-seven for cavalry, includes those references where the number given applies to both groupings, as it does at 1.18.6 when Procopius sets out the army at Callinicum.
151 Procop. Wars 1.13.19.
152 Rance 2005.
153 Procop. Wars 5.18.18, 5.27.23, 5.28.21, 6.1.1 (horse battles); Procop. Wars 8.23.30, 8.23.35 (foot battles). Incidentally, Agathias only uses the word foot battle, and does so twice, once as a verb (πεζομαχεῖν, 2.5.4), and once as a noun (πεζομαχία, 5.22.8).

cavalry, even if certain tactics were given extra attention in some of the engagements. Indeed, this very issue—privileging one troop type over another, is the subject of the next, extended, section.

In sum, the favouring of cavalry over infantry is apparent in Procopius' *Wars*, much as we would expect. On the other hand, it is not as marked as we might have suspected, and Procopius often does so by means of subtle language choices, especially by using numbers for cavalry troops but not infantry ones.[154]

4.2 Hippotoxotai

That Procopius privileges cavalry is not surprising. But how does this fit into broader studies of military change in the sixth century (generally speaking)? Moreover, where do horse archers, the *hippotoxotai*, fit into all this? A few years ago, David Graff published a book entitled *The Eurasian Way of War*, which compared the military practices of seventh century Byzantium with those of seventh century Tang China. He noted a remarkable number of similarities in their military systems, and attributed these to their shared interactions with the peoples of the steppes. While scholars have already commented on the influence of steppe armies on Rome's armies,[155] discussion of a wider Eurasian impact on Rome's military development has been restricted to analyses of changes in cavalry usage. Indeed, Graff's book echoes a surge of interest in the impact of the steppe world on late antique Rome in particular,[156] and a growing appreciation of the benefits of adopting a pan-Eurasian perspective in world history in general.[157] If Graff is right, and the seventh century East Roman state employed a "Eurasian way of war", it is worth delving deeper into when this came about, especially given Procopius' important role in all of this. In this section I will address the appropriateness of Graff's term "Eurasian way of war"; whether any value should be given to the term in the late Roman military context; and discuss what evidence, if any, we have for the adoption of a Eurasian way of war by the late Roman military, with a focus on the sixth century and the age of Justinian. Graff covers quite a lot of ground in his analysis, from resources and institutions and weapons and tactics to the army on campaign. The combat of steppe peoples is generally agreed to have consisted

---

[154] Kaldellis (2004b: 198) argued that it is not possible to determine what proportion of the invasion force in Italy in 535 was composed of cavalry.
[155] Eadie 1967, Bivar 1972.
[156] Kim 2013, 2016; Maas 2015; Cosmo and Mass 2018.
[157] Cunliffe 2015; Frankopan 2015.

of mounted archers, and in some contexts heavily-armoured cavalry, using tactics that included a mixture of encirclement, feigned flight, and ambush.[158] To keep the discussion manageable, I will be restricting my focus to tactics, particularly those concerned with cavalry, the heavily armoured cataphracts and *clibanarii*, and the horse archers. The principal benefit of this is that it allows us to keep Procopius squarely in our sights.

We know, for instance, that the number of cavalry soldiers gradually increased over the course of the first two centuries.[159] This is even true for some specific regions. The Moesias, the part of the Roman Empire that regularly witnessed attacks by steppe peoples,[160] saw a gradual increase in the number of cavalry, both soldiers and units, from the reign of Augustus to the reign of Severus Alexander.[161] This is especially true for Moesia Inferior, which covers much of modern day Bulgaria, where the proportion of cavalry that made up the province's garrison rose from just under a quarter of the total in 93 CE, to nearly a third of the total in 170 CE.[162]

While a rise in the number of cavalry alone is not proof of an adoption of the Eurasian way of war, it does imply the Romans were interested in increasing their mobility. The Sarmatians, usually considered steppe peoples themselves, are the only ones with any real tradition of using heavily-armoured cavalry.[163] By all accounts, they had a significant impact on the Roman military, especially Roman arms, from the second century on, with the ring-pommel sword the best example.[164] Some have even spoken of the Sarmatization of Roman military culture.[165] They feature as Dacian allies on Trajan's column, and it is on that famous monument that we find their famous horsemen, with both rider and horse covered in mail, and the Sarmatian cavalryman carrying a lance. Some decades later, we find our first reference to a Roman soldier who might have been armoured in the same way, and from the aforementioned Moesia Inferior, no less. The *ala I Pannoniorum et Gallorum* had been recorded

---

158 This is the verdict of Hildinger (2013: 10) though others note the same proclivities (Alofs 2014a, 2014b, 2015a, 2015b; Janniard 2015).
159 Colombo 2009. See too Treadgold (1995: 50–52) and Whitby (2004: 160).
160 Coulston 2003; Batty 2007; Whately 2016b.
161 Whately 2016b: 78–82.
162 Whately 2016b: 81. Rather interestingly, during the major build-up in troop numbers for Trajan's Dacian Wars, 100 CE to be exact, amongst auxiliary soldiers the most significant increase in the number of units and soldiers in Moesia Inferior were for cavalry, and in Moesia Superior infantry. Whately 2016b: 81–82.
163 Hildinger 1997: 47.
164 Haldon 2002: 66–68; Coulston 2003: 432; James 2011: 213. See too James 2006.
165 Coulston 2003: 430, James 2011: 2014.

as is for several diplomas from the first half of the second century before an Italian inscription, which dates to the reign of Antoninus Pius, recorded the unit as the *ala I Pannoniorum et Gallorum catafracta*.[166] "Cataphract" is probably the best-known term for the heavily-armoured cavalry of the ancient world. They might also be called *clibanarii*, usually translated as something like "oven men".[167] There was also an *ala Ulpia Contariorum* based in Pannonia Superior as early as 112.[168] Given that a *contus* is a lance, the weapon of choice for heavily-armoured horsemen of the age, this might well have been heavily-armoured too, though we cannot know for certain.

If we jump ahead two centuries, we find many more cataphracts and the like fighting for Rome, and this came after an apparent spike in their deployment in the third century.[169] They play an important role in the Battle of Strasbourg, which pitted Julian and the Romans against the Alamanni in 357.[170] Ammianus also refers to Persian cataphracts in the build-up to the siege of Amida in 359, which the historian himself famously witnessed firsthand.[171] By the end of the century a number of units of *cataphractarii* and *clibanarii* appear in the *Notitia Dignitatum*, with the majority listed in the eastern list rather than the western one. They make up about 15% of the total cavalry units in the field armies in the *Notitia Dignitatum*.[172] A century after that, however, they had all but disappeared. There are several sixth-century papyri that name an *arithmos* of *Leontoklibanarii*, but the documents refer to the mundane and their origins are obscure.[173] Outside of those soldiers based in Egypt, we have no direct evidence at any other point in the sixth century, even if the soldiers from Procopius' preface were heavily armed. We are ill-informed about sixth-century armour, at least in comparison to earlier periods of Roman history.[174] As it happens, the best-documented cavalry of the Roman world hail from the

---

166   CIL 11.5632; Whately 2016b: 40.
167   Harl 1996: 626. Cf. Speidel 1984, Coulston 1986: 63. Note too Ammianus Marcellinus, who had firsthand experience with both Roman and Persian heavily-armoured cavalry and says cataphracts and *clibanarii* are the same thing (Amm. Marc. 16.10.8).
168   Holder 2003: 135.
169   CIL 3.14406a, 5.6784, 13.848, 13.3493, 13.3495, 13.6238, Eadie 1967: 173.
170   Amm. Marc. 16.12.
171   Amm. Marc. 18.8.8.
172   Hoffmann 1969/70; Elton 1996: 106–107; Haldon 2002: 68. Graff (2016: 158) counts fourteen units of heavy cavalry in the east and four in the west near the end of the fourth century.
173   See Diethart and Dintsis 1984: 81. As for the papyri, see CPR 8.61, 24.20, 24.21, and several more.
174   Haldon 2002: 65; Decker 2013: 105. The evidence for late Roman weaponry also tends to be better represented in northern Europe rather than the Mediterranean (Sarantis 2013: 154).

third century thanks to the spectacular finds at Dura Europos.[175] While there might well have been heavily-armoured cavalry still fighting for Rome, these were likely few in number.[176]

Heavily-armoured horsemen are only one side of the coin, however, for the quintessential tactical component of the steppe armies are the mounted archers who regularly engaged in feigned flight in combat. This warrior-type and tactical approach was a feature of steppe combat for nearly 2000 years.[177] The earliest recorded horse archers fighting for Rome, however, which were found among the auxiliary units, had no direct link with the steppe world, and appeared as early as the reign of Caligula. The first such units were based in the eastern half of the empire and, at least initially, originated in the Levant. Some of the units were based in the Pannonias,[178] some in Syria,[179] and some in Mauretania.[180] We cannot say where the soldiers who served in those units hailed from, it is likely that many, at least initially, came from the Near East. One unit's called the *Ala Augusta Ituraeorum sagittariorum*, another the *Ala Augusta Parthorum et Araborum Sagittaria*, and yet another the *Ala I Hamiorum Syrorum Sagitariorum*, and the name of each unit consists of at least one ethnic ethnonym (*Ituraeorum, Parthorum, Araborum, Hamiorum,* and *Syrorum*) that suggests some sort of eastern heritage. None of the peoples from which the names originate, Arabs, Hamians, Ituraeans, Parthians, or Syrians, are necessarily from the steppe themselves, except for the Parthians.[181] Indeed, James has argued that, Sarmatians influence on the Roman military notwithstanding, the steppe impact might have come through an intermediary, at least initially, like the Parthians.[182] This, in itself, would support claims, made by Alofs in particular, that mounted horse-archery had a long and continuous history in the Middle East.[183] Although debate rages over the degree to which auxiliary units kept their ranks filled with recruits locally or from a unit's homeland, Haynes has made a strong case that the Romans employed a mixed local, regional, and

---

175   James 2004: 113–115; Sarantis 2013: 172.
176   Haldon 2002: 69. See too Syvänne 2004: 169–181, and Maur. *Strat.* 8.2.
177   Hildinger 2013: 10.
178   *Ala Augusta Ituraeorum sagittariorum*, Spaul 1994: 154; *Ala I Thracum Veteranorum sagittariorum*, Spaul 1994: 223; *Ala III Augusta Thracum sagittariorum*, Spaul 1994: 234.
179   *Ala Gallorum et Thracum Antiana sagittaria*, AE 2005, 1730; AE 2011, 1810, Spaul 1994: 27; *Ala III Augusta Thracum sagittariorum*, Spaul 1994: 234.
180   *Ala Augusta Parthorum et Araborum Sagittaria*, Spaul 1994: 176; *Ala I Hamiorum Syrorum Sagitariorum*, Spaul 1994: 140.
181   For a detailed, recent, study of Rome's use of Parthian auxiliaries, see Wheeler (2016a, 2016b).
182   Coulston 1986; James 2006: 371–374; James 2011: 214–215. Cf. Bivar 1972.
183   Alofs 2014a, 2014b, 2015a, 2015b.

provincial recruitment programme which varied from place to place.[184] A special case has sometimes been claimed for mounted archers, with Mann saying that these kinds of soldiers tended to be recruited from an original group.[185] Haynes has forcefully refuted the argument for special recruitment practices continuing over long periods of time,[186] which implies that regardless of the origins of the initial mounted archer recruits, decades and more later they were Roman in some capacity or other, and likely trained by their comrades if they had entered service not yet accomplished riders and archers.

If we jump to the end of the fourth century and the *Notititia Dignitatum*, we find many more mounted archer units fighting for Rome, and their names too betray an eastern connection rather than a steppe one, with good examples being the *Equites sagittarii Parthi* and the *Equites sagittarii Cordueni* based in the west. There are a handful of indigenous units based in the east, particularly the Near East, though there is little more we can say about them. In general, the mounted archers were split between east and west. As far as Ammianus' account is concerned, while he refers to cataphracts, especially Persian ones, on several occasions, he is far more Spartan in his references to horse archers. There were some, presumably mounted, in the service of Julian at Strasbourg,[187] some others based in Amida during the Persian invasion just a couple of years later,[188] a cohort of mounted archers in North Africa,[189] and perhaps some others serving along with Valens a few years later.[190] But to get back to the point about special recruitment, perhaps too we should draw attention to Ammianus' praise of Constantius II, who notes the emperor's skill at riding and archery.[191] Whether Ammianus' praise is genuine or otherwise, or even whether his views in anyway matched those of his or Constantius' contemporaries, it implies that, at least on some level, skill at mounted archery was valued by members of the Roman elite in the fourth century.

---

184 Haynes 2013: 121–134.
185 Mann 1963: 147.
186 Haynes 2013: 135–142.
187 Amm. Marc. 16.12.7.
188 Amm. Marc. 18.9.4.
189 Amm. Marc. 29.5.20. This is probably the Equites quarto *sagittari* based under the Comes Africae listed in the *Notitia Dignitatum*.
190 Amm. Marc. 30.1.11. Valens apparently sent ahead 1000 nimble and light-armed archers after some skirmishes. Ammianus does not explicitly say they are mounted, but the speed that he refers to suggests to me that they might be.
191 The *missorium* of Kerch displays him on horseback, though wielding a lance.

4.3 Horse Archers: The Procopian Ideal and the Reality

We have now seen the context. Roman armies used heavily-armoured and mounted archery for centuries before Procopius and Justinian. Significantly, for the sixth century, Procopius is often adduced as a key source for this shift in how the Roman state fought. Indeed, right from the start of his 8-book *Wars* he sets the stage for this Roman approach to war by comparing what purport to be contemporary horse-archers with their Homeric forbearers. This surprising comparison has puzzled scholars for some time, with some seeing it as a genuine reflection of the dominant soldier-type and mode of combat in the sixth century, others as an anachronistic representation-cum-subtle criticism of the spate of reforms of the current regime.[192] I have argued elsewhere that the mounted archer of the introduction should be understood as an ideal warrior best suited to the heroic, even vaguely Homeric, warfare described in the Gothic Wars, which reached its peak during the 537/538 siege Rome.[193] But ideal does not mean most common. Indeed, what I did not do in *Battles and Generals* is look at their ubiquity in Procopius' narrative, our best evidence for the practice of sixth-century combat.

Kaldellis, for one, argues that horse archers were rare in the sixth century,[194] though Petitjean has made a forceful rebuttal.[195] Alofs, the author of four detailed articles on mounted archers, regularly uses Procopius' *Wars* as evidence for warmaking in the east Roman state. Much like Graff, Alofs does not focus on cavalry tactics alone even though it is the linchpin of his studies; rather, he too ranges more widely. Ultimately, Alofs posits a Romano-Persian "military culture of armoured horse archers".[196] Graff does not use Procopius nearly as much as Alofs for obvious reasons—Procopius was writing a century too soon. That said, he does argue that "Procopius' accounts of battles [are] decided by the actions of versatile, rather lightly-armored horsemen, equally adept with lance and bow, riding unarmored horses".[197] So how often does Procopius provide evidence of heavy cavalry or mounted archers?

---

192 See Basso and Greatrex (2017) and Kruse (2017a).
193 Whately 2016a: 181–188.
194 Kaldellis 2004b.
195 Petitjean 2014. See too Breccia (2004).
196 Alofs 2014a: 426.
197 Graff 2016: 56. See too Haldon (1999: 215), who notes that the Byzantines of Procopius' day had the advantage of using mounted archery against those unused to the tactics, while against those with many formations filled with archers, they could at least match them.

Alofs identifies twenty different passages from Procopius in support of his argument on the dominance of mounted archers.[198] As it happens, there are many more places in the *Wars* where Procopius refers to bows, arrows, or archers.[199] What Procopius does not often specify is whether these archers were on foot or mounted. An obvious source of a few references to archery is the horse-archer comparison from the introduction (1.1.12–14). Its position at the start of the *Wars* does point to a strong role for mounted archers. Some references to archers have little to do with the Romans or their foes, however.[200] Arrows fly between the Romans and the Persians in the Battle of Dara, but Procopius does not specify whether these are mounted archers firing off these missiles or not.[201] The next time we find them is the Battle of Callinicum. There too Procopius does not indicate whether mounted archers are involved.[202] We also get Procopius' oft-cited comparison of Roman and Persian archers which, it should be stressed, does not in any way suggest that they were mounted. In both battles the flying arrows come at the beginning of the fighting itself. That Procopius indicates that the quantity of arrows was such to black out the sky, which he says was also the case at Dara, suggests to me that it is not likely cavalry alone that is involved in these opening volleys.[203] Feigned fights involving mounted archers are unlikely to have created the visual effect that Procopius describes.

There are plenty of other references to archery in the *Wars*. Some are incidental details about the death of a combatant, as we find in Procopius' account of the Siege of Sura.[204] A number of examples involve siege warfare, and, from the perspective of the defenders, in those circumstances it is unlikely there were mounted archers firing from the battlements. We find defenders from the battlements and attackers from the base of the walls firing at their foes at the sieges of Antioch, Petra, and Edessa.[205] Near the end of the *Persian Wars*, Belisarius employs a ruse to mislead the Persian king Khusro about his

---

198   Procop. *Wars* 1.1.12–14, 1.14.35–6, 1.18.31–35, 1.18.41–8, 2.21.7, 5.22.20, 5.28.1–18, 5.28.21, 5.29.17, 5.29.37–8, 5.29.42, 6.1.20, 7.4.21–30, 7.5.7–12, 8.8.30–1, 8.8.32–4, 8.13.4, 8.29.23, 8.31.5, 8.35.19. Many of the examples produced by Alofs do not describe quite what he implies they do.

199   There are 82 such uses in the *Wars*, and 1 each in the Buildings and Secret History. While all refer to missiles of some sort, some are the missiles shot from artillery.

200   Procop. *Wars* 1.7.8, 3.8.27.

201   Procop. *Wars* 1.14.35.

202   Procop. *Wars* 1.18.31–35.

203   Syvänne (2004: 169) assumes the archers who opened fire at the beginning of battles were mounted.

204   Procop. *Wars* 2.5.12.

205   See Procop. *Wars* 2.8.7, which refers to defenders at the siege of Antioch, and 2.8.10 and 2.8.15, which refer to the attackers; 2.17.14–15 the attackers at Petra; and 2.26.28 the defenders at Edessa.

SOLDIERS IN THE FIELD

troop numbers. The stratagem entailed Roman soldiers walking around nonchalantly without their armour and with assorted weapons, including swords, axes, and bows to mislead the Persians about their numbers and readiness.[206] Significantly, Procopius does not specify whether any of those carrying bows were mounted archers.[207]

There are plenty of references to archery in the Vandal and Gothic wars, wars of conquest set in ostensibly foreign lands. Beginning with Vandal Africa, Procopius identifies bowmen a few times, but as is his practice earlier, very rarely does he specify whether they are on foot or on horse.[208] There are cases where the archers are almost certainly on foot, as is the case with the siege of Mt. Papua when some men, who recently ran to the top of a rock, kept their attackers at bay by means of their bows.[209] That said, there are instances of single combat in which the participants are clearly horse archers, as is the case in the duel involving two men named Althias and Iaudas.[210] In fact, it is not until the very end of the *Vandal Wars* that we find mounted archers engaged in combat, as when John killed Stotzas, both of whom happened to be mounted, with his bow.[211]

Procopius' *Gothic Wars* is full of references to archery, especially during the suitably epic siege of Rome of 537/538. The first archers we find, however, are on foot posted to the tops of the masts of Roman ships to shoot at the Goths at Palermo.[212] Many of the rest come during that siege. Belisarius, for instance, shoots and kills one of the Goths as he comes near Rome's moat.[213] Shortly thereafter, Belisarius ordered the entire Roman army to shoot at the Goths using their bows.[214] The peak in the deployment of horse archers, however, comes a few chapters later when Belisarius sometimes dispatched small bands of these mounted soldiers from the gates of Rome against the Goths encamped outside a few times.[215] After the third such sortie, our narrator Procopius jumps in to alert us to the tactical failings of the Gothic king Vittigis.[216] But Vittigis does not learn his lesson and sends another group of Gothic horsemen to engage

---

206 Procop. *Wars* 2.21.8.
207 Procop. *Wars* 2.21.4.
208 Procop. *Wars* 3.15.36. For an overview of the war in Africa with occasional discussion of the role of mounted archers, see Sarantis (2017b).
209 Procop. *Wars* 4.10.9.
210 Procop. *Wars* 4.13.15.
211 Procop. *Wars* 4.24.11.
212 Procop. *Wars* 5.5.16.
213 Procop. *Wars* 5.22.4.
214 Procop. *Wars* 5.22.7.
215 Procop. *Wars* 5.27.4–5, 11, 14.
216 Procop. *Wars* 5.27.15.

the Romans. In fact, in response, Belisarius dispatches the commander Bessas against Vittigis' troops, and he and his 1,000 men perform textbook steppe-tactics: they encircle the Goths, shoot arrows at them from behind, and initially, at least, hold off from meeting them hand-to-hand.[217] At the end of this chapter, Procopius intervenes again to comment on the differences between Gothic and Roman cavalry, noting that nearly all the Romans and their allies, the Huns especially, are good archers while not one of the Goths are.[218]

Less than a chapter later, while speaking to his assembled soldiers during the same siege in anticipation of a pitched battle, Belisarius implores his men not to spare their horses, bows, or any other weapon they might have.[219] When the fighting begins a chapter later, archery, as is to be expected, plays a key role in the opening stages, and takes a heavy toll on the Goths.[220] Given we know that nearly all the Romans were mounted in this encounter it seems likely we are dealing with mounted archers here.[221] Quite a bit later, however, archery is just a part of the Roman armament in this battle, for Procopius refers to the use of javelins,[222] and the hacking of combatants at close-quarters, an indication of the use of swords.[223] The Hunnic allies were mounted and noteworthy archers.[224] Some of Procopius' guardsmen were mounted too, for one Chorsomantis, in a drunken stupor and determined to avenge a wound to his leg, trotted out of the Pincian gate at noon with several arrows and proceeded to take out a number of Gothic adversaries.[225] That Belisarius' bodyguards were often mounted archers is implied by a comment a little while later. At the start of book seven Procopius gives a pseudo-eulogy of Belisarius. While gushing over the commander's beneficence, he notes that whenever a soldier lost a horse or a bow in battle, he would replace it.[226]

The last flurry of references to archers comes in book eight, which was published after the first seven books of the *Wars*; it covers combat against both the Persians and the Goths. In the Battle of the River Hippis, which pits the Persians and their allies against the Romans and theirs, the arrows of the

---

217 Procop. *Wars* 5.27. 19.
218 Procop. *Wars* 5.27.27–28. See too Whately (2016a: 184–187).
219 Procop. *Wars* 5.28.13.
220 Procop. *Wars* 5.29.17.
221 Procop. *Wars* 5.28.21–22.
222 Procop. *Wars* 5.29.22. Granted, it is Moors whom Procopius highlights here. But see Procop. *Wars* 5.29.42.
223 Procop. *Wars* 5.29.41.
224 Procop. *Wars* 6.1.9.
225 Procop. *Wars* 6.1.30.
226 Procop. *Wars* 7.1.8.

participants are referred to regularly.[227] Though they fight much of the battle on foot, they began on horseback: what Roman cavalry there were dismounted when they thought they could not bear the charge of the Persian horsemen.[228] The Romans then form a phalanx and thrust out their spears to meet the charge.[229]

Some of the remaining cases where archers feature involve sieges.[230] We find archers in one of the few naval battles of the *Wars*, fought by Romans and Goths, and clearly no place for mounted combat.[231] Archers surface in the final battles of the Gothic War, and the text as a whole. The eunuch commander Narses had some mounted archers as he ranged across the countryside in Italy.[232] In the penultimate battle, Busta Gallorum, they feature prominently. One of the most detailed episodes in the battle involves two men of fifty, a Paulus and a Ansilas, both infantrymen whom Narses had tasked with holding a hill.[233] They discard their swords and fight off their cavalry foes with their bows and arrows alone.[234] These fifty were only a portion of the total foot archers on the Roman side, for Procopius later notes about 8,000 of them on both wings of their formation.[235] At several points in the battle the archers play a significant role, but again they are on foot.[236]

When Procopius introduces the Franks, his observation that their infantry was armed with neither bows nor spears suggests that a significant proportion of the Roman infantry were.[237] And yet Rance has argued that the presumed emphasis on cavalry over infantry in the *Wars* is overstated;[238] moreover, the text usually wielded in support of this presumed age of cavalry, Maurice's *Strategikon*, may not actually reflect a world where infantry has been all but replaced. Rance has also argued that the text was originally conceived as a cavalry-only manual. Indeed, one of the *topoi* of military manuals is the statement that some branch of the military, if not the whole institution, is in a sad state; hence the need for said manual. To get back to Procopius' preface, while archery is the element of the contemporary soldier that he highlights, he notes

---

227   Procop. *Wars* 8.8.32–37.
228   Procop. *Wars* 8.8.29–30.
229   Procop. *Wars* 8.8.31.
230   Procop. *Wars* 8.14.11, 31.
231   Procop. *Wars* 8.23.30, 32, 34.
232   Procop. *Wars* 8.28.8.
233   Procop. *Wars* 8.29.13.
234   Procop. *Wars* 8.29.22–28.
235   Procop. *Wars* 8.31.5.
236   Procop. *Wars* 8.32.5, 9.
237   Procop. *Wars* 6.25.3.
238   Rance 2005.

that some archers would also wield spears (1.1.13), others would have swords (1.1.12). This ideal warrior of the preface reflects some wider trends in the sixth century including the despecialization of the cavalry; Procopius' archers, much like the cavalrymen whom Maurice spends so much time with, can use a range of weapons effectively.[239] In sum, mounted archers feature occasionally in the *Wars*, and they tend to be confined to particular circumstances. Although I have not discussed it, this is also true for heavily-armoured cavalry: there is no clear evidence for their use in the *Wars*.

Procopius is often vague in his differentiation of troops types, per the classicizing genre and as we have seen in this book so far. Even so, we have limited evidence for mounted archery—it was deployed in very specific contexts—and none for heavily-armoured cavalry, at least amongst the Romans. Procopius' evidence, then, does not show a wholehearted shift to a Eurasian way of war.

What is more, if the Romans had long had mounted archers, their increase was gradual, and their total number was modest at best, what does this mean for this supposed shift to a Eurasian way of war? For one, any claims that a shift in organization to compensate for the adoption of steppe techniques was a revolution is an overstatement.[240] Along those same lines, any determinist explanations, whether technological or otherwise would also be incorrect: there is no clear evidence of any significant shift, within a short period of time, to either horse archery and/or heavily-armoured cavalry during the period under review. Any changes that we have seen have been gradual. The existence of gradual changes does not obviate an impact from the steppe world. Indeed, it would be hard to argue that they had no impact. Rather, the impact seems much subtler than has sometimes been argued, particularly recently.[241] The arrival of the Huns at the end of the fourth century undoubtedly had an impact on how Rome fought. The same is true for the arrival of the Avars nearly two centuries later. It is not so much a question then of was there an impact, but what was its scale. Agathias' note on Narses' use of feigned flight in Italy, a stratagem he specifically associates with the Huns, does not mean that the Romans had become wholly Eurasianized.[242] Though Maurice refers to Avar adaptations to the Roman cavalry on a few occasions (neck pieces, lances,

---

239 Haldon 1975: 12; Rance 2007: 357–358. Note, for example, the duel involving Anzalas at 7.4.21–30.
240 Kim 2016: 160. Kennedy (2001: 122–123) argues similarly with regard to the adoption of mounted archery by the armies of the early Islamic world.
241 See Kim (2016: 160–163) in particular.
242 Agathias 1.22.1. cf. Kim 2016: 160.

SOLDIERS IN THE FIELD   131

and tents for instance), that he felt compelled to specify this is telling.[243] Procopius' comment in the *Secret History* that certain young members of the Constantinopolitan public wore their hair in the Hunnic fashion should also be grouped together into this category.[244] In truth, Procopius implies that Rome's mounted archers were best used in certain contexts, such as combat against the Goths.[245]

5   Conclusion

In conclusion, we should no longer equate στρατιῶται with the *comitatenses* that played such a key role in late antique armies. *Comitatenses* and *foederati* were often hard to distinguish in Procopius' works, even if the two were distinct categories in his African and Italian catalogues of forces. One group whom he does distinguish is the *bucellarii*. The distinction between Roman and non-Roman is not so neat either. To my mind, this shows not the barbarization of the military but the growing despecialization in sixth-century soldiers, who might have a range of skills.

Procopius' soldiers could be any kind of soldier, even if he devoted much more attention to those armies in the field than to those on the frontier, the subject of the next chapter. That said, Procopius provides few concrete details about the lives or experiences of those soldiers, or about their units and structures. But this is not specific to field army soldiers, for there is also limited detailed evidence for federates and allies.

We have also seen the limitations to Procopius' descriptions of combat. Cavalry is privileged over infantry, but not necessarily because of any perceived skewing of his factual record. Rather, Procopius manipulates the sixth century's tactical history by focusing a little more on cavalry, and giving more figures for cavalry soldiers than infantry ones. The horse archers that feature so prominently in the preface to the *Wars* are an ideal, but their role is far from common—and their history is long. They had existed in the Roman military for some time, so reflecting the growing Eurasian character of Roman armies. It is also far from clear that these were non-Roman soldiers. The one group of soldiers, from the basic types discussed earlier, left out are the *limitanei*. They are the subject of the next chapter.

---

243   Maur. *Strat.* 1.2.
244   Procop. *SH*. 7.10.
245   Janniard 2016: 21; Whately 2016a: 181–188. See too Curta (2016: 85–86).

TABLE 4.1 *Magistri Militum* in Procopius' works

Number	Name	*Magister Militum* type	Location (in Procopius)
1.	Amalafridas	Unknown	8.25.11–15
2.	Aratius	Vacans	1.12.21, 6.13.17, 7.34.40, 7.40.34, 8.19.3, 8.25.11, 8.27.13
3.	Artabanes 2	Thracias, Praesentalis	4.24.2, 4.27.9, 4.28.27–33, 7.31.10, 7.39.8, 8.24.1, 8.25.24
4.	Babas	Unknown	8.9.5, 8.13.8
5.	Belisarius	Orientem	1.11.21, 1.12.20, 3.11.21, 8.21.1, *SH* 4.4, 4.39
6.	Beros	Vacans?	2.24.14, 7.27.3, 7.37.28
7.	Bessas	Vacans, Armeniam	1.8.3, 5.5.3, 5.16.2, 5.19.15, 6.30.2, 7.6.8, 7.19.14, 8.9.4, 8.11.40, 8.12.29–34
8.	Buzes	Armeniam, Vacans	1.13.5, 2.3.28, 2.20.20, 7.32.41, 7.34.40, *SH* 4.4
9.	Chilbudius	Thracias	7.14.2
10.	Conon	Vacans?	6.5.1, 7.6.2, 7.17.2, 7.30.7
11.	Constantianus 1	Vacans	2.24.3, 2.28.2
12.	Constantianus 2	Illyricum, Vacans	5.7.26, 5.16.1, 15, 6.30.2, 7.2.8, 7.3.4, 7.6.8, 7.32.41, 7.34.40, 7.40.34
13.	Constantinus	Vacans	5.5.3, 5.16.1, 5.19.16, 6.1.4, 6.8.1–18, *SH* 1.24–30
14.	Cutzinas	Vacans	2.28.50, 8.17.21
15.	Cyprian	Vacans	3.11.5–15, 4.7.11, 5.23.19, 6.23.2, 7.5.4,
16.	Dagisthaeus	Armeniam	2.29.10, 8.8.1–16, 8.9.4, 8.26.13, 8.33.24
17.	Demetrius	Vacans	5.5.3, 6.23.2, 7.6.13
18.	Domnicus	Vacans	4.16.1, 4.19.1, 6.29.1

TABLE 4.1   *Magistri Militum* in Procopius' works (*cont.*)

Number	Name	*Magister Militum* type	Location (in Procopius)
19.	Dorotheus 2	Armeniam	1.15.3, 3.11.5–15, 3.14.14
20.	Germanus 1	Thracias, Praesentalis	2.6.9, 4.16.1, 4.19.1, 7.37.24–26, 7.39.9, 7.40.6, 7.40.9
21.	Gilacius	Vacans?	7.26.24
22.	Gontharis 2	Vacans	4.19.6–9, 4.25.1, 4.26.33, 4.28.27–33
23.	Hypatius	Thracias, Praesentalis	1.11.24
24.	Ildiger	Vacans	2.24.13, 4.8.24, 4.15.49, 4.17.6, 6.7.15, 7.1.1
25.	Irenaeus	Vacans	1.12.14–15
26.	John 6	Vacans?	3.11.5–15, 4.5.5, 4.16.2
27.	John 7 Tzibus	Vacans?	2.15.9, 2.17.4
28.	John 9	Vacans	4.19.1, 4.22.3, 4.24.6–14
29.	John 12 Troglita	Africam	2.14.12, 4.17.6, 4.28.45, 8.17.20, 8.24.33
30.	John 14 of Vitalian	Vacans, Illyricum	6.5.1, 6.10.8–10, 6.21.23, 6.30.2, 7.6.8, 7.13.20
31.	Justinian	Armeniam, Orientem	7.40.10, 8.25.1–11
32.	Justinus 1	Illyricum	6.13.17, 6.21.16, 6.23.2, 7.5.1–4, 7.13.19, 8.28.4
33.	Justinus 2	Armeniam	7.32.14–15, 7.40.34, 8.25.1–11
34.	Justus	Vacans	1.24.53, 2.20.20, 2.24.15, 2.28.1
35.	Leontius	Vacans	4.19.1, 4.20.19
36.	Libelarius	Orientem	1.12.23
37.	Marcellus 3	Vacans	2.28.2
38.	Martinus	Orientem, Armeniam	1.21.27, 2.13.16, 2.24.13, 3.11.5–15, 4.14.39, 5.24.18, 6.21.13, 7.1.1, 8.17.12, *SH* 4.13
39.	Mauricius	Vacans	5.7.1

TABLE 4.1 *Magistri Militum* in Procopius' works (*cont.*)

Number	Name	*Magister Militum* type	Location (in Procopius)
40.	Mundus	Illyricum, Orientem	1.24.43, 5.5.2, 5.7.5
41.	Narses 1	Vacans?	1.15.31, 6.13.16, 7.13.21, 8.21.6, 19, 8.26.13, 8.33.1, 8.35.33
42.	Narses 2	Unknown	1.12.21, 2.24.12, 2.25.23, 6.13.17
43.	Nazares	Illyricum	7.11.18, 7.40.34
44.	Paulus 2	Vacans	6.5.1, 6.7.16
45.	Peranius	Vacans	2.24.15, 2.28.1, 5.5.3, 5.23.13, 6.19.1
46.	Petrus 3	Vacans	1.12.9 2.16.16, 2.24.13, *SH* 4.4)
47.	Philemouth	Vacans?	2.24.14, 6.22.8, 7.13.21, 7.34.42, 8.26.13
48.	Pompeius	Vacans	1.24.19
49.	Rufinus 2	Vacans	4.19.1, 4.20.19
50.	Scholasticus	Unknown	7.40.34
51.	Sergius	Vacans	4.21.1, 4.22.1, 4.24.16, 7.27.2, *SH* 5.28–33
52.	Sittas	Armeniam, Praesentalis	1.12.20, 1.15.3, 2.3.25–27
53.	Solomon 1	Vacans	3.11.5–15, 3.24.19, 4.8.23, 4.11.47, 4.19.1, 4.21.28
54.	Suartuas	Praesentalis (?)	8.25.11
55.	Theoctistus	Africam	2.8.2, 2.24.13
56.	Theodorus 2 the Cappadocian	Vacans	4.8.24, 4.14.32, 4.15.6, 4.15.49, 4.17.6
57.	Thomas Guzes	Vacans	2.30.4–5
58.	Valerian	Vacans, Armeniam, Orientem	2.14.8, 3.11.5–15, 4.14.40, 5.24.18, 7.1.1, 7.27.3, 8.23.4, 8.33.2
59.	Vitalian	Thracias, Praesentalis	1.8.3, *SH* 6.27, *Build.* 4.11.20
60.	Vitalius	Illyricum	6.22.7, 6.28.2, 7.1.34, 7.10.2, 7.11.11

TABLE 4.2   Roman infantry in Procopius' *Wars*

Number	Location	Specifics (and battle, if applicable)[a]
1.	1.13.22	Infantry army, Dara
2.	1.18.6	20,000 infantry (and cavalry) Callinicum
3.	1.18.26	All the infantry, Callinicum
4.	1.18.42	Phalanx of infantry, Callinicum
5.	1.18.44	The infantry, Callinicum
6.	1.26.5	Posted [in] a roster[b] of infantry
7.	3.11.2	10,000 infantry
8.	3.11.7	Infantry
9.	3.11.8	All the leaders of the infantry
10.	3.19.1	All the infantry, Ad Decimum
11.	3.19.11	The infantry, Ad Decimum
12.	3.20.1	The infantry
13.	4.1.21	The infantry
14.	4.2.2	Infantry army, Tricmarum
15.	4.3.6	The infantry, Tricamarum
16.	4.3.19	The infantry, Tricamarum
17.	4.3.20	The infantry, Tricamarum
18.	4.5.5	An infantry company
19.	4.12.17	1,000 infantrymen, Mt. Bourgaon
20.	4.15.50	An infantry register, Carthage
21.	4.16.2	The infantry army
22.	4.17.4	All the infantry, Scalae Veteres
23.	4.17.5	On the left of the infantry, Scalae Veteres
24.	4.17.17	Upon the infantry, Scalae Veteres
25.	5.5.3	Rosters ... of infantry, Salona and Sicily
26.	5.14.1	300 from the infantry register
27.	5.19.18	Commanders of the infantry rolls, Naples
28.	5.23.2	With an infantry roll, Rome
29.	5.23.3	Infantry component, Rome
30.	5.28.21	Most of the infantry, Rome

a   The standard term for infantry is πεζός on its own, and unless other indicated, this is what Procopius uses (in a variety of cases and numbers). Occasionally, he uses πεζός, an adjective, with a noun like army (στρατός), as he does at 4.2.2, πεζῷ στρατῷ.
b   καταλόγῳ τεταγμένος πεζῶν. In this and the next table, katalogos is translated interchangeably as register, roster, and roll. For more on why, see the discussion in chapter three.

TABLE 4.2 Roman infantry in Procopius' *Wars* (*cont.*)

Number	Location	Specifics (and battle, if applicable)
31.	5.28.22	The infantry, being few, Rome
32.	5.28.24	Phalanx of the infantry, Rome
33.	5.28.25	Commanders of the infantry, Rome
34.	5.28.26	All the commanders of the infantry, Rome
35.	5.28.28	A few infantry, Rome
36.	5.28.29	Fleeing to the infantry, Rome
37.	5.29.13	Stationed infantry in the centre, Rome
38.	5.29.37	To the phalanx of infantry, Rome
39.	5.29.38	The infantry, Rome
40.	5.29.39	With some few of the infantry with them, Rome
41.	5.29.40	The rest of the infantry, Rome
42.	6.10.14	All the infantry, Rome
43.	6.11.6	Unsupported infantry, Petra
44.	6.11.21	Many of the infantry, Petra
45.	6.11.22	The infantry, Petra
46.	6.23.2	500 infantry, Osimo
47.	6.23.27	The infantry, Osimo
48.	6.23.34	Infantry trumpet, Osimo
49.	7.6.13	Leading an infantry register, Naples
50.	7.19.6	Infantry
51.	7.19.11	Infantry army
52.	7.27.16	200 infantry
53.	7.28.4	The infantry
54.	7.30.1	2,000 infantry soldiers, Rusciane
55.	7.30.6	100 infantry, Rusciane
56.	7.39.6	Infantry rolls, Reggio
57.	8.8.16	With the infantry of both, River Hippis
58.	8.8.29	The infantry with Goubazes and Dagisthaeus, River Hippis
59.	8.20.34	The custom for infantry
60.	8.29.13	50 infantry from the register, Busta Gallorum
61.	8.31.5	Making them infantry, Busta Gallorum
62.	8.32.9	8,000 infantry, Busta Gallorum

TABLE 4.3 Roman cavalry in Procopius' *Wars*

Number	Location	Usage
1.	1.13.19	Many cavalry, Dara
2.	1.13.20	600 cavalry, Dara
3.	1.13.21	Many cavalry, Dara
4.	1.13.21	600 cavalry, Dara
5.	1.13.22	Rosters of cavalry, Dara
6.	1.15.15	All cavalry, Satala
7.	1.18.6	20,000 infantry and cavalry, Callinicum
8.	1.18.26	The cavalry, Callinicum
9.	1.18.37	Roman cavalry, Callinicum
10.	2.3.19	Both were cavalry, Oinochalakon
11.	2.21.2	1,000 cavalry
12.	2.21.18	1,000 cavalry
13.	3.11.2	5,000 cavalry
14.	3.11.7	Cavalry soldiers
15.	3.19.11	All the cavalry, Ad Decimum
16.	3.19.12	With the cavalry, Ad Decimum
17.	4.2.1	All the cavalry, except 500, Tricamarum
18.	4.2.2	500 cavalry, Tricamarum
19.	4.3.4	Rosters of cavalry, Tricamarum
20.	4.3.6	500 cavalry, Tricamarum
21.	4.7.21	Number of cavalry
22.	4.10.5	Cavalry registers
23.	4.14.17	Five cavalry registers
24.	4.15.50	Cavalry register, Carthage
25.	4.17.5	Best of the cavalry, Scalae Veteres
26.	4.23.6	Leading a roster of cavalry
27.	5.5.3	Rosters of cavalry, Salona and Sicily
28.	5.10.1	Cavalry register
29.	5.17.17	Cavalry register
30.	5.18.1	1,000 cavalry, Tiber
31.	5.18.3	By cavalry on both sides, Tiber
32.	5.18.37	Some of the cavalry
33.	5.27.1	1,600 cavalry (most of whom were Huns, Sclaveni, and Antae), Rome
34.	5.27.4	200 cavalry of the shieldmen, Rome

TABLE 4.3   Roman cavalry in Procopius' *Wars* (cont.)

Number	Location	Usage
35.	5.27.13	300 cavalry, Rome
36.	5.28.16	Cavalry register, Rome
37.	5.28.22	The cavalry, Rome
38.	5.28.26	Rest of the cavalry, Rome
39.	5.28.29	Ant division of cavalry, Rome
40.	5.29.13	Cavalry on both wings, Rome
41.	5.29.38	Cavalry, Rome
42.	5.29.42	With some cavalry, Rome
43.	6.1.2	Cavalry, Rome
44.	6.1.20	Cavalry, Rome
45.	6.1.21	A few cavalry, Rome
46.	6.2.9	600 cavalry, Rome
47.	6.4.3	A few cavalry, Rome
48.	6.4.5	Many of his cavalry, Rome
49.	6.5.1	800 Thracian cavalry, Rome
50.	6.5.2	300 cavalry, Rome
51.	6.5.9	1,000 cavalry, Rome
52.	6.5.21	Cavalry, Rome
53.	6.7.3	100 cavalry, Rome
54.	6.7.15	With a few cavalry, Rome
55.	6.7.25	Many cavalry, Rome
56.	6.10.1	2,000 cavalry, Rome
57.	6.10.14	Most of the cavalry, Rome
58.	6.11.4	1,000 cavalry, Petra
59.	6.11.7	2,000 cavalry, Petra
60.	6.23.27	Cavalry trumpets, Osimo
61.	7.1.9	The cavalry
62.	7.1.20	7,000 cavalry
63.	7.3.5	(plains which are suitable) for cavalry, Verona
64.	7.19.16	Cavalry, River raid
65.	7.19.25	100 cavalry amongst those soldiers Belisarius had stationed there, River raid
66.	7.19.29	Cavalry, River raid
67.	7.26.2	The most illustrious cavalrymen
68.	7.27.16	700 cavalry
69.	7.28.5	All the cavalry

TABLE 4.3   Roman cavalry in Procopius' *Wars* (*cont.*)

Number	Location	Usage
70.	7.30.6	300 Illyrian cavalry, Rusciane
71.	7.34.40	10,000 cavalry
72.	7.36.16	Cavalry roll, Rome
73.	7.36.17	400 cavalry, Rome
74.	7.38.5	He led the cavalry rosters
75.	7.39.18	Cavalry rosters
76.	8.8.14	The cavalry of the Lazi
77.	8.8.16	The cavalry, River Hippis
78.	8.8.29	Their cavalry, River Hippis
79.	8.26.13	All cavalry
80.	8.31.6	1,500 cavalry, Busta Gallorum

140 CHAPTER 4

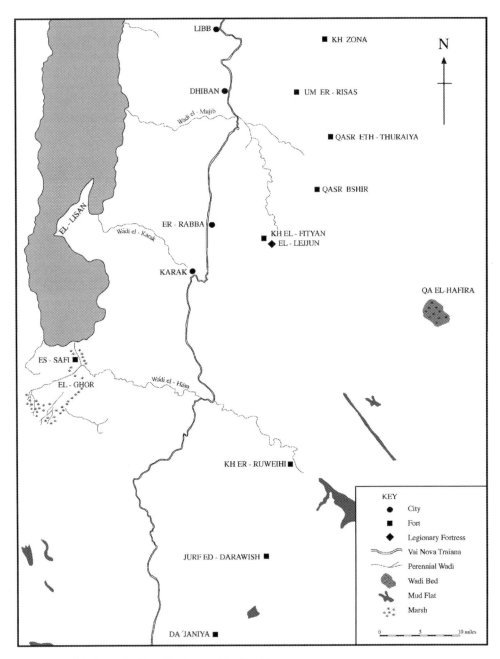

1.1   Map of the Limes Arabicus Southeast of the Dead Sea

CHAPTER 5

Limitanei in the Age of Justinian

1 Introduction

In this penultimate chapter we come to the *limitanei*, the most overlooked category of soldier in Procopius' oeuvre. They feature, by name, only once in Procopius' works, in the *Secret History*. That is where this chapter begins. After that, we scour the rest of Procopius' works for traces of their presence, especially in the *Buildings*, before turning to the evidence on the ground, at least such as we find it in Rome's southeast, though also North Africa. We finish the chapter by investigating their role in Rome's foreign policy.

2 Procopius on the End of the *limitanei* in the *Secret History*

2.1 *Rome's Frontier Soldiers*

From the second century CE through the third and into the fourth, the Roman military underwent significant changes. This included the crystallization of a distinction between those soldiers in regiments fixed to particular locations and those sent regularly off on campaigns. The former came to be known as the *limitanei*, the latter as the *comitatenses*. The distinction between the two classes of soldiers continued into the fifth and sixth centuries after which, by some accounts, it became murky.[1]

From the beginning, however, their merit has been questioned. For nearly a century, scholars have characterized the *limitanei* as little more than peasant militia.[2] Stein agreed: "but their [the *limitanei's*] military valour did not cease to diminish".[3] Van Berchem and Jones were more positive in their assessments, even if they were qualified.[4] Despite the convincing assertions of the *limitanei's* effectiveness by Isaac, Elton, and Nicasie, doubts still remain, as the works of Richardot, and Le Bohec, and to a lesser degree Southern and Dixon, and Greatrex indicate.[5] In turn, the assessment of Southern and Dixon is a bit more positive than those of Richardot and Le Bohec.

---

1 Carrié 1995: 33; Whitby 1995: 70–71.
2 Grosse 1920: 63–70; 275–276.
3 Stein 1949: 86.
4 Van Berchem 1952: 20–21; Jones 1964: 649–654.
5 Isaac 1990: 208–213, Elton 1996: 200–208, Nicasie 1998: 18–22; Richardot 2005: 171–175, Le Bohec 2006: 143–144, Southern and Dixon 1996: 35–37, Greatrex 1998: 34–36.

The term *limitanei* applies to the frontier soldiers themselves rather than their regiments, for they were enrolled in units with a number of different names.[6] Using the *Notitia Dignitatum*, which provides an accurate list of the empire's regiments in the eastern empire around 400 CE, we discover that there were at least six different kinds of units deployed in the frontier armies (*limitanei*).[7] There were infantry *auxiliares*, *cohortes*, and *legiones*, and cavalry *alae*, *cunei equitum*, and *equites* (*Illyriciani* and *indigenae*).[8] We also occasionally find the terms *milites* and *numeri* associated with the soldiers themselves. The *Notitia* itself hardly ever uses the term *limitanei*, with the term only used for the lists of regiments under the *Comes Africae* and the *Comes Tingitanae*, both in North Africa.[9] In those two cases, the naming pattern varies considerably, with *limitis* and the name of a location under a *praepositus* used for the *Comes Africae* like the *praeopositus limitis Zabensis*,[10] and named cohorts under a tribune, like the *Tribunus cohortis tertiae Asturum* for the *Comes Tingitanae*.[11]

Although the *limitanei* are listed throughout the *Notitia Dignitatum*, usually with the name of their base, many questions remain. Not all the sites listed in the *Notitia* have been identified in each and every province; moreover, there are plenty of cases where we have remains of Roman fortifications, but we do not know what the place was called in antiquity. There is another category, those sites for which we have independent evidence about their identity and/or operations, but which are not recorded in the *Notitia* or otherwise. A case in point is Qasr Bshir in Jordan, one of the best-preserved fortresses from the late Roman world. That fort preserves a dedicatory inscription atop the main entrance on the face of a lintel, which names the emperors Diocletian and Maximinus and an Aurelius Asclepiades, the *praeses* of Arabia at the time.[12] The inscription also names the fort as *Castra Praetorii Mobeni*. Mobeni is not found in the *Notitia Dignitatum* for the appropriate territories, in its day Palestine, or even Arabia.[13] Under the duke of Palestine, the only sites that at first glance seem vaguely similar are Menochiae and Mohile, both garrisoned

---

6 For a detailed examination of the development of the term *limitanei*, see Isaac (1988: 139–146).
7 On the accuracy of the eastern list, see Pollard (2013) and Kaiser (2015). On some of the issues with the *Notitia*, see Kulikowksi (2000). See too the works of Brennan (1980, 1996, 2007, 2015).
8 Brennan 2015: 1050.
9 *Not. Dign. occ.* 25.21, 26.13.
10 *Not. Dign. occ.* 25.26.
11 *Not. Dign. occ.* 26.19.
12 CIL 3.14149.
13 On the Roman political organization of *provincia Arabia* through the centuries see Bowersock (1983).

by a unit of *equites*. There is a Moenoenum castrum listed in the *Codex Theodosianus*, which might well be Menochiae, but this is only conjecture.[14] This does not help us identify Mobeni, unfortunately; there is no similarly named location under the Duke of Arabia, even if this is the most likely official under whom the soldiers operated. The case of Qasr Bshir is but one of many such examples.[15] Whether all these units continued in operation into the sixth century CE is another matter that we will return to below after we have had a chance to look closely at what Procopius has to say.

2.2 *Procopius*[16]

One of the most significant moments in the history of the *limitanei* came around the year 530 CE when Justinian undertook significant reforms to the military, the scale of which has been debated.[17] The discussion about the change in fortunes of the *limitanei* stems in its entirety from an over-quoted, but poorly understood, passage from Procopius' *Secret History*.[18] When it is

---

14 *Cod. Theod.* 7.4.30.
15 See Kennedy (2004: 53–54) for a summary of the places in Roman Arabia found in the *Notitia Dignitatum*.
16 The word *limitanei* is rare in Greek, though the *Suda* does provide the following definition, which betrays the compiler(s)'s familiarity with Procopius' *Secret History*. The *Suda* specifically refers to the *Secret History* in its entry on Procopius at π, 2479: "The Roman emperors in earlier times in every direction of the extremities of their domain stationed a very great number of soldiers as guards over the borders of the Roman empire, and especially in the eastern part, thereby repulsing the attacks of both Persians and Saracens. They used to call them 'border-troops.' These men Justinian treated so triflingly and thoughtlessly that within 4 or 5 years those who defrayed the costs of the soldiers' pay were behind on their payments. But when a peace was declared for both Romans and Persians, these were forced to forgive the treasury if they did not receive the payments that were owed within a stated time. Note that, for the Romans, a limitatus [sic] field is one abandoned by the enemy." Sud. Λ, 549, trans. Gibson (Suda Online). Λιμιτανᾶοι. οἱ Ῥωμαίων βασιλεῖς ἐν τοῖς ἄνω χρόνοις πανταχόσε τῶν τῆς πολιτείας ἐσχατιῶν πάμπολυ κατεστήσαντο στρατιωτῶν πλῆθος ἐπὶ φυλακῇ τῶν ὁρίων τῆς τῶν Ῥωμαίων ἀρχῆς καὶ κατὰ τὴν ἑῴαν μάλιστα μοῖραν, ταύτῃ τὰς ἐφόδους Περσῶν τὲ καὶ Σαρακηνῶν ἀναστέλλοντες, οὕσπερ λιμιταναίους ἐκάλουν. τούτοις Ἰουστινιανὸς οὕτω δὴ παρέργως καὶ φαύλως ἐχρῆτο, ὥστε δ' ἢ ἑαυτοῖς ἐνιαυτῶν τῶν συντάξεων τοὺς χορηγοὺς ὑπερημέρους εἶναι ἐπειδὰν δὲ Ῥωμαίοις τε καὶ Πέρσαις εἰρήνη γένοιτο, ἠναγκάζοντο οὗτοι χρόνου ῥητοῦ τὰς ὀφειλομένας συντάξεις μὴ λαμβάνοντες τῷ δημοσίῳ χαρίζεσθαι. σημείωσαι ὅτι λιμίτατος ἀγρός ἐστι κατὰ Ῥωμαίους ὁ ἀπὸ πολεμίων ληφθείς.
17 For two recent, opposed, views on the scale of Justinian's military reforms, see Heather (2018—minimal changes) and Koehn (2018—major changes).
18 The passage in question comes from Procopius' *Secret History* (Procop. SH. 24.12–14). Much of the following discussion is drawn from Whately (2013a).

read in its broader context and in light of Procopius' broader themes in the *Secret History*, the peculiarities of the passage are brought into clearer focus.[19]

In chapter twenty-four, while going through the sufferings of the various groups in the empire under Justinian, Procopius has this to say about the *limitanei* in this, the sole passage in which he explicitly names them:

> a long time ago those who ruled Rome deployed a host of soldiers at all of the furthest points of the commonwealth to guard the frontiers of the Roman Empire, especially the eastern part from Persian and Saracen incursions; they called these troops *limitanei*. The emperor Justinian at first treated these men harshly and as second-class troops, so that those responsible for paying their wages were four or five years in arrears, and whenever peace broke out between the Romans and Persians, the poor souls were forced, since they were meant to benefit from the blessings of peace, to give freely to the office of the public treasury that which was owed to them for some time; later they were deprived of this classification as legitimate soldiers.[20]

Debate continues to rage about the historicity of the *Secret History*, with scholars split on its value: some seem to see it as containing real nuggets of information of demonstrable historical value, while others are more dismissive. Most of this has centred on Theodora, at least recently; indeed, Procopius' characterization of the empress is anything but straightforward.[21] In contrast, relatively little scholarship has explored what the complexities and rhetorical exaggerations of the *Secret History* mean for understanding of the transformation of this maligned group of soldiers, the *limitanei*. Before we move on to

---

19 The *Secret History* is perhaps the most problematic of Procopius' texts, without necessarily being the most complex, a point raised some time ago by Cameron (1985: 49ff). Amongst the many new works on the *Secret History*, see, for example, Karantabias (2017) and Kruse (2017b).

20 Procop. *SH*. 24.12-13. Προσθήσω δέ τι τούτοις καὶ ἕτερον, ἐπεί με ὁ τῶν στρατιωτῶν λόγος ἐς τοῦτο ἄγει. οἱ Ῥωμαίων βεβασιλευκότες ἐν τοῖς ἄνω χρόνοις πανταχόσε τῶν τῆς πολιτείας ἐσχατιῶν πάμπολυ κατεστήσαντο στρατιωτῶν πλῆθος ἐπὶ φυλακῇ τῶν ὁρίων τῆς Ῥωμαίων ἀρχῆς, [καὶ] κατὰ τὴν ἑῴαν μάλιστα μοῖραν ταύτῃ τὰς ἐφόδους Περσῶν τε καὶ Σαρακηνῶν ἀναστέλλοντες, οὕσπερ λιμιταναίους ἐκάλουν. τούτοις (Ἰουστινιανὸς) ὁ βασιλεὺς κατ' ἀρχὰς μὲν οὕτω δὴ παρέργως τε καὶ φαύλως ἐχρῆτο, ὥστε τεσσάρων ἢ πέντε αὐτοῖς ἐνιαυτῶν τῶν συντάξεων τοὺς χορηγοὺς ὑπερημέρους εἶναι, καὶ ἐπειδὰν Ῥωμαίοις τε καὶ Πέρσαις εἰρήνη γένοιτο, ἠναγκάζοντο οἱ ταλαίπωροι οὗτοι ἅτε καὶ (αὐ)τοὶ τῶν ἐκ τῆς εἰρήνης ἀγαθῶν ἀπολαύσοντες χρόνου ῥητοῦ τὰς ὀφειλομένας σφίσι ξυντάξεις τῷ δημοσίῳ χαρίζεσθαι· ὕστερον δὲ καὶ αὐτὸ τὸ ⟨τῆς⟩ στρατείας ὄνομα αὐτοὺς ἀφείλετο οὐδενὶ λόγῳ.

21 See Brubaker 2004, 2005; Potter 2015; Cooper 2016.

frontier soldiers in Procopius' other works, a few comments about its place in the *Secret History* are in order.

This passage is tied to the wider administrative reforms undertaken by Justinian and is part of a longer series of complaints that Procopius airs in the text. About midway through the *Secret History* Procopius turns his attention from his issues with Belisarius, Antonina, and Theodora, to Justinian's depredations of the empire, which unsurprisingly, take up most of the text. Although Procopius has a number of gripes in the text, there are three particular issues that are pertinent here, all of which probably had an impact on Procopius himself: economic matters, foreign policy, and those groups wronged by Justinian.[22] In this passage, from his discussion of the sad plight of all sixth century soldiers,[23] Procopius is afforded the chance to check off all three of his biggest complaints, and this is how we should understand this passage: an opportunity for Procopius to kill three birds with one stone. He has discussed the foreign policy blunders of Justinian, the plight of people such as the landowners, and his economic depredations, and this passage enables Procopius to bring all of these issues together. That said, Procopius provides further support for his claims, the downgrading of the *limitanei*, in his two other texts, the *Buildings* and the *Wars*. A closer look at his reference to the frontier soldiers in those works shows the lengths to which Procopius went to minimize their role in the sixth-century wars.

2.3   Limitanei *in the* Wars *and* Buildings

In chapter three, we saw that vagueness in the size of units and in Procopius' *Wars* is a problem. For the *Buildings* the issue is comparable, namely his regular reference to garrisons, using a couple of different terms. Rather than give the identity of those soldiers—which regiment they belong to—the information he provides is basic.[24] The two words he uses are φρούριον and φυλακτήριον (tables 5.2 and 5.3).[25] When he identifies garrisons, the only qualifier he usually uses is soldier in the genitive. This is the case when he discusses Pheison at 3.3.6 and Citharizon at 3.3.8 for instance. Occasionally, he will associate a duke with a fortress, which would seem to allow us to identify the soldiers resident as frontier soldiers given the traditional association of dukes with the frontiers.[26]

---

22   The former issue, economic matters, has been signalled by Sarris (2006: 5–6).
23   Procopius focuses on soldiers from 24.1 to 24.29.
24   Note Cameron (1985: 104).
25   Note that Sarantis (2016: 105) touches on Procopius and these terms noting their ambiguous character, at least in the Balkans, where they need not be fortress. They could be fortified civilian settlements instead. Ultimately, the difference between the two, fortresses and civilian settlements, is murky.
26   Note the discussion of Greatrex (2007).

But he uses the word sparingly—and not always to designate the duke of a particular place.[27] The word duke also seems to have become associated with cities or fortresses, rather than frontier regions in general, which raises questions about the status of the soldiers (i.e., can we still call them *limitanei*).

On the one hand, you could make a case that his practice is not unlike what we find in the frontier lists that comprise a significant proportion of the *Notitia Dignitatum*. To take one example, the following table illustrates the disposition of the Arabian army under the *Dux Arabia*.

TABLE 5.1   The garrison of the *Dux Arabiae* from the *Notitia Dignitatum*

Passage number	Regiment name	Location
Not. Dign. or. 37.14	Equites scutarii Illyriciani	Motha
37.15	Equites promoti Illyriciani	Tricomia
37.16	Equites Dalmatae Illyriciani	Ziza
37.17	Equites Mauri Illyriciani	Areopoli
37.18	Equites promoti indigenae	Speluncis
37.19	Equites promoti indigenae	Mefa
37.20	Equites sagittari indigenae	Gadda
37.21	Legionis tertiae Cyrenaicae	Bostra
37.22	Legionis quartae Martiae	Betthoro
37.23	Equites sagittarii indigenae	Dia—Fenis
37.25	Ala nona miliaria	Auatha
37.26	Ala sexta Hispanorum	Gomoha
37.27	Ala secunda Constantiana	Libona
37.28	Ala secunda Miliarensis	Naarsafari
37.29	Ala prima Valentiana	Thainatha
37.30	Ala secunda felix Valentiniana	Aditha
37.31	Cohors prima miliaria Thracum	Adtitha
37.32	Cohors prima Thracum	Asabaia
37.33	Cohors octava voluntaria	Ualtha
37.34	Cohors tertia felix Arabum	castris Arnonensibus
37.35	Cohors tertia Alpinorum	Arnona

---

27   The one reference in the *Wars*, for example, is for dukes in general (1.17.46). The relevant entries in the *Buildings* are for Circesium (2.6.9), Armenia in general (3.1.28), Martyropolis (3.2.1), Citharizon (3.3.8), Artaleson (3.3.14), and Horonon (3.6.18).

I will not go through the entire garrison for the province, but a quick glance at a few of those units listed should underscore something of the practice employed, at least in this one region. The units come in a variety of different types: there are legions, cohorts, *alae*, and *equites*. Of the twenty-one units named, seven are explicitly classified as infantry, the legions and the cohorts, while the rest are cavalry. Many of the names follow the traditional pattern used during the early and high imperial era. Let us take the *Cohors tertia felix Arabum* as an example, which includes the kind of regiment, like *cohors*, the number, like *tertia*, and the cognomen, like *felix Arabum*.[28] Others are more generic, like the various *equites*, which are only distinguished by the kind of mounted unit they are, and the apparent origin of their soldiers like the *Equites sagittari indigenae*.[29] They were mounted archers evidently indigenous to their home base, Gadda. But even here, in regiments like this, the units include far more technical information than in any of the cases we have looked at so far.

The *Buildings*, of course, is much more focused on the role of physical defences than soldiers, and so we should not be totally surprised by his comparative silence on the troops themselves. Our most important imperial pronouncement on frontier defence matters, 1.27 from the *Codex Justinanus* on civil and military administration in Africa post conquest, puts most of the discussion on troops rather than structures, so providing the opposite to what we find in the *Buildings*. And so, perhaps, we should not begrudge Procopius for his comparative silence on the soldiers garrisoning those forts.

The *Buildings* focuses on Justinian's considerable efforts to transform the physical, built environment in the Roman Empire of his day. Much of the work is focused on Constantinople and the east. Some buildings, like Hagia Sophia in Constantinople, are described in significant detail, while elsewhere entire towns and cities are only recorded in lists. Many of the sites that Procopius names are fortifications, or cities that underwent considerable fortification work (or so Procopius). And, it should not come as much of a surprise, given the focus of the text, that when Procopius does describe fortification work his emphasis is on the role of the physical structures in protecting the empire's citizens rather than on the soldiers. This makes it difficult to find evidence for those soldiers based in the empire's cities and forts, though not impossible.

The following sites, presented in the order in which we find them in the *Buildings*, are identified along with their local garrison (in some form or other): Dara (2.1.4), Rhabdios (2.4.1), Circesium (2.6.2), the Thannourioi (2.6.14), Zenobia (2.8.8), Sura (2.9.1), Hemerium (2.9.10), Zeugma and

---

28   *Not. Dign. or.* 37.34.
29   *Not. Dign. or.* 37.20.

Neocaesarea (2.9.18), Pheison (3.3.6), Citharizon (3.3.7), Melitene (3.4.15), Theodosiopolis (3.5.1), Sisilisson (3.6.22), Tzanzacon (and Schamalinichon) (3.6.26), Pelopennesse (in general—4.2.28), Byzantium/Constantinople (4.9.11), Gallipoli (4.10.17), Caesarea (in Cappadocia—5.4.7), Mt Sinai (5.8.1), Paratonium and Antipyrgum (6.2.2), Aumetra (6.6.18), Dabusis and Gaeana (6.7.8), and Septum (6.7.15). Of those twenty-seven locations, only six had a garrison of *limitanei* a century and a half earlier (the date of the eastern portion of the *Notitia Dignitatum*). Let us take a closer look, starting with those places that could be equated with sites garrisoned by frontier soldiers named in the *Notitia*.

The first location that had a confirmed frontier garrison in the *Notitia* was Circesium. Procopius says that Justinian found it "unguarded" (2.6.2) and that "he established a commander of select troops [στρατιωτικῶν δὲ καταλόγων], who they call dukes, who would be established there continuously" (2.6.9).[30] Circesium is found in the *Notitia*; it is listed as the base for the prefect of the *legio IV Parthica*.[31]

Procopius identifies two Thannourioi at 2.6.14. Near the larger of these Justinian built a very large tower "in which he has established a very considerable [ἀξιολογωτάτην] garrison" (2.6.16).[32] The physicality of Justinian's initiatives is important here, but so too are the men who make up the garrison. At least one (if not both) of these Thannourioi are in the *Notitia*, for just after Circesium we find the *ala prima nova Diocletiana* under the *Dux Oshorene* between Thannurin et Horobam.[33] Horobam is likely the Aborrhas river that Procopius mentions as flowing nearby one Thannourios (2.6.15). The other, smaller Thannourios as Procopius calls it, is more difficult to pin down—though it might also be easier. In a province over under the *Dux Mesopotamia* the *Notitia* lists an *equites sagittarii indigenae* at a Thannurin.[34] None of the cities that Procopius mentions in the vicinity of the Thannourioi, like Vimisdeon, Themeres, and Vidamas and others are found under Mesopotamia (2.6.14). On the other hand, in Procopius' eyes, his discussion of the Thannourioi falls under the broader geographic category of Mesopotamia (2.7.1). By this logic, this could well be the Big Thannourios that Procopius had in mind. Either way, the main point for us is that this "considerable garrison" was most likely composed of *limitanei*.

---

30 Procop. *Wars* 2.6.9, καὶ στρατιωτικῶν δὲ καταλόγων ἄρχοντα τῇδε καταστησάμενος, ὃν δοῦκα καλοῦσι, διηνεκὲς ἐνταῦθα καθιζησόμενον.
31 *Not. Dign.* or. 35.24.
32 ἐνταῦθά τε φρουρὰν ἀξιολογωτάτην καταστησάμενος.
33 *Not. Dign.* or. 35.31.
34 *Not. Dign.* or. 36.28.

Next is a place Procopius calls Zenobia (2.8.8ff). There "he stationed a commander of select troops and a thoroughly adequate garrison" (2.8.11).[35] A bit later Procopius says that there were "homes for those under the military standards" found at Zenobia (2.8.24).[36] There is no Zenobia in the *Notitia*, though there is a Palmira in the *Notitia*.[37] A *legio prima illyricorum* was garrisoned there. At quick glance, Zenobia would seem a likely stand in for Palmyra, given it is the name of the famous third century CE queen who ruled Palmyra.[38] The catch is Procopius also refers to Palmyra a few books over at 2.11.10. Procopius says that the place had fallen into desuetude, and that Justinian had restored it, which included adding a garrison (2.11.12).[39] What is more, Zenobia has been identified with modern Halabiye in Syria.[40]

Procopius describes Sura, as well as Resafa/Sergiopolis, in detail starting at 2.9.1. According to Procopius, Justinian established "a garrison of soldiers" there (2.9.8).[41] Sura is in the *Notitia* as the base of the *legio XVI flavia firma*, which is under the command of the *Dux Syriae*.[42]

Zeugma and Neocaesarea are discussed from 2.9.18, which he considers in tandem until he gets to the garrison and then he refers to them in the singular, for he says, "since the garrison of the town had no place whatever where they might stand and carry on the defence" (2.9.19).[43] Neocaesarea as it happens, is in the *Notitia*. There we find it as the home of the *equites Mauri Illyriciani* under the *Dux Syriae* in Syria Eufratensis.[44]

When Procopius turns to Melitene at 3.4.15, we find one of the more interesting and technical descriptions of all frontier garrisons named in the *Buildings*. Procopius says that "a detachment [λόχος] of Roman soldiers" was based at Melitene (3.4.15).[45] What is more, he says that the "detachment [λόχος] was called a legion [λεγεών]" (3.4.16).[46] There was a legion headquartered at Melitene based on the evidence of the *Notitia*, the *legio XII fulminata*.[47] Procopius includes other interesting details about the garrison of the city

---

35 ἄρχοντά τε στρατιωτικῶν καταλόγων καὶ διαρκὲς ἄγαν καταστησάμενος φυλακτήριον.
36 στρατιωτικῶν σημείων οἰκίας.
37 *Not. Dign.* or. 32.30.
38 On Zenobia, see Lauffray (1983).
39 φυλακτηρίου στρατιωτῶν ἐμπλησάμενος. On Palmyra, see Intagliata (2018).
40 Butcher 2018.
41 φρουρὰν τῇδε στρατιωτῶν.
42 *Not. Dign.* or. 33.28. On Resafa, see Fowden (1999) and Hof (2020).
43 οὐκ ἐχόντων τὸ παράπαν τῶν ἐνταῦθα φρουρῶν ὅποι ἂν ἑστῶτες ἀμύνοιντο.
44 *Not. Dign.* or. 33.26.
45 ἐφ᾽ οὗ δὴ λόχος Ῥωμαίων στρατιωτῶν ἵδρυτο.
46 λεγεὼν δὲ ὁ λόχος ἐπωνομάζετο.
47 *Not. Dign.* or. 38.14.

and its structures, like how in past times they built "barracks for the soldiers and provided a place where they could deposit their standards" (3.4.16).[48] Melitene is the last location for which we can use the *Notitia* with profit. For the next set of locations, I will be going through those fortifications to which Procopius attributes a garrison of some sort or other. At the end, I will return to the difficulty in distinguishing *limitanei* from *comitatenses* using Procopius' comments.

2.4 Ambiguous Garrisons in the Buildings

In most cases all we find are the barest of accounts. Procopius is, in general, much more interested in the role of the physical defences of fortifications in ensuring a site's security while references to the garrisons are limited.[49] At Dara, Procopius notes the "men serving in the army in this place" (2.2.10),[50] and the "numerous barracks for the soldiers" (2.3.26).[51] At Hemerium, Procopius notes that Justinian established "a crowd of guards" (2.9.10), who are to make the defence of the place more secure.[52] The next set of accounts come in subsequent books.

In book two, which deals with Armenia, Procopius says near the start and in reference to the region as a whole that "it did not have men on the military rolls there" (3.1.16).[53] Such a claim would fit with the legislation Justinian passed concerning the reorganization of Armenia's administration, which was part of Justinian's larger reorganization of the military, a point to which I return below.[54] When Procopius brings up Roman soldiers a bit later, his discussion is very generic (3.1.24, 3.1.27). In truth, much of this early discussion is concerned with Justinian's reorganization efforts, which included putting two dukes in charge of Armenia (3.1.28–29).[55] In that vein, Procopius says that "he established a vast amount of registers of Roman soldiers to help them guard the boundaries/frontiers of the Romans" (3.1.29).[56] Procopius' discussion here is one of the few ones in the *Buildings* where he puts more weight behind the new soldiers than he does in the physical structures.

---

48   τοῖς τε στρατιώταις ἀποχρῶντος ἐς καταλύσεις ἔχον καὶ ὅπως σφίσι τὰ σημεῖα τῇδε ἐναποκείσονται.
49   For more on this, see Whately (forthcoming b).
50   Τῶν τις ἐκείνῃ στρατευσαμένων.
51   τοῖς στρατιώταις καταλυτήρια ἐδείματο παμπληθῆ.
52   φρουρῶν ὅμιλον.
53   οὐ παρόντων αὐτῇ στρατιωτικῶν καταλόγων.
54   *Iust. Nov.* 21 and 31.
55   On Armenia and the military in the age of Justinian, see Adontz (1970).
56   οἷς δὴ ξυνεστήσατο μὲν Ῥωμαίων στρατιωτῶν καταλόγους παμπληθεῖς, ἐφ᾿ ᾧ τὰ Ῥωμαίων ξυμφυλάξουσιν αὐτοῖς ὅρια.

A little later, Procopius gets into the sites. At Pheison, Justinian established "an incomparable garrison of soldiers" (3.3.6).[57] Procopius has a great deal to say about Citharizon from 3.3.7, which includes his somewhat technical comment that Justinian stationed there "the second duke, as I have said, with more than sufficient garrison of soldiers there" (3.3.8).[58] A bit later at 3.3.14, Procopius says that "he stationed military registers".[59] Theodosiopolis too witnessed a great deal of fortification and defence work, which is recounted from 3.5.1. Among other things, he notes that Justinian stationed "all the forces and the general in the Armenias" there.

As he turns to Tzanica at 3.6.9, Procopius again emphasizes Justinian's military efforts in general. Procopius says that the emperor "built forts in all parts of the land, assigned to them strong guards of Roman soldiers all over the place there" (3.6.13).[60] For Sisilisson, Procopius says Justinian restored the place, a fort, and established "a sufficient number of Roman soldiers" (3.6.22).[61] There is a Sisila in the *Notitia* which had a *cohors miliaria Germanorum* in garrison, but it is not clear that these two are one in the same; hence its inclusion here.[62] Procopius has little to say about Tzanzacon and Schamalinichon, though he says that Justinian posted "another commander/leader of soldiers" there (3.6.26).[63]

Book four shifts the geographical focus to the Balkans. As before, Procopius goes over all of Justinian's supposed work on the frontiers and forts of the region, which includes discussing his efforts to established a number of fortifications and by Procopius' reckoning, their "garrisons of soldiers beyond reckoning" (4.1.6).[64] A good deal of his pronouncements about soldiers and forts are general, as they had been for the previous book (3). For instance, he notes that Justinian distributed forts along the Danube, and that thanks to him there were "garrisons of troops everywhere" (4.1.33).[65]

There are exceptions, however, particularly when he pushes south into Greece and then back to the environs of Constantinople. Procopius had a good deal to say about Thermopylae. He touches on its walls before turning to the

---

57 στρατιωτῶν φρουρὰν ἀνανταγώνιστον καταστησάμενος.
58 τὸν ἕτερον δοῦκα, ᾗπέρ μοι εἴρηται, ξὺν στρατιωτῶν ἐνταῦθα φρουρᾷ ἱκανωτάτῃ ἱδρύσατο.
59 στρατιωτικοὺς καταλόγους τῇδε ἱδρύσατο.
60 καὶ φρούρια δὲ οἰκοδομησάμενος πανταχόθι τῆς χώρας φρουρούς τε ἐνταῦθα Ῥωμαίων στρατιωτῶν ἱδρυσάμενος βεβαιότατα.
61 διαρκὲς Ῥωμαίων στρατιωτῶν ... φυλακτήριον κατεστήσατο.
62 *Not. Dign. or.* 38.30.
63 ἔνθα δὴ καὶ ἄλλον ἄρχοντα στρατιωτῶν κατεστήσατο.
64 στρατιωτῶν ἀμύθητα φυλακτήρια.
65 φυλακτήριά τε στρατιωτῶν πανταχόθι.

troops and Justinian's establishment of a "garrison soldiers to the number of about 2000" (4.2.14).[66] Further south, the Peloponnese in general was fortified by means of fortresses and the establishment of "garrisons" there (4.2.28).[67] Back at the Danube (4.5.1ff) and the interior of Illyricum, Procopius returns to generalities, with comments about the "garrisons of soldiers" there (4.5.1).[68] Thereafter, Procopius talks about all sorts of fortified places, including some with only one tower in which were stationed "a few men" (4.5.4).[69] These later books are devoid of any attempts at technicality, or in many respects specificity, that occasionally surface in the earlier sections. For instance, he says that Justinian fortified pretty much the whole area, and that he had established "garrisons of soldiers" (4.6.37) in all the places.[70] When he gets to Constantinople, he says that each tower of the walls had "guards" (4.9.11).[71] At the long walls at the Cheronsonese, Justinian stationed "men on the military rolls" (4.10.17).[72]

With book five, Procopius returns to the east and the rest of Asia. He mentions Caesarea in Cappadocia (5.4.7ff) and says the extant fortifications were not good enough for a garrison to defend; but, Justinian improved things both physically and by giving it a "sufficient garrison" (5.4.14).[73] Procopius does discuss soldiers in the context of the Samaritan uprising, but they are just generic soldiers (5.7.13) (στρατιώτας), which is no more helpful to the "guards" (φρουρούς) he referred to a bit earlier (5.7.12).[74] To the southwest, Mt Sinai was given a "most noteworthy garrison of soldiers" (5.8.9).[75]

Book six, the final book, shifts the focus to Africa. Procopius says that Justinian established in Libya two garrisons at Paratonium and Antipyrgum (6.2.2).[76] Much of his later discussion hints at the conquest and the troops involved, but his emphasis is squarely on the expeditionary forces (στόλος, 6.6.8), not the later frontier garrison.[77] Along the same lines, a few lines later

---

66   στρατιώτας τε φρουρούς ἐς δισχιλίους μάλιστα τῇδε ἱδρύσατο. Procopius' comments about the garrison here have engendered some debate. Note the comments of Cherf (2011: 104).
67   Φρούριά. Procopius also discusses this work at Thermopylae in the *Secret History* (*SH* 26.31).
68   φυλακτηρίοις στρατιωτῶν.
69   ἄνθρωποί τε ὀλίγοι.
70   στρατιωτῶν φρουράς.
71   φρουροί … τοῖς φρουροῖς.
72   στρατιωτῶν καταλόγους.
73   διαρκεῖ δὲ αὐτὸ φυλακτηρίῳ.
74   On the Samaritan revolt, see Adshead (1996) and Sivan (2008: 107–142).
75   φυλακτήριόν τε στρατιωτῶν ἀξιολογώτατον. On the garrison here, see Ward (2015: 111–127).
76   δύο καὶ φυλακτήρια.
77   On the often-difficult relationship between the invading troops and the residents of North Africa, see Conant (2012: 310–311).

he mentions a Roman army using quite different language than he had for this expeditionary force (6.6.10).[78] At last, he finally turns to the frontier garrison first at Aumetra, where, besides building a fort, he established a "garrison of soldiers" (6.6.18).[79] Justinian also ensured the safety of Numidia by means of forts and garrisons (6.7.1).[80] At the forts of Dabusis and Gaeana Justinian set up "garrisons of soldiers" (6.7.8),[81] and then at Septum, besides strengthening the location by means of a wall and a garrison (φυλακτηρίῳ, 6.7.15). In the very last paragraph of the whole text and in regard to the whole empire he gives an important phrase: "Emperor Justinian strengthened the Empire, not with fortresses alone, but also by means of garrisons of soldiers, from the bounds of the East to the very setting of the sun" (6.7.17).[82] This sums up Procopius' approach in the *Buildings* nicely. Before we look into the specifics, we now turn to the *Wars*.

These are the garrisons in the *Buildings* some or many of which might be composed of *limitanei*. But how accurate is his information? Procopius' *Buildings* has attracted no shortage of attention.[83] Some have raised doubts about the accuracy of the descriptions of the cities and buildings that he includes, with Dara the object of much debate some decades ago.[84] More recently, Thermopylae has been the subject of debate, with Cherf discounting much of what Procopius says about the building work in and around the famous Greek site.[85] A great deal of the debate has centred on the degree to which Justinian deserves credit for the building work as Procopius argues, or if enough of it dated earlier. But some work, by Whitby in particular, has argued that there is real value in the *Buildings*, though it is largely a question of giving each site its own careful consideration.[86] Some more recent work has been more positive on what Procopius has to say, notably about the empire's waterworks.[87]

But all that work has focused on the cities and places of the empire and their architecture, not, so much, their garrisons, the frontier soldiers and others that

---

78 τοῦ Ῥωμαίων στρατοῦ.
79 φρουροὺς στρατιωτῶν.
80 στρατιωτῶν φυλακτηρίοις.
81 φυλακτήρια δὲ στρατιωτῶν.
82 ἀμφίλεκτον δὲ οὐδὲν γέγονεν, ἀλλ' ἔνδηλον ἀνθρώποις διαφανῶς πᾶσιν, ὡς ἐκ τῶν ἑῴων ὁρίων ἄχρι ἐς δύοντά που τὸν ἥλιον, ἃ δὴ πέρατά ἐστι τῆς Ῥωμαίων ἀρχῆς, οὐκ ἐρύμασι μόνοις, ἀλλὰ καὶ στρατιωτῶν φυλακτηρίοις Ἰουστινιανὸς βασιλεὺς τὴν πολιτείαν ἐκρατύνατο.
83 See Greatrex (2014a: 101–104).
84 Croke and Crow 1983; Whitby 1986b.
85 Cherf 2011. See too Gregory (2000) and Brown (2010).
86 Whitby 1986a, 1987, 1989.
87 Pickett 2017. See too Howard-Johnston (2000).

inhabited them. It is also the case that my concern has not been on whether soldiers were put in a fortress by Justinian or someone else, but whether they were there in the first place, and what kind of soldier they were. Procopius highlighted Justinian's deployment of garrisons to undermanned fortifications in the *Buildings*, but was not interested in the specifics of those garrisons. This, most basic of information, likely recorded on documents like the annual and quarterly reports referred to earlier, seem like the kind of sources that Procopius would have had access to.

So, I am prepared to accept that there were soldiers based in a location if Procopius said so. The truth is that in the absence of comparative evidence, including references in the *Notitia Dignitatum* (of minimal value) and verifiable inscriptions, we are left with little alternative besides tossing all his notices out. The other option is to test for consistency in Procopius' oeuvre. If there are places in the *Buildings* mentioned in the *Wars* and we find soldiers based in both, that is enough of a reason for me to accept Procopius' notices. If they are all correct, we could even consider all other notices as accurate, at least at the most basic of level. I will return to this question after I go through the potential references to *limitanei* in the *Wars* in the next section.

On the other hand, in keeping with the general pattern that we have observed in the book so far, the information he provides is minimal. Procopius likely did have access to the names of the units and the number of soldiers (at least on paper) in the various places, but he usually leaves out this information. As with other soldiers in Procopius' works, these soldiers are faceless, even if he does, regularly, give them an important role in the empire's defence, a point to which we will return below.

2.5   Limitanei *in the* Wars

In this section I will concentrate on books one and two because this is the part of the empire that witnessed a significant invasion and that he describes in considerable detail. As Sarantis has noted, Procopius has little to say about the various conflicts in the Balkans despite Justinian's demonstrable efforts there.[88] I will start with what could be called the more direct evidence for *limitanei* in the *Wars*. Then I will turn to the less direct material.

One of the earliest conflicts that Procopius discusses is Kavadh's attack on Amida (502–503 CE). Procopius does mention an army sent to intercept, but the most likely identity of this force in this context is a field army, or part of one. Procopius' language is vague, and when he refers to the army he does so

---

88   Sarantis 2016.

LIMITANEI IN THE AGE OF JUSTINIAN

mostly in terms of its commanders.[89] The same is true for Pseudo-Zachariah the rhetor, who also describes the siege: "Their commanders were Patricius, the great general ... and Hypatius and Celer the *magister officiorum*, and eventually also Areobindus. With them was the *comes* Justin".[90] He adds later that many horses and riders perished escaping, which provides some insight into its makeup—though not whether it comprised frontier or field army soldiers; his comments on Farzman (Pharesmanes) and the 500 horsemen is no more useful.[91] Pseudo-Joshua provides more detail in general, but not about Farzman's men.[92] He does have more to say about other components of the army, however, including three of the commanders named by Pseudo-Zachariah, and the size of some of the armies brought against Amida. Plus, Pseudo-Joshua provides some information on some of the other Roman armies that participate, like the armies of the *duces* of Tella and Melitene.[93]

Getting back to Procopius, when the action turns to Martyropolis, we get what is probably the most direct evidence, for Procopius tells us that Buzes and Bessas had been deployed to guard the city (1.21.5).[94] A bit earlier, Procopius had said that Buzes was based in Lebanon, "they (Buzes and Cuzes) led the soldiers in Libanon then" (1.13.5).[95] Buzes later appears at the battle of Dara "with many horsemen" (1.13.19).[96] Whether this means he was using *limitanei* at Dara or not is question to which we will return later.

In the discussion of the *Buildings*, I covered Sura. In the *Wars* Procopius says that Arsaces, an Armenian by birth, "led the soldiers there" (2.5.11).[97] These soldiers play an active role in the siege, for they get posted among the parapets (2.5.11). Later in the course of the same narrative, he refers to guards at the spot when the Persians enter the city, and they could be these men, or some of them (2.5.23).[98] Procopius provides similar information about Beroea, where soldiers were stationed and who were to guard the city (2.7.7).[99] These Roman

---

89   On the differences between the accounts of Pseudo-Joshua the Stylite and Procopius on the siege of Amida, see Debié (2004). Pseudo-Zachariah the Rhetor does not include details on Amida's garrison either, though his description of the siege is detailed (*EH*. 7.4).
90   Ps.-Zach. *EH* 7.4.g, trans. Phenix and Corn.
91   Ps.-Zach. *EH* 7.5.a. Farzman is listed as Pharesmanes 3 in the *PLRE* (Martindale 1980: 872–873).
92   Ps.-Josh. *Chron*. 56.
93   See Ps.-Josh. *Chron*. 51.
94   See Whitby (1984).
95   οἳ τῶν ἐν Λιβάνῳ στρατιωτῶν ἦρχον.
96   ξὺν ἱππεῦσι πολλοῖς.
97   τῶν ἐνταῦθα στρατιωτῶν ἄρχων.
98   οἵ τε φύλακες ἔτι μᾶλλον ὠθοῦντές.
99   ξὺν τοῖς ἄλλοις στρατιώταις, οἳ δὴ ἐνταῦθα ἐπὶ φυλακῇ ἐτετάχατο.

soldiers valiantly defend the city when it has been broached, but do not have much success (2.7.12).[100]

There are other locations in which we find soldiers. When Dara is besieged at 2.13.16–29, Procopius implies that it is chance that Martin happens to be there; moreover, Procopius does not assign him any men even if he says he is a general (2.13.16). In his account of the capture of Petra, Procopius says John was there with the Roman army (2.17.4).[101] Sergiopolis was also the sight of some activity, and Procopius says it had no more than 200 soldiers there to guard it (2.20.14).[102]

Procopius' description of the second siege of Edessa is detailed, but he has hardly anything to say save about the Roman soldiers who worked with the citizens to defend the city (2.26.7).[103] Interestingly, some of the soldiers with some of the citizens make a sally against Persians. A bit later, we learn that Peter, a Roman general, and Martin and Peranius happened to be there, evidently with some Huns (2.26.25),[104] and some guardsmen (τῶν τις δορυφόρων), for at least one of them, Argek, killed 27 of the enemy (2.26.26). Procopius' account of the siege of Archaeopolis in Lazica described at 8.14.1–44 might provide one other case. Given the region's status as an allied kingdom, it is unlikely to have had any Roman frontier troops based in the fortification. The siege, however, could be considered as special circumstances. When the siege kicked off, Procopius notes that Odonachus and Babas had been there with some soldiers (8.14.14).[105] A bit earlier Procopius had noted that "Venilus, the brother of Buzes, had also been sent there already with an army, as well as Odonachos, Babas from Thrace, and Uligag of the Heruls" (8.9.5).[106] At 8.13.8, Procopius had said that there had been 3,000 soldiers based here, though he implies that they were presented on a temporary basis.[107] Later Procopius says the commanders let the army (τὸ στράτευμα) out through a gate (8.14.22).

There are two cases which provide less direct evidence for frontier soldiers. One is the siege of Antioch (540 CE); the city had been home to *fabricae* in

---

100 μὲν Ῥωμαίων στρατιῶται καρτερῶς ἀμυνόμενοι.
101 τὸ Ῥωμαίων στράτευμα.
102 στρατιώτας γὰρ οὐ πλέον ἢ διακοσίους ἔχοντες ἔτυχον.
103 Ῥωμαίων δὲ στρατιωτῶν.
104 Πέτρος δὲ ὁ Ῥωμαίων στρατηγὸς ἐνταῦθα γὰρ ξὺν Μαρτίνῳ καὶ Περανίῳ ἐτύγχανεν ὢν τοὺς ταῦτα ἐργαζομένους ἀναστέλλειν ἐθέλων Οὔννων τῶν οἱ ἐπομένων τινὰς ἐπ' αὐτοὺς ἔπεμψεν.
105 Τότε δὴ Ὀδόναχός τε καὶ Βάβας, εἴτε ἀρετὴν ἐνδεικνύμενοι εἴτε τῶν στρατιωτῶν ἀποπειρᾶσθαι βουλόμενοι, ἢ καί τι αὐτοὺς θεῖον ἐκίνησεν, εἴασαν μὲν τῶν στρατιωτῶν ὀλίγους τινάς.
106 οὗ δὴ καὶ Βενῖλος, ὁ Βούζου ἀδελφός, ξὺν στρατῷ ἤδη σταλεὶς ἔτυχε καὶ Ὀδόναχός τε καὶ ὁ Βάβας ἐκ Θράκης καὶ Οὐλίγαγος Ἔρουλος γενος.
107 ἀλλ' ἐν μὲν τῷ ἐν Ἀρχαιοπόλει φυλακτηρίῳ τρισχίλιοι ἦσαν, ὧν Ὀδόναχός τε καὶ Βάβας ἦρχον.

the *Notitia*.[108] Procopius implies that Antioch did not have its own soldiers at the time of the siege; indeed, the *Notitia* implies that, at the end of the fourth century at least, the city was home to *fabricae* alone. Rather, Theoctistus and Molatzes, "who led the soldiers in Libanon" (2.8.2) came up and brought 6,000 men.[109] Later we learn they are involved in fighting, but so too are its citizens. Procopius even claims that had 300 of the soldiers managed a sortie, things might have improved (2.8.13).[110] The size reported by Procopius, 300, could hint at the size of the subdivisions operating at Antioch, but we have no way to verify this. A little later, we read that Buzes was going to come with an army, but that is all we get (2.8.17).[111] The other case is Sergiopolis, which had a *fabrica* (factory) that produced *Scutaria et armamentaria*.[112] I want to focus on the case for Antioch, however.

In his article on *limitanei*, Isaac provided evidence for their service in campaign armies in the sixth century, and the evidence he adduced came from Procopius' account of the Persian wars. There were four passages in particular that provided evidence for this.[113] Below I provide them all in full. The first passage comes at 1.13.5 and reads:[114]

> he ordered another army to go there and also Cutzes and Buzes, who at that time commanded the soldiers in Lebanon. These two were brothers from Thrace, both young and reckless in engaging with the enemy.[115]

The second passage comes at 2.8.2:

> Some of the Antiochenes therefore picked up and left their city with their money, each one fleeing as he could. And all the rest likewise intended to do the same thing and would have done so had not the commanders of the soldiers in Lebanon, Thectistus and Molatzes, who arrived in the

---

108   The *scutaria et armorum Not. Dign. or.* 11.21, and the *clibanaria* at 11.22. On Antioch, see Brands (2016).
109   οἱ τῶν ἐν Λιβάνῳ στρατιωτῶν ... ξὺν ἑξακισχιλίοις ἀνδράσιν.
110   τοῦ Ῥωμαίων στρατοῦ ξὺν τριακοσίοις.
111   ξὺν στρατῷ.
112   *Not. Dign. or.* 11.23.
113   Isaac 1988: 147. For a different view, see Liebeschuetz (1977).
114   The translation of all four passages are Kaldellis' (slightly modified).
115   ἐνθένδε τῷ παρόντι στρατῷ ἀποκρούεσθαί, ἄλλην τε στρατιὰν ἐπήγγελλεν αὐτόσε ἰέναι καὶ Κούτζην τε καὶ Βούζην, οἳ τῶν ἐν Λιβάνῳ στρατιωτῶν ἦρχον τότε. τούτω δὲ ἀδελφὼ μὲν ἐκ Θρᾴκης ἤστην, νέω δὲ ἄμφω καὶ οὐ ξὺν τῷ ἀσφαλεῖ τοῖς πολεμίοις εἰς χεῖρας ἰόντε.

meantime with six thousand men, buttressed their resolve with hope and prevented their departure.[116]

The third at 2.16.17 reads:

> But Recithanc and Theoctistus, the commanders of the soldiers in Lebanon, said that, while they too wanted the same as the others concerning the invasion, they feared that if they abandoned the country of Phoenicia and Syria, al-Mundhir would plunder it at his leisure, and that the emperor would be angry at them for not guarding and preserving unplundered the territory under their command, and for this reason they were quite unwilling to join the rest of the army in the invasion.[117]

Finally, the fourth at 2.19.33–34 reads:

> The whole army, therefore, was eager to depart from there and return as quickly as possible to their own land, and most of all the commanders of the soldiers in Lebanon, Recithanc and Theoctistus, who saw that the time that was sacred to the Saracens had in fact already passed. They went frequently to Belisarius, entreating him to release them immediately and protesting that they had basically given over to al-Mundhir the lands of Lebanon and Syria, and were sitting there for no good reason.[118]

Do these passages provide evidence for *limitanei*?

Martindale in volume three of the *PLRE* ranks all those named commanders as frontier dukes, with Buzes the *dux phoenice libanensis* in 528,[119] Cutzes

---

116 Ἀντιοχέων δέ τινες μὲν ἐνθένδε ξὺν τοῖς χρήμασιν ἐξαναστάντες ἔφευγον ὡς ἕκαστός πη ἐδύνατο. ταὐτὸ δὲ τοῦτο διενοοῦντο καὶ οἱ λοιποὶ ξύμπαντες, εἰ μὴ μεταξὺ ἥκοντες οἱ τῶν ἐν Λιβάνῳ στρατιωτῶν ἄρχοντες, Θεόκτιστός τε καὶ Μολάτζης, ξὺν ἑξακισχιλίοις ἀνδράσιν ἐλπίσι τε αὐτοὺς ἐπιρρώσαντες διεκώλυσαν.

117 Ῥεκίθαγγος μέντοι καὶ Θεόκτιστος, οἱ τῶν ἐν Λιβάνῳ στρατιωτῶν ἄρχοντες, ταῦτα μὲν τοῖς ἄλλοις ἀμφὶ τῇ ἐσβολῇ βούλεσθαι καὶ αὐτοὶ ἔφασαν, δεδιέναι δὲ [p. 402] μὴ σφῶν ἐκλελοιπότων τά τε ἐπὶ Φοινίκης καὶ Συρίας χωρία, κατ' ἐξουσίαν μὲν Ἀλαμούνδαρος ταῦτα ληίζηται, βασιλεὺς δὲ σφᾶς δι' ὀργῆς ἔχοι, ἅτε οὐ φυλάξαντας ἀδῄωτον τὴν χώραν ἧς ἦρχον, καὶ δι' αὐτὸ συνεισβάλλειν τῷ ἄλλῳ στρατῷ οὐδαμῇ ἤθελον.

118 ἅπας μὲν οὖν ὁ στρατὸς ἐνθένδε τε ἀπαλλάσσεσθαι καὶ ὅτι τάχιστα ἐς τὴν οἰκείαν γῆν ἐπανήκειν ἐν σπουδῇ εἶχον, μάλιστα δὲ ἁπάντων οἱ τῶν ἐν Λιβάνῳ καταλόγων ἄρχοντες, Ῥεκίθαγγός τε καὶ Θεόκτιστος, ὁρῶντες ὅτι δὴ καὶ ὁ χρόνος τὸ Σαρακηνῶν ἀνάθημα παρῴχηκεν ἤδη. Βελισαρίῳ γοῦν συχνὰ προσιόντες ἐδέοντο σφᾶς αὐτίκα ἀφεῖναι, μαρτυρόμενοι ὡς Ἀλαμουνδάρῳ τά τε ἐπὶ Λιβάνου καὶ Συρίας χωρία ἐνδόντες κάθηνται αὐτοῦ οὐδενὶ λόγῳ.

119 Martindale 1992: 255.

dux phoenices libanensis at Damascus in 528,[120] Molatzes *dux* in *phoenice libanensis* in 540,[121] Recithanc *dux* in *phoenice libanensis* at Damascus or Palmyra in 541,[122] and Theoctistus *dux* in *phoenice libanensis* at Damascus or Palmyra 540–543.[123] The evidence for all five attributions, however, is Procopius himself, and his language is ambiguous. In all four passages, Procopius says that the men were the commanders of the soldiers in Lebanon and he uses a form of οἱ τῶν ἐν Λιβάνῳ στρατιωτῶν ἦρχον (1.13.5).[124] If we go back, again, to the *Notitia Dignitatum* we find some clues, though few of limited value. There was a *dux Foenicis*, which corresponds in part to the *phoenice libanensis* that equates to Procopius' Lebanon, but the *Notitia* does not indicate his headquarters, and Procopius does not say where those commanders were based. That said, as we saw above, Procopius does indicate the (albeit vague) defensive measures undertaken by Justinian in Phoenicia by Lebanon (i.e. *Phoenice Libanensis*) at Palmyra, even if he does not outline any action at Damascus.[125] One of Justinian's edicts is concerned specifically with the governorship of Phoence-Libanensis, *Edict* 4 dated to 536. That legislation makes a few references to dukes who were responsible for the military in the province.[126] It does not say much about the identity of the soldiers, though it includes references to a phylarch and a regiment called the *Tertiodalmatae* (τερτιοδελμάτων).[127] There is an *Equites Dalmatae Illyriciani* based at Latavi under the *Dux Foenicis*, which could be the same unit, though it is missing the number three, which, in turn, might have been descended from the *cohors III Dalmatae equitata* previously based in Dacia until 257 if not later.[128] Regardless, the law dictates that the unit is to be transferred to the governor's command, effectively removing it from the sorts of operations that Procopius describes.

As Greatrex notes, our best comparative evidence for this and other *duces* of the east in the sixth century comes from Pseudo-Joshua the Stylite supplemented by Malalas and Pseudo-Zachariah.[129] What this information reveals is that the *Notitia*'s list of regiments, as we might expect, provides an incomplete

---

120   Martindale 1992: 366.
121   Martindale 1992: 894.
122   Martindale 1992: 1084.
123   Martindale 1992: 1226.
124   2.8.2—οἱ τῶν ἐν Λιβάνῳ στρατιωτῶν ἄρχοντες; 2.16.17—οἱ τῶν ἐν Λιβάνῳ στρατιωτῶν ἄρχοντες; 2.19.33–34—ἁπάντων οἱ τῶν ἐν Λιβάνῳ καταλόγων ἄρχοντες.
125   Procop. *Build.* 2.11.10–12.
126   Iust. *Ed.* 4.2.
127   Iust. *Ed.* 4.2.
128   Not. Dign. or. 32.21. On the earlier unit, see Spaul (2000: 302–314). Roxan (1976), who discusses the pre-Severan auxilia in the *Notitia Dignitatum*, leaves out this cohort.
129   Greatrex 2007b.

record of the region's military organization in the first half of the sixth century. Dukes were more likely to be put in charge of cities rather than entire provinces, at least if the evidence of Joshua was anything to go by.[130] Some of the *novels* of Justinian dealing with provincial reform mention how the local duke or dukes are to interact with the civilian officials; some of the laws in the code discuss the duties of dukes as well.[131]

At this point it should be obvious that Procopius only focused on the garrisons of a few select locations, and about many others he was silent. For Liebeschuetz, this is evidence that many of the fortifications had been abandoned, a point picked up some of those working on the fortifications in the southeast, to which we will return later.[132]

I want to finish this section by looking at the overlap between the accounts in the *Buildings* and the *Wars*, which I alluded to above. Of the cities listed along with garrisons in the *Buildings*, a few reappear in the *Wars* with a local military presence. At Dara, Martin happened to be there with an army at the time of Khusro's siege.[133] Note, regarding Zenobia Procopius says that when Khusro came upon it, because it was unimportant and with little land of value, he bypassed it.[134] Sergiopolis, on the other hand, was a wealthy city (or so Procopius) with a garrison of its own, thought numbering no more than 200 soldiers.[135] Although the citizens and soldiers defend the city admirably, it was the actions of Ambrus that saved the city.[136] Citharizon makes an appearance, and is garrisoned by Isaac, under whom were Philemouth and Beros, and some Heruls.[137] Theodosiopolis gets named, principally for Anastasius' efforts in buttressing the defences of the city.[138] Furthermore, of those garrisons identified in the *Buildings* and the *Wars*, only one is listed along with a local regiment in the *Notitia*, Sergiopolis, which I discussed above.[139]

Before we move on to the comparative evidence, there is one last issue to discuss: what do we make of those locations that Procopius alleges had a garrison in the *Buildings* but which he did not discuss in the *Wars*? Perhaps this is evidence for the presence of the garrisons to which Procopius refers, and

---

130 Greatrex 2007b: 90.
131 See, for example, *Cod. Iust.* 1.27.2.8, 12.35.17, 12.35.18, and *Iust. Nov.* 8, 102, 103.
132 Liebeschuetz 1977: 490–494.
133 Procop. *Wars* 2.13.16.
134 Procop. *Wars* 2.5.7.
135 Procop. *Wars* 2.20.13.
136 Procop. *Wars* 2.20.14–16.
137 Procop. *Wars* 2.24.14.
138 Procop. *Wars* 1.10.19.
139 *Not. Dign.* or. 33.28.

perhaps they did their job admirably. Indeed, if Khusro (or Kavadh) and the Persians found certain locations to be too much trouble because of the resistance they were likely to face, that could be proof enough for the effectiveness of their garrisons. It is worth noting that Procopius did not identify all known forts and garrisons in his works. Those in the southeast, to which we will return below, are left out, like Umm el-Jimal and el-Lejjūn, though they play no role in the geographic course of events that he describes. Plus, it could be that they did not receive ample attention from Justinian; hence their exclusion from the *Buildings*. Qasr el-Hallabat would seem to be an exception, however, and if nothing else it highlights Procopius' selectivity.[140] Despite the abundance of material that Procopius includes in the *Buildings*, he makes no claims to being complete. Indeed, his purpose was not to identify all fortifications in the empire, but only those whom Justinian had had a hand in reinforcing.

3 Rome's Frontier Soldiers across the Empire in the Sixth Century

Procopius' reporting on the sixth century *limitanei* is incomplete, but we have plenty of additional evidence for their role from other sources. One of the most important, though possibly even overlooked, documents for understanding the role of the *limitanei* is the *probatoria* from Egypt which we will discuss in chapter six. This recruitment document, the only one of its kind to survive from late antiquity (so far as I know), reveals the considerable effort that went into the recruitment of frontier soldiers, which calls into question a significant part of the background of the soldiers, at least as is commonly understood.[141]

The attention devoted to the recruitment of the *limitanei* is only part of the story, for we find them operating in a range of other capacities. In fact, we find them in all parts of the empire, old and new. They played an important role in Justinian's policy in the Balkans, a region vitally important to Justinian but one which Procopius downplays. What is more, not only were the frontier soldiers in the Balkans tasked with keeping watch from their fortifications, but they also participated in offensive operations.[142]

One prominent piece of Justinian's legislation refers to *limitanei*, the novel (103) on the proconsul of Palestine. Therein, he classifies them as one of the

---

140 PUAES 3.18. That inscription is dated to 529 CE.
141 I believe that P. Ness. 3.35 is also a recruitment document of sorts, for it lists both camels and camel riders, and even identifies (presumably) local officers. Its specific function and character require more work, however; this is an issue I plan to return to in. For the moment, see Whately (2016c).
142 Sarantis 2016: 394–395 (see too 25–26).

three primary classes of soldier under the command of the *dux* of the region in this part (Palestine) of the sixth-century Roman Empire.[143] The other two categories are soldiers and *foederati*.[144] The reference to soldiers seems ambiguous, although most categorize the soldiers as field soldiers, or *comitatenses*, as Koehn has.[145]

The next issue that we need to briefly discuss is the presence and use of *limitanei* in the sixth century. There are, in fact, a number of sources, both literary and papyrological, that suggest that they continued to have a prominent role.[146] They seem to be attested at Elephantine in southern Egypt, as both papyri and a few comments in Procopius' *Wars* make clear.[147] Procopius himself discusses the soldiers at Elephantine noting that a very large number had been based there since at least the reign of Diocletian, and that they serve to keep the barbarians, here Blemmyes, in check.[148] Justinian's *Novel* 103 notes the importance of the *limitanei* in Palestine in the first half of the century.[149] Generally, the novel maintains the distinction between civilian and soldiery in the province,[150] though as a result of the unrest involving the Samaritans,[151] the proconsul was able to co-opt frontier soldiers based in the province to quell any serious disturbances. Tackling civilian unrest is different from fighting an organized army; nevertheless, in some ways the former can be more challenging than the latter, and so here we have evidence for the *limitanei's* continued importance. Staying with Roman Palestine, we also have evidence

---

143   *Iust. Nov.* 103.3.1. ἔσονται δὲ διακεκριμένοι τοῖς ὅλοις ὅ τε περίβλεπτος τῶν τόπων δοὺξ καὶ ὁ τὴν ἀνθύπατον ἔχων ἀρχήν. καὶ ὁ μὲν ἡγήσεται στρατιωτῶν τε καὶ λιμιτανέων καὶ φοιδεράτων καὶ εἴ τι κατὰ τὴν χώραν ὁπλιτικὸν ὅλως ἐστί, πλὴν τῶν ἀφωρισμένων τῷ ἀνθυπάτῳ στρατιωτῶν, ὁ δὲ τὴν ὑπὲρ τῶν πολιτικῶν προσώπων τε καὶ πραγμάτων καὶ προσεδρευόντων αὐτῷ στρατιωτῶν ἕξει πρόνοιάν τε καὶ φυλακήν.

144   στρατιωτῶν τε καὶ λιμιτανέων καὶ φοιδεράτων.

145   Koehn 2018: 34.

146   In Isaac's (1998: 462) words: 'To conclude, it must be said again that so far there is little evidence of any large-scale reduction of the provincial army in Palestine before the early seventh century.'

147   The papyri pertaining to Elephantine are collected and translated by Porten (1996). The pertinent passage in Procopius is found at 1.19.27–37, in which he summarized the military and diplomatic history of the region as he knew it.

148   Procop. *Wars* 1.19.27–36. On Procopius' comments here, see Dijkstra (2008: 11–14, 23–36). See too Dijkstra 2014.

149   *Iust. Nov.* 103. The province in question was *Palestina Secunda*. On this interesting piece of legislation see Meyerson (1988: 65–71).

150   This process was initiated by Diocletian. Barnish, Lee, and Whitby (2000: 199) sensibly note, however, that this distinction was difficult to maintain in practice. cf. Isaac (1998: 467–469) on this unit of camel-riders, and Justinian's treatment of *limitanei*.

151   Meyerson (1988) 68.

for the existence of units of *limitanei* from 505, or, 548, to the end of the sixth century from Nessana,[152] as well as in the middle of the sixth century from the fortresses at Upper Zohar, and En Boqeq.[153] Units of *limitanei* also seem to have been used in Syria during this period, as a passage in John Malalas dated to 527 indicates.[154]

As we noted in the previous chapter, over a hundred years ago, Maspero published a detailed study of the garrisons of the Roman frontier in Egypt at the end of antiquity. Using the invaluable papyrological evidence among other things like the list of Hierocles, he singled out fifty-five locations as the bases of frontier troops, thirty-five of which were *poleis*, fourteen *kastra*, and six which do not fall into either of the two previous categories.[155] In Maspero's opinion, the *kastra* were occupied by *limitanei*, while the *poleis* were occupied by *arthmoi*. In his exhaustive discussion of the military works of Byzantine North Africa, Pringle carefully went through the evidence, such as it was in 1981, for the fortifications and frontier soldiers of that new frontier.[156] He noted that the epigraphic evidence for the presence of *limitanei* was limited; but using Maspero's much older work as a springboard, he did identify a few examples.

Pringle found evidence for a few units in and around Hippo Regius including a *numerus Bis Electorum* and a *numerus Hippo Regii*.[157] An inscription from Algiers attested to a deceased soldier from the *numerus Primi Felices Justiniani*. There are no other *numeri* directly attested in North Africa, though inscriptions identifying tribunes might allude to their presence.[158] The *numerus* of *Numidi Justiniani*, which appears in some Egyptian papyri, might have been raised in North Africa, even if it is not attested there.[159] For Pringle, all of these *numeri* were composed of *comitatenses*, not *limitanei*, which were not as well attested beyond one unclear inscription, which refers to a *castrum* constructed during the reign of Tiberius II.[160] But the arguments for *comitatenses* are weak, and largely come down to which structures the different soldiers were thought to inhabit, the degree to which the *limitanei* were considered to be full-fledged soldiers or part-time militia, and Justinian's own instructions in his legislation

---

152 Kraemer (1958: 5) dates the archive to the period between 505 and 596, while Isaac (1990: 209) says that the Theodosian *numerus* was there from at least 548.
153 Magness (1999).
154 Mal. *Chron.* 18.2.
155 Maspero 1912: 90.
156 See, especially, Pringle (2001: 72–94).
157 Pringle 2001: 72–73.
158 Pringle 2001: 73–74.
159 Pringle 2001: 73. BGU 12.2197, P. Cair. Masp. 1.67056, 67058.
160 Pringle 2001: 74, 106; *CIL* 8.4354.

on North Africa. But as I noted, Maspero's model for Egypt was also a major source of inspiration.

One of the difficulties stems from how we should identify the regiments of the different classes of soldiers, and as we have seen in this book, Procopius' language is not much help. *Limitanei* were deployed in a range of units, usually styled *numeri* or *arithmoi*, as we have seen, and they could be based right on the frontier or throughout the province, both in forts and in towns and cities.[161] After the re-conquest of Africa in 533, Justinian attempted to reassert imperial control by deploying *limitanei* and *comitatenses* to the new province. The relevant legislation is 1.27, which is concerned with the duties of the praetorian prefect and the organization of the new territory. It discusses the different types of troops to be deployed to manage and safeguard the provinces.[162] The law also puts a lot on stock in the importance of detailed records, particularly for appointments, which are to be kept in secure places.[163] It also includes a long list of officials and payments, not unlike Slab C in the Perge edict, only much longer and more extensive.[164]

The second chapter of the law is the portion specifically concerned with armed forces, *armata militia*, and the dukes of the frontier, *duces limitum*.[165] The law is filled with comments about where the soldiers, initially styled as *milites*, should be stationed, and what regions they are to guard, like the strait of Gibraltar (opposite Spain in its own language) and besides the mountains to watch over the Barbaricini.[166] After setting out the regions to be defended, it provides more detail about the soldiers themselves, stating that the officials, the dukes, shall station "as many soldiers, whether infantry or cavalry, as those who command them should have to guard the provinces and cities".[167] What it does not do is specify what kinds of soldiers they are to be, though a little later it provides more detail:

> For the deployment of frontier troops—because it seems necessary to Us that in addition to field troops frontier soldiers be stationed in camps, who could defend the camps and cities on the frontier and work the land ... we have drawn up as an example one unit [*unius numeri limitaneorum*], so that ... Your Greatness may station them in camps and places as you

---

161 Greatrex 1998: 35.
162 *Cod. Iust.* 1.27.1.16.
163 *Cod. Iust.* 1.27.1.18.
164 *Cod. Iust.* 1.27.1.21–42.
165 *Cod. Iust.* 1.27.2.pr.
166 *Cod. Iust.* 1.27.2.2–3.
167 *Cod. Iust.* 1.27.2.4b, trans. Dillon.

shall see fit in aa similar way to Our example; but in such a way that if you should find suitable men in the provinces or from among those they previously had as soldiers, you shall station them as frontier troops in each frontier region; thus, if some disturbance should arise, the frontier troops themselves, without the field troops ... may help the places where they are stationed, and neither the frontier troops nor their Dukes need go far beyond the frontier, so that the aforementioned frontier troops shall suffer no loss at the hands of the Dukes or their officers, nor shall the latter fraudulently divert payments from the troops' wages to their own profit.[168]

This section makes it clear that the *limitanei* are to play an important role in the territory's defence, and that they are to work in concert with the field army soldiers. What the law does not discuss is the origins and source of those field troops. To my mind, then, they are the soldiers initially dispatched to Africa as part of Belisarius' expeditionary army. It is these soldiers, largely field army soldiers, who were to stay behind and work on the transition to imperial rule. Indeed, the language of the law implies that these newly raised frontier soldiers are to become the primary party involved in the military organization of the region.

The law goes on to discuss other relevant issues, like periods of leave, pay, and familiar concerns over corruption, which I will return to in the discussion of recruitment below and as we find in the Anastasius edicts on the frontiers. In fact, the end of the law includes another set of payments, these for the officers in the military command, and many of their ranks appear in Slab C from Perge, which contains similar information.[169] There is even a nod to the size of

---

168 *Cod. Iust.* 1.27.2.8, trans. Dillon. I included and discussed part of this passage above in the chapter on field army soldiers. *Pro limitaneis vero ordinandis (quia necessarium nobis esse videtur, ut extra comitatenses milites per castra milites limitanei constituantur, qui possint et castra et civitates limitis defendere et terras colere, ut alii provinciales videntes eos per partes ad illa loca se conferant) exemplum fecimus unius numeri limitaneorum, ut secundum exemplum, quod nos misimus, per castra et loca, quae providerit tua magnitudo, eos ad similitudinem nostri exempli ordinet, sic tamen ut, si inveneris de provinciis idonea corpora, aut de illis, quos antea milites habebant, limitaneorum constituas numero in unoquoque limite, ut, si forsitan commotio aliqua fuerit, possint ipsi limitanei sine comitatensibus militibus una cum ducibus suis adiuvare loca, ubi dispositi fuerint, non longe limitem exeuntes nec ipsi limitanei nec duces eorum, ut nullum etiam dispendium a ducibus vel ducianis praedicti limitanei sustineant, nec aliquas sibi consuetudines de eorum stipendiis per fraudes ad suum lucrum convertant. haec autem non solum in limitaneos volumus observari, sed etiam in comitatenses milites.*

169 *Cod. Iust.* 1.27.2.20–34; Onur 2012, 2017.

some fortifications; the emperor has a desire that smaller sites be constructed so that they can be manned effectively, which is not possible when big sites are occupied by few men.[170]

The legislation on North Africa is only part of the story, however, for there are a handful of other laws in the Code and the Novels that deal in part with *limitanei* and these, in turn, point to a continued important role for the frontier soldiers. One of the those, sent to the *magister officiorum* and dated to 443, stresses the importance of training the *limitanei* to keep them up to par.[171] Additionally, one of the laws from book eleven deals specifically with frontier soldier properties. Parts of it date to the same year as the other law just discussed, dating to 443.[172] The bulk of the content has to do with the lands on the frontiers and how they are managed, as well as taxation and how the soldiers might be misused.[173] It also hints at farming, which another law specifies was one of the activities that soldiers were not to get involved in.[174]

There is no explicit use of the term *limitanei* in the papyri, though as we saw in the previous chapter, they mention them in all other sorts of ways. We do find plenty of references to *riparii*, which are usually styled as police officers.[175] Indeed, so far I have been focusing on *limitanei*, but this was not the only legal term for a frontier soldier, for there were plenty of others including, notably, *ripariensis*. One piece of Justinianic legislation, however, raises the possibility that a *riparius* might, in fact, be another phrasing for frontier soldier, for it is contrasted with *comitatenses*.[176] By all accounts, the fourth century officer Abinnaeus was a frontier officer, and much of what he did could be classified as policing duties.[177] At least one inscription uses the term *riparius*, though it does not deal explicitly with policing.[178] Another inscription, the Anastasius edict from Qasr el-Hallabat, refers to *limitanei*, using that particular phrase, a number of times, though it is the only one so far known.[179]

---

170 *Cod. Iust.* 1.27.2.14. On the fortifications themselves, see Pringle (2001: 171–304).
171 *Cod. Iust.* 1.46.4.2. See too Jones (1964: 661–663), Whitby (1995: 113–114), and Greatrex (1998: 34).
172 *Cod. Iust.* 11.60.3.
173 *Cod. Iust.* 11.60.1–3.
174 *Cod Iust.* 12.35.15.
175 See, for example, Ruffini (2018: 36).
176 *Cod. Iust.* 12.35.14pr.
177 On the archive, see Bell (1962). On soldiers and policing in the earlier empire, see Furhmann (2012).
178 Marek, Kat. Kaisareia Hadrianop. 10, SEG 35.1360.
179 SEG 32.1554. The relevant parts of the inscription are: τὸν παραλαμβάνειν βοηθόν· ὥ[στε τὸν ἡρογ]άτορα μηκέτι [τῇ ἀ]ναβολῇ κεχρῆσθαι περὶ τὴν ἀπαίτησιν τῶν [παραλειπο]μένων τοῖς λ[ιμι]ταναίοις μήτε τόκους ... εἰς ὁλόκληρον παρα[......] λόγῳ τῆς αὐτῆ[ς ἐ]πινημέσεως

But it is also worth drawing attention to the comments we find in the one other sixth-century author who mentions *limitanei*, Malalas. He mentions them in two places in his *Chronograph*, first while going over the reforms of Diocletian, and then again when he comes to the sixth century. In the first instance, Diocletian notes that they were stationed in the new fortifications that he built in the east from Egypt northwards to Persia so echoing in short Procopius' comments on Justinian's own efforts in the *Buildings*.[180] The second instance comes right at the beginning of book eighteen, which coincides with Justinian's accession.[181] This too has to do with reforms, particularly some improvements to the defensive works in the east, and Palmyra especially. Malalas says Patricius was appointed *comes Orientis*, and that he was given instructions to rebuild the city and garrison it with an *arithmos* of soldiers to supplement the *limitanei* already there.

This concise survey of the evidence for the *limitanei* in the sixth century demonstrates their continued importance. It is now time to take a closer look at one of the regions that I have already discussed, one touched on by Procopius but only in passing, and so one for which we must draw on additional sources of information.

4   Case Study: The *limitanei* in the Southeast[182]

Having looked at the evidence of Procopius and beyond, is time to cast the net wider and look at what the other sixth-century sources have to say about *limitanei*. But before we go further, it is worth highlighting the limitations of

---

δηληγατευθέντα τοῖς λι[μιταναί]οις χρήματα ... καὶ] ἐν μηνὶ Σεπτεμ[βρί]ῳ τὴν ῥόγαν [τ]ῶν λιμιταναίω[ν καὶ τῶν στρα]τιωτῶν ὑπὲρ τῆ[ς π]εντεκαιδεκ[ά]της ἰνδικτιόνος ... τῆς αὐτῆς πρώ-τη[ς δ]ηληγατευό[μ]ενα τοῖς λιμιτ[αναίοις ...]ις ... The inscription is in the process of being re-edited by Feissel. Once published, it should help make more sense of the assorted fragments. For the moment, Feissel et al. (2014) provides a good overview.

180 12.40.4 Ἔκτισεν δὲ καὶ εἰς τὰ λίμιτα κάστρα ὁ αὐτὸς Διοκλητιανὸς ἀπὸ τῆς Αἰγύπτου ἕως τῶν Περσικῶν ὅρων, τάξας ἐν αὐτοῖς στρατιώτας λιμιτανέους, προχειρισάμενος καὶ δοῦκας κατὰ ἐπαρχίαν ἐνδοτέρω τῶν κάστρων καθέζεσθαι μετὰ πολλῆς βοηθείας πρὸς παραφυλακήν. There are other sources that mention *limitanei* operating near the end of the third century CE and beginning of the fourth.

181 18.2.6 Ὁ δὲ αὐτὸς βασιλεὺς ἐπὶ τῆς ἕκτης ἐπινεμήσεως τῷ ὀκτωβρίῳ μηνὶ προηγάγετο κόμητα ἀνατολῆς ἐν Ἀντιοχείᾳ ὀνόματι Πατρίκιον, Ἀρμένιον· ᾧτινι δέδωκε χρήματα πολλά, κελεύσας αὐτῷ ἀπελθεῖν καὶ ἀνανεῶσαι πόλιν τῆς Φοινίκης εἰς τὸ λίμιτον τὴν λεγομένην Πάλμυραν καὶ τὰς ἐκκλησίας καὶ τὰ δημόσια, κελεύσας καὶ ἀριθμὸν στρατιωτῶν μετὰ τῶν λιμιτανέων καθέζεσθαι ἐκεῖ καὶ τὸν δοῦκα Ἐμίσσης πρὸς τὸ φυλάττεσθαι τὰ Ῥωμαϊκὰ καὶ Ἱεροσόλυμα.

182 This discussion is based on Whately (forthcoming b).

the evidence. While we know a great deal about some aspects of the fifth century in the Mediterranean, like the role of law and the emperor in running the empire, for other matters like military affairs, we are, effectively, in the dark.[183] Indeed, it is no wonder that Jones' detailed discussion of the late Roman army is divided into two sections, one which focuses on the fourth century, and another which focuses on the sixth.[184] One of many unknowns about military organization in the sixth century Roman Empire is what happened to the regiments between the creation of the eastern list of the *Notitia Dignitatum* and the beginning of the sixth century, if not later, a period between 100 and 150 years.

At the beginning of this chapter I noted how the *limitanei* have often been disparaged by scholars; it is easy to see why. Justinian himself, at the opening of one particular piece of legislation, says: "Therefore We order that all those who serve under arms, whether of greater or lesser rank—We call soldiers both those who are known to tolerate service under the high Master of Soldiers and those who are counted in the eleven most elevated corps (*scholae*), as well as those who have been decorated as allies under diverse officials (*optiones*)".[185] The first line seems to make it clear that he means every soldier, while the latter part, where he subdivides the soldiery into three groups, would exclude *limitanei*. Such a definition would support the relative silence of Procopius.

Some of the physical evidence provided by the remains of the empire's fortifications has also been used to disparage the frontier soldiers, or at least support Procopius' claims in the *Secret History*. One of the difficulties we have is in identifying the garrison of those fortifications, which, in most instances, is not yet (if ever) possible. The most thorough catalogue of Roman fortifications in the east is Gregory's. On the eastern frontier, which runs from Pontus in the north to Arabia in the south, she identifies 122 sites, with the majority of those found in Arabia: 8 in Pontus, 5 in Cappadocia, 15 in Mesopotamia, 9 on the Euphrates (banks), 29 in south Syria, and 56 in Arabia.[186]

The most important piece of evidence for late antique military organization, the *Notitia Dignitatum*, includes not just the names of units but their locations.[187] And, so far as we have it, it is pretty accurate for the late fourth century,

---

183   See Millar (2015) for imperial administration and communications in the fifth century. For a snapshot of life in the first half of the fifth century (428 CE), see Traina (2009).
184   Jones 1964: 607–654, 654–679.
185   Cod. Iust. 4.65.35, trans. Kehoe.
186   Gregory 1997 (volume 2).
187   For other attempts to use the *Notitia* to understand frontier military organization, see Collins (2012: 38–54) and Whately (2015a: 7–15).

at least for the east.[188] One of the principal difficulties, however, is that we do not know the identity of all of the bases that the *Notitia* names, and this is no less true for Arabia and Palestine, the regions we are concerned with, than any other region. In some ways, it is easier to identify fortifications and garrisons with larger forts like that at el-Lejjūn, which was garrisoned by a legionary unit.[189] In the case of Arabia and Palestine, however, we are dealing with a much smaller sample size: there are two legions under the duke of Arabia, and twenty-one smaller units (*alae*, *cohortes*, and *equites*).

If there is any overlap between the list of forts and the list of units,[190] it is in the sheer number of each: there are plenty of smaller Roman forts and fortlets in Jordan that could only ever have held a small number of men, and there are plenty of smaller units listed in the *Notitia Dignitatum*. What is more, the fortifications are fairly evenly distributed along the two major routes in the frontier, the *Via Nova Traiana* and the *Strata Diocletiana*. This suggests an interest in responding to threats on a smaller-scale rather than large-scale. Furthermore, at least half of the regiments in Palestine and Arabia were mounted, if not closer to three quarters.[191] And this is to say nothing of the mobility of the Arab allies, who had an important role fighting alongside the regular Roman troops.[192]

Although the *Notitia* shows that many forts had garrisons in the late fourth century, we are in the dark for the fifth and sixth centuries.[193] Some still hold to the view that the forts in the southeast were abandoned at this time.[194] The evidence for this is slim, however, despite some claims to the contrary.[195] In terms of the physical evidence, it usually comes down to arguments for Ghassanid occupation and Roman abandonment of fortified sites. A case in point for the former is Qasr el-Hallabat, and the latter el-Lejjūn. Justinian's *Novels* 102 and 103, both dated to 536, demonstrate the continued presence of Roman soldiers in the region, even if a phylarch is referred to in the former. Indeed, the

---

188 Pollard 2013, Kaiser 2015. Jones (1964) saw the *Notitia* as an official document. Others have questioned its value, at least in certain contexts Kulikowski (2000). For some sort of middle ground, see Brennan 1998.
189 Whately 2013; Whately 2015a.
190 Kennedy's (2004) book includes both ancient and modern names where available. There are a handful of other pieces of evidence that are extremely valuable when it comes to reconstructing late antique Jordan: the Madaba Map, a mosaic from the church of St. Stephen at Umm er-Resas, Eusebius' *Onomasticon*, and the Beersheba tax edict.
191 Lewin 2015: 180–181.
192 Fisher 2011; Edwell et al. 2015: 230–253; Lewin 2015: 175–179.
193 Note Parnell's (2017: 14) comments.
194 Parker 2006: 562–571.
195 This discussion is based on Whately (forthcoming b).

reference to a *numerus* in *Novel* 102 points to the presence of frontier soldiers. The Anastasius edict from Qasr el-Hallabat itself includes the term *limitanei*, which points to their presence, if not in that city, then at least in Umm el-Jimal, where the inscription originated.[196] On the other hand, the inscription put up by the duke Flavius Anastasius at Qasr el-Hallabat, dated to 529, points to a continued Roman military presence at the fort, whatever form that might have taken.[197] Thus, while Roman forts, like Qasr el-Hallabat, might have been transformed into Jafnid monasteries and palaces much later in the sixth century,[198] this alleged widespread demilitarization and transformation, if it happened at all, does not seem to have happened until at least 551, well after the context of Procopius' comments.[199]

Upper Zohar, a smaller fort, was occupied into the early seventh century from the fifth.[200] The same was true for Ein Boqeq.[201] Umm el-Jimal, often thought to have been abandoned by regular soldiers, might well have been occupied by soldiers well into the sixth century.[202] There were soldiers in Jerash too, though we know less about them.[203] Plus, there is a good deal of evidence for regular military personnel operating in the region near the end of the sixth century. A few papyri from Petra and the Beersheba edicts point to the continued military presence in some of the sites listed in the *Notitia Dignitatum*.[204] Indeed, in some instances the soldiers were first stationed in the region in the middle of the sixth century, as might be the case at Nessana.[205]

Perhaps the best-known set of comparative evidence is composed of the forts and fortifications of the frontiers, which many take as a starting point in discussions of eastern strategy. One reasonably well known set of fortifications can be found in Jordan, the southeastern frontier, running approximately in a line from the northwest corner of the Wadi Sirhan west towards Umm el-Jimal

---

196 Arce, Feissel, Weber 2014.
197 PUAES 3.18: "Under Flavius Anastasius, the most excellent and renowned, of the rank of the ex-consuls and dux, the camp was restored in the year 424, in the time of the 7th indiction [March 22–Sept 1, 529 AD]". See Sartres 1982: 108–109; Greatrex and Lieu (2002, 267, n. 31); Greatrex 2015: 134.
198 Arce 2006, 2008, 2010: 464. Parker (in De Vries (1998: 140)) questioned whether this was the case at Umm el-Jimal, even though many had accepted Butler's (PUAES 2.171) suggestion that the soldiers' quarters had been converted into a monastery.
199 Genequand 2015: 174–175; Greatrex 2015: 133–134.
200 Harper 1997.
201 Magness 1999.
202 De Vries 1998: 233; Greatrex 2015: 133, n. 40.
203 Lichtenberger and Raja 2016: 643.
204 P. Petr. 3.23; Fiema 2002: 228–231; Di Segni 2004.
205 This is Isaac's (1990: 209) suggestion. See too Whately (2016b).

TABLE 5.2 Select southeastern frontier fortifications[a]

Name	Date of Roman military construction	Size
Qasr el-Azraq[b]	292–306 CE[c]	80 × 72m
Deir el-Kahf[d]	306 CE[e]	62 × 61 × 60 × 61m
Umm el-Jimal	early fourth century[f]	100 m[g]
Qasr el-Hallabat	early third century[h]	c. 38m square
Al-Hadid	end of the third century[i]	158 × 107m
Khirbet er-Zona	late third or early fourth century[j]	44 × 40m
Qasr eth-Thuraiya	late third or early fourth century[k]	37.5 × 34.5m[l]
Umm er-Resas (Mefaat)	Late third or early fourth century[m]	158 × 139m
Qasr Bshir	Aurelius Asclepiades (293–305 CE)[n]	56.75 × 57.05 × 55.3 × 54.35m
El-Lejjūn (Betthorus)	300 CE	247 × 190m
Khirbet el-Fityan	300 CE[o]	78.8 × 76.8 m
Udruh (Adrou)	in 300 CE[p]	248 × 207 × 246 × 177m
Rujm es-Sadaqa (Zodocatha)	reoccupied in the third century[q]	c. 250 × 150m[r]

a For a much more complete and updated catalogue, see Ross (2016: 8–46).
b Parker 1986: 19.
c Parker 1986: 19–20.
d Kennedy and Riley 1990: 181.
e Parker 1986: 21–24.
f See Parker (1986: 26–29), Gregory (1997: 273), and Kennedy (2004: 83).
g Parker (1986, 29) does state that its function may not have been military in nature. Gregory (1997: 266) has identified a fortified town with a monumental gateway, a fort, and barracks, which suggests that at least a portion of the site had a military function.
h Kennedy 2004: 99. Ross (2016: 15) says it dates to Marcus Aurelius but he means Caracalla.
i Parker's (1986: 33–4) date does seem plausible based on the presumed connection with other similar sites but Gregory (1997: 326) does note the parallels with other sites that seem to be Iron Age in origin.
j Parker 1986: 45.
k Kennedy 2004: 133.
l Parker 1986: 50.
m Kennedy 2004: 138.
n Gregory 1997: 338.
o Parker 1986: 78–9; Kennedy 2004: 150.
p Gregory 1997: 383.
q *Not. Dign. or.* 34.24.
r Kennedy 2004: 177.

TABLE 5.2   Select southeastern frontier fortifications (*cont.*)

Name	Date of Roman military construction	Size
El-Quweira	late third and early fourth century.[s]	32.5 × 31.5 m
Khirbet el-Khalde (Praesidium)	late third or early fourth century.[t]	54 × 53 m
Humayma (Huara)	Later second century[u]	150 × 200m
Aqaba (Aila)	Fourth century (?)[v]	Unknown as yet

s   Parker 1986: 105–108.
t   Parker 1986: 108–109.
u   Ross 2016: 9.
v   Kennedy 2004, 208; Ross 2016: 8.

and then south to Aqaba. Many date to the reign of Diocletian. Some were big enough to house late antique legions, and some are included in the table above. Others, though smaller, like Qasr Bshir, had a number of watchtowers in their vicinity.[206] Table 5.2 provides a summary of many of the better-preserved forts, of many different sizes, in Jordan.[207]

While the forts and fortlets cannot speak for themselevs, their positioning betrays an interest in defensive concerns. Qasr el-Azraq was located at a strategic point near an outlet of the Wadi Sirhan.[208] Deir el-Kahf guarded the southeast Hauran and was founded in 306 CE.[209] Khirbet er-Zona was situated in a strong defensive position overlooking a wadi with an excellent view in all directions, save the north.[210] Qasr eth-Thuraiya, though at a point where there is little inherent defensibility, affords a good view of the surrounding area.[211] Khirbet el-Fityan controlled access into the valley from the north and west and commanded an excellent view in all directions.[212] Udruh offers good views of the desert in most directions, and where there are deficiencies there might well have been a system of watchtowers built on those hills to compensate for

206   Kennedy 2004: 53.
207   More detailed overviews can be found in Gregory (1997), on the entire eastern frontier; Kennedy (2004), on Jordan in particular; and Ross (2016), on Jordan and Syria.
208   Parker 1986: 19.
209   Parker 1986: 21–24.
210   Parker 1986: 45.
211   Parker 1986: 50.
212   Parker 1986: 78–9; Kennedy 2004: 150.

this problem.[213] There is a tower at el-Quweira on the northeast edge of this outcrop which provides an excellent view of the road in both directions.[214] Nearly every site was superbly placed in order to optimize observation, and where this was not the case and part of the view was obstructed, more often than not watchtowers were found close by to compensate for this fallibility.[215]

We do not know the history of each of the sites in the list, or many others besides. What is more, when their histories came to an end is a matter of some debate. Many scholars prefer a date in the early sixth century, if not earlier, for the abandonment of most military sites in Jordan and Israel/Palestine.[216] As I suggested a few pages earlier, in some cases, particularly in the north of Jordan and the south of Syria, the thinking is that these military sites were re-occupied by monks or Ghassanids, as is the case with Qasr el-Hallabat and Umm el-Jimal.[217] Some more recent research has questioned this, however, especially when it comes to the forts at el-Lejjūn, En Boqeq, Upper Zohar, Umm el-Jimal, and Qasr el-Hallabat.[218] Most of these sites were located either close or adjacent to a major road, or were located near a body of water (whether permanent or seasonal). Although they were constructed nearly two hundred years before Justinian, their continued use presupposes a recognition of their utility and value.[219]

4.1 *Frontier Soldiers in Action: Checking Barbarians*[220]

To get a sense of the importance of the frontier soldiers, I will focus on those based on the eastern frontier, and the southeast in particular. In the *Buildings*, Procopius leaves out the defensive works of Palestine/Arabia in his extended description of the empire's larger defensive network. He draws attention to the troubles that had beset Asia, and the fortification works that had been built in response.[221] On the other hand, as we saw earlier in the chapter, he does hint at its role in the larger system a few times. Procopius highlights two fortifications

---

213 Parker 1986: 94–5.
214 Parker 1986: 105–108.
215 Parker 1986: 83–4.
216 Parker 1986.
217 De Vries 1998, Shahîd 2002, Arce 2015.
218 Casey 1996, Harper 1997, Whately 2013b, Genequand 2015. See too Greatrex (2015) and Lewin (2015).
219 El-Lejjūn, one of the best excavated of the lot, and which started its life as a military installation, was occupied until the middle of the sixth century. See Whately 2013b. For the continued use of forts in a different desert frontier, west of the Nile of Egypt, see Kucera (2016).
220 This discussion is based on Whately (forthcoming b).
221 Procop. *Build.* 5.1.3.

in Syria for their roles in checking Saracen raids, Palmyra and Thannourios.[222] At the other end of the eastern frontier, Mt. Sinai was fortified for similar reasons, with a view to preventing Saracen raids—and in Procopius' eyes from sneaking into the rest of Palestine.[223] The physical defences were to work in concert with the soldiery; this was the purpose of the *limitanei*, or so Procopius says in the *Secret History*: prevent invasions, particularly of the Persians and Saracens in the east.[224] The theme of Saracen raiding is not specific to the *Buildings*, for Procopius highlights this particular threat in both the *Secret History* and the *Wars*, though the Saracens were not unique in this regard.[225] In the *Secret History*, the Saracens were just one of the barbarian groups who engaged in raiding,[226] and sometimes suffered as a result, at least when the defences were working properly.[227] Indeed, those Saracens who fought with Rome were characterized positively, which is in stark contrast to those allied to Persia.[228] The issue of raiding, its prevention, and its impact are themes that connect all three of Procopius' texts. They are also the primary strategic issue pertaining to the southeast we find in Procopius' works.

Although Procopius may have been conspicuously silent on the role of the *limitanei* in safeguarding the empire's residents, some of his strategic considerations show their importance should not be overlooked. In the *Buildings* more than in the other texts, we find a number of comments on strategy. At the start of book two, where Procopius describes the eastern fortifications, we discover how Justinian surrounded the empire with defensive fortifications.[229] We also read, however, about how fear guided some Roman actions, such as the haste with which they constructed fortifications at Dara.[230] Moreover, there was an expectation that most Persian attacks would involve a siege, and the implication is that the defensive system was established for just this purpose, and Dara in particular,[231] though the same could be said for most of the fortifications

---

222   Procop. *Build.* 2.11.10ff, 2.6.15.
223   Procop. *Build.* 5.8.9.
224   Procop. *SH.* 24.12.
225   In the *Wars* Procopius calls the Saracens "the cleverest of all men at plundering" (2.19.12). On Saracen raiding, see Caner (2010: 59), Ward (2015: 111–127), and Whately (2016c: 132). Some of the Safaitic graffiti from the basalt desert refer to raids, some of which could have been directed at Romans.
226   Procop. *SH.* 11.3–11.
227   Procop. *SH.* 18.25.
228   Those Saracens based further south in Arabia are called cannibals (Procop. *Wars* 19.15). cf. Whately (2014: 222–224).
229   Procop. *Build.* 2.1.2.
230   Procop. *Build.* 2.1.7.
231   Procop. *Build.* 2.1.11–27.

so described. Procopius highlights the defensive characteristics of the east's fortifications: an expectation of siege warfare was the purpose of these reconstruction measures. If strong enough, Procopius alleges that they could be a deterrent: Sergiopolis' defences were so strong that Khusro abandoned his siege of the city not long after he had invested it.[232] In other spots, Procopius highlights some of Justinian's long-term military planning.[233] For example, Procopius praises Justinian's foresight regarding the defensive measures implemented at Dara.[234] Some comments, as in the *Wars*, even reveal what could be characterized as a defence-in-depth policy; troops were established in barracks in Dara, which, in theory, could be dispatched to meet an invading force.[235] What is more, there was a line of fortifications from Dara to Amida, the bulk of which had been refortified, so acting, in Procopius' own words, as a bulwark against Persian incursion.[236] Indeed, Procopius even went so far as to claim that Justinian had made Mesopotamia impenetrable to Persians.[237] On the other hand, there was a recognition that not all fortifications were given the same treatment, for Sisauranon was left unguarded.[238] And, when Procopius finished his account of Mesopotamia, he said that some regions offered little of value, and so were not worth fighting for.[239] There were good reasons that some fortifications received attention while others did not, and for Procopius Justinian's ultimate goal when it came to eastern fortifications was to ensure the safety of the Roman people.[240]

The organization of the fortifications and the character of their garrisons point to mobility. A few scattered comments in inscriptions, papyri, and law codes give us a good indication what their strategic function might have been. Of particular importance are the decree of Anastasius from Cyrenaica,[241] one of the longest pieces of legislation in *Codex Justinianus*, 1.27 on North Africa,[242] a handful of military orders from Egypt from the reign of Justinian,[243] and a papyrus containing a list of military camels from Nessana, from the second

---

232   Procop. *Build.* 2.9.9.
233   Procop. *Build.* 2.1.8–10.
234   Procop. *Build.* 2.2.20–21.
235   Procop. *Build.* 2.2.26.
236   Procop. *Build.* 2.4.14. On the dating and character of the fortifications at Amida, see Crow (2007).
237   Procop. *Build.* 2.4.21.
238   Procop. *Build.* 2.4.10. Granted, Sisauranon was a Persian fort.
239   Procop. *Build.* 2.8.4–5.
240   Procop. *Build.* 2.9.11.
241   SEG 9.356 and 414, Oliverio 1936: 135–163.
242   *Cod. Iust.* 1.27.
243   P. Cair. 3.67321, SB 18.13127, SB 5.8028, P. Lond. 5.1663.

half of the sixth century.244 All these documents discuss, or allude to, how to deal with barbarians, and each is concerned with a frontier region.

The piece of legislation, contained within the *Justinianic Code*, details the administration of North Africa in the wake of its reconquest by Belisarius. At 1.27.4b, the decree, ostensibly a letter from Justinian to Belisarius, expresses the hope that the soldiers, under dukes (responsible for commanding frontier soldiers), would keep the province "intact in safety and peace … and … kept unharmed by the vigilance and labours of the most devoted soldiers".245 A few lines later, it reads as follows: "Your Greatness shall, at your discretion, station for each frontier region [*limitem*] as many soldiers, whether infantry or cavalry, as those who command them should have to guard [*ad custodiendas*] the provinces and cities".246 The rest of the section goes into even more detail. As for the nature of the threat, the concern seems to be whether a *commotio*, a disturbance, arises. Several of the later novels deal with administrative changes in parts of the empire, and they seem to hint at the sort of commotion alluded to in Africa. This is true for the novels on Psidia,247 Thrace,248 and Cappadocia.249

The frontier troops based in Nessana, in Israel/Palestine, were on at least one occasion dispatched to Caesarea, though for reasons that are not clear.250 Incidentally, individual soldiers (George Zonenos and Thomas Victor) were sent to Egypt, as the same papyrus tells us.251 As for the Egyptian papyri, the relevant passage from four documents dating to the mid-sixth century are virtually identical, even if they were recovered from different locations, and their dating seems to vary slightly.252 All contain the phrase: "an *arithmos* of the loyal Justinian Numidians, five hundred and eight men, [is] to guard the eparchy of the Thebaid and repulse every inroad of barbarians".253 These stated duties are not unlike those espoused by Anastasius in his edict from Cyrenaica: "The soldiers in the camp shall take utmost precautions that no person shall pass

---

244   P. Ness. 3.37.
245   Trans. Dillon.
246   *Cod. Iust.* 1.27.5, trans. Dillon.
247   *Nov.* 24.
248   *Nov.* 26.
249   *Nov.* 30.
250   P. Ness. 3.37.40.
251   P. Ness. 3.37.15. It is possible that more than those two soldiers were sent to Egypt, though it is not clear.
252   P. Cair. 3.67321, SB 18.13127, SB 5.8028, P. Lond. 5.1663.
253   Trans. Hunt (slightly modified), ἀριθμὸν τῶν εὐκαθοσιωτῶν Νουμιδῶν Ἰουστινιανῶν, ἀνδρῶν πεντακοσίων ὀκτὼ, πρὸς παραφυλακὴν τῆς Θηβαίων ἐπαρχείας καὶ [πρὸς ἐκδί]ωξιν πάσης β[α]ρβαρικῆς [ἐπ]ιδρομῆ. The Greek here is taken from P. Cair. 3.67321. See too the comments of Koehn (2018: 20).

through to the barbarians for commercial purposes or make contracts with them, but they shall watch the roads that neither Roman nor Egyptian nor anyone else may cross over to the barbarians without a permit."[254] The consensus from this varied collection of documents is that the frontier soldiers were to protect their region, and, more often than not, keep barbarians in check.[255]

This purpose, keeping barbarians in check, echoes some of Procopius' own comments, for he notes the role fear played in Roman war strategies; fear seems to have guided Roman actions, or so Procopius, in the *Buildings*, appears to say.[256] This fear of an enemy's forces, and of invasion, reads a lot like the defensive imperialism mentality—even the realism advocated by Eckstein—that has been associated with Rome's rise during the republican period.[257] Greatrex has even argued for a similar mentality in late antiquity.[258] There are at least two aspects of strategy alluded to in the *Secret History* that overlap with strategic comments in the other texts. One concerns the meticulous records the Romans kept. Although we have less evidence for Roman military paperwork for the sixth century than for the second century, some of the inscriptions, laws, and papyri we do have imply that the total was still substantial.[259] Procopius' comments about the stationing of troops in Dara and Justinian's creation of the *magister militum per Armeniam* in the *Wars* points towards the existence of detailed records of troops numbers and their dispositions. On this basis, if we follow Kagan, who reduces grand strategy to a state's resource allocation for military purposes, there seems clear evidence for grand strategy here.[260]

254　SEG 9.356, 11. Trans. Johnson. ὥ[σ]τε τοὺς καστρ(η)σιανοὺς μετὰ πά(σ)ης ἐπιμελίας παρα[φ]υλάττιν, καὶ μὴ σ[υνω]νῆς χάριν τινὰ παρειέναι ἐπὶ τ[ο]ὺϛβαρβάρους μήτε τ[ὰ] ἀλλάγματα πρὸς αὐτοὺς τιθ[έν]αι· ἀλλὰ φυλάττιν αὐτοὺς καὶ τὰς ὁδοὺς ἐπὶ τῷ μήτε Ῥωμαίους μήτε Αἰγυπτίο[υς μ]ήτε ἕτερόν τ(ι)να δίχα [πρ]οστάγματος τὴν πάροδον ἐπὶ τοὺς βαρβάρους [π]οιεῖ(ν)· [το]ὺς δὲ ἐκ τοῦ ἔθνου[ς τ]ῶν Μακῶν διὰ γραμμάτων τοῦ λα(μπροτάτου) πραιφέκτου συγχωρῖσθαι ἐπὶ τὰ χωρία [Πε]νταπόλεως παραγίνεσθαι.

255　Due to constraints of space, I have had to omit discussion of the character of that threat, on this frontier the Saracens. On the nature of this threat, and the relationship between pastoralists and nomads, see, among others, Graf (1978, 1989), Shaw (1982), Shahîd (1984), Banning (1986), Whately (2014: 220–224), Edwell et al. (2015: 218–228).

256　Parnell (2017: 77) argues that fear guided the emperor's actions in all sorts of military-scenarios.

257　Eckstein 2006.

258　Greatrex 2007a.

259　Note, for instance, the various edicts of Anastaius, the papyri from the soldiers archive (P. Ness. 3.14–30) at Nessana, the Beersheba edict (Di Segni 2004), and assorted comments in the legislation (*Cod. Iust.* 1.27.5, 1.42.2).

260　Kagan 2006b.

Procopius' comments on the joint responsibilities of forts and soldiers seem to betray the existence of a defence-in-depth strategy, particularly Procopius' comments about the line of fortifications in Mesopotamia and the establishment of the aforementioned *magister militum per Armeniam* command. Defence-in-depth is how Luttwak famously characterized the strategy of the Roman Empire that emerged in the wake of the third century crisis.[261] More recently, Vannesse described the defensive system of Italy in late antiquity, in the process elucidating its complexities.[262] He too dismisses the defence-in-depth model, though his characterization of the military units and his emphasis on their mobility and responsiveness suggests that some sort of defence-in-depth system was in place. Getting back to the east, Howard-Johnston has recently carried out a comparable analysis to Vannesse.[263] He characterizes Rome's eastern frontier at the end of antiquity as a bipartite defensive zone, so not unlike Luttwak's defence-in-depth.[264] This defence-in-depth strategy seems to be what Procopius is alluding to when he describes Belisarius' responses to Persian invasions. Even Procopius' description of the nature of the later conflict, the one which included the sack of Antioch, would seem to hint at such a system: Khusro invades, the main opposition he meets is that based in the cities he encounters, and the Romans eventually send a mobile force to meet the opposition. Along the way, many well-defended cities are bypassed, like Circesium,[265] which as we saw above had an established garrison, while others were not.

Before we conclude, it is worth considering why Procopius was silent on the southeast frontier. Some have taken this as evidence of his overt bias against the Ghassanids/Jafnids,[266] while others have claimed this indicates that there was nothing significant there for him to discuss.[267] Recent research on Procopius' account of the frontier in other parts of the empire, however, provides an alternative explanation for Procopius' silence. Sarantis has proved beyond a doubt that Justinian invested heavily in the conflicts in the Balkans.[268] The Balkans, like the southeast, are an area that Procopius glossed over, though this is less pronounced for that frontier than it is for the southeast. The point is, Procopius is always selective, and his silence should not be equated with absence.

In the end, what are we left with? Sarantis has emphasized the importance of Rome's military infrastructure for its success, even survival, in late

---

261 Luttwak 1976: 127–190.
262 Vannesse 2010.
263 Howard-Johnston 2013.
264 Howard-Johnston 2013: 885. See too Greatrex (2007a: 152).
265 Procop. *Wars* 2.5.3.
266 Shahîd 2002.
267 Arce 2015.
268 Sarantis 2016.

antiquity.[269] In particular, Sarantis argued that it was Rome's network of fortifications that allowed it to fare comparatively well. What is more, perhaps the most famous expression about strategy is a Roman one, and a late Roman one at that, namely Vegetius' *"qui desiderat pacem praeparet bellum"* (those who desire peace should prepare for war), often reported as *"si vis pacem, para bellum"* (if you want peace, prepare for war).[270] There is, thus, a sense that soldiers, fortifications, and strategy were a big part of Rome's success in late antiquity, and that those in power and who wrote about military affairs had a genuine awareness of their existence and effectiveness. Procopius' strategic comments focus on the role of soldiers and forts in defending various parts of the empire against raids; the forts, many of which continued to be occupied in the sixth century, were constructed to garrison small, mobile groups of soldiers able to respond to small-scale threats; the official documentation that we have stresses the duty of soldiers to protect the frontiers from barbarian inroads. We have, then, considerable overlap between the various types of evidence. It is also clear that the *limitanei* played a significant role in this defensive policies.

5   Conclusion

In this chapter we have seen that Procopius' record on the *limitanei*, like so much else, is inconsistent. While the *Secret History* might be damning about their role in Justinianic combat, the *Wars* is much more circumspect. The *Buildings*, once you scratch beneath the surface, does offer them a role, though it comes out indirectly and it is usually subordinated to larger strategic issues, and the important role of the empire's physical infrastructure in its defence policy. In other words, with the *limitanei*, as with so much else besides, Procopius has been very deliberate in what he does describe, and very selective; classicizing tendencies abound (no technicalities, names of *limitanei*, or their units). There are plenty of reasons why this might have been so, and we will return to this issue in the conclusion to this book. As we close this chapter, however it is worth taking stock, for as we have also seen the *limitanei* continued to play an important role in sixth-century military operations.

For some, the downgrading of the *limitanei* has been connected to the blurring of the distinction between them and the *comitatenses*.[271] A law dated to

---

269   Sarantis 2013.
270   Veg. *Mil.* 3. Pr. 8.
271   Treadgold (1995: 193) argued that their pay was halted, or at least diminished, because of the financial challenges borne by the outbreak of the plague. While I do not deny that the plague had a significant impact on the state's ability to recruit soldiers, as I will discuss in chapter six, I do not think the *limitanei* suffered quite as much as he insisted.

400 but used in the *Codex Justinianus* suggests otherwise. The law in question, 12.35.14, reads:

> We do not want our soldiers to be transferred from one unit to another contrary to the public advantage. Let the counts and dukes, therefore, to whom the responsibility of commanding the soldiery is entrusted, take notice that not only is it impermissible for soldiers to be transferred from the field and palatine units to other units, but neither has the prerogative been accorded to any of them of transferring a soldier from the field legions or from **the riparian** or the garrison of any other forces, unless Our August Majesty has ordered this to be done for the public good, because an increase in honour should come to each and every one not by corrupt solicitation, but by labour. Those who act to the contrary may know that a pound of gold will be demanded of them for every soldier.[272]

This law strongly contradicts any supposition that the *limitanei* were secondary troops in the sixth century. It was not easy for troops to be transferred between any unit, not just field army ones.

For others, the downgrade is connected to the rise of Rome's Arab allies, who are seen to have taken their place. Indeed, the *foederati* play an important role in much sixth-century combat, and in Justinian's own legislation the Arab phylarchs are given a prominent place. To what degree are these replacements, however, or simply intended to complement the existing *limitanei*? This question is a big one and beyond the scope of this book.[273] The material that I have looked at here, only the tip of the iceberg, implies that they were not replaced. Rather, they continued to play an important role in the empire's defence. If it were not for Procopius downgrading of the *limitanei* in the *Wars* and *Buildings*, though especially the *Secret History*, I suspect that their role would not now be in doubt.

---

272 *Cod. Iust.* 12.35.14, trans. Pazdernik. *Contra publicam utilitatem nolumus a numeris ad alios numeros milites nostros transferri. sciant igitur comites vel duces, quibus regendae militiae cura commissa est, non solum de comitatensibus ac palatinis numeris ad alios numeros milites transferri non licere, sed ne ipsis quidem seu de comitatensibus legionibus seu de **riparensibus** castricianis ceterisque cuiquam eorum transferendi militem copiam attributam, nisi hoc augusta maiestas publicae utilitatis gratia fieri iusserit: quia honoris augmentum non ambitione, sed labore ad unumquemque convenit devenire.*

273 I am currently working on a book more narrowly focused on the frontier soldiers in the southeast, which will, in part, address this question.

LIMITANEI IN THE AGE OF JUSTINIAN 181

TABLE 5.3 Garrisons/guards (φρούριον or φρουρός) in Procopius' *Buildings*

Number	Location	Usage
1.	2.1.20	The Guards
2.	2.3.28	The fortresses
3.	2.4.14	All the other forts
4.	2.4.18	Building[a] a fort
5.	2.4.19	The fort is named
6.	2.4.19	Forts around Amida
7.	2.4.22	Fort Baras
8.	2.4.22	Inside the fort
9.	2.4.23	Of the fortification
10.	2.4.24	Not only is the fortress place
11.	2.5.9	For they call forts *castella* in the Latin tongue.
12.	2.6.1	A fortress of Romans
13.	2.6.4	Diocletian constructed this fortress
14.	2.6.5	A protection [the water] for this fort
15.	2.6.7	Unwalled side of the fortress
16.	2.6.11	Restored it to the guards there
17.	2.6.12	Is an ancient fort
18.	2.6.13	Those forts which lie about the city
19.	2.6.16	A most noteworthy garrison
20.	2.7.13	A certain part of the enclosing-wall of Edessa contains a fort
21.	2.7.18	The fortress at Batnae
22.	2.8.5	Have built forts carelessly of unbaked brick
23.	2.8.7	Had built three forts
24.	2.8.8	From this fort on the road
25.	2.9.8	A garrison of soldiers
26.	2.9.10	All the towns and forts
27.	2.9.10	Considering the fortresses altogether
28.	2.9.19	He established a throng of guards
29.	2.11.4	And great number of guards
30.	2.11.9	The other towns and forts of the Syrians
31.	3.2.1	In a fortress which they call Citharizon
32.	3.3.3	Fortress of Citharizon

a It should come as little surprise and that most references involve Justinian building a fort or forts of some sort or other.

TABLE 5.3 Garrisons/guards (φρούριον or φρουρός) in Procopius' *Buildings* (*cont.*)

Number	Location	Usage
33.	3.3.6	Garrison of soldiers
34.	3.3.7	Established a fortress
35.	3.3.8	A garrison of soldiers
36.	3.3.14	Impregnable fortress
37.	3.4.5	Fortress not far from Satala
38.	3.4.6	A certain fortress
39.	3.4.10	He constructed forts
40.	3.4.11	He built a new fortress
41.	3.5.2	He built … a fort
42.	3.5.4	On which stood the fortress of Theodosius
43.	3.5.11	Fashioning each tower as a fortress
44.	3.6.13	He built forts in all parts of the land
45.	3.6.13	And established garrisons of Roman soldiers
46.	3.6.14	He built these forts
47.	3.6.16	A very strong fortress
48.	3.6.20	He built a new fortress
49.	3.6.22	There is a fort named Sisilisson
50.	3.6.24	Built a fort there
51.	3.6.25	This fort there
52.	3.6.26	He made two forts
53.	3.7.5	Built a fortress called Losorium
54.	3.7.8	Two fortresses
55.	3.7.8	And seize these fortresses
56.	3.7.11	He made fortresses there
57.	3.7.16	No city or fortress
58.	4.1.17	Close to the fortress
59.	4.1.28	Rebuilt the entire fortress
60.	4.1.35	Either been converted into a stronghold
61.	4.1.38	He built forts
62.	4.2.4	And in the fortress
63.	4.2.12	He constructed many forts
64.	4.2.13	In the fortresses
65.	4.2.14	Around 2,000 soldiers as guards
66.	4.2.28	He built forts there and established garrisons
67.	4.3.13	Applied to a fort in the mountains

LIMITANEI IN THE AGE OF JUSTINIAN 183

TABLE 5.3 Garrisons/guards (φρούριον or φρουρός) in Procopius' *Buildings* (*cont.*)

Number	Location	Usage
68.	4.3.14	The fortress of Eurymene
69.	4.3.15	Many other forts
70.	4.3.29	Having neither fortress nor any other defence
71.	4.3.30	Built a new fort
72.	4.4.1	We were making this catalogue of forts
73.	4.4.3	The following new forts were built
74.	4.4.3	The following new forts
75.	4.4.3	Fort of Come
76.	4.4.3	Two forts of St. Donatus
77.	4.4.3	These forts were restored
78.	4.5.2	He built towns and fortresses
79.	4.5.16	Another new fortress of exceptional strength
80.	4.6.4	Transformed into a great fortress
81.	4.6.5	The forts of
82.	4.6.5	A number of other forts
83.	4.6.8	There is a fort
84.	4.6.15	He built two forts
85.	4.6.17	Both these forts
86.	4.6.20	The fortress called Dorticum
87.	4.6.21	He made it a most splendid fortress
88.	4.6.25	More complete fortress
89.	4.6.27	A very strong fortress
90.	4.6.28	A fortress which had not existed
91.	4.6.33	An ancient fort
92.	4.6.34	This fort of Hunnon
93.	4.6.35	He built a fort
94.	4.6.36	He built a fort
95.	4.6.36	Into a notable fortress
96.	4.6.37	Garrisons of soldiers
97.	4.7.4	Built the fortress
98.	4.7.6	He preserved the fortress
99.	4.7.7	Built the fort
100.	4.7.7	The emperor of the Romans built a fort
101.	4.7.13	A new fort named Adina
102.	4.7.14	Built the fortress of Tilieion

TABLE 5.3 Garrisons/guards (φρούριον or φρουρός) in Procopius' *Buildings* (cont.)

Number	Location	Usage
103.	4.7.16	The first fortress named for St. Cyrillus
104.	4.7.20	He built a new fortress
105.	4.7.20	Lies another fortress
106.	4.8.4	There is a fortress
107.	4.8.20	Built a fortress
108.	4.8.22	By the guards there
109.	4.9.8	All the guards
110.	4.9.9	For the sake of the guards
111.	4.9.11	The guards there
112.	4.9.11	Safety for its guards
113.	4.10.8	Was neither fort nor any other stronghold
114.	4.10.9	Frightening off the guards
115.	4.10.25	An altogether inaccessible fortress
116.	4.10.27	Built a fortress
117.	4.10.28	He founded the fortress
118.	4.11.16	So as to be a strong fort
119.	4.11.20	He established countless fortresses
120.	4.11.20	These fortresses
121.	5.1.2	All the fortifications of cities and the fortresses
122.	5.4.15	A certain fortress
123.	5.4.16	An ancient fortress
124.	5.7.8	A garrison of soldiers
125.	5.7.12	The guards there
126.	5.8.9	A very strong fortress
127.	6.5.11	Made it an impregnable fortress
128.	6.5.15	A fortress which they call Tucca
129.	6.6.6	A garrison of soldiers
130.	6.6.18	He constructed a fort
131.	6.6.18	Garrisons of soldiers
132.	6.7.8	Two forts
133.	6.7.11	Two forts
134.	6.7.14	A fortress on the Libyan shore
135.	6.7.16	Making this fortress impregnable

LIMITANEI IN THE AGE OF JUSTINIAN 185

TABLE 5.4   Garrisons (φυλακή or φυλακτήριον) in Procopius' *Secret History and Buildings*

Number	Location	Usage
1.	1.3.9	Invincible fortifications
2.	2.6.9	Sufficient protection[a]
3.	2.8.11	Sufficient garrison
4.	2.11.12	A garrison of soldiers
5.	3.6.23	He established a sufficient garrison of Roman soldiers
6.	4.1.6	Untold garrisons of soldiers
7.	4.1.33	Garrisons of soldiers everywhere
8.	4.2.14	The garrisons maintained in the fortresses
9.	4.2.28	He established garrisons
10.	4.5.1	Garrisons of soldiers
11.	4.10.8	No further protection
12.	5.4.13	Neither could the garrison
13.	5.4.13	Keep guard
14.	5.4.14	A sufficient garrison
15.	5.8.9	A garrison of soldiers
16.	6.2.2	He established two garrisons
17.	6.2.20	Would be a protection
18.	6.7.1	Garrison of soldiers
19.	6.7.8	A garrison of soldiers
20.	6.7.15	By means of a garrison
21.	6.7.17	Garrisons of soldiers

a   Occasionally, as here, Procopius uses the adjectival form, φυλακτήριος, which means something like "protection" rather than "fortress", "garrison", etc.

CHAPTER 6

Recruitment

1   Introduction

In this last chapter we return to the soldiers as a collective, and in particular how the empire went about collecting them, a process Procopius touches on at several points in his oeuvre. The issue of army recruitment in Late Antiquity continues to be an object of debate, with some scholars arguing for a dearth of recruits on the basis of imperial legislation (along with many references to deserters), while others view the opposite on the basis of that same evidence.[1] I argued before that there is less room for movement in the debate on recruitment unless new evidence is brought to light. In this chapter and to that end, I will test whether we can squeeze any additional insight from Procopius' works. To do so, I will examine the mechanics of recruitment in general amongst all classes of soldier, *comitatenses*, *foederati*, and *limitanei*, but also *bucellarii*. Then I turn to some of the demographic challenges borne out by consideration of recruitment, both respect to Procopius and the plague, but also with regard to the corruption that afflicted the military in the sixth century. Ultimately,

---

1   There has been quite a lot of discussion of recruitment problems in the sixth century in the wake of the wars of Justinian, not to mention the devastating impact of the plague, though some have minimised its impact (Teall 1965; Fotiou 1988; Liebeschuetz 1993. Contra, Whitby (1995: 100–103)). As contentious is the issue is 'barbarisation', with one modern camp seeing the empire and its armed forces as becoming increasingly barbarised, this then forming a key factor in the 'fall of Rome' (Ferrill 1986; Liebeschuetz 1990). However, even here there is recognition that the Roman military had long contained a mixture of 'Roman' and 'non-Roman' soldiers ever since the days of the Republic when Rome's Italian allies frequently served alongside the Romans, and long before they gained citizenship in the aftermath of the Social War (*ca.* 89 BCE). Other scholars have by contrast contended that the impact of 'barbarisation' was negligible, or rather that its impact was not deleterious (Whitby 1995, 2004; Elton 1996; Nicasie 1998). Nevertheless, our primary sources do imply that significant numbers of barbarians enlisted were employed in various guises in Late Antiquity and at all levels (Carrié 1995, 2002, 2004; Goffart 2006; Parnell 2010: 56–107). As regards the derivations of these barbarian recruits, the state often sought out people whom it perceived as possessing identifiable martial valour, particularly those from the Balkans and central and southern Asia Minor (Lee 2007b: 83–84; Lee 2011: 156–157). Indeed, Parnell suggests that many of the stereotypes associated with barbarians, especially in instances of combat, might to some degree be based upon the established martial valour of the barbarian combatants active in the imperial rank and file (Parnell 2010: 186–187. See now Parnell 2012, 2015). For additional bibliography, see Whately (2013a: 227–228).

I will argue that it is in the category of recruitment that Procopius is most useful as a source for sixth-century rank and file soldiers, so long as his comments are used in conjunction with our other evidence.

2 Procopius on Recruitment

2.1 The Mechanics of Recruitment

Procopius talks about recruitment in two of his three works, the *Wars* and the *Secret History*, but the references are scattered and, on the surface, disjointed. If we look closely, however, we can collate those references to build a well-rounded image of the mechanics of recruitment, particularly when used along with the material from our other varied pieces of evidence. With this in mind, this section offers a reconstruction of the mechanics of recruitment that starts at the top, at the level of the emperor, and works its way to the bottom, at the level of the low-ranking soldier.

The responsibility for procuring troops for whatever purpose fell to the commander-in-chief, depending on the context, with the emperor the final word on the decision-making. That we have two major campaigns in faraway lands, Africa and Italy, makes this a bit easier. The opening books of the *Vandal War* include detailed arguments both for and against going to war; they also include an outline of the numbers involved in the Roman contingent.[2] Procopius crafts his story in such a way that the ultimate dispatch of Roman troops was due to Justinian's receipt of a letter from Goda, who was in charge of Sardinia, and who had asked the emperor for help, including soldiers.[3] Immediately thereafter, Procopius says Justinian resolved to send troops to help overthrow Gelimer and the Vandals—though admittedly, he had already determined to do just this.[4] The *Gothic War* included a couple of instances in which a commander, here Belisarius, wrote the emperor Justinian asking for more men. In one later case, the letter was a report setting out the Romans' progress (or lack thereof).[5] This letter might have resembled the sort of report discussed in chapter one above and referred to in the *Codex Justinianus*, the quarterly report. Only, in this case, it was specific to this wartime context. The most famous example of one of these from the *Wars* was the one that came earlier, and which might have been composed by Procopius himself.

---

2 Procop. *Wars* 3.11.1–18.
3 Procop. *Wars* 3.10.29–31.
4 Procop. *Wars* 3.10.32.
5 Procop. *Wars* 7.13.21.

> For though we did travel most diligently through Thrace and Illyria, the soldiers we gathered are a small and pitiful band, without a single weapon in their hands, and altogether unpractised in fighting ... It is therefore imperative that my spearmen and guardsmen [*doryphoroi*] should be sent to me and, beside them, a large force of Huns and other barbarians is needed, to whom money must be given immediately.[6]

Sending letters, which seems to have been the usual means of procuring troops from the emperor, did not always work. As a result, commanders might turn to the sixth-century equivalent of lobbyists, individuals who might petition the emperor, or the emperor's close confidants, in person in the hopes of securing more men. Such a role was filled by Antonina during Belisarius' second sojourn to Italy.[7] Throughout the *Wars*, Antonina regularly plays a significant role in managing the supplies and manpower in the expeditionary armies, both in Africa and in Italy.[8] That being said, in this particular instance, Belisarius' campaign was starting to unravel and Antonina's trip to the capital to meet with the empress might have had more to do with these challenging circumstances.

Lobbyists were not always necessary, however. When Narses set out from Salona against Totila and the Goths in book eight, Justinian gave him sufficient money, apparently, to collect soldiers on his own, without the requisite imperial permission needed once the troops had been selected.[9] This implies that, once given imperial permission, a general would be given the funds needed to get the soldiers himself. Narses had significant financial support, and with that money he did what others in the *Wars* had done, visit perspective regions to find recruits:

> He not only took with him many Roman soldiers from Byzantium, but he also collected many from the lands of Thrace and Illyria. John accompanied him too with his own army and that left by his father-in-law Germanus. Moreover, Audoin, the ruler of the Lombards, was won over by the emperor Justinian and by much money, and, in accordance with the treaty of alliance, selected 2,500 of his men who were capable warriors and sent them to fight with the Romans; and they were attended by

---

6   Procop. *Wars* 7.12.4, 10. Θρᾷκας μὲν γὰρ καὶ Ἰλλυριοὺς ἐνδελεχέστατα περιελθόντες στρατιώτας ξυνήγομεν κομιδῇ ὀλίγους οἰκτροὺς οὐδέ τι ὅπλων ἐν χερσὶν ἔχοντας καὶ μάχης ὄντας παντάπασιν ἀμελετήτους ... δορυφόρους τοίνυν καὶ ὑπασπιστὰς τοὺς ἐμοὺς μάλιστά μοι πάντων σταλῆναι προσήκει, ἔπειτα πάμπολύ τι πλῆθος Οὔννων τε καὶ ἄλλων βαρβάρων, οἷς καὶ χρήματα ἤδη δοτέον.
7   Procop. *Wars* 7.30.3.
8   Africa: Procop. *Wars* 3.12.2; 3.13.24; 3.19.11; 3.20.1. Italy: Procop. *Wars* 5.18.43; 6.4.6; 6.4.20; 6.7.4.
9   Procop. *Wars* 8.26.5–6.

more than 3,000 fighting men as servants. He also had with him more than 3,000 of the Herul nation, all horsemen, commanded by Filimuth and others, besides great numbers of Huns. Dagisthaeus too was there with his followers, having been released from prison for this purpose; also Kavadh with many Persian deserters.[10]

That said, it was not always clear whether commanders like Belisarius and Narses were gathering individuals from those regions to serve in far-flung campaigns, or units based in those regions to take along. The general Germanus, dispatched to Italy to fight the Goths, assembled an army seemingly comprising both men and units. He gathered guardsmen (*bucellarii*) who served other commanders, some of whom came from Constantinople, some from Thrace and Illyria.[11] Germanus also took some from the cavalry registers in Thrace.[12] Not all of those who volunteered were Romans, however, for Procopius tells us that quite a lot of barbarians from all over the Roman world enlisted, including the Lombards.[13] Sometimes these men would become soldiers in the *foederati*,[14] though more on this later.

As noted, when troops were needed in the field, it was up to the commander-in-chief to write to the emperor to request reinforcements.[15] In the darkest days of his second sojourn to Italy, Belisarius wrote Justinian asking for reinforcements. Here, I pick up the passage referred to a couple of pages earlier:

> We have arrived in Italy, most mighty emperor, without men, horses, arms, or money, and no man, I think, would ever be able to carry on a war without a plentiful supply of these things. For though we did travel most diligently through Thrace and Illyria, the soldiers we gathered are a small

---

10 Procop. *Wars* 8.26.10–13. ἔκ τε γὰρ Βυζαντίου ἐπηγάγετο Ῥωμαίων στρατιωτῶν μέγα τι χρῆμα κἀκ τῶν ἐπὶ Θρᾴκης χωρίων ἔκ τε Ἰλλυριῶν πολλοὺς ἤθροισε. καὶ Ἰωάννης δὲ ξύν τε τῷ οἰκείῳ στρατεύματι καὶ τῷ πρὸς Γερμανοῦ τοῦ κηδεστοῦ ἀπολελειμμένῳ ξὺν αὐτῷ ᾔει. καὶ Αὐδουΐν, ὁ Λαγγοβαρδῶν ἡγούμενος, χρήμασι πολλοῖς ἀναπεισθεὶς Ἰουστινιανῷ βασιλεῖ καὶ τῇ τῆς ὁμαιχμίας ξυνθήκῃ, πεντακοσίους τε καὶ δισχιλίους τῶν οἱ ἑπομένων ἀπολεξάμενος ἄνδρας ἀγαθοὺς τὰ πολέμια ἐς ξυμμαχίαν αὐτῷ ἔπεμψεν, οἷς δὴ καὶ θεραπεία εἵπετο μαχίμων ἀνδρῶν πλέον ἢ τρισχιλίων. εἵποντο δὲ αὐτῷ καὶ τοῦ Ἐρούλων ἔθνους πλέον ἢ τρισχίλιοι, ἱππεῖς ἅπαντες, ὧν ἄλλοι τε καὶ Φιλημοὺθ ἦρχον, καὶ Οὖννοί τε παμπληθεῖς καὶ Δαγισθαῖος ξὺν τοῖς ἑπομένοις ἐκ τοῦ δεσμωτηρίου διὰ τοῦτο ἀπαλλαγείς, καὶ Καβάδης, Πέρσας ἔχων αὐτομόλους πολλούς.

11 Procop. *Wars* 7.39.17.
12 Procop. *Wars* 7.39.18.
13 Procop. *Wars* 7.39.20.
14 Procop. *Wars* 7.33.13.
15 For some, like Koehn (Koehn 2018: 96), these requests were invariably for *foederati*, although I am not wholly convinced.

> and pitiful band ... Meanwhile, we see that the men who were left in Italy are both insufficient in number and in abject terror of the enemy, their spirit humbled by the many defeats they have suffered at their hands. These are not men who happened to escape by chance from their enemies, but they abandoned their horses and flung their weapons to the ground ... if you want to overcome your foes in the war, it is necessary to make other provisions too. For I think that no man can be a general without men to support him. It is therefore imperative that my spearmen and shield bearers should be sent to me and, beside them, a large force of Huns and other barbarians is needed, to whom money must be given immediately.[16]

Assuming the requested troops arrived and they did not arrive in pre-existing units, they would move on to the next stage in the process.

Once they had been enrolled on the military registers, soldiers would receive official, written, documentation from the emperor which demonstrated this. Procopius uses the generic term γράμματα, a piece of writing.[17] It is hard to know which document Procopius had in mind here, but it is most likely to have been the *probatoriae*, which were the enlistment papers found in assorted pieces of legislation and a papyrus from Egypt.[18] We are fortunate to have a complete one, which dates to a few decades after Justinian's reign (May 6, 578 CE). In full, the document reads:

> The Board of Leading Men of the Regiment of the soldiers of the fortress of Elephantine [τοῦ ἀριθμοῦ [τ]ῶν στρατιωτῶν τοῦ φρουρίου Ἐλεφαντίνης], through those found to have signed below, to Fl. Patermouthis son of Dios, new recruit of the same (regiment) of our (fortress of) Elephantine, greetings. We have received your recruitment certificate together with (those) of the other persons (which), by the authority of your master, Fl.

---

16 Procop. *Wars* 7.12.3–5, 9–10. Ἀφίγμεθα εἰς τὴν Ἰταλίαν, ὦ βασιλεῦ κράτιστε, ἀνδρῶν τε καὶ ἵππων καὶ ὅπλων καὶ χρημάτων χωρίς. ὧν οὐδ ἄν τις μὴ διαρκῶς ἔχων πόλεμον, οἶμαι, διενεγκεῖν οὐ μή ποτε ἱκανὸς εἴη. Θρᾷκας μὲν γὰρ καὶ Ἰλλυριοὺς ἐνδελεχέστατα περιελθόντες στρατιώτας ξυνήγομεν κομιδῇ ὀλίγους οἰκτροὺς οὐδέ τι ὅπλων ἐν χερσὶν ἔχοντας καὶ μάχης ὄντας παντάπασιν ἀμελετήτους. ὁρῶμεν δὲ καὶ τοὺς ἀπολελειμμένους [p. 250] ἐνταῦθα οὔτε αὐτάρκεις ὄντας καὶ κατεπτηχότας τοὺς πολεμίους δεδουλωμένους τε τὸ φρόνημα τῷ πρὸς ἐκείνων πολλάκις ἡσσῆσθαι, οἵ γε οὐδὲ εἰκῇ τοὺς ἐναντίους διέφυγον, ἀλλὰ τούς τε ἵππους ἀφέντες καὶ τὰ ὅπλα ἐς τὴν γῆν ῥίψαντες ... εἰ δὲ περιεῖναι βούλει τῷ πολέμῳ τῶν δυσμενῶν, καὶ τὰ ἄλλα ἐξαρτύεσθαι δεῖ. στρατηγὸς γάρ τις, οἶμαι, τῶν ὑπουργούντων χωρὶς οὐκ ἂν γένοιτο. δορυφόρους τοίνυν καὶ ὑπασπιστὰς τοὺς ἐμοὺς μάλιστά μοι πάντων σταλῆναι προσήκει, ἔπειτα πάμπολύ τι πλῆθος Οὔννων τε καὶ ἄλλων βαρβάρων, οἷς καὶ χρήματα ἤδη δοτέον.

17 Procop. *SH*. 24.7.

18 *Cod. Iust.* 1.31.5pr, 12.17, 12.35.17; P. Muench 1.2.

Marianios Michaelios Gabrielios Ioannes Theodoros Georgios Marcellos Julianos Theodoros Julianos, the most excellent Commander and all-praiseworthy Prefect of the Justinians, with (the grace of) God *dux* and *Augustalis* of the Thebaid, orders us to enter your name onto our roster from the calends of January of the most present twelfth indiction in the thirteenth year of the reign of our most divine and most pious master Fl. Justinus the eternal Augustus, Emperor, and greatest benefactor, (space) and in the fourth year of Fl. Tiberius Minor Constantine, the most benevolent and most fortunate thrice-great benefactor Caesar, in the tenth year after the second consulship of sour s[a]me most serene maste[r]. And we, fearing the highly regarded (authority) of our honorable Eminence, are ready to fulfill all orders (given) to us, and for your assurance we have made for you this notification, a written receipt of the recruitment certificate of your military service, being valid and warranted as aforementioned. We, the Fl(avians) Dios son of Paminios, with (the grace) of God a *primic(erius)* and Georgios son of Dios and Pelagios son of Pasmes and Ioannes son of Sarapamon and Makarios son of Isakos and Paon son of Theophanos and Dios son of Pa[o]uos and Dios son of Serenos, *ordinarii*, and the rest of the *priores* of the regiment of Elephantine, the aforementioned, we have had drawn up for you this written acceptance of the recruitment certificate of your military service. Everything written in it is satisfactory to us as aforementioned. I, Fl. Makarios son of Isakos, *ordinarius* of the same regiment, having been invited and instructed, wrote on their behalf since they are not literate. Farewell. Written by me, Fl. Makarios son of Isakos, *ordinarius* and *adiutor* of the same regiment. Farewell. VERSO (2nd hand) Acceptance of the recruitment certific(ate) of military servi(ce) of Patermouthis son of Dios, recruit of the regiment of Elephanti(ne).[19]

---

19 P. Muench 1.2 = D31, trans. Porten. ὁ κοινὸς τῶν πρωτευόντων τοῦ ἀριθμοῦ [τ]ῶν στρατιωτῶν τοῦ φρουρίου Ἐλεφαντίνης διὰ τῶν ἑξῆς ὑ(*)πογράφειν εὑρισκομένων vac. ? Φλ(αυίῳ) Πατερμουθίῳ υἱ(*)ῷ Δίου νεοστράτῳ(*) τείρονι τοῦ αὐτοῦ ἡμετέρου Ἐλεφαντίνης χαίρειν. vac. ? ἐδεξάμεθα τὴν σὴν προβατορίαν μεθ᾽ ἑτέ[ρ]ων ὀνομάτων ἐπὶ τῆς ἐξουσίας τοῦ κυρίου ἡμῶν Φλ(αυίου) Μαριανοῦ Μιχαηλίου Γαβριηλίου Ἰ(*)ωάννου Θεοδώρου Γεωργίου Μαρκέλλου Ἰ(*)ουλιανοῦ Θεοδώρου Ἰ(*)ουλιανοῦ τοῦ τὰ πάντα ὑ(*)περφυεστάτου στρατηλάτου καὶ πανευφήμου πραιφέκτου Ἰ(*)ουστινιανῶν σὺν θ(ε)ῷ δουκὸς καὶ ἀγουσταλί[ο]υ τῆς Θηβαίων χώρας τὴν παρακελευομένην ἡμας(*) καταγαῆναι τὴν σὴν προσηγορίαν εἰς τὴν ἡμετέραν μάτρικα ἀπὸ καλανδῶν Ἰ(*)ανουαρίου τῆς παρούσης δωδεκάτης ἐπινε[μ]ήσεως βασιλείας τοῦ θειοτάτου καὶ εὐσεβεστάτου ἡμῶν δεσπότου Φλ(αυίου) Ἰ(*)ουστίνου τοῦ αἰωνίου Αὐγ[ούσ]του Αὐτοκράτορος καὶ μεγίστου εὐεργέτου vac. ? ἔτους τρισκαιδεκάτου(*) καὶ Φλ(αυίου) Τιβερίου Νέου Κωσταντίνου τοῦ φιλανθρωποτάτου καὶ εὐτυχεστάτου τρισμεγίστου εὐεργέτου Καίσαρος ἔτους τετάρτου τοῖς μετὰ τὴν δευτέραν ὑ(*)πατείαν τοῦ α[ὐ]τοῦ γαλληνοτάτου(*) ἡμῶν δεσπότο[υ] ἔτους δεκάτου. καὶ ἡμεῖς ἔχοντες τὸν φόβον τῆς ἀκαταφρονήτου τῆς ὑ(*)μετέρας ἐνδόξου

As Keenan noted, this papyrus is full of important information.[20] For one, several officials are responsible for signing off on Flavius Patermouthis' enlistment, including an *adiutor*, a *primicerius*, and a few *ordinarii*. We also know that the soldier and unit are both on the frontier and that this document is dealing with a unit of *limitanei*, frontier soldiers, in part based on the author's terminology for unit or regiment, *arithmos*. As we saw in chapter three, *arithmos* is the standard term for unit or regiment in the sixth century CE, and several papyri use it. The highest-ranking commander of this document is the duke of the Thebaid, a commander of *limitanei* listed in the *Notitia Dignitatum*.[21]

The *probatoriae* appear in the legal evidence from Justinian's reign. In the *Codex*, at 12.17, a law dated to 472 CE discusses *probatoriae*. According to this law, decisions on recruitment were ultimately the responsibility of the emperor with no clear distinction drawn between types of soldiers. It reads:

> No one hereafter is to be enrolled in any unit of cavalry or infantry, or on any frontier, without an imperial certificate of appointment from Our Divine Majesty. The custom heretofore in force, which gave the Master of Soldiers and the Dukes the right to issue military certificates of appointment [*probatorias*] or to enlist anyone in the army, is obsolete, so that only persons who have obtained certificates of appointment from Our Divinity may serve in the field units or on the frontiers. It is for the currently serving Most Eminent Masters of Soldiers and the *viri spectabiles* Dukes, if they think it necessary to replenish units or account of losses sustained through fatalities to declare in their recommendations to Our Clemency, after investigating the facts, which soldiers ought to be enlisted and how many and in what unit or on what frontier, so that only those who are endorsed by the imperial signature in the manner resolved upon by Our Majesty shall join the military.[22]

ὑ(*)περοχῆς ἕτοιμοί ἐσμεν πᾶσι τοῖς προστεταγμένοις ἡμ[ῖ]ν τὸ ἱ(*)κανὸν ποιεῖν καὶ εἰς σὴν(*) ἀμερ[ι]μνίαν ταύτην σοι πεποιήμεθα τὴν δηλωτικὴν ἔγγραφον ἀπόδειξιν τῆς προβατορίας τῆς σῆς στρατίας κυρίαν οὖσαν καὶ βεβαίαν ὡς πρόκ(ειται). Φλ(αύιοι) Δῖος Παμινίου σὺν θ(ε)ῷ πριμικ(ήριος) καὶ Γεώργιος Δίου καὶ Πελάγιος Πασμῆτος καὶ Ἰ(*)ωάννης Σαραπάμωνος καὶ Μακάριος Ἰ(*)σακίου καὶ Πάων Θεοφάνου καὶ Δῖος Πα[ο]υῶτος(*) καὶ Δῖος Σερήνου ὀρδινάριοι καὶ οἱ λοιποὶ πρίορες ἀριθμοῦ Ἐλεφαντίνης οἱ προκ(είμενοι) ἐθέμεθα σοὶ ταύτην τὴν ἔγγραφον ἀποχὴν τῆς προβατορίας τῆς σῆς στρατίας(*) καὶ στοιχεῖ ἡμῖν πάντα τὰ ἐν αὐτῇ γεγραμμένα ὡς πρόκ(ειται). Φλ(αύιος) Μακάριος Ἰ(*)σακίου ὀρδινάρ(ιος) τοῦ αὐτοῦ ἀριθμοῦ παρακληθεὶς καὶ ἐπιτραπεὶς ἔγραψα ὑ(*)πὲρ αὐτῶν γράμματα μὴ εἰδότων. δι' ἐμοῦ Φλ(αυίου) Μακαρίου Ἰ(*) σακίου ὀρδιναρ(ίου) καὶ ἀδιούτορ(ος) τοῦ αὐτοῦ ἀριθμοῦ ἐγράφη.

20 Keenan 1990: 142.
21 *Not. Dign. or.* 31.
22 *Cod. Iust.* 12.35.17, trans. Pazdernik. *Neminem in ullo numero equitum vel peditum vel in quolibet limite sine nostri numinis sacra probatoria in posterum sociari concedimus,*

This law describes how the *probatoria* from Egypt came into being, and makes it clear that frontier soldiers were subject to a set of standard procedures in the recruitment process. This is not the only legislation of relevance, however, for one of the first laws to appear in the *Codex Justinianus* touches not only on training (more on this below), but on recruitment. It stipulates that the dukes are to be kept on the frontier where they are to recruit new soldiers, albeit under the supervision of the Masters of Soldiers.[23] In fact, although the law seems to be a revision of the previous policy, that it specifies that recruitment had previously been the ultimate responsibility of either dukes or masters of soldiers implies that all different types of soldiers were meant. Plus, it does not absolve those officers of any role in the matter; rather, masters and dukes were to send reports to the emperors that noted any losses through death. Then, the emperor—or I imagine someone he might appoint—would carry out an investigation to determine whether a request for new troops was legitimate or not.

The investigative part of the recruitment process is touched on in some other pieces of legislation. One is a law on quarterly reports, both civil and military, although it does not specify what their content might be.[24] Another, on the office of the Master of Offices, specifically refers to a *probatoria*, an imperial certificate, in the context of recruitment for the imperial guard.[25] That said, the Master of Offices is given responsibility for *limitanei* in another law dated to 443, a measure reiterated a few decades later in 470 CE.[26] The record of the imperial guard, a higher-ranking class of soldier, was to be kept up-to-date, and was stored by the Sacred Bureau of the Register.[27] The process was similar for *limitanei* and other soldiers, like *comitatenses*, as we have seen.

---

    consuetudine quae hactenus tenuit antiquata, quae magisteriae potestati vel ducibus probatorias militum facere vel militibus adiungere licentiam tribuebat, ut ii tantum in numeris vel in limitibus militent, qui a nostra divinitate probatorias consequuntur. Viros autem eminentissimos pro tempore magistros militum nec non etiam viros spectabiles duces, si supplere numeros pro his qui fatalibus sortibus decrescent necessarium esse putaverint, veritate discussa per suggestionem suam nostrae mansuetudini declarare, qui et quanti et in quo numero vel limite debeant subrogari, ut ita demum, prout nostrae sederit maiestati, divina subnotatione subnixi militiam sortiantur; officio, quod tuae sublimitatis actibus obsecundat, centum librarum auri dispendio feriendo, si ex aliqua parte, quae statuit nostra serenitas, fuerint violata.

23   Cod. Iust. 1.46.4.pr.
24   Cod. Iust. 1.42.1.
25   Cod. Iust. 1.31.5.pr.
26   Cod. Iust. 1.46.4.pr, 12.59.8.
27   Cod. Iust. 1.31.5.2.

2.2 *Volunteers and Conscripts*

What Procopius does not do is stipulate whether those troops the commanders managed to find were volunteers or conscripts, excluding cases like the Persians or Vandals, defeated foes forced to fight for Rome.[28] Perhaps the only clue he provides about this comes, like much else, from the *Gothic War*, when the Illyrian troops flee the Italian theatre for home when they learn of threats to their families and homes.[29] While this anecdote is not conclusive, that these men seem to have been free, to some degree, to leave as they wished, hints at their service having been voluntary, and perhaps this was not an example of desertion even if Procopius' description is vague. Ordinarily their actions would not have gone unpunished. Some legislation does threaten punishment if soldiers desert the field, though we lack concrete examples of this on the ground.[30] In the case of these Illyrian soldiers, they only seem to have escaped punishment when the emperor learned of their motives: to save their families who had fallen victim to Hunnic raids.[31]

When Belisarius went round Thrace in advance of his second trip to Italy, Procopius specifies that he was in search of recruits, but Procopius does not specify if he was looking for volunteers.[32] The *Secret History*, however, does provide one concrete example of the use of volunteers in the military. At 6.2–3, Procopius says:

> When Leon was holding the imperial power in Byzantium, three young farmers, Illyrians by race, Zimarchus, Dityvistus and Justinus from Vederiana, men who at home had to struggle incessantly against conditions of poverty and all its attendant ills, in an effort to better their condition set out to join the army. And they came to Byzantium, walking on foot and themselves carrying cloaks slung over their shoulders, and when they arrived they had in these cloaks nothing more than toasted bread which they had put in at home; and the Emperor enrolled them in the

---

[28] A fundamental issue surrounds the methods of recruitment, with debate focused on the degree to which troops were conscripted, or whether they served as volunteers (Parnell 2017: 25). Conscription was favoured in the fourth and fifth centuries, and although procedures were perhaps already changing in the last quarter of the fourth century, there are good arguments in favour of conscription's continued use into the sixth century (Zuckerman 1998; Carrié 2004; Whitby 1995, 2004).
[29] Procop. *Wars* 7.11.12–18.
[30] Dig. 49.3.16. On combat motivation in the sixth-century military, see Whately (2018).
[31] Procop. *Wars* 7.11.16.
[32] Procop. *Wars* 7.10.1–3.

ranks of the soldiers and designated them for the Palace Guard. For they were all men of very fine figure.³³

These men were, admittedly, special, for the latter of the three went on to become the emperor Justin I. Assuming this story is true—and I have no reason to discount it—it does speak to a certain appeal to military service, even if the men end up serving in the Palace Guard, the *excubitors*.³⁴

Volunteers could be found in the provinces and out in the frontiers too. Keenan noted that we have evidence for a man (Aurelius Paeion) who first appears in a papyrus as a civilian in amongst the papyri from Syene, who shows up in an arbitration document dated to 574.³⁵ In 581, he returns as a soldier and witness in the sale of a boat. In other documents we read about additional members of the family, though there are questions about his status given he kept the appellation Aurelius, which is usually restricted to civilians, rather than Flavius.³⁶ We do not only find locals enlisting and serving in their home region in Egypt, however, for there are scattered cases elsewhere, like further west in the newly conquered north Africa.³⁷

As for finding recruits to put on lists, some recruits were already on different lists, tax lists, from which their names were extracted to be conscripted in the military.³⁸ Evagrius refers to one such instance from a few decades after Procopius, "the army owed great respect to [Gregory], since some he had welcomed with money, others with clothes and food and other things when they were passing through his see after being enrolled from the register."³⁹ All in all, our evidence for conscripts is limited. There is no direct evidence for conscription in Procopius, though we do have some tax registers dated to a year or two before Justinian's accession from Aphrodito in Egypt.⁴⁰ Whether conscript or volunteer, so far as we know, all the recruits were freemen, though it seems

---

33 Λέοντος ἐν Βυζαντίῳ τὴν αὐτοκράτορα ἀρχὴν ἔχοντος, γεωργοὶ νεανίαι τρεῖς, Ἰλλυριοὶ γένος, Ζίμαρχός τε καὶ Διτύβιστος καὶ Ἰουστῖνος ὁ ἐκ Βεδεριάνης, πράγμασιν ἐνδελεχέστατα τοῖς ἀπὸ τῆς πενίας οἴκοι μαχόμενοι τούτων τε ἀπαλλαξείοντες ἐπὶ τὸ στρατεύεσθαι ὥρμησαν. καὶ πεζῇ βαδίζοντες ἐς Βυζάντιον ᾔεσαν, σισύρας ἐπὶ τῶν ὤμων αὐτοὶ φέροντες, ἐν αἷς δὴ ἄλλο οὐδὲν ὅτι μὴ διπύρους ἄρτους οἴκοθεν ἐμβεβλημένοι ἀφίκοντο, ταχθέντας τε ἐν τοῖς στρατιωτικοῖς καταλόγοις βασιλεὺς αὐτοὺς ἐς τοῦ Παλατίου τὴν φυλακὴν ἐπελέξατο. κάλλιστοι γὰρ ἅπαντες τὰ σώματα ἦσαν.
34 Martindale 1980: 648–651. On Justinian under Justin, see Croke (2007).
35 Keenan 1990: 142; P. Muench 1.1.
36 P. Muench 1.4. On the use of the name Flavius by soldiers, see Keenan (1973, 1974).
37 See *Cod. Iust.* 1.27.2.8, for example, and note Pringle's (2001: 67) comments.
38 Whitby 2000: 301, n. 39.
39 Evag. *EH* 6.11, trans. Whitby.
40 Zuckerman 2004.

there were sometimes exceptions, with slaves sometimes recruited to serve in the *scholarii*, at least up until the reign of Justin I.[41]

2.3   Character Traits

From unwillingness to serve I turn to character traits. Procopius does not focus on the proposed traits of soldiers from different regions, even if he does provide a varied impression of the origins, at least in general, of the empire's soldiers.[42] So, there are none of the sorts of comments we find in authors like Vegetius, who talks about what sort of individuals are best for service, namely those from temperate climes and who are from the country, but not those who hold down certain kinds of jobs.[43] These sorts of comments also appear in an important recruitment document from Egypt, dated to 505:

> Flavius Constantinius Theophanes, count, vir illustris, count of the most faithful household troops and of the military administration of the Thebaid frontier to Flavius ... Alias Theodotus the most faithful tribune stationed at Hermopolis. Since I shall be taking steps in accord with the sacred order of our lord Anastasius ... whereby young men of strong physique are to be attached to units to bring them up to strength, this my order hereby instructs Heracleon, son of Constantinus, a native of the city of Hermopolis to serve in the troop at present entrusted to your care; if he is of military family, is neither of senatorial nor of gubernatorial rank and is not ... weak physique and is not enrolled on the census list, see to it that his name is entered on the register of the said unit ...[44]

---

41   Procop. *SH*. 24.18.
42   For an overview of Rome's tendency to recruit soldiers from specific regions, see Whitby (2015: 817–820).
43   Veg. *Mil.* 1.2 (temperate), 1.3 (country), 1.7 (jobs). On the exclusion of certain jobs from the ranks of the military in late antiquity, see Bond (2016: 164–166).
44   P.Ryl 4.609, trans. papyri.info. The Latin reads: [⳨ *Fl(avius) Cons]tantinuṣ theofanes(*) com(es) et ṿịr inl(ustris)(*) com(es) dev(otissimorum) dom(esticorum) et ṛei miḷ(itaris) ṭḥ[e]b(aici) lim(itis) \fl(avio)/.... u ṛte sive Tḥẹodoti v(iro) d(evotissimo) trib(uno) Hermupọḷi deg(enti) [cum] opḍulero(*) sacra iussione domini nostri Anastasii ... [e qua n] ụmeriṣ ṣụpplementi causạ i[u]niorẹs robustis corporibus adsociarentur Heracleon fil(ium) Constantinii 5[ortum e] civitati Ḥermupolitana in vexillatione pṛudentiae tuae pro tempore credita edictio mea ṃiḷiṭarẹ prae[cip]it [eiusq]ụe nomen ṣị ex gene(*) oritur mịlitaṛi et neque curialis nec praesidaḷiṣ(*) eṣt neç invecill[o](*) [c]orpoṛe ṇ[ec] [invalid]ụs nec censibus adscribtos(*) matriculis eiusdem numeri inseri ...

Of course, it is hard to know just what a "good physique" is, how stringent they were in recruiting such men, and whether it applied to all soldiers given this particular notice focuses on the *protectores domestici*. Still, what is mentioned in this document implies that it was a factor at least considered at the official level. It is also not the sort of detail we would expect from Procopius—and, unsurprisingly, we do not find any cases like this.

We do have a bit more information about what happened to recruits, the procedures, after they enlisted, and some of this even comes from the works of Procopius. The bodyguards who served with, and fought alongside, the Roman officers had to swear an oath, perhaps not unlike the earlier *sacramentum*.[45] Upon enlisting, "it was an old custom among all Romans that no one could become a spearman of one of the officers unless he had first taken the most dread oaths and given pledges of his loyalty toward both his own commander and the emperor of the Romans".[46] Once equipped and ready for service, recruits would be distributed to would-be regiments and, in turn, assigned to squads.[47]

Procopius, supplemented by other sixth-century sources, does allow us to build up a fuller image of the mechanics of recruitment than might have been expected, but there are some details still to consider.[48] In the previous chapter, I spent a lot of time going over the nuances of the word *katalogos* and Procopius' use of the term. We have only a few of these *matrices*, but one papyrus, from later in the sixth century CE, notes that the recruit, Flavius Patermouthis, would be placed on a roster after enlistment.[49] These registers, which would include the names of all soldiers in a given unit, would be in the possession of the commanders for a given post or army. In turn, they would use these to keep track of the number of men at their disposal. Fortunately, Procopius does provide us with a reference to one of these documents in action. When describing the war in Vandal Africa, Procopius notes, "when they sailed into Carthage, Germanus counted the soldiers whom they had and, upon looking over the books of the secretaries where the names of all the soldiers were registered, he found that a third of the army was in Carthage and the other cities while all the rest were arrayed with the tyrant against the Romans."[50]

---

45   Veg. *Mil.* 2.5. On the oath, see Hebblewhite (2016).
46   Procop. *Wars* 4.19.6.
47   Maur. *Strat.* 1.4, 1.5.2. Maurice uses the term τάγμα (plural τάγματα) for units, and ἀκία, from the Latin *acies*, for squads (Dennis' translation).
48   Whitby 1995: 74.
49   P. Muench 1.2 = D31.
50   Procop. *Wars* 4.16.3.

2.4 Origins of Recruits

What we have not yet addressed is the geographical origins of these soldiers, a fundamental part of the topic, and one only hinted at so far. Some soldiers were defeated foes. In one famous passage, found in his catalogue of the expeditionary force off to Vandal Africa, he notes that the *foederati* used to be drawn from groups who had formed treaties (*foedera*) with the Romans, but that their ranks were now filled with anyone who so desired.[51] On that note, defeated Roman foes could still be sent off to fight in other fronts, as was the fate of some of the Vandals, who went off and served as the Justinianic Vandals.[52] The Moors too were eager to fight for Rome in the Vandal war; their leading men went so far as to assert they were slaves to the emperor by ancestral tradition.[53] Some men went the other way, for Procopius notes that some Persians had been sent west to fight for Rome.[54] The Persian fighters were first referred to in the *Persian War* in the context of the capture of Sisauranon, when Persian soldiers were dispatched to Constantinople.[55]

We know that quite a lot of soldiers came from the Balkans. When Justinian sent Constantianus to Italy, he went via Illyria to round up some soldiers.[56] Sometime later, Martin and Valerian had a contingent of cavalry composed of Huns, Slavs, and Antai from across the Danube.[57] In fact, if there is a pattern, at least for the war in Italy, it was that generals would pass through the Balkans to collect troops before continuing west. There are several generals in the *Wars* who did just this. For example, on his way to Italy for a second time, Belisarius stopped in Thrace to get soldiers, and managed to get 4,000 volunteers.[58]

While some Balkan soldiers were Thracians and some were Illyrians, some were Goths too. Indeed, some other sixth-century literary sources hint at the role of the Balkans in supplying troops through their use of the ethnonym, Goth, to mean soldier. John of Ephesus, or the version that we have, calls soldiers fighting for Rome Goths.[59] In the course of attacks near Constantinople, Justinian sent John, the count of the Pontic Shore, against them "with a force full of Goths", according to Malalas.[60] Malalas also says that when Belisarius

---

[51] Procop. *Wars* 3.11.3–4. For Koehn (2018), the *foederati* were empire's elite troops. Note his comments (Koehn 2018: 94–96) on their recruitment.
[52] Procop. *Wars* 4.14.17.
[53] Procop. *Wars* 3.25.1. On the Moors in late antiquity, see Modéran (2003).
[54] Procop. *Wars* 7.3.10.
[55] Procop. *Wars* 2.19.23–25.
[56] Procop. *Wars* 5.7.26.
[57] Procop. *Wars* 5.27.1.
[58] Procop. *Wars* 7.10.1–3.
[59] John of Ephesus, *EH* 3.13.
[60] Mal. *Chron.* 18.14, trans. Jeffreys, Jeffreys, Scott et al. ἀποστείλας αὐτὸν μετὰ βοηθείας Γοτθικῆς.

was sent after the rioters during the Nika riot he was sent with a large force of Goths.[61] There are even papyri from Egypt that reveal the presence of Goths in the region in the sixth century.[62] In Syriac, the term Goth was often used as a generic term for a soldier, which is best exemplified by the story of Euphemia and the Goth, which takes place at the very end of the fourth century CE.[63] Pseudo-Joshua the Stylite, for instance, adopts similar practices.[64] The Syriac usage of Goth and the eastern focus of this material implies that, for many in that part of the empire, the sixth-century soldier was a Goth—ostensibly from the Balkans. This can help us understand, at least to some degree, Procopius' penchant for referring to recruitment trips in that part of the empire.[65] But as dominant as the Balkans seem to have been as a source of recruits, they were not the only region. A closer look at a few select passages combined with a careful consideration of the ethnic names Procopius uses allows us to round out our picture of the geography of sixth-century recruitment.

Rome's military was heterogeneous in the sixth century, as it had been for most of its history.[66] To some degree this is reflected in Procopius' works; he uses a dizzying array of different ethnic names when referring to the soldiers of Rome's armies.[67] What is not always is clear is whether he is referring to individuals from a particular region or to the sort of ethnic epithets that the Romans had long used in their armed forces.[68] That said, Greatrex notes that "local or regional identity seems to have flourished in the sixth century".[69] It can be hard to know if Procopius is referring to specific ethnic regiments when he refers to Isaurian or Gothic soldiers, to give but two examples. One of the first scholars to do this was Müller over a century ago. He identified the following barbarian groups in Justinian's armies: Antai, Gepids, Heruls, Huns, Lombards, Moors, Ostrogoths, Saracens, Slavs, and Tzani.[70] Some of these were the *symmachoi* that we touched on in chapter five, while others served in

---

61 Mal. *Chron.* 18.71. μετὰ πλήθους Γοτθικοῦ.
62 PSI 8.953, 8.956; Underwood 2014.
63 Pollard 2000: 158; Sidebottom 2004: 50; Petersen 2014: 101, n. 25.
64 Ps.-Josh Styl. 310–313.
65 Procop. *Wars* 5.7.26, 7.10.1, 7.11.15–16, 7.12.3, 8.26.10.
66 Teall 1965.
67 Kaldellis (2013: 10–17) argues that Procopius constructed his barbarians in such a way as to give voice to criticisms of Justinian and his policies. Cesa (1981, 1982) has taken a much more expansive view of Procopius' take on barbarians, as has Greatrex (2018), more recently.
68 Müller 1912. For Romans and barbarians in the sixth-century military, see Parnell (2017: 33–76). Note too Sarantis (2017a), who focuses on the Balkans in particular.
69 Greatrex 2018: 336.
70 Müller 1912: 111–114.

units of *foederati*. Procopius' provides clues as to their recruitment in the *Wars*, but like much else, they are few and far between. He discusses the recruitment of the Heruls, for instance, when he says that Justinian sent out Narses to recruit some Heruls to fight in Italy. Many of them agreed, and they came from Thrace under their own commanders.[71] He provides similar details about the Lombards: a long, diplomatic exchange involving them, the Romans, and the Gepids led the Lombard king to send 10,000 cavalry to Constantianus.[72] Procopius does not describe how the Antai came to serve with Rome, though he does cover other matters. The same is true for the Tzani.[73] That said, the consensus, for these most barbaric of allies (in Procopius' eyes), is that they entered service with Rome by means of a diplomatic arrangement borne out of military encounters or more peaceful contacts.[74]

But those troops were only part of the story, for there were all those other groups whom Procopius identifies: Armenians, Illyrians, Isaurians, and Thracians. Some of those groups were local, some, by Roman and Procopius' reckoning, were more barbaric. In the description of the Battle of Callinicum, Procopius notes that 2,000 Isaurians participated, which sounds like an ethnic unit, given Isauria (in Asia Minor) was inside the Roman Empire.[75] Procopius also implies that his use of a form of Isaurian was something of a generalization, for, in his eyes, they played a key role in the Roman defeat, "for they were thoroughly inexperienced in this business, as they had recently left off farming and entered into the perils of warfare, which before that time were unknown to them … They were not in fact all Isaurians but the majority were Lycaones."[76] As it happens, several books later, Procopius returns to this very group in his account of the *Lykokranitai* soldiers.[77] These soldiers, from Pisidia, were called wolf skulls—the meaning of *Lykokranitai*—not because of the shapes of their heads, but the shape of a mountain in the region where they were recruited. While this story seems strange—and I should add Procopius does not tell us

---

71   Procop. *Wars* 7.13.21–22.
72   Procop. *Wars* 7.34.1–40. See too Procop. *Wars* 7.39.16–20.
73   Procop. *Wars* 2.19.10. On the Tzani in late antiquity, see Intagliata (2018).
74   This is a big topic. On diplomacy in late antiquity, see, among others, Lee (1993) and Nechaeva (2014). On diplomacy in the Balkans, where many of these peoples originated, see Sarantis (2009, 2016). Some of these groups have themselves been the subject of considerable discussion. On the Saracens, for instance, note the discussions of Shahîd (1995a, 1995b, 2002, 2010) and Fisher (2011, 2015).
75   Procop. *Wars* 1.18.5–7.
76   Procop. *Wars* 1.18.39–40. ἀπειρίᾳ γὰρ τοῦ ἔργου τούτου πολλῇ εἴχοντο, ἐπεὶ ἄρτι τῆς γεωργίας ἀφέμενοι ἐς κίνδυνον πολέμου κατέστησαν, ἀγνῶτα σφίσι τὰ πρότερα ὄντα … οὐ μὴν οὐδὲ Ἴσαυροι ἅπαντες, ἀλλὰ Λυκάονες οἱ πλεῖστοι ἦσαν.
77   Procop. *Wars* 7.27.20.

what kind of soldier they were—we find confirmation in the pages of Malalas and in Justinian's novel on Pisidia (not Lycaonia).[78] Malalas called them "not a small number of infantry", but that does not help us determine what type of soldier they were.[79] They were sent to deal with the Lakhmids, though we do not know what became of them in this excursion.[80] This is the only local group that gets this level of attention in Procopius' works, however, and there is no indication that they formed a particular unit. Interestingly, in the novel on the praetor of Lycaonia, we find the following, relevant, details: "the area is one of strong men ... it is good horse country, and supports numerous men and horses, with a large number of big villages, and of men who are good riders and archers."[81] Although their names and place of origin are similar, the "wolf-heads" seem to have been infantry (as befits their mountain origin), while these other Lycaonians could serve as cavalry. Nevertheless, this valuable detail provides some insight into recruitment practices within individual regions of the empire.

As we saw in chapter three, the sixth-century military continued to have units with individual names, for these occasionally surface in the literary texts, and more regularly in the assorted documentary material, like law codes, papyri, and epigraphy. The number of units with epithets, or which at least appear that way in the sources, is not inconsiderable, even if the evidence is incomplete. It includes the following: the *Daci*, the *Perso-Iustiniani*, and the *Felices Perso-Armenii* in Italy; the *Sexto Dalmatae* in Constantinople; the *Tertio Dalmatae* and the *Vandali Iustiniani* in the east; the *Equites Mauri Scutarii*, the *Macedoni*, the *Numidae Iustiniani*, and the *Scythae Iustiniani* in Egypt; and the *Libyes Iustiniani* in Libya.[82] The nomenclature of a few of those were specific creations from the reign of Justinian. The two units known as the *Perso-Iustiniani* and the *Vandali Iustiniani* were full of soldiers taken from their homelands and dispatched elsewhere to fight for Rome. I touched on these at the start of this section. Three of those, though ostensibly possessing ethnic names, instead seem to be relying on much older epithets, like the *Sexto Dalmatae*, the *Tertio*

---

78   Mal. *Chron.* 18.34; *Iust. Nov.* 24.1; Ravegnani 2005: 190. The Justinianic novel complains about the lawlessness of the region: "bandit-ridden, murderous regions situated on the mountain ridge called the Wolf's Head, known as the homeland of the 'Wolfheads'; and that it is campaigning against this area in a hit-and-run sort of style, instead of in proper military fashion" (trans. Miller).
79   οὐκ ὀλίγην βοήθειαν πεζικήν.
80   See Greatrex (1998: 151–153).
81   *Iust. Nov.* 25.1, trans. Miller.
82   On the appearance of a number of new units during the reign of Justinian, see Koehn (2018: 48–53), who situates their creation to the emperor's wide scale military reforms.

Dalmatae, and the *Macedoni*. The *Tertio Dalmatae* unit dates back to at least the fourth century CE, as does the *Sexto Dalmatae* unit, which was a vexillation under a *magister militum praesentalis*.[83] The *Macedoni* found in the Egyptian papyri were not a unit of Macedonians; rather, their unit was the contemporary vestige of a long-lived legion, the *Legio V Macedonica*, which ultimately dates back to the end of Rome's republican era.[84] The *Equites Mauri Scutarii*, which appear in a papyrus dated to 528 (or so), likely owe that name to an earlier part of their history.[85] They appear both in the *Notitia Dignitatum* and from papyri dated a couple of decades later.[86] That leaves the *Perso-Iustiniani*, the *Felices Perso-Armenii*, the *Numidae Iustiniani*, and the *Scythae Iustiniani* as potential ethnic units that we could liken to some of those groups named by Procopius. The *Numidae Iustiniani* appear in a handful of papyri from Egypt that date to the reign of Justinian.[87] The *Scythae Iustiniani* are also found in Egyptian papyri.[88] Scythian legions appear in the *Notitia*, and this Justinianic Scythian unit might simply have been rebranded during the reign of Justinian.[89]

The *Felices Perso-Armenii* appear only briefly in an Italian document dated to 591, so their origins are hard to pin down, though they should probably be connected to the Persians Belisarius led and whom Procopius mentions.[90] The *Daci*, who also in Italy, appear in one, sole, document from Ravenna dated to the very end of the sixth century CE. Jones argued they were stationed there after the conquest, having previously been stationed in Egypt, and though they do appear in the papyrological record, they also appear in the *Notitia Dignitata* as one of the palatine legions.[91] There remain two further units to discuss: the *Tertio Dalmatae* and the *Libyes Iustiniani*. They too, on the surface, hint at the presence of ethnic troops, but like all the units discussed in the previous

---

83   IGLSyr 21,4 50 (*Tertio*) and Not. Dign. or. 7.27; P. Cair. Masp. 2.67126 (*Sexto*) and Not. Dign. or. 6.37. See too Ravegnani (2005: 189).
84   P. Cair. Masp. 1.67002. On the legion's earlier history, see Whately (2016c: 12–13).
85   P. Cair. Masp. 1.67091—"τοῦ ἀριθμοῦ] τῶν γενναιωτάτων(*) Μ[αύ]ρω[ν". See Jones 1964: 655, 1272, n. 110.
86   Not. Dign. or. 31.23–24; BGU 12.2137, BGU 12.2139.
87   BGU 12 2197, P.Cair.Masp. 1.67056, P.Cair.Masp. 1.67058, P.Cair.Masp. 3.67321, and P.Lond. 5 1663, among others.
88   See P. Cair. Masp. 1.67002, P. Cair. Masp. 1.67009, and P. Cair. Masp. 1.67057, for example.
89   Not. Dign. or. 6.44. See Koehn (2018: 49) comments on Justinian's rebranding of existing units. See too Jones (1964: 660–661).
90   P. Dip. 122. Procop. Wars 7.3.10.
91   P. Ital. 18–19. Jones 1964: 655. See Not. Dign. or. 6.43 and Stud. Pal 20.139. It could be the unit went from the palatine army in about 400 to Egypt by 530, before being transferred to Italy at some point after 540. Procopius' language, as we have seen, is unhelpful, for he does not refer to the movement of any Egyptian units to Italy for the war.

paragraph, their names have a much older history. The *Tertio Dalmate* unit had at the end of the fourth century been part of the field army in the east.[92] In Justinian's fourth edict on the governorship of Phoenice-Libanensis, the unit, already stationed in Phoenice at the time (536), was transferred to the control of the moderator (governor).[93] The lengthy thirteenth edict, on Alexandria and the Egyptian provinces (which includes the Libyan frontier), details the transfers of soldiers from two units, the *Libyes Iustiniani* and the *Paraetonitae Iustiniani*, to the dux of Libya.[94] These units seem to have been frontier soldiers, which could mean that they were enrolled with local men, Libyans, but there is insufficient evidence to support this.

At the end of this brief survey of known units with potential ethnic names, we find that in no case do they provide evidence of ethnic units, with the exception of the Persian and Vandal troops, whom we have already discussed.[95] It is also the case that none of these individual units are named in any of Procopius' works. Procopius' penchant for ethnic epithets would seem to be a literary practice rather than a reflection of the military structures such as we have them.

2.5 Recruitment Gaps

This reconstruction, such as I have provided, is not without its problems. For one thing, these recruitment procedures perhaps should be characterized as special acts for wartime contexts. We have some later evidence that paints a similar picture. A few authors refer to the efforts of the emperor Tiberius II (r. 574–582) to recruit troops. As Tiberius was heading east to deal with the Persians, he collected troops from the west, for John of Ephesus the aforementioned Goths, who left their families behind in Constantinople.[96] Theophylact Simocatta and Theophanes are a littler vaguer in their accounts, simply referring to the number of new recruits.[97] Evagrius is much more helpful, however, even if he does exaggerate the number of recruits: "by recruiting the best men both from the tribes beyond the Alps in the vicinity of the Rhine, and those on this side of the Alps, the Massagetai and other Scythian nations, and those near

---

92 *Not. Dign. or.* 7.27; Jones 1964: 661.
93 *Iust. ed.* 4.2.
94 *Iust. ed.* 13.18. These units might be some of those alluded in the long, detailed edict put up by Anastasius (*SEG* 9.356). Jones (1964: 661) argues that the units in the Anastasian edict were full of *comitatenses*, but there is no evidence of this in the inscription itself.
95 See Pringle 2001: 73. As Haynes (2013) demonstrated in his detailed analysis of the earlier imperial Roman auxiliaries, these ethnic epithets started to lose their original meaning not long after they were instituted in the first place.
96 John of Ephesus *HE* 3.13, 3.26.
97 Theophyl. Sim. 3.12.4; Theoph. A.M. 6074.

Paeonia, and Mysians, Illyrians and Isaurians, that he established squadrons of excellent horsemen almost 150,000 in number."[98] This, like those recruitment drives referred to by Procopius, seems to have been for specific circumstances. What is notable, however, is the scope of the process, with Tiberius drawing troops from a wide variety of locations. Although Procopius does not describe any recruitment drives for the east, this later anecdote combined with the comments about Goth and Syriac above show that wars in the east could elicit these sorts of changes.

Another problem is that many of these recruitment details in Procopius surface solely in the *Gothic War*, which adds to the concerns about how representative it is of wider Roman practices. Indeed, there has been some speculation that a significant proportion of the soldiers fighting for Rome in Italy in the sixth century, the federates and *bucellarii*, were short-term soldiers for this particular conflict.[99] Is this what Procopius is implying in his discussion? Most of the commanders who are described scooping up recruits before heading to Italy stop in Thrace and Illyria en route, as I noted earlier. While the Balkans were a primary recruiting ground, a point long recognized, this could be a matter of access. On that note, Rance describes at length the army Narses led against Totila to Busta Gallorum.[100] He argues that a great number of the soldiers brought from Byzantium comprised rank and file Roman soldiers from the praesental army combined with new troops transferred from the Thracian and Illyrian armies.[101] Conant, on the other hand, suggested that the abundance of Thracian soldiers in Africa, many of whom he argued did not stay behind post-conquest, might be due, at least in part, to Belisarius' and other officers' personal connections to the region.[102] The only place where we seem to have evidence of recruitment of local individuals into the Roman military comes in the wake up the uprising that rocked the region in the late 530s and 540s. When Solomon was dispatched to Africa around 539/540, he enrolled a number of new soldiers, presumably in Africa, so following the precepts set out in Justinian's decree.[103] Justinian's decree specifically focused on *limitanei*,

---

98   Evag. *HE* 5.14, trans. Whitby (ἔκ τε τῶν ὑπὲρ τὰς Ἄλπεις ἐθνῶν τὰ ἀμφὶ τὸν Ῥῆνον ἀριστίνδην στρατολογήσας, τά τε ἐντὸς τῶν Ἄλπεων, Μασσαγετῶν τε καὶ ἑτέρων Σκυθικῶν γενῶν, καὶ τὰ περὶ Παιονίαν, καὶ Μυσούς, καὶ Ἰλλυριούς, καὶ Ἰσαύρους, ὡς σύνεγγυς πεντήκοντα καὶ ἑκατὸν χιλιάδων ἴλας ἱππέων ἀρίστων ἐγκαταστήσασθαι). For more on Tiberius' recruitment drive and warfare in the 570s, see Whitby (1995: 87–92).
99   Rance 2005: 443.
100 Rance 2005: 446.
101 Procop. *Wars* 8.26.10; Rance 2005: 446.
102 Conant 2012: 230–231.
103 Procop. *Wars* 4.19.3; *Cod. Iust.* 1.27.2.8.

and those might well have been the soldiers identified here, but Procopius' language is ambiguous.

It is also worth considering the degree to which the recruitment we see in Procopius was part of a larger phenomenon, like the expansion of the armed forces that Koehn advocates.[104] One of the big administrative-cum-military changes was the creation of the Armenian army under the *magister militum per Armeniam*. Procopius describes this change in the *Buildings*, as does Malalas.[105] The change itself was formalized in a piece of Justinianic legislation.[106] Koehn argued that the existing *limitanei* in the region were not dissolved, but rather converted into units of *comitatenses*.[107] The evidence for this comes from the aforementioned passage of Malalas, where he says, "The emperor gave Sittas *numeri* of soldiers from the two *magistri militum praesentales* and the *magister militum per Orientem* ... he [Sittas] also took four *numeri* from the *magister militum per Orientem* and from that time he became a great bulwark for the Romans."[108] The imperial rescript in the *Codex Justinianus* confirms what Malalas says, though, for all its detail, it is short of specifics concerning the character of all the units to be based in the new region. It refers to certain units (*certosque ... numeros*), both new ones, but also some soldiers from masters of soldiers at court (*praesentales*) and in the east. The soldiers transferred from pre-existing commands would have been units of *comitatenses*. This army features only rarely in the *Wars*, and Procopius provides little insight into its structures.[109]

It is fitting, I think, that this piece of legislation on the creation of the Armenian army follows another rescript on the existing restrictions regarding troop transfers, both collectively under the larger discussion of masters of soldiers (*magistri militum*).[110] For our purposes, the important part of the passage reads as follows:

> We order that soldiers may not be transferred from the places where they are stationed to other places without the special authorization of Our Serenity ... But if perchance some urgent and compelling reason arises, the Most Exalted Praetorian Prefecture as well as your office shall immediately provide for the public interest and safety and address your reports

---

104   Koehn 2018: 48–53.
105   Procop. *Build.* 3.1.27–29; Mal. *Chron.* 18.10. See too Greatrex and Lieu (2002: 83–84).
106   *Cod. Iust.* 1.29.5.
107   Koehn 2018: 48.
108   Mal. *Chron.* 18.10, trans. Jeffreys et al.
109   Procop. *Wars* 2.14.8, 3.11.5, 7.27.3.
110   *Cod. Iust.* 1.29. On military affairs in sixth century Armenia, see Ayvazyan (2012).

to Our ears, indicating both the places from which the soldiers should be transferred and those to which they must go, the names of the most courageous units [*nominaque fortissimorum numerorum*] in which the aforementioned soldiers are enrolled, as well as the amount of rations and above all the reason on account of which the aforementioned soldiers should be transferred, so that after receiving such information appropriate action may be taken on Our authority.[111]

This law seems to explain why, in some places, we find Procopius referring to the recruitment of new soldiers for several campaigns. It also fits in with what we discussed above: if soldiers and their units were needed elsewhere, the commanding officer had to write the emperor to ask and explain why this was so.

While some of the reinforcements described by Procopius refer to the transfer of units, in some cases they refer to the recruitment of new soldiers, what has been the subject of most of this chapter to this point. Part of the problem with determining whether the circumstances where generals visit regions to garner troops were exceptional is that Procopius never specificies this himself. Even if we take a conservative figure for the total number of soldiers under Rome's command, like 150,000, to keep the military up to strength they would need about 6,000 new recruits a year at a minimum, a not insignificant total.[112] Still, uncertainty remains. If we are to get any sense of the regularity of this pattern, we need to look more closely at what Procopius has to say about that one type of soldier I have not yet discussed here, the *bucellarii*.

So far, the discussion on recruitment has centred on the three primary classes of soldier in the military, the *comitatenses*, the *foederati*, and the *limitanei*. As we have seen, Procopius usually shies away from technical terminology. He never uses the term *bucellarius*. Instead, he often uses some form of the phrase οἱ οἰκεῖοι, "the household ones", to refer to these men.[113] In Procopius' oeuvre we find them serving alongside several of the empire's leading commanders,

---

111   *Cod. Iust.* 1.29.4, trans. Dillon. *Milites de locis, in quibus consistunt, ad alia loca sine speciali nostrae serenitatis auctoritate nullatenus transferri praecipimus, nec eorum expensae in locis, in quibus consistunt, minuantur. Sed si forte quaedam urguens et necessaria causa emerserit, utilitati ac securitati publicae tam amplissimam praetorianam praefecturam quam tuam sedem sine ulla procrastinatione prospicere protinus oportet et suggestiones ad nostras aures destinare, indicantes tam loca, de quibus milites transferendi sunt, quam ea, ad quae pervenire eos oportet, nominaque fortissimorum numerorum, in quibus idem milites referuntur, nec non quantitatem annonarum et ante omnia causam, ob quam idem milites transferendi sunt, ut post talem suggestionem a nostra auctoritate competentia procedant.*
112   Whitby 1995: 85.
113   Note the comments of McMahon (2014: 26–27).

though Belisarius especially. In fact, the clearest statement of their role and size comes in Procopius' mini-eulogy in book seven. There, Procopius says that he used to equip "7,000 horsemen from his household".[114] Whether that was 7,000 men at once is another matter to which I will return presently. Schmitt, at least, thinks that most commanders never possessed more than 300 *bucellarii*. Though private soldiers ostensibly under individual generals, most argue that they remained loyal to the emperor and the state, who provided their food and weapons.[115] Indeed, in a passage quoted above, Procopius notes that bodyguards would swear oaths of loyalty to both their generals and the emperor.[116] As for their origins, Jones argues the could have either Roman or non-Roman backgrounds, an important point if we are to determine what role, if any, their recruitment plays in Procopius' works.[117]

In the second chapter, I noted that these men were sometimes seen as some of the principal oral sources for Procopius, and that they featured throughout the *Wars*, with Procopius using forms of δορυφόρος (spearman) and ὑπασπιστής (shield bearer) dozens of times each.[118] More often than not, the words are used in the plural to indicate generic spearmen or shield bearers. For example, the first time Procopius uses the word ὑπασπιστής it is to highlight the number and quality of these soldiers collectively, "leading a strong and formidable force, in particular a large number of his spearmen and shield bearers who were trained in the actual struggles and dangers of war."[119]

The two classes of *bucellarius*, the spearman, the officer, and the shield bearer, the lower-ranking soldier, figure most prominently in the two invasions of Africa and Italy. They are named amongst the units found in the two catalogues of forces, though Procopius provides no specifics about their numbers, nor does he indicate how they came to serve with Belisarius.[120] It is possible that some of the recruitment drives that he alludes to throughout the text could have involved *bucellarii*, though evidence of this in his works is hard to find. Sometimes, however, officers collected *bucellarii* by stealing them from their fellow officers, as happened in the midst of the *Gothic War*.[121] As to how they stole the guardsmen in this episode, it came down to Germanus' financial

---

114 Procop. *Wars* 7.1.20.
115 Schmitt 2015: 121. See too Jones (1964: 666–667) and Lenski (2009: 159).
116 Procop. *Wars* 4.14.17.
117 Jones 1964: 667.
118 In terms of numbers, a search of *TLG* reveals that Procopius uses a form of δορυφόρος 118 times, and ὑπασπιστής 47 times.
119 Procop. *Wars* 1.24.40.
120 Procop. *Wars* 3.11.19, 5.5.5.
121 Procop. *Wars* 7.39.16–20.

resources (provided by the emperor) and his personality, or so Procopius. As a result of this, Germanus managed to win over the *bucellarii* of other commanders. On occasion too, generals might employ guardsmen from other commanders because they were concerned about their behaviour, as seems to have been the case when Germanus hired Maximinus, an action that ultimately failed.[122] Indeed, as Parnell argued, Roman generals were often competitive, striving to achieve fame and fortune in their careers.[123] To do so, they often relied heavily on their *bucellarii*.

Ultimately, it is difficult if not impossible to say definitively whether Procopius meant for these recruitment missions to which he alludes to be temporary measures or something more lasting, and the occasional references to *bucellarii* do not provide much needed clarity. That said, that they are usually found in exceptional wars of conquest (i.e., not the war in Persia) combined with the legal evidence, suggests to me that these measures evinced aspects of both. Although they were initially short term recruitment operations, the legal evidence shows that this involved established procedures, and that many of the soldiers so enrolled would take up long term posts.

3   Demographics

One of the big issues in the context of recruitment is manpower, in particular getting enough soldiers to fight in the first place. By some measures, the Roman state did not suffer any notable population problems as the total number of soldiers likely never made up more than a small percentage of the empire's total population.[124] Indeed, Treadgold estimated that the population of the empire of in 540 was 26,000,000, with soldiers making up 374,300 of the total, or 1.4%.[125] At the end of Justinian's reign, by his reckoning the population had dropped to 19,500,000, while the number of soldiers had increased to 379,300, or 2.0% of the total.[126] That said, for a large proportion of the populace military service was unpopular, and this might be reason enough to explain the prolonged use of conscription and hereditary service, even if they both had a long pedigree.[127]

---

122 Parnell 2017: 167–168.
123 Parnell 2017: 103–129.
124 Lee 2007a: 78.
125 Treadgold 1995: 162.
126 Treadgold 1995: 162.
127 Fear 2007: 429–31.

Now that we have looked closely at what Procopius has to say about the mechanics of recruitment, I will move to the bigger picture to look at the relationship between recruitment and demographic questions. Three issues that Procopius does touch on are the plague, the trouble with finding recruits, and the corruption that sometimes ensued during the recruitment process.

3.1   Recruitment and the Plague

In this section, I will focus on the plague, a major sixth-century event for which Procopius is one of our most important sources. As we well know, Procopius provided a detailed account of the plague in Constantinople focusing on its character and impact.[128] Just as Procopius used Thucydides' account of the disease that ravaged Athens during the Peloponnesian war, so too did Procopius serve as a model for later sources, like John Kantakouzenos.[129] As noted, Thucydides' account of the plague comes in the midst of the war, and it was to have a marked impact on Athens' fortunes: for one thing, Pericles, the great Athenian orator and statesman, succumbed to the yet-unknown disease.[130]

Thucydides' narrative went something like this. The first invasion of Attica runs from 2.10–2.23. Shortly thereafter, Thucydides describes Athenian preparations including the migration from the countryside, with refugees flooding into Athens itself.[131] After assorted skirmishes, Thucydides eventually turns to Pericles' famous funeral oration, which immediately precedes his account of the plague.[132] It is followed by a second invasion of Attica and Athenian counterattacks, and yet another speech given by Pericles, who dies shortly thereafter. In the course of Thucydides' eulogy of Pericles, he sets out the reasons for Athens' eventual defeat.[133]

The specific relationship between plague and war in Procopius has not attracted the same amount of attention.[134] On the surface, this makes sense, as the plague plays a different role in Procopius' narrative. And yet, one of the biggest potential recruitment challenges in the age of Justinian was the outbreak of plague in 541. Could it be that Procopius includes more subtle comments on the plague's role in Roman military success that have escaped notice?

---

128   His account, found at *Wars* 2.22–23, is but one of many, with those of Evagrius (10.4.1) and John of Ephesus (Witakowski 1996: 74–98) also notable for their vividness.
129   Brand 1976: 7; Miller 1976; Hunger 1976, 1978: 45; Scott 1981; Cameron 1985: 40; Meier 1999, 2004.
130   Thuc. 2.47.1–2.55.1.
131   Thuc. 2.13–2.14.
132   Thuc. 2.34–46 (oration), 2.47–54 (plague).
133   Thuc. 2.65.
134   Though note the comments of Sarris (2002: 179, 2007: 131).

The plague has been the subject of lots of work in the past decade or so, with two—opposed—positions emerging, the maximalist and the minimalist, with the former arguing for a significant demographic impact caused by its outbreak, and the latter a much more limited one.[135] Several parts of Roman life were impacted on some level or another by plague. There is evidence for a new official responsible for burials in Constantinople, and a lack of concern in response to the financial hardships faced by the populace (i.e. no tax relief). At the cultural level, Cameron argued for a rise in the use of icons, especially those connected to the worship of the Virgin Mary.[136] Despite some arguments to the contrary, even extant legislation highlights some of the problems generated by the plague. The issue that interests us most, of course, are the potential demographic shortages.[137] By some accounts, there were 5,000 to 10,000 deaths per day in Constantinople, with perhaps a 1/3 of the total population perishing.[138] Some places might even have been abandoned, at least temporarily.

Let us return to Procopius: what would we have expected him to say to stress the impact of the plague on Rome's ability to wage war? The structure of the *Wars* does complicate matters: though the text proceeds in chronological order for the most part, it is also divided into three theatres. So, events in Persia come before events in Africa or Italy, even if, chronologically speaking, they came after. It is tempting, then, to look at later parts of the *Wars* to see which events took place after the plague broke out. But it is not clear that this is how we are meant to read the *Wars*.

The most straightforward option is to look at what comes before and what comes after his discussion of the plague, at least sequentially in the text, the book that came before (21) and the one that came after (24). In the chapter immediately preceding, Procopius details the aftermath of Khusro's invasion of the Roman Empire and describes the episode in which he sent a secretary, named Abandanes, to investigate Belisarius. Belisarius discovers this,

---

135 The scholarship is vast and growing. The chapters in Little (2007) provide a good overview of the disparate aspects of the plague, though we know more about it now than we did then. More recently, Meier (2016, 2020) has argued forcefully that the plague had a significant impact on Roman society, a view shared by Harper (2017, 2018) and Greatrex (2020). On the other hand, scholars like Haldon et al. (2018), Eisenberg and Mordecai (2019), and Sessa (2019) minimizes its long-term impact.

136 Cameron 1978.

137 For a detailed discussion of this very matter, see Meier (2016: 270–282). For some other discussions of the plague's demographic impact, see Mitchell (2014: 466–496, 2018), McCormick (2015, 2016), and Mordechai and Eisenberg (2019). Treadgold (1995: 16–17; 159–162, 165), whose focus is military matters, also discusses the impact of the plague.

138 Procop. *Wars* 2.23.1–2.

RECRUITMENT

and employs several ruses taken right out of the pages of a military manual, like Maurice's *Strategikon*, where generals are urged to mislead their opponents on the number of men at their disposal.[139] It worked, for Abandanes returned to Khusro and advised the shah to leave because of the perceived number of Roman soldiers.[140] Shortly thereafter, the third Persian invasion (according to Procopius) drew to a close and Justinian summoned Belisarius to Constantinople to send him off to Italy, where the war had turned sour for the Romans.[141] For Procopius, this "victory" was no mean feat, for he claims that Belisarius had managed to defeat Khusro, whose army vastly outnumbered his—myriads versus an army few in number.[142]

Two books later, when Procopius returns to the story in the east, a year or two had passed (it was now 542 or 543 CE), and Khusro readied yet another invasion of Roman territory, this time through Persarmenia.[143] Khusro's plans were curtailed by the plague, however, and, according to Procopius (though others too), the revolt of his son, Anush-Zad.[144] Indeed, Procopius says that Khusro himself was infected and was forced to withdraw to recover, a detail shared by Dinawari. What is more, Procopius claims that the plague affected the entire Persian army.[145] The Roman army found out, thanks to the information they gleaned from negotiations with Armenia, and decided to take advantage of this apparent Persian weakness.[146] A substantial and varied Roman army gathered near Martyropolis, which numbered 30,000 soldiers and counted among its complement Martin and the eastern army and many others besides.[147]

Ultimately, then, besides being an important contemporary event in and of itself, the plague did play an important role in the course of war in the latter part of the *Persian War*. It comes on the heels of some significant setbacks

---

139 Maurice, for example, notes the value in concealing numbers for the purpose of an ambush (Maur. *Strat.* 4.1).
140 Procop. *Wars* 2.21.13–15.
141 Procop. *Wars* 2.21.34.
142 Procop. *Wars* 2.21.20.
143 Procop. *Wars* 2.24.1.
144 On the revolt, both in Procopius and the Persian tradition (history of Dinawari, the *Shahnameh*, and the *Chronicle of Seert*) see Bonner (2020: 195–199).
145 Procop. *Wars* 2.24.8.
146 Procopius' note that the entire army had suffered from the plague seems an exaggeration. There is little doubt that the Persian army was weakened by the plague however, with Bonner (2011: 85–87, 2020: 194) suggesting that it might have been this that led to the increased recruitment of non-Persians in the military during the reign of Khusro. Note too the comments of Rubin (1995: 294). For a concise overview of recruitment in the Persian military, see McDonough (2013: 605–608); for a more detailed treatment, see Farrokh (2017: 18–22).
147 Procop. *Wars* 2.24.12–16.

suffered by the Romans, punctuated by the sack of Antioch in 540 CE. Belisarius' "victory" over the numerically superior Persian force involved significant subterfuge. That said, despite the plague's significant impact on the populace of Constantinople, which Procopius sets out in vivid detail, he said nothing about its impact on the Roman military. Instead, in the subsequent book, he marks out the devastation it wrought in Persia, which enabled the Romans to gather a much larger army. And yet, in the absence of a leader like Belisarius, the Romans were not able to take advantage and even suffered some defeats, as happened at Anglon when a smaller Persian force defeated a larger Roman one.[148] In terms of war at least, the plague allowed for a complete reversal in Roman fortunes. What it does not do is play a role in the recruitment and relative manpower of Rome's military in Procopius' *Persian War*. To find traces of its impact on manpower in the text, we have to look harder.

Although Procopius does not ascribe a particular military-demographic role to the plague where we find it in the *Persian War*, two comments in the *Secret History* indicate that he did feel that the plague's larger impact was substantial. In the two places where he refers to the plague, he says it both afflicted everyone living in the Roman Empire and that it killed off about half of the entire population.[149] Procopius might not provide us details of the specific demographic challenges the plague brought to the military, but we should not take his silence as evidence for business as usual. If half the Roman world died and Khusro's entire army caught the disease, it is unlikely there were no repercussions for Rome's military. To resolve this uncertainty, we should look more closely at Procopius' numbers.

To set up Procopius' take on this, for some context I turn to another of Procopius' esteemed classical predecessors. Though Polybius did not have a plague of his own to describe in his *Histories*, he did give sufficient attention to the demographic challenges posed by Hannibal during his invasion of Italy.[150] Polybius gave the strength of the Roman military at the dawn of the war at 2.24, and these figures have been used to give the population of Italy.[151] According to Polybius, Rome had 2 consuls, 2 legions and allies, including 15,000 infantry, and 1,000 cavalry each. The allied Sabines and Etruscans numbered 50,000 infantry and 400 cavalry. Umbrians, Sarsinates, Veneti, and Cenomani on the

---

148 Procop. *Wars* 2.25.5–35. See too Rubin (1957: 398), Syvänne (2004: 441–442), and Petersen (2013: 530). On the Roman failures at Anglon and Procopius' characterization of these, see Whately (2016a: 92, 97, 99).
149 Procop. *SH*. 6.22, 18.44.
150 The demographic challenges posed by the Hannibalic War have attracted lots of attention, from the classic work of Brunt (1971) to the more recent work of Rosenstein (2004).
151 For a more recent account of these and related issues, see De Ligt (2012).

frontier with Gaul numbered 40,000. Back in Rome, there were 20,000 Roman infantry and 1,500 cavalry, and 30,000 allied infantry and 2,000 cavalry. There were a number of additional troops which, when added together, gave Rome a fighting capacity of 700,000 infantry and 70,000 cavalry.

Procopius provides no figures anything like this before or after his discussion of the plague. Indeed, at no point does he give the fighting capacity of the Roman state, which is not the case with Agathias. Agathias argues that Justinian was to blame for the drop in the size of the military, from a high of 645,000 down to a new low (for him) of close to 150,000.[152] He does not associate this specifically with the plague, however. To complicate matters, one of the few figures he gives for a Roman army about to do battle, the army under Narses at Casilinum, numbered about 18,000, which is well in keeping with the sort of figures we find, for example, in the two big set-piece battles in the Procopius' *Persian War*, Dara and Callinicum.[153] Plus, in his description of Kutrigur siege of Constantinople, Agathias makes it out that the aged Belisarius and his ragtag group of fellow defenders—veterans, civilians, and peasants—were enough to fight them off.[154] In other words, Agathias' drop is probably exaggerated, and even if not, his own account makes it clear that 150,000 might not have shortchanged the Romans as much as the low number might make it seem.

The truth is, it can be difficult to disentangle the impact of the plague from the impact of war in the evidence.[155] That the two were simultaneous threats facing the state is worth stressing. When Justinian took up the top post, the empire was in good financial shape, thanks in large part to the fiscal policies of Anastasius.[156] Haarer has plausibly suggested that it was this full treasury that enabled Justinian to undertake the ambitious projects that he did.[157] Later in his reign Justinian had trouble paying his troops, with military unrest becoming a significant concern from the late 530s onwards.[158] Justinian was very interested in maximizing his income from taxes, and enacted legislation in 539, for example, that strove to eliminate the corruption that limited its quantity in

---

152   Agathias 5.15.7–8.
153   Agathias 2.4.10.
154   See Agathias 5.16.2–3 for the numbers.
155   Note Lee's (2005: 128) comments regarding the difficulties in disentangling evidence for disruption caused by natural disaster from disruption caused by warfare in the material evidence.
156   Haarer 2006: 193–222.
157   Haarer 2006: 253. Note too the comments of Heather (2018: 43–68).
158   Procop. *Wars* 4.18.2–9, 4.26.10–12. Kaegi 1981: 49–52; Lee 2007b: 400.

Egypt.[159] To make matters worse, the state suffered lost tax revenues due to the plague. In this light, Justinian's decision to resort to the payment of indemnities to the Persians and other foes, rather than direct military engagement, most likely reflects the changed fiscal situation.[160] The plague is likely to have caused some manpower problems, but it would have affected not just Rome, but its foes, such as Sasanid Persia.[161]

Some Roman legislation hints at the impact of the plague on Roman society more generally. Accordingly, the following novels had some impact: 117, a novel on marriage dated to 542; 118, which has to do with children and dates to 543; 119, also on marriage and children, which dates to 544; 120, concerned with ecclesiastical land not in used and dated to 544; and 122, on skilled workmen.[162] There is one other novel, relevant for us here, 116 on soldiers; it is concerned specifically with soldiers not performing the duties they are supposed to be performing: "soldiers are to return to their units and *foederati* to their *optiones*, and fight on behalf of the common good. In future, we are in no way permitting our soldiers or *foederati* to be employed for any private purposes at all".[163] It had long been illegal for soldiers to serve in the private employ of landowners, and the plague only exacerbated these manpower demands.[164]

3.2   *Recruitment and Corruption*

To get a better sense of the relationship between recruitment and the plague and Procopius, I will turn to some of the problems connected to the plague's impact. Notably, the plague seems to have added to the corruption problems that were often rife in the military, and which Procopius laments. Two important issues in this regard directly pertaining to recruitment that surface in Procopius' works are the plague of corruption and the difficulty in soliciting new recruits. What legislation we have stresses the need for care and rigour in evaluating requests for new soldiers, so that there are no unexpected, or nonexistent, recruits. Procopius touches on these very issues in the recruitment process in the infamous *Secret History* passage discussed above, and he identifies some legitimate concerns. Procopius says the "Logothetes … would not allow the names of the deceased to be removed from the rolls, even when great

---

159   *Iust. Edict.* 13; Sarris 2006: 212–217.
160   Börm 2008.
161   Note the discussion of Bonner (2020: 191–195) on the impact of the plague on Sasanian Persia.
162   Sarris and Miller 2018: 751, n. 1; 767, n. 1; 775, n. 1; 781, n. 1; 799, n. 1.
163   *Iust. Nov.* 116.1, trans. Miller.
164   Sarris and Miller 2018: 747, n. 1. Treadgold (1995: 165) highlighted the long term demographic impact of the plague on the empire as a whole.

numbers died at one time from other causes [the plague possibly included], and especially, as was the case with the most, in the course of the numerous wars. Furthermore, they would no longer fill out the muster-rolls, and that too for a long period."[165] This means that the concerns with recruitment checks-and-balances in the legislation were warranted, and all branches of the military were likely to fall victim to this practice. But before we look closer at Procopius' comments, I want to highlight some outwardly unusual pieces of legislation, which have some bearing on this discussion.

In the collection of newer laws, the *Novels*, we find a piece of legislation, *Novel* 117 and dated to Dec 14, 542 CE, on the dissolution of marriage, which states:

> We command that for however many years they remain on active service, their wives are to wait, even if they have received no letter or reply from their husbands. If any such wife hears that her husband is dead, we do not let her enter into a second marriage even then, unless the wife first puts in an appearance (either in person or through her parents, or through any other person) before the *priores* and the *chartularii* of the unit in which her husband was serving, and asks them or the tribune (if he is present) whether it is true that her consort has died. They are then to depose, with the gospels displayed, and with an entry in the records, as to whether it is true that her husband is dead.[166]

That law is a revision of an earlier one (Nov 22), published just a few years earlier, March 18, 536 CE, which reads, in section 14:

> Therefore a wife ... is not to go to a second husband before a period of fully ten years has elapsed, during which she has been constantly pestering her husband by sending him letters, or messages by others; and either he has distinctly renounced his marriage to her, or nothing at all has been heard from him; and she was put in notice to either the Most Illustrious

---

165 Procop. *SH* 24.5, trans. Dewing.
166 *Iust. Nov.* 117.11, Trans. Miller. καὶ κελεύομεν ὁσουσδήποτε ἐνιαυτοὺς ἐν ἐξπεδίτῳ μείνωσι, περιμένειν τὰς τούτων γαμετάς, κἂν μὴ γράμματα ἢ ἀπόκρισίν τινα παρὰ τῶν ἰδίων ἀνδρῶν δέξωνται. εἰ δέ τις ἐκ τῶν τοιούτων γυναικῶν τὸν ἴδιον ἄνδρα ἀκούσει τετελευτηκέναι, οὐδὲ τότε εἰς ἑτέρους αὐτὴν ἐλθεῖν γάμους ἐπιτρέπομεν, εἰ μὴ πρότερον παραγένηται ἡ γυνὴ δι' ἑαυτῆς ἢ διὰ τῶν ἰδίων γονέων ἢ δι' ἄλλου οἱουδήποτε προσώπου πρὸς τοὺς πρίορας τοῦ ἀριθμοῦ καὶ τοὺς *cartularios*, ἐν ᾧ ὁ ταύτης ἀνὴρ ἐστρατεύετο, καὶ τούτους ἤτοι τὸν τριβοῦνον, εἴ γε πάρεστιν, ἐρωτήσῃ, εἰ ταῖς ἀληθείαις ἐτελεύτησεν ὁ αὐτῇ συνοικήσας, ὥστε ἐκείνους τῶν ἁγίων εὐαγγελίων προκειμένων ἐπὶ πράξεως ὑπομνημάτων κατατίθεσθαι, εἰ ταῖς ἀληθείαις ὁ ἀνὴρ τετελεύτηκε.

general, or Admirable *dux*, or Most Distinguished *tribunus* under whom the soldier concerned is serving.[167]

Though on the surface they are part of the interminable legislation on marriage in the Roman world, these two laws provide some unexpected insight into the potential traumatic experiences of sixth-century military wives.[168] While we know that plenty of men died in battle, what is surprising about these laws is the possibility that their wives might not know that this had happened for some time afterwards. Since we lack detailed, firsthand accounts from the military families themselves, laws like these give us some idea of the trauma they might have suffered.[169] But how is it that a soldier's wife might not know about his death for many years afterwards, and why were these laws implemented in the first place?

The two laws noted at the start, when viewed in isolation, make it seem that Justinian took a harsher stance over time when it came to the wives of soldiers, especially when those laws are compared with an earlier iteration (originally dated to 337), which read as follows:

> A wife whose husband set out on military service and who has been able to secure no evidence of his well-being after a period of four years, and so has considered marrying another man, and yet did not marry before approaching his (her husband's) commanding officer through a document disclosing her intentions, is not deemed to have entered upon a secret marriage, nor to be liable to the loss of her dowry, nor to be vulnerable to the capital penalty (*capitalis poena*), since she, after such a long period of time, is shown to have begun a new marriage not rashly or secretly but publicly, by submitting a declaration (of her intent). 1. On that account the rule must be upheld that, if there is no reason to suspect adultery and no secret union is uncovered, women shall fear no risk from the men to whom they are joined, since, it is (only) if the marriage bed

---

167 *Iust. Nov.* 22.14, Trans. Miller. τὸ γὰρ πράξεσι πολεμικαῖς ἐνησχολημένῳ τῷ γήμαντι γυναικὸς ἐπάγειν στέρησιν οὐχ ἥττων ἐστί ποινὴ τοῦ παρὰ πολεμίοις ἁλῶναι. Ὥστε μὴ πρότερον εἰς ἀνδρὸς φοιτάτω δευτέρου ἡ τοιαύτη γυνὴ ὁποίαν ὁ νομοθέτης οὗτος ὑπέθετο, πρὶν ἂν καὶ δεκαετὴς διέλθοι χρόνος, καὶ αὐτὴ διενοχλήσειε τὸν ἄνδρα στέλλουσα γράμματα ἢ διά τινων ῥήμασι χρωμένη πρὸς αὐτόν, ὁ δὲ ἢ σαφῶς ἀπείποι πρὸς τὸν γάμον τὸν αὐτῆς ἢ καθάπαξ σιγήσειε, τηνικαῦτά τε διδασκαλίαν ἐπιδοίη ἢ τῷ ἐνδοξοτάτῳ στρατηγῷ ἢ τῷ περιβλέπτῳ δουκὶ ἢ τῷ λαμπροτάτῳ τριβούνῳ, ὑφ' οὓς ὁ στρατιώτης ἐκεῖνός ἐστι.

168 Note the evocative discussion of Sessa (2018: 131).

169 For the experience of civilians, especially women, in wartime in the sixth century, see Fan Chiang (2015, 2018).

were knowingly violated in secret that criminal law policy would demand a suitable punishment.[170]

This fourth-century version gave women the chance to remarry after only four years, and they required less proof that they had made every effort to contact their missing husbands. This makes Justinian seem harsh indeed. If we look closer at some comparative legalisation, however, a different image emerges. In this final section, I want to address two questions: first, why might Justinian have implemented this legislation; and secondly, is this legislation more or less favourable than what existed for other marriages (i.e. not involving soldiers)?[171] Even if Roman law, such as we have it, is not the best barometer of day-to-day practice, it at least illuminates something of the official position on the issue, and in the absence of suitable evidence from the ground it should be considered.[172]

A search for an explanation for Justinian's revised legislation on deceased-soldiers' wives reveals some interesting details. For one thing, quite a lot of the legislation on the military pertinent to our discussion seems to have been designed with a view to making service more attractive to those on duty.[173] Soldiers could make a will in nearly any situation, so long as they were on campaign.[174] Along the same lines, if a soldier had his rights restricted while he was away, they would be restored.[175] If an ex-wife had been charged with adultery but had fled the province before a soldier received justice, he would be allowed to seek her out once his duties permitted.[176] Even commanders would not be allowed to leave their post for the sake of a trial if similar circumstances occurred.[177] There are plenty of other laws that deal with exceptions made for

---

170   Cod. Iust. 5.17.7. trans. McGinn. *Uxor, quae in militiam profecto marito post interventum annorum quattuor nullum sospitatis eius potuit habere indicium atque ideo de nuptiis alterius cogitavit nec tamen ante nupsit, quam libello ducem super hoc suo voto convenit, non videtur nuptias inisse furtivas nec dotis amissionem sustinere nec capitali poenae esse obnoxia, quae post tam magni temporis iugitatem non temere nec clanculo, sed publice contestatione deposita nupsisse firmatur.*

171   For a more complete discussion of this and other related issues, with an emphasis on the legal material, see Arjava (1996). For the life and experiences of women in late antiquity in general, see Clark (1994).

172   This is much easier to do for other subjects, like the sixth-century economy. Note Sarris (2006: 149–176), for example. For a good discussion of how law worked in late antiquity, see Harries (1999).

173   On this matter, see the comments of Jones (1964: 668).

174   *Cod. Iust.* 6.21.17.

175   *Cod. Iust.* 2.50.1.

176   *Cod. Iust.* 9.9.15.

177   *Cod. Iust.* 9.9.19.

soldiers on campaign.[178] On rare occasions, these exceptions even extended to the members of their *familiae*. If a soldier's wife happened to accompany him on campaign and suffered herself, she too would get reparation for any harm she received while away with him.[179] All this said, the law was pretty clear that these privileges expired when the expedition was over and they were back home.[180]

Publicly, Justinian seems to have been very interested in incentivizing would-be and serving soldiers, and with good reason, for he might well have been trying to counter some negative press.[181] Soldiers were known to desert, sometimes for more than four years, due to prolonged leaves of absence. In this light, one explanation for these marriage laws was that, in some situations, the state could not be certain that soldiers had died or abandoned their posts.[182] Indeed, the change in Justinian's legislation on the remarriage of military widows likely had less to do with concern over the morality of the women, and more to do with concern over the whereabouts of the empire's soldiers, who in 542 were likely not only fighting on several fronts, but also likely suffering the impact of the plague. Justinian had manpower and morale problems.

An important part of our understanding of these marriage laws lay in Justinian's stipulation that proof of death must be proffered. A significant problem highlighted in some of the sixth-century evidence is the corruption of the empire's officers, at least in some capacities.[183] The most relevant for us is the corruption connected to the muster rolls that Procopius reports in the *Secret History*. According to Procopius,

> But when they [the soldiers] have grown old and are on the point of being discharged from the army, the pay is very much more imposing, to the end not only that they may, when in future they are living as private citizens, have sufficient for their own maintenance, but may also, when it is their lot to have completely measured out the term of life, be able to leave from their own property some consolation to the members of their households ... But the *Logothetes*, as they are called, would not allow the names of the deceased to be removed from the rolls, even when great numbers died at one time from other causes, and especially, as was the case with

---

178   *Cod. Iust.* 2.50.3–7, 3.23.2, 3. 28.37, 4.52.4, 7.35.1.
179   *Cod. Iust.* 2.51.
180   *Cod. Iust.* 2.50.8.
181   Book 24 of Procopius' *Secret History* is filled with complaints about the state of the soldiers, especially their low morale.
182   *Cod. Iust.* 12.42.2–3.
183   See Kaegi (1981: 41–101).

the most, in the course of the numerous wars. Furthermore, they would no longer fill out the muster-rolls, and that too for a long period. And the result of this practice has proved unfortunate for all concerned—first, for the State in that the number of soldiers in active service is always deficient; secondly, for the surviving soldiers, in that they are elbowed out by those who have died long before and so find themselves left in a position inferior to what they deserve, and that they receive a pay which is lower than if they had the rank to which they are entitled; and, finally, for the *Logothetes*, who all this time have had to apportion to Justinian a share of the soldiers' money.[184]

If Procopius is to be believed, keeping track of just who was enrolled in the military and who was not was a real issue for Justinian. In fact, there are several pieces of legislation and assorted edicts that allude to problems with the muster rolls throughout the first half of the sixth century CE, or which at least stress the importance of keeping track of the number of troops. In the long edict concerned with the management of the newly conquered territory in North Africa, Justinian lists one of the new governor's tasks as keeping track of how many frontier troops there were and where they were stationed.[185] Importantly too, a few sections later the edict gets into the payment of those based in the province.[186] A later law notes that there should be quarterly military reports. Though it does not specify what exactly these would entail, the references to the secretary, bookkeeper, paymasters, accountant, and his assistant are suggestive.[187] It could well be, then, that this strenuous insistence on

---

184 Procop. *SH* 24.3–6. Trans. Atwater. Γεγηρακόσι μέντοι καὶ μέλλουσι τῆς στρατείας ἀφίεσθαι πολλῷ ἔτι κομπωδεστέρα ἡ σύνταξις, ὅπως αὐτοί τε τὸ λοιπὸν ἰδίᾳ βιοῦντες ἐς τὸ ἀποζῆν διαρκῶς ἔχοιεν, καὶ ἐπειδὰν αὐτοῖς ξυμμετρήσασθαι τὸν βίον ξυμβαίη, παραψυχήν τινα τῶν οἰκείων ἀπολιπεῖν τοῖς κατὰ τὴν οἰκίαν δυνατοὶ εἶεν. ὁ τοίνυν χρόνος τῶν στρατιωτῶν τοὺς καταδεεστέρους ἐς τῶν τετελευτηκότων ἢ τῆς στρατείας ἀφειμένων τοὺς βαθμοὺς ἀεὶ ἀναβιβάζων πρυτανεύει κατὰ πρεσβεῖα τὰς ἐκ τοῦ δημοσίου συντάξεις ἑκάστῳ. ἀλλ' οἱ λογοθέται καλούμενοι οὐκ εἴων τάξεις ἑκάστῳ. ἐκ τῶν καταλόγων ἀφαιρεῖσθαι τὰ τῶν τετελευτηκότων ὀνόματα, καίπερ ὁμοῦ διαφθειρομένων, ἄλλως τε καὶ κατὰ τοὺς πολέμους συχνοὺς γινομένους, τῶν πλείστων. οὐ μὴν οὐδὲ τοὺς καταλόγους ἔτι ἐπλήρουν, καὶ ταῦτα χρόνου συχνοῦ. καὶ ἀπ' αὐτοῦ περιειστήκει τῇ μὲν πολιτείᾳ τὸν τῶν στρατευομένων ἀριθμὸν ἐνδεέστερον ἀεὶ εἶναι, τῶν δὲ στρατιωτῶν τοῖς περιοῦσι πρὸς τῶν πάλαι τετελευτηκότων διωθουμένοις ἐπὶ μοίρας παρὰ τὴν ἀξίαν τῆς καταδεεστέρας ἀπολελεῖφθαι, τάς τε ξυντάξεις ἐλαττόνως ἢ κατὰ τὴν προσήκουσαν κομίζεσθαι τάξιν, τοῖς δὲ λογοθέταις διαλαγχάνειν Ἰουστινιανῷ τῶν στρατιωτικῶν χρημάτων πάντα τοῦτον τὸν χρόνον.
185 *Cod. Iust.* 1.27.13.
186 *Cod. Iust.* 1.27.19–35.
187 *Cod. Iust.* 1.42.2.

making absolutely sure that someone's husband was dead came down to a concern that there might have been some misappropriation of state funds.

Military problems aside, there are other important considerations to bear in mind when trying to understand Justinian's legislation on these issues. For, corruption aside, the law also recognized the possibility that someone might be captured "by the enemy" (*ab hostibus*) and then returned, though it does not specify who this enemy might be.[188] While examples of this might be few and far between in the literature, they do exist, such as those soldiers captured by the Moors who later escaped, Sergius' nephews' bold attempt to elude his Moor captors, and, in a different context, the narrator in Pseudo-Nilus' *Narrations*.[189] This would, in fact, be a good explanation for silence on the part of a soldier husband: he did not reply because he was an enemy prisoner. Indeed, one of those laws, 5.16.27, even implies that it was impossible to know whether someone married (either husband or wife) who had been captured had died in captivity. *Novel* 22 even includes a clause on captivity.

On the other hand, it is also worth bearing in mind that marriage was an important issue for Justinian, and several pieces of legislation from his legal corpus deal with marriage, from its formation to its dissolution—and its consequences. As it happens, this legislation on soldiers' wives is not out of keeping with the other Justinianic legislation we have for marriage and remarriage. Much Roman law punished women who sought remarriage too soon, though evidence from Egypt suggests that in practice much of this was overlooked by the authorities.[190] Remarriage was a regular facet of Roman life, while marriage itself was, for some in the sixth century CE, the peak of human achievement.[191] Quite a significant proportion of Justinianic law was concerned with protecting the rights of women, undoubtedly due to the influence of Theodora.[192] Indeed, the very law that allowed Justinian to marry Theodora in the first place, promulgated by Justin, made offhand comments about improving women's rights.[193] People regularly got divorced and remarried. In the case of women, when their husbands died they were well within their rights to remarry, so

---

188 *Cod. Iust.* 2.53.5, 5.16.27, 7.35.6.
189 Procop. *Wars* 4.23.17 (soldiers), 4.22.12–17 (Sergius); Caner (2010: 84–135).
190 Arjava 1996: 168, n. 34.
191 *Novel* 2 dated to 535, for instance, a long piece of legislation on remarried women and their rights of preference, amongst other things, takes the existence of their remarriages for granted. The opening lines to *Novel* 140, dated to 566, reads "Mankind has nothing more admirable than marriage: from it stem children and successive generations, the peopling of villages and cities, and society's best bond" (trans. Miller).
192 Beaucamp 1990: 225–231; Miller and Sarris 2018: 65, n. 1.
193 *Cod. Iust.* 5.4.23pr; Potter 2015: 91.

long as the appointed period of mourning (the length of which is unclear) had passed.[194] While remarriages were common, there were strict rules concerning whom one could and could not marry; these were mostly concerned with marriage between blood relatives, those of different religious backgrounds, and adulterous wives.[195] One of the main issues surrounding marriage in late antiquity was the relative position of the two parties: those with unequal social statuses were not permitted to marry.[196] All this being said, divorce was only permitted with just cause, and widows were encouraged to practise chastity.[197] Like Augustus long before him, Justinian had a strong moralizing agenda, and so was keen to regulate marriage as much as possible.[198]

Novel 22, specifically concerned with remarriage, dated to 536, and one of the novels discussed that opened this chapter, also happens to be one of the longer of Justinian's pieces of legislation. As noted earlier, it contains a clause on captivity. Basically, if the husband or the wife are unfortunate enough to suffer capture, the marriage could be dissolved.[199] If one or the other party becomes enslaved, the law dictates that their marriage must be dissolved because of their differing status. On the other hand, if it is a question of whether the person is alive, the other partner must wait at least five years before the marriage could be annulled. *Novel* 117, the source of the other passage discussed in the beginning, includes a number of clauses on the dissolution of marriage, and makes a point of clamping down on the abundance of dissolutions (of marriage) that Justinian felt had taken place too easily.[200]

While it is difficult to say whether there was a methodical attempt by sixth-century lawmakers to ensure all possible legalities concerning marriage would be addressed, the breadth of the coverage on marriage in Justinian's corpus is remarkable. There is even a body of legislation on marriage involving soldiers and similar matters. A law from the *Codex* dated to 426 permits all soldiers from all backgrounds to marry freeborn women with or without a contract.[201] This same stipulation is repeated in a later, much more extensive, novel, 74, where the lowest-ranking soldiers, called *caligati milites* (στρατιώτας ἐνόπλους, οὓς ὁ νόμος καλιγάτους καλεῖ), are given permission, which is in stark contrast

---

194   *Cod. Iust.* 5.9.3.
195   Miller and Sarris 2018: 167, n. 1. On the different standards for extramarital affairs in late antiquity between men and women, see Sessa (2018: 182).
196   Potter 2015: 93; Sessa 2018: 92.
197   Miller and Sarris 2018: 233, n. 1; Sessa 2018: 93.
198   Sessa 2018: 93.
199   *Iust. Nov.* 22.7.
200   *Iust. Nov.* 117.8.
201   *Cod. Iust.* 5.4.21.

to men of illustrious rank, like the empire's senators.[202] The only exception, set out in yet another piece of legislation, is that they should stay away from slave women.[203] But there are plenty of other relevant pieces of legislation. As noted, some legislation even sought to improve the lot of women in the sixth century, and with good reason.[204] There were stories of soldiers going off on campaign married men and then returning with a "new" wife: this was, strictly speaking, illegal.[205]

All in all, there is little in the legal evidence to suggest that Justinian singled out the wives of the empire's soldiers. Rather, Justinian worked to stamp out the corruption that plagued the sixth century military and improve the morale and working conditions of the soldiers, and one of the unfortunate consequences was the extra set of requirements to ensure a soldier, who seemed to be dead, really was.[206] As a result, their wives would be left in limbo, with little consideration for the impact all of this would have on their wellbeing. Although Procopius claimed Justinian hated the soldiers, Justinian's legislation implies that the opposite was true.[207] Or rather, Justinian was willing to go to some lengths to keep up the soldiers' spirits, a necessity in a period of significant recruitment challenges. The plague had undermined Justinian's tax revenues and reduced the number of soldiers in the military.[208] With wars being waged on multiple fronts, he could ill afford to let those still serving abandon their posts. Additionally, the state could not afford the sort of corruption that seems to have been rampant in the military at this time at the higher levels and which Procopius himself addresses. For Procopius, the plague did have an impact on recruitment, but his discussions of this subject are scattered throughout his three works.

4   Conclusion

In the first section of this chapter, I discussed the recruitment of *bucellarii*, with specific reference to an episode involving Justinian's cousin Germanus.

---

202   *Iust. Nov.* 74.4.1–3.
203   *Cod. Iust.* 5.16.2.
204   *Cod. Iust.* 5.11.7, 5.14.11, 6.40.3.
205   Sessa 2018: 132; *Cod. Iust.* 5.5.1.
206   It also highlights the significant gaps in the empire's ability to collect important information about its own soldiery. On this problem at a larger level (running an empire), see the comments and discussion of Kelly (2004: 115, and passim).
207   Kruse (2017b), concerned with the sixth-century consulship, discusses similar issues and makes a good case for the consideration of the legal evidence when evaluating Procopius.
208   Note Sarris' (2017) discussion of related matters.

RECRUITMENT 223

That passage is worth quoting in full, for it provides a neat summary of the recruitment practices described, or better alluded to, by Procopius. Therein, Procopius says the following:

> Then, by spending great sums of money, part of which was provided by the emperor but most of which he furnished unstintingly from his own resources, he easily succeeded, contrary to expectation, in raising a great army of very warlike men in a short amount of time. For among the Romans, men who were experienced fighters disregarded the officers whose spearmen and shield bearers they were and followed Germanus; they came from Byzantium and also from the towns of Thrace and Illyria, and his sons Justin and Justinian displayed great zeal in this recruitment drive, for he had taken them also on his departure. He also chose some of those from the cavalry rolls encamped in Thrace, with the emperor's permission. The barbarians also, who had their homes near the Danube river kept coming in great numbers, attracted by the fame of Germanus, and, upon receiving large sums of money, joined the Roman army. Other barbarians too kept flocking to his standards, collected from the whole world. The ruler of the Lombards also made ready a thousand heavy-armed soldiers and promised to send them immediately.[209]

For one thing, this passage stresses the importance of Germanus' financial resources to raising troops successfully for this campaign. It was not only a matter of resources, however, but personality, at least in Procopius' telling. Non-Roman recruits rushed to Germanus' side because of his personal appeal—though also the money. It also illustrates some of the varied sources of Rome's soldiers. Besides the barbarians (unnamed), there were Lombards who sent soldiers of their own. Soldiers also flocked to Germanus from Illyria, Thrace, and Constantinople. Some were new recruits, while others were enrolled on the rosters of pre-existing units. One other important point that the passage raises, however, is the role of the general, especially vis-à-vis the

---

209   Procop. Wars 7.39.16–20. ἔπειτα δὲ χρήματα μεγάλα τὰ μὲν ἐκ βασιλέως, τὰ δὲ πλείω οἴκοθεν οὐδεμιᾷ φειδοῖ προϊέμενος στρατιὰν ἐκ τοῦ ἀπροσδοκήτου πολλὴν ἀνδρῶν μαχιμωτάτων ἀγεῖραι δι᾽ ὀλίγου εὐπετῶς ἴσχυσε. Ῥωμαῖοί τε γάρ, ἄνδρες ἀγαθοὶ τὰ πολέμια, τῶν ἀρχόντων πολλοὺς ὧν δὴ δορυφόροι τε καὶ ὑπασπισταὶ ἦσαν, ἐν ὀλιγωρίᾳ πεποιημένοι, Γερμανῷ εἵποντο, ἔκ τε Βυζαντίου καὶ τῶν ἐπὶ Θρᾴκης χωρίων καὶ Ἰλλυριῶν οὐδέν τι ἧσσον, Ἰουστίνου τε καὶ Ἰουστινιανοῦ, τῶν αὐτοῦ παίδων, πολλὴν ἐνδειξαμένων περὶ ταῦτα σπουδήν, ἐπεὶ καὶ αὐτοὺς ἐπαγαγόμενος ἀπιὼν ᾤχετο. τινὰς δὲ καὶ ἐκ καταλόγων ἱππικῶν οἳ ἐπὶ τῆς Θρᾴκης ἵδρυντο, δόντος βασιλέως, ξυνέλεξε. καὶ βάρβαροι πολλοὶ οἵπερ ἀμφὶ ποταμὸν Ἴστρον διατριβὴν εἶχον, κατὰ κλέος τοῦ Γερμανοῦ ἥκοντες καὶ χρήματα πολλὰ κεκομισμένοι, ἀνεμίγνυντο τῷ Ῥωμαίων στρατῷ. ἄλλοι τε βάρβαροι ἐκ πάσης ἀγειρόμενοι ξυνέρρεον γῆς. καὶ ὁ τῶν Λαγγοβαρδῶν ἡγούμενος ὁπλίτας χιλίους ἐν παρασκευῇ πεποιημένος αὐτίκα δὴ μάλα ὑπέσχετο πέμψειν.

emperor. Germanus went off to elicit troops from a variety of sources, but he did so only with the emperor's permission, which, as we saw above, he would have had to secure before this process began. That Germanus had Justinian's financial backing suggests that he did. Thus, for all Procopius was concerned with other aspects of military history like battles and generals, a closer look at recruitment reveals that he provides much of the outline material that our other sixth-century evidence supplements well. The rank and file soldiers are there in Procopius' works. If you scratch below the surface, you can find traces not only of their existence, but also their experiences.

Conclusion

In chapter one, I looked at the manifold ways that Procopius privileges commanders, generals particularly, over the course of his works, though the *Wars* especially. Regular, low-ranking, soldiers feature only as somewhat indeterminate masses, who are rarely named, let alone highlighted. The contrast with the generals could not have been more marked. I highlighted the considerable concrete evidence that Procopius minimizes, to a significant degree, the amount of detail that he affords the rank-and-file soldiery.

Procopius did many of the things that classical and classicizing historians do to stress their authority. What is more, Procopius did make a perfectly reasonable case for his accurate reporting in his preface, engaged in autopsy, and had some real experience in the waging of war in the sixth century. There are problems, however, for Procopius' naming of high-ranking officials might be suggestive of the identity of his sources; but it is also sound historiographical practice. Moreover, the abundance of spearmen and shield bearers likely has more to do with the exigencies of the wars of conquest than any gratitude Procopius felt because of their value as sources of information. The hunt for documentary sources has also revealed little. In short, Procopius had access to the kinds of sources that would inform him about these soldiers. There were plenty of firsthand opportunities for Procopius to see low-ranking soldiers. He likely knew officers who had information about these men, and we have every indication that documents existed that documented their lives. What we have also seen, however, is there are a few scattered traces of these sources in Procopius' works, at least based on what we have seen so far.

In chapter three, I turned back to the rank-and-file soldiers as collectives through the perspective of units and regiments. Ultimately, I argued that *arithmos* is the correct term for a generic unit, while *katalogos* is not. Nor does it denote particular units, like regiments of *comitatenses*. Procopius' use of *katalogos* was likely due both to his experiences organizing men in the army using official *matrices*, and his desire to give a nod to a truly classical structure, the Athenian *katalogos*, or conscription list. But it also allowed him to minimize the soldiers, whom he glosses over regularly, in a new way. Procopius' plentiful experiences with the military arranging of new troops conditioned how he saw groups of soldiers. It also provided a means for him to minimize the common soldier's role in the narrative.

In chapter four, I showed why we should no longer equate στρατιῶται with the *comitatenses* that played such a key role in late antique armies. *Comitatenses* and *foederati* were often hard to distinguish in Procopius' works, even if the two were distinct categories in his African and Italian catalogues of forces. One group whom he does distinguish is the *bucellarii*. The distinction between Roman and non-Roman is not so neat either. To my mind, this shows not the barbarization of the military but the growing despecialization in sixth-century soldiers, who might have a range of skills. Procopius' soldiers could be any kind of soldier, even if he devoted much more attention to those armies in the field than to those on the frontier, the subject of the next chapter. That said, Procopius provides few concrete details about the lives or experiences of those soldiers, or about their units and structures. But this is not specific to field army soldiers, for there is also limited detailed evidence for federates and allies.

We have also seen the limitations to Procopius' descriptions of combat. Cavalry is privileged over infantry, but not necessarily because of any perceived skewing of his factual record. Rather, Procopius manipulates the sixth century's tactical history by focusing a little more on cavalry and giving more figures for cavalry soldiers than infantry ones. The horse archers that feature so prominently in the preface to the *Wars* are an ideal, but their role is far from common—and their history is long. They had existed in the Roman military for some time, so reflecting the growing Eurasian character of Roman armies. It is also far from clear that these were non-Roman soldiers.

Turning to *limitanei* in chapter five, while the *Secret History* might be damning about their role in Justinianic combat, the *Wars* is much more circumspect. The *Buildings*, once you scratch beneath the surface, does offer them a role, though it comes out indirectly and it is usually subverted to larger strategic issues, and the important role of the empire's physical infrastructure in its defence policy. In other words, with the *limitanei*, as with so much else besides, Procopius has been very deliberate in what he does describe, and very selective; classicizing tendencies abound (no technicalities, names of *limitanei*, or their units).

In chapter six I looked at that one aspect of the sixth-century' rank and file soldiers about whom Procopius reveals the most, recruitment. I carefully set out the mechanics of the process starting from the highest level and working my way down to the lowest, the experiences of those soldiers, at least where possible. Having set that out, I turned to the demographic problems the empire faced regarding military manpower, at least insofar as what we find in Procopius' own works. The empire's attempts to counter these issues, as reflected in assorted pieces of legislation, can also be found in some select comments in Procopius' oeuvre.

My initial plan had been to write a detailed analysis of Procopius the military historian. I got waylaid along the way, as the end result should make clear. One reason is the increasing attention that I have paid to Ammianus Marcellinus, the other great late antique classicizing historian, whose approach to war and history, though vaguely similar to Procopius', is also significantly different. There are (at least) two areas in which this was most apparent to me: first, in the detail with which he occasionally affords the military units he discusses. He names far more units, and in greater detail, than does Procopius, as is the case in the build-up to the Siege of Amida when he names the specific legions involved in the city's defence.[1] The other area is his attention to the suffering of the soldiers, the face-of-battle approach to battle narrative, that has attracted so much attention. We see this, for instance, in his account of Strasbourg.[2] To my mind, despite some recent forceful arguments to the contrary, Procopius does not devote this level of attention to the rank and file soldiers, the hallmark of face-of-battle approaches.[3] And indeed, as I demonstrated above, the rank and file soldiers, even the lower-ranking shield bearers, who, as a rule, tend to get more attention than the common ones, are rarely named or directly involved in the action. These are only a couple of examples, but they have shown to me just how different their approaches are.

Another formative influence has been two trips to Jordan, one in February of 2017, the other in February of 2018, both funded by SSHRC.[4] Seeing the frontier fortifications in person brought home the important role of these structures and those who inhabited them, not just in Jordan but in the empire in general, in the empire's military policies. Significantly too, these forts and their residents are hardly mentioned by Procopius, which means to understand them fully, or as fully as we can manage, we need to use evidence completely independent of Procopius and other literary sources like him (Agathias for instance).[5] Indeed, while in Jordan I was reminded of the Anastasius edict in Qasr el-Hallabat, an important near contemporary inscription that deserves more attention—though it is in the process of being edited and republished.

---

1 Amm. Marc. 18.9.3.
2 Amm. Marc. 16.12.52–56.
3 Koehn 2018: 189–197. This subject, how different late antique authors describe battle, is the subject of the third of four books from this extended project (with *Battles and Generals* and now this book the first and second components). It will focus on pitched battle narrative in the works of the historians of the age of Justinian, like Procopius, but also Zosimus, Jordanes, Procopius, Agathias, and Theophylact Simocatta.
4 Social Sciences and Humanities Research Council of Canada.
5 This will be the subject of the fourth book in this quartet, the frontier soldiers and their communities in the late antique southeast. It will start with the material in the second half of chapter five and delve deeper, exploring the people, relationships, and lives of those in the sixth-century frontier communities.

As a result, it became quite clear in the research and writing of this book that a military history of Procopius would be a monumental project, and one far more difficult than I had first imagined. Indeed, with *Battles and Generals* in print and this one not far off, I do think they provide the foundation for such a study. Indeed, they could be considered parts one and two of a prolegomenon to a study of Procopius the military historian.

What this book and the previous one have revealed are the myriad challenges that Procopius' three texts provide anyone who would undertake such a study of Procopius the military historian. The evidence of Procopius the author abounds throughout his work. By that I mean we can see throughout the works that Procopius has taken great care to manipulate his subject matter, highlighting some details, ignoring others, and more besides. Indeed, one of the points of this book has to been to show some of the ways that Procopius' selectivity hinders our understanding of war and warfare in the sixth century CE by providing a narrow perspective of the military and its component parts.

In *Battles and Generals*, my inclination had been to excise Procopius the author (i.e. not Procopius the narrator) as much as possible from the text with the proviso that the author is dead, and knowing about him should or would have had no impact on how we understand his approach to battle. In the end, the chapter on Procopius' background was included largely to provide the necessary context for interested readers. In this book, Procopius the author has played a much more significant role, in part because of some changes in my thinking, in part because this is the way the evidence, and some recent research, has led me. I put great stock in the consideration of Procopius' experiences and the sources he used and had access to.

A big part of this book has been looking into accessibility. Where Procopius gets things wrong, like what he said about *limitanei* in the *Secret History*, or more likely excludes certain details, like the role of the *limitanei* in the action that he describes in the *Wars* and *Buildings*, was this because he was not able to get the information that he needed? That is, to what degree was Procopius' apparent reticence at identifying rank and file soldiers and giving their names dictated by the kinds of information that Procopius had access to?

As I argued, there was plenty of material available to him, both in general, and more specifically. In general, because we have lots of evidence for the documentary history of the sixth-century military, even if nearly all of the documents themselves no longer exist. Specifically, because of Procopius' own experiences, which by his own account, at least in Italy, involved managing the records for the troops during the campaign, the sort of records, the lists, that Germanus consults, "the books [τὰ βιβλία] of the secretaries", upon his arrival in Carthage.[6] For all we know, Procopius might also have been involved in asking Justinian for reinforcements. In short, Procopius was in a position to get all of the documents that he might have needed to write about the subject matter which he did not have firsthand accounts of.

By and large, as we have seen, he did not use them. While it is easy to see this in his references to soldiers and regiments, we can see it too when he turns to combat. So much of what he says is focused on Belisarius and generals, and so little on the rest. He has carefully manipulated the relative efforts of infantry and cavalry in the empire's wars, and put a lot of stock on horse archers, which were by no means exceptional, despite their role in the Italian conflict.

On the one hand, what we have seen throughout this book is the problem with focusing too much attention on Procopius. Indeed, by focusing too much on Procopius we are just about as guilty as Procopius for spending too much time on Belisarius. In the end, my intention in this book has not been to muddy the waters by deconstructing Procopius to such an extent that there is little of real, historical, value left, at least that does not pertain solely to the realm of intellectual history. Rather, it has been to remove the covers and so reveal the scale of the challenge for those interested in giving Procopius' value as a military historian due consideration. But it has also been to highlight some of the important other evidence we have for military affairs in the sixth century: the law codes, the inscriptions, the papyri, even the material evidence, which I have hardly had occasion to discuss, deserve much more attention.

And yet, though Procopius was beholden to his classicizing perspective, which meant an obligation to focus on generals and war from a top-down perspective, scattered beneath the surface are plenty of details on the rank and file soldiers, at least in certain respects. On the one hand, the dominant role played by the field army soldiers is not as apparent as it might have initially seemed, and στρατιώτης (soldier) should not be used a synonym for a field army soldier, a *comitatensis*. In fact, there was considerable overlap in Procopius' works between the different kinds of soldiers, at least as he described them. On the other hand, though seemingly downgraded if not erased from most actions, there are more *limitanei* in Procopius' oeuvre, and in the sixth century more generally, than might have been expected. What is more, Procopius is a veritable goldmine for the question of recruitment in the sixth century, both at the level of mechanics and larger demographic issues, especially vis-à-vis the plague.

---

6   Procop. *Wars* 4.16.3.

And so, to close, it is worth going back to Flower's pronouncements on Xenophon, which I highlighted in the introduction. Three important considerations raised by Flower were whether what Xenophon had to say was probable, and whether his work was internally consistent, the importance of looking at other sources, and the degree to which he was internally consistent. To test Procopius' value as a source for the rank-and-file soldiers, in the preceding chapters I resorted to the kinds of practices advocated by Flower for Xenophon. Regarding recruitment, Procopius' account is probable and consistent, and this is confirmed by external sources. In playing close attention to Procopius' use of two important terms κατάλογος and στρατιώτης, it is clear that he is consistent through all three works. Finally, while Procopius includes plenty of evidence for rank and file soldiers, and though his writing is conditioned by his personal and literary context, it is the other sixth-century sources, the inscriptions, papyri, and law codes, among other things, that will ultimately allow us to get a more complete picture of soldiers and military affairs in the sixth century.

APPENDIX

Soldiers in Procopius' *Wars*, *Buildings*, and *Secret History*

Numbers	Location	Usage[a]	Type[b]
1.	Wars 1.6.18	All the soldiers	Persian
2.	1.7.4	The Amidenes had no soldiers present	Soldiers at Amida (lack thereof)
3.	1.8.2	Those leading the soldiers in Byzantium	Soldiers in Constantinople, possibly bodyguards
4.	1.8.4	Each man led the soldiers	Roman (in general)
5.	1.9.2	Seeing the soldiers distressed	Roman (in general)
6.	1.9.7	Roman soldiers	Roman (in general)
7.	1.9.14	1000 soldiers	Roman (in general)
8.	1.9.23	The generals … reproached the soldiers	Roman (in general)
9.	1.10.11	Support the soldiers	Roman (possibly frontier but ambiguous)
10.	1.12.18	Roman soldiers be stationed	Roman (in garrison, so maybe frontier)
11.	1.13.5	Who led the soldiers in Lebanon	Possibly frontier
12.	1.13.30	Not a soldier nor one who ever practises war	Roman (in general, amongst the entire army at Dara)
13.	1.14.1	Ten thousand soldiers	Persian
14.	1.14.25	Serve the soldiers	Persian
15.	1.14.28	Drew up the soldiers	Roman (in general at Dara)
16.	1.15.33	He ordered the soldiers	General (ultimately Roman)

a Note that Procopius uses the standard word, στρατιώτης, for soldier, and he uses it in a variety of different cases and numbers—and standard forms. The first usage, for instance, is dative plural (στρατιώταις—masculine). All that said, I have not included the adjectival form: στρατιωτικός. On the other hand, I have excluded those instances where Procopius used a verbal form of soldier, like "serve on campaign", στρατόω, or even "enlist in the military", στρατεύω, from my table.

b By type, I mean larger imperial group (Persian, Roman), smaller regional group (Thracian), or kind of soldier (bodyguard).

(cont.)

Numbers	Location	Usage	Type
17.	1.17.34	Great number of soldiers	Roman (in the cities of Mesopotamia and Osroene)
18.	1.17.36	Desolate of soldiers	Roman (Antioch)
19.	1.17.39	Soldiers in Mesopotamia	Roman (frontier maybe)
20.	1.17.42	The generals and the soldiers	Roman (in Mesopotamia, frontier maybe)
21.	1.17.43	He captured all the soldiers	Roman
22.	1.17.46	Commander of the Roman soldiers	Frontier (led by *duces*)
23.	1.18.12	Both the commander and soldiers	Roman (army at Callinicum)
24.	1.18.24	Some of the commanders joined the soldiers	Roman (at Callinicum)
25.	1.18.52	Each of the soldiers takes one arrow	Persian
26.	1.18.53	The number of soldiers	Persian
27.	1.19.29	A very great number of soldiers	Roman (possibly frontier, reign of Diocletian)
28.	1.19.33	Fear of the soldiers	Generic (but Roman, and probably frontier)
29.	1.19.37	Led the soldiers	Roman (frontier, Elephantine/Philae)
30.	1.22.3	The one who led the soldiers in Mesopotamia	Roman (frontier, at Dara)
31.	1.22.16	No longer anyone in charge of soldiers in Dara	Roman (frontier, at Dara)
32.	1.23.25	The soldiers under his command	Persian
33.	1.24.39	All the soldiers	Rome (both those at the imperial court and the rest)
34.	1.24.44	Garrison of soldiers	Roman (from the palace)
35.	1.24.44	He ordered the soldiers	Roman (presumably the same as above)
36.	1.24.45	Since the soldiers had decided	Roman (presumably the same as above)

(cont.)

Numbers	Location	Usage	Type
37.	1.24.47	The soldiers of the palace garrison	Roman
38.	1.24.49	Soldiers of Hypatius	Roman (unclear, maybe bodyguards)
39.	1.24.51	When they saw the armoured soldiers (στρατιώτας ... τεθωρακισμένους)	Roman (possibly the soldiers of Belisarius and Mundo, who had fought against Persia, some of whom were spearmen and shield bearers)
40.	1.24.56	The soldiers executed both of them	Roman (general, but including those just noted above)
41.	1.25.24	With many soldiers	Roman (from the palace guard)
42.	1.26.5	With some of the soldiers	Roman (possibly infantry soldiers at Dara, possibly frontier)
43.	1.26.8	Some soldiers came to an agreement	Roman (possibly same as above)
44.	1.26.9	The soldiers were not the first	Roman (same as above)
45.	1.26.11	These very soldiers	Roman (some of the same ones as above)
46.	1.26.12	Fearing the soldiers	Roman (some of the same as above)
47.	2.1.9	Soldiers in Palestine	Roman (possibly frontier)
48.	2.3.52	Majority of Roman soldiers	Roman (general)
49.	2.5.11	Who led the soldiers	Roman (at Sura, possibly frontier)
50.	2.5.11	He led the soldiers	Roman (at Sura, possibly frontier)
51.	2.6.22	Garrisoned with soldiers	Roman (at Hierapolis, possibly frontier)
52.	2.7.7	The soldiers who had been stationed there	Roman (at Beroia, possibly frontier, possibly more temporary)

(cont.)

Numbers	Location	Usage	Type
53.	2.7.12	The Roman soldiers	Roman (at Beroia, possibly frontier, possibly more temporary)
54.	2.7.37	A few of the soldiers	Roman (at Beroia, possibly frontier, possibly more temporary)
55.	2.8.2	Commanders (Theoctistus and Molatzes) of the soldiers in Lebanon	Roman (possibly frontier)
56.	2.8.11	Not just the soldiers	Roman (possibly frontier, based temporarily at Antioch)
57.	2.8.17	The soldiers with Theoctistus and Molatzes	Roman (possibly frontier, based temporarily at Antioch)
58.	2.8.19	The soldiers ... sparing no one	Persian
59.	2.8.23	He saw the soldiers fleeing	Roman (possibly frontier, based temporarily at Antioch)
60.	2.8.24	The Roman soldiers	Roman (possibly frontier, based temporarily at Antioch)
61.	2.8.25	The Roman soldiers with their commander	Roman (possibly frontier, based temporarily at Antioch)
62.	2.8.26	Escaped with the soldiers	Roman (possibly frontier, based temporarily at Antioch)
63.	2.8.27	The Roman soldiers had moved on	Roman (possibly frontier, based temporarily at Antioch)
64.	2.8.33	Large number of his best soldiers	Persian
65.	2.10.1	The standards of the soldiers	Roman (at Antioch, frontier possibly)
66.	2.10.2	The soldiers showed this	Romans (at Antioch, possibly frontier)

(cont.)

Numbers	Location	Usage	Type
67.	2.10.23	Their own soldiers	Persian
68.	2.12.1	All the soldiers who were there	Roman (at Chalkis, possibly frontier)
69.	2.12.2	As for soldiers	Roman (at Chalkis, possibly frontier)
70.	2.12.2	Andonachus who led the soldiers there	Roman (at Chalkis, possibly frontier)
71.	2.13.14	Neither a garrison of soldiers	Roman (at Constantine—but none present)
72.	2.14.12	Led the soldiers in Mesopotamia	Roman (at Mesopotamia, so maybe frontier)
73.	2.15.6	Roman soldiers started to be based in Lazica	Roman (among the Lazi, possibly frontier)
74.	2.16.2	Equipping the soldiers	Roman (Belisarius was gathering his army from everywhere, organizing and equipping them, so maybe mixed force)
75.	2.16.17	Who led the soldiers in Lebanon	Roman (in Lebanon, under Recithanc and Theoctistus)
76.	2.18.8	He stationed the soldiers in such number and quality	Persian
77.	2.18.13	When soldiers are defending it [wall]	Persian
78.	2.19.13	Some of our soldiers who are good fighters (μαχίμων)	Roman (general or varied)
79.	2.19.15	1,200 soldiers	Roman (mixed, "most of whom were his spearmen")
80.	2.19.31	Many of the soldiers	Roman (varied)
81.	2.19.39	Our most efficient soldiers	Roman (presumably the same as the 1,200, mixed)
82.	2.20.14	No more than 200 soldiers	Roman (at Sura, possibly frontier)
83.	2.20.19	Whether commanders or soldiers	Roman (possibly general, possibly frontier)
84.	2.20.26	Guard of soldiers	Roman (possibly frontier—generic territory)

(cont.)

Numbers	Location	Usage	Type
85.	2.21.3	He arranged the soldiers	Roman ("he [Beliarius] arranged the soldiers as follows. On either side ... Thracians and Illyrians, with Goths beyond them, and next to them Heruls, and finally Vandals and Moors"
86.	2.21.14	And soldiers such as he	Roman (in general)
87.	2.21.20	So many myriads of barbarians with soldiers	Persian
88.	2.21.31	The rest without soldiers remained there	Roman (in general)
89.	2.23.6	He posted soldiers from the palace	Roman (from the palace)
90.	2.25.14	The soldiers marched	Roman (mixed)
91.	2.26.7	But Roman soldiers and some of the populace	Roman (at Edessa, possibly frontier)
92.	2.27.23	Not only the soldiers but even the peasants	Roman (at Edessa, possibly frontier)
93.	2.27.34	Repelling the enemy ... with the soldiers	Roman (at Edessa, possibly frontier)
94.	2.27.42	Peranius with many soldiers	Roman (at Edessa, possibly frontier)
95.	2.28.32	A large force of soldiers	Persian
96.	2.30.5	He led the soldiers	Roman (in general)
97.	3.2.31	From the Romans and the soldiers there	Roman (in Britain, collectively, so mixed, but not explicitly specified by Procopius)
98.	3.2.36	A great number of soldiers	Roman (from Constantinople/Byzantion—east in general)
99.	3.3.5	One of the soldiers there	Roman (soldiers in Rome)

SOLDIERS IN PROCOPIUS' WARS, BUILDINGS, AND SECRET HISTORY 237

(cont.)

Numbers	Location	Usage	Type
100.	3.6.1	Both soldiers and sailors	Roman (sent by Leo)
101.	3.6.20	The soldiers together with the sailors	Roman (Leo's expedition)
102.	3.6.22	Plundered the soldiers	Roman (Leo's expedition)
103.	3.7.19	By the soldiers of the court	Roman (of the court)
104.	3.10.2	Reciting how many soldiers had perished	Roman (Leo's expedition)
105.	3.10.5	The soldiers ... recently returned	Roman (veterans who had fought against Persia)
106.	3.10.31	Send soldiers	Roman (general)
107.	3.10.32	Promised ... soldiers	Roman (general
108.	3.10.34	His wish to have soldiers	Roman (general)
109.	3.11.1	400 soldiers	Roman
110.	3.11.2	10,000 foot soldiers	Roman (infantry—from the registers and *foederati*)
111.	3.11.2	5,000 horsemen	Roman (cavalry—from the registers and *foederati*)
112.	3.11.7	Cavalry (στρατιωτῶν δὲ ἱππέων)	Roman (general)
113.	3.12.2	One of the soldiers	Roman (recently baptized—Kaldellis, p. 171, speculates this is Theodosius, who hada been adopted by Belisarius, SH 1.15ff)
114.	3.12.10	Even by Roman soldiers	Roman (Vandal expedition soldiers)
115.	3.13.10	Drew up the soldiers	Roman (Vandal expedition soldiers)
116.	3.13.11	Many of the soldiers died	Roman (Vandal expedition soldiers)
117.	3.13.14	How he destroyed the soldiers	Roman (Vandal expedition soldiers)
118.	3.13.15	The bread that soldiers are assigned	Roman (those in camp, and so soldiers in general)
119.	3.13.15	When such bread is distributed, the soldiers ... receive	Roman (as above)

(cont.)

Numbers	Location	Usage	Type
120.	3.13.19	Dispensed ... to the soldiers[c]	Roman (Vandal expedition soldiers)
121.	3.13.20	The soldiers became sick	Roman (Vandal expedition soldiers)
122.	3.14.2	He was disturbed by the soldiers	Roman (Vandal expedition soldiers)
123.	3.15.20	The soldiers said openly earlier	Roman (Vandal expedition soldiers)
124.	3.15.22	The soldiers would be blameless	Roman (Vandal expedition soldiers)
125.	3.15.32	Ordered both the soldiers and sailors	Roman (Vandal expedition soldiers)
126.	3.15.36	All the soldiers bivouacked in the camp	Roman (Vandal expedition soldiers)
127.	3.16.1	Some of the soldiers went out	Roman (Vandal expedition soldiers)
128.	3.17.6	He kept the soldiers in line	Roman (Vandal expedition soldiers)
129.	3.17.6	Served the soldiers	Roman (Vandal expedition soldiers)
130.	3.17.10	Each of the soldiers pitched his tent	Roman (Vandal expedition soldiers)
131.	3.19.6	A soldier who is ill-disposed	Roman (generic)
132.	3.20.2	Prevent his soldiers	Roman (Vandal expedition soldiers)
133.	3.20.11	Archelaus and the soldiers ordered them	Roman (Vandal expedition soldiers—some of them)
134.	3.20.18	He reminded the soldiers	Roman (Vandal expedition soldiers)
135.	3.21.9	Roman soldiers not accustomed	Roman (in general)
136.	3.21.10	Drew up their list of soldiers	Roman (Vandal expedition soldiers)
137.	3.23.3	Killed many from the Roman army, not soldiers	Roman (Vandal expedition slaves and servants)

c   The bread, distributed to the soldiers, is divvied up by *choinix* and *medimnos*, so using measurements that you find in the papyri from Egypt. See Mitthof (2001).

(cont.)

Numbers	Location	Usage	Type
138.	3.23.4	They had slain enemy soldiers	Roman (supposedly soldiers but in fact slaves and servants)
139.	3.23.13	One of the soldiers roused from sleep	Roman (Vandal expedition soldiers)
140.	3.24.17	Happened upon some Roman soldiers	Roman (some, general)
141.	4.1.4	Roman soldiers who followed the doctrine of Arius	Roman (Arians, otherwise unspecified)
142.	4.4.3	The soldiers were extremely poor men	Roman (Vandal expedition soldiers)
143.	4.4.7	Heaping reproaches upon all, soldiers and commanders alike	Roman (general)
144.	4.4.11	Gathered the soldiers hastily	Roman (general)
145.	4.4.12	With soldiers to guard them	Roman (general)
146.	4.4.22	Soldiers no longer pressed the pursuit	Roman (general)
147.	4.4.25	The soldiers said	Roman (general)
148.	4.4.28	He chose out the soldiers	Roman (some of the expeditionary soldiers)
149.	4.7.20	Might of soldiers (στρατιωτῶν δυνάμει)	Vandal
150.	4.8.21	Soldiers were both few ... along the frontier	Roman (all or part of the expeditionary army minus Belisarius' spearmen and shield bearers)
151.	4.10.2	Barbarians had destroyed the soldiers	Roman (in Byzacium and Numidia, including Massagetae and Thracians)
152.	4.11.32	A good soldier derives his confidence from himself	Roman (in general)
153.	4.11.51	No less than 500 soldiers	Roman (with Solomon, general?)
154.	4.11.56	The soldiers secured as booty all the camels	Roman (as above)
155.	4.12.11	The soldiers were intimidated	Roman (with Solomon, general?)

(cont.)

Numbers	Location	Usage	Type
156.	4.12.20	The soldiers were completely at a loss	Roman (with Solomon, general?)
157.	4.13.31	The soldiers brought themselves and their horses	Roman (with Solomon, general?)
158.	4.14.7	Mutiny among the soldiers in Libya	Roman (possibly frontier already)
159.	4.14.8	The Roman soldiers took their wives and daughters	Roman (expeditionary ones)
160.	4.14.10	The soldiers did not think	Roman (expeditionary ones)
161.	4.14.10	Slaves and ... other things ... should go to the soldiers	Roman (expeditionary ones)
162.	4.14.10	Both become and be called soldiers	Roman (expeditionary ones)
163.	4.14.12	Not fewer than 1000 soldiers of the Arian faith	Roman (barbarian, some Herul)
164.	4.14.18	Vandal soldiers	Vandal (but ones sent east to fight for Rome)
165.	4.14.20	The soldiers who were planning the mutiny	Roman
166.	4.14.30	Being done by the soldiers	Roman (in general)
167.	4.14.36	Houses that had no soldiers to defend them	Generic
168.	4.14.40	Some of the soldiers known to him	Roman (general—mutineers)
169.	4.14.42	Treatment at the hands of his own soldiers	Roman (emperor's own)
170.	4.15.16	In the minds of his soldiers	Roman (Belisarius')
171.	4.15.20	The mass of Roman soldiers	Roman (in general)
172.	4.15.34	As soldiers you will be required to spend all your lives in the dangers of war	Roman (emperor's)
173.	4.15.47	He gave to the soldiers	Roman (general)
174.	4.15.58	The soldiers listened to his words	Roman (listening to Stotzas)
175.	4.16.3	Germanus counted the soldiers	Roman (general)

(cont.)

Numbers	Location	Usage	Type
176.	4.16.3	the names of the soldiers	Roman (general on the rolls counted by Germanus)
177.	4.16.4	Defend the soldiers	Roman (mutineers)
178.	4.16.8	The defection of more of his soldiers	Romana (mutineers)
179.	4.16.9	The soldiers in Carthage	Roman (possibly frontier)
180.	4.17.22	The soldiers of the emperor	Roman (of the emperor—general)
181.	4.17.22	A soldier of Germanus	Roman (general, in Germanus' army)
182.	4.17.29	The soldiers, finding it easy to plunder	Roman (Germanus' army)
183.	4.18.2	Most of the soldiers	Roman (under Maximinus, a spearman of Theodorus)
184.	4.18.9	Many soldiers were standing in disorder	Roman (part of the conspiracy of Maximinus)
185.	4.19.3	Enrolling new soldiers to take their place	Roman (enrolled for continued unrest in Africa)
186.	4.20.12	An infantryman among the soldiers (ἐν τοῖς στρατιώταις πεζός)	Roman (optio of the roster, a Roman paymaster)
187.	4.20.27	The Roman soldier ... drew his sword quietly	Roman (general)
188.	4.20.28	The soldiers, now emboldened	Roman (under Solomon)
189.	4.21.24	The soldiers were dissatisfied and protested	Roman (under Solomon)
190.	4.22.2	The soldiers disliked him	Roman (in general)
191.	4.23.1	Having a few soldiers	Roman (under Stotzas)
192.	4.23.7	With the soldiers under him, numbering 50	Roman (under Severianus, a Phoenician)
193.	4.23.10	Any of his soldiers	Roman (under Himerius)
194.	4.23.10	Handed his soldiers over	Roman (under Himerius)
195.	4.23.12	With some of those soldiers following Stotzas	Roman (under Stotzas)
196.	4.23.14	Commander of all the soldiers in Byzacium	Roman (possibly frontier)

(*cont.*)

Numbers	Location	Usage	Type
197.	4.23.21	Only a few soldiers	Roman (in general)
198.	4.23.23	The garments that Roman soldiers are accustomed to wear	Libyans (dressed like Roman soldiers)
199.	4.23.31	Many Roman soldiers following him	Roman (under Stotzas)
200.	4.24.1	A few soldiers	Roman (sent by the emperor under Areobindus)
201.	4.24.4	The rosters of soldiers	Roman (to be under Sergius and Areobindus)
202.	4.25.10	1,500 Roman soldiers	Roman (under Antalas, to be at Byzacium)
203.	4.26.10	To the soldiers	Roman (under and allied to Areobindus)
204.	4.26.10	The soldiers, fighting both with hunger and the Moors	Roman (in general)
205.	4.26.11	Captured by the soldiers and ruthlessly put to death	Roman (in general)
206.	4.26.12	[give] to the soldiers money of his own	Roman (in general)
207.	4.27.1	Deprive him of … soldiers	Roman (formerly under Areobindus)
208.	4.27.6	The soldiers … stationed in Byzacium	Roman (possibly frontier)
209.	4.27.7	Soldiers of Stotzas	Roman (in general)
210.	4.28.50	John rallied the soldiers	Roman (in general—survivors of wars)
211.	5.1.4	The prestige of the Roman soldiers declined	Roman (in general)
212.	5.3.21	Mistake made by soldiers	Roman (in general)
213.	5.5.2	4,000 soldiers from the rolls and the *foederati*	Roman (from the rolls and *foederati*)
214.	5.7.29	Land … full of soldiers	Roman (seemingly many myriads)
215.	5.8.43	Losing many of the soldiers	Roman (under Belisarius)
216.	5.9.4	Soldiers of the emperor	Roman (in general—part of a story)

SOLDIERS IN PROCOPIUS' WARS, BUILDINGS, AND SECRET HISTORY 243

(cont.)

Numbers	Location	Usage	Type
217.	5.9.5	Soldiers of the emperor	Roman (in general—part of a story)
218.	5.9.6	A few of the soldiers	Roman (under the emperor)
219.	5.10.17	Soldiers in a state of perplexity	Roman (attacking Naples)
220.	5.10.19	The soldiers, laying hold of it	Roman (attacking Naples)
221.	5.10.21	Ordering the soldiers to mount them	Roman (under Belisarius at Naples)
222.	5.10.23	The soldiers got above the level	Roman (attacking Naples)
223.	5.10.24	The soldiers were unable	Roman (attacking Naples)
224.	5.10.34	He reconciled the soldiers to civilians	Roman (under Belisarius)
225.	5.10.37	Holding them in no less honour than his own soldiers	Roman (in general—compared to Goths at Naples)
226.	5.12.13	The Arborychi had become soldiers of the Romans	Roman (in general)
227.	5.12.16	Other Roman soldiers	Roman (frontier at Gaul)
228.	5.12.51	2,000 soldiers	Gothic
229.	5.15.2	A small number of soldiers	Roman (under Belisarius)
230.	5.16.14	Summoned the soldiers holding all the fortresses there	Roman (frontier at Salones/Dalmatia)
231.	5.16.16	Filling their ships with soldiers	Barbarian (under Asinarius)
232.	5.17.14	Stationed in it a garrison of soldiers	Roman (under Belisarius)
233.	5.17.17	Roman soldiers from the cavalry register of Innocentius	Roman (under Innocentius)
234.	5.17.19	All the soldiers … keeping guard	Roman (in general)
235.	5.18.4	Began to fight in the front ranks like a soldier	Roman (Belisarius fighting like a soldier)
236.	5.18.34	Gathered the soldiers	Roman (in general)
237.	5.22.2	He ordered the soldiers to remain quiet	Roman (under siege at Rome)
238.	5.22.16	Since he had a few soldiers	Roman (under siege at Rome)

(cont.)

Numbers	Location	Usage	Type
239.	5.23.14	The soldiers in Vivarium	Roman (under siege at Rome)
240.	5.23.18	Allowed the soldiers to defend the wall	Roman (under siege at Rome)
241.	5.24.2	Stationed a great number of soldiers in Sicily and Italy	Roman (under siege at Rome)
242.	5.24.8	Let both arms and soldiers be sent to us	Roman (request for reinforcements)
243.	5.25.3	He ordered the soldiers	Roman (under siege at Rome)
244.	5.25.11	The number of soldiers	Roman (in general—insufficient to surround walls at Rome)
245.	5.25.11	Mingled soldiers and civilians together	Roman (under siege at Rome)
246.	5.25.17	He sent some of the soldiers	Roman (though Moors too)
247.	5.27.1	1,600 cavalry (στρατιώτας ἱππεῖς)	Huns, Sclaveni, Antae (fighting for Rome)
248.	5.28.25	Cowardice of the soldiers	Roman (under siege at Rome)
249.	5.29.16	The soldiers on both sides	Roman and Goth
250.	5.29.23	Thinking they were soldiers	Roman (thinking they were soldiers)
251.	5.29.25	Not all soldiers	Roman (under siege at Rome)
252.	5.29.28	Caused the soldiers	Roman (under siege at Rome)
253.	5.29.49	A very great number of soldiers	Roman (under siege at Rome)
254.	6.2.1	The money the emperor owed the soldiers	Roman (in general)
255.	6.2.6	Held his soldiers near the gates	Roman (under siege at Rome)
256.	6.3.1	Some grain for the soldiers	Roman (under siege at Rome)
257.	6.3.8	The most daring of the soldiers	Roman (under siege at Rome)

(cont.)

Numbers	Location	Usage	Type
258.	6.4.2	Gather all the soldiers who had arrived from Byzantium	Roman (newly arrived from Constantinople)
259.	6.4.19	500 soldiers there	Roman (in Campania which Procopius collected)
260.	6.5.1	1,000 others soldiers from the cavalry rolls	Roman (from the cavalry under various commanders)
261.	6.7.25	Abundantly supplied with soldiers	Roman (based at Rome)
262.	6.9.12	Not many soldiers left there	Roman (based at Rome)
263.	6.10.10	Ability to endure hardship unsurpassed by any ... soldier	Roman (in general—John has these qualities)
264.	6.12.14	So he armed his soldiers	Roman (under John)
265.	6.12.40	The soldiers were not keeping watch of the wall	Roman (at Milan)
266.	6.13.9	Together with the soldiers	Roman (under Conon at Auximus)
267.	6.13.9	Destitute of soldiers	Roman (at Auximus)
268.	6.13.13	Received the soldiers	Roman (in general)
269.	6.13.17	1,000 soldiers followed	Roman (under Narses from Byzantium)
270.	6.16.11	Number of soldiers	Goths (Narses discussing Goths)
271.	6.16.14	A soldier who had escaped from Ariminum	Roman (escaped from Goths)
272.	6.18.5	The greater part of the soldiers	Roman (under Belisarius and potentially Narses)
273.	6.21.11	Hopes of the soldiers	Roman (at Milan)
274.	6.21.20	Inexpedient for soldiers	Roman (in general—Belisarius to Narses)
275.	6.21.27	The soldiers remain free from harm	Roman (under Mundilas)
276.	6.21.29	Give pledges to Mundilas and the soldiers	Roman (under Mundilas)
277.	6.21.30	Called all the soldiers together	Roman (under Mundilas)
278.	6.21.38	Not one of the soldiers	Roman (generic—under Mundilas)

246　　　　　　　　　　　　　　　　　　　　　　　　　　　　APPENDIX

(cont.)

Numbers	Location	Usage	Type
279.	6.22.5	Bringing some few soldiers	Roman (under Narses)
280.	6.23.23	To urge the soldiers on	Roman (generic—of old)
281.	6.23.24	Give appropriate commands to the soldiers	Roman (generic—of old)
282.	6.23.27	Urge on the soldiers	Roman (generic)
283.	6.23.34	And this signal, soldiers, will be given by the trumpet	Roman (under Belisarius)
284.	6.23.35	The soldiers, seeing the enemy near	Roman (under Belisarius)
285.	6.26.5	The soldier, won over by the money	Roman (Burcentius, a Besi, under Narses)
286.	6.27.21	Belisarius ordered the soldiers	Roman (under Belisarius)
287.	6.27.31	The soldiers would not allow	Roman (under Belisarius)
288.	6.28.17	Multitude of soldiers	Roman (whom the emperor can enlist)
289.	7.1.8	Love ever felt for him by soldiers	Roman (who served Belisarius)
290.	7.1.8	His treatment of the soldiers	Roman (who served Belisarius)
291.	7.1.8	When a soldier had lost a horse	Roman (who served Belisarius)
292.	7.1.19	Looked upon by commanders and soldiers	Roman (who served under Belisarius and besides)
293.	7.1.23	Mercy of the soldiers	Roman (in Italy without Belisarius)
294.	7.1.23	Obedience to their commands on the part of the soldiers	Roman (in Italy without Belisarius)
295.	7.1.25	Many of the Roman soldiers	Roman (those deserting to Ildibadus)
296.	7.1.29	Always making charges against the soldiers	Roman (suffering at the hands of Alexander, the Logothete)
297.	7.1.29	The soldiers were both few and poor and reluctant to face the perils of war	Roman (in general)

SOLDIERS IN PROCOPIUS' WARS, BUILDINGS, AND SECRET HISTORY 247

(cont.)

Numbers	Location	Usage	Type
298.	7.1.33	He [Alexander] disappointed the soldiers by the niggardliness of the reckoning with which he repaid them for their wounds and danger	Roman (in general)
299.	7.1.33	Not one of the soldiers	Roman (in general)
300.	7.4.11	A great number of soldiers	Roman (Totila speaking to Goths of Roman soldiers in garrison in Italy)
301.	7.6.7	The soldiers ... showing themselves subordinate	Roman (in Italy)
302.	7.6.9	Furnish the soldiers with provisions	Roman (in Italy—to be under Maximinus as praetorian prefect)
303.	7.6.10	Thracian and Armenian soldiers	Roman (Thracian and Armenian reinforcements for Maximinus)
304.	7.6.18	The soldiers at Rome	Roman (left as garrison at Rome)
305.	7.7.16	All his soldiers	Roman (under Conon)
306.	7.7.17	All the soldiers with Conon	Roman (under Conon)
307.	7.8.6	Conon and the soldiers with him	Roman (under Conon)
308.	7.8.20	A great many soldiers	Goth (Totila in a speech to his men)
309.	7.9.1	The commanders of the Roman army with the soldiers	Roman (in Italy)
310.	7.9.1	The soldiers ... showing themselves ... subordinate	Roman (in Italy)
311.	7.9.4	The soldiers ... unable to defend them	Roman (in Italy)
312.	7.9.14	The soldiers ...	Roman (in letter from Totila to Roman senate)
313.	7.9.14	... and commanders of soldiers	Roman (in letter from Totila to Roman senate)
314.	7.10.1	An especially small number of soldiers	Roman (under Belisarius—he gathers Thracians)

(cont.)

Numbers	Location	Usage	Type
315.	7.10.3	The Illyrian soldiers	Roman (Illyrian soldiers under Vitalius)
316.	7.11.1	The Roman soldiers	Roman (in Ravenna)
317.	7.11.3	The treatment of his soldiers	Roman (Belisarius in speech to soldiers, general)
318.	7.11.11	The Illyrian soldiers	Roman (Illyrian under Belisarius)
319.	7.11.18	Commander of the Illyrian soldiers	Roman (in Illyricum under Nazares)
320.	7.11.19	1,000 soldiers	Roman (sent under spearmen Thurimuth, Ricilas, Sabinianus)
321.	7.11.27	One of the soldiers ... deserted	Roman (deserter who tells all to Totila)
322.	7.11.31	Clothing of the soldiers	Roman (their servants, weapons, and clothing captured)
323.	7.12.2	The few soldiers	Roman (serving the state, but owed money)
324.	7.12.4	Travel about ... through Thrace and Illyricum, the soldiers we gathered	Roman (from Illyricum and Thrace, new and unpractised recruits)
325.	7.12.7	Fallen behind ... the payment of the soldiers	Roman (in general)
326.	7.12.14	The soldiers	Roman (garrison in Spoleto)
327.	7.12.20	The soldiers of Cyprian	Roman (at Perugia, loyal to emperor)
328.	7.13.20	An army of barbarian and Roman soldiers	Roman and barbarian (an army of both under John, Isaac the Armenian, and Narses, sent by the emperor)
329.	7.15.2	Most warlike of the soldiers in Rome	Roman (in Rome under Bessas)
330.	7.15.3	3,000 soldiers with him	Roman (the soldiers under Bessas at Rome)

(cont.)

Numbers	Location	Usage	Type
331.	7.15.7	A certain soldier of Innocentius	Roman (under Innocentius)
332.	7.17.1	The soldiers, however, had not exhausted	Roman (in Rome)
333.	7.17.10	The soldiers were constantly taking	Roman (the garrison under Bessas and Conon in Rome)
334.	7.17.16	The soldiers of the emperor	Roman (in Rome under Bessas and Conon)
335.	7.18.21	The emperor's soldiers	Roman (the emperor's)
336.	7.18.23	The soldiers no longer entertained any suspicion	Roman (in Italy, at least some of them)
337.	7.18.26	The Roman soldiers	Roman (who deserted, with some Moors, to Totila)
338.	7.18.28	Killed many of the ... Roman soldiers	Roman (many of the deserters along with the Moors, John kills)
339.	7.19.5	Most warlike soldiers	Roman (under Belisarius to man the dromons)
340.	7.19.6	Foot soldiers and cavalry (στρατιώτας ... πεζούς τε καὶ ἱππεῖς)	Roman (infantry and cavalry to guard the Tiber)
341.	7.19.14	Grain ... sent to Rome ... for the soldiers	Roman (in Italy, but Rome especially)
342.	7.19.14	Providing for the soldiers	Roman (in Italy, but Rome especially)
343.	7.19.25	And from the soldiers	Roman (100 cavalry based at Portus)
344.	7.20.1	The soldiers who so wished	Roman (at Rome under Bessas)
345.	7.20.10	Many Roman soldiers	Roman (at Rome, most likely)
346.	7.20.17	Most of the Roman soldiers	Roman (at Rome)
347.	7.20.23	There perished among the soldiers	Roman (during the escape from Rome 26 died along 60 civilians)

(cont.)

Numbers	Location	Usage	Type
348.	7.21.4	200,000 warlike soldiers	Goths (Totila referring to the past)
349.	7.23.4	Winning the friendship of 15 soldiers	Roman (at Spoleto won over by Martinianus)
350.	7.23.7	In company with 15 soldiers	Roman (those with Martinianus)
351.	7.23.8	1,000 soldiers	Roman (under Belisarius)
352.	7.24.2	A few of the soldiers	Roman (under Belisarius left at Portus)
353.	7.24.11	Most warlike of soldiers	Roman (at Rome under Belisarius)
354.	7.26.10	70 Roman soldiers	Roman (who had deserted to the Goths)
355.	7.26.12	The men followed the soldiers in flight	Roman (who had fled Rome)
356.	7.26.14	With the 70 soldiers	Roman (who had deserted to the Goths but now gone back to John and Romans)
357.	7.27.14	Not sufficient for soldiers	Roman (in general, Valerian's belief)
358.	7.28.4	Brought in for the soldiers	Roman (in general, Belisarius struggling to supply his troops)
359.	7.28.9	The soldiers of Belisarius	Roman (under Belisarius)
360.	7.30.1	2,000 foot soldiers	Roman (reinforcements sent by emperor)
361.	7.30.7	The soldiers detailed by Belisarius for the garrison of Rome	Roman (garrison at Rome)
362.	7.30.21	As for the soldiers	Roman (at Rusciane, besieged by Totila)
363.	7.31.10	General of the troops in Byzantium and commander of the *foederati*	Roman (Artabanes made commander of the soldiers in Constantinople and the *foederati*)

(cont.)

Numbers	Location	Usage	Type
364.	7.33.13	Some of them have become soldiers of Rome	Roman (Heruls, who have become Roman soldiers after enlisting among the foederati)
365.	7.36.5	The soldiers there	Roman (in Rome)
366.	7.37.11	Challenged him and the soldiers	Roman (under Diogenes)
367.	7.38.9	Topirus … had a garrison of soldiers	Roman (garrison at Toperus)
368.	7.38.11	The soldiers keeping guard there	Roman (garrison at Toperus)
369.	7.38.15	The support of the soldiers	Roman (at Toperus)
370.	7.39.22	Roman soldiers	Roman (fighting for the Goths)
371.	7.40.39	The soldiers began to be resentful	Roman (angry with officers at Adrianople)
372.	7.40.39	Paying no heed to the soldiers	Roman (angry with officers at Adrianople)
373.	7.40.41	Many of the best soldiers died	Roman (at Adrianople)
374.	8.2.16	Rolls of Roman soldiers	Roman (based in Colchis during reign of Trajan)
375.	8.4.4	Garrison of soldiers	Roman (garrison at Sebastopolis and Pityous)
376.	8.4.5	Rolls of Roman soldiers	Roman (in garrison from Trebizond to Saginae—as noted at 8.2.16)
377.	8.4.6	The Roman soldiers succeeded	Roman (in garrison at Petra)
378.	8.5.13	As the other Roman soldiers did	Roman (both Goths who fought in the *foederati*)
379.	8.8.25	Two of the Roman soldiers	Roman (who had been under Valerian, general in Armenia, possibly frontier)
380.	8.9.10	Roman soldiers … began to be quartered among them	Roman (in garrison amongst Abasgi)
381.	8.9.20	Disembarked the soldiers	Roman (under John sent to the Caucasus)

(cont.)

Numbers	Location	Usage	Type
382.	8.11.32	Roman soldiers chosen for their valour in groups of no less than 40	Roman (besieging Petra)
383.	8.12.3	Ordered one of the Roman soldiers	Roman (besieging Petra under Bessas)
384.	8.12.17	Most notable of all his soldiers	Persian
385.	8.12.17	Fell to each soldier	Roman (in general when they had taken Petra)
386.	8.13.18	These soldiers … being hard pressed by the lack of necessary supplies, abandoned these fortresses	Roman (in garrison at Skanda and Sarapanis in territory at Lazi, so maybe frontier)
387.	8.14.14	A few of the soldiers	Roman (under Odonachus and Babas)
388.	8.14.14	Fellow-soldiers	Roman (under Odonachus and Babas)
389.	8.14.52	Small number of Roman soldiers	Roman (in garrison at Outhimereos)
390.	8.16.3	Roman soldiers	Roman (in general, in Lazica)
391.	8.20.1	Island soldiers	British (maybe—could be soldiers based in Jutland too—Brittia is the island Procopius refers to)[d]
392.	8.23.13	To the soldiers	Roman and Gothic (in general)
393.	8.24.34	Fleet of ships and a great number of soldiers	Roman (John, commander of the army in Libya, sends forces to Sardinia)
394.	8.25.24	The soldiers who constituted the garrison	Roman (at Crotone under Palladius)
395.	8.26.6	Pay the soldiers in Italy	Roman (those in Italy)

[d] On this point, see Carlson (2017).

(cont.)

Numbers	Location	Usage	Type
396.	8.26.10	A great number of soldiers	Roman (in Constantinople and from Thrace and Illyria)
397.	8.26.15	Commanders and soldiers	Roman (who had benefitted from leadership of Narses)
398.	8.27.9	All commanders and soldiers	Roman (sent into Thrace and Illyria)
399.	8.27.15	Gave the soldiers the usual orders	Roman (in general, under Aratius, Recithanc, Leonianus, Arimuth, and others)
400.	8.27.18	The soldiers, finding themselves without commanders	Roman (without commanders)
401.	8.31.3	The other soldiers	Roman (at Busta Gallorum—other soldiers from the spearmen, shield bearers, and barbarian Huns)
402.	8.31.5	8,000 foot archers from the roster of soldiers	Roman (at Busta Gallorum)
403.	8.31.8	He kept encouraging the soldiers	Goth (Totila exhorting them)
404.	8.31.12	The Roman soldiers	Roman (Kokkas who had deserted Rome for the Goths)
405.	8.32.2	As a private soldier	Goth (Totila armed himself as a private soldier)
406.	8.32.20	Great number of the old Roman soldiers	Roman (those who had deserted to the Goths)
407.	8.32.34	In the fashion of a simple soldier	Goth (Totila armed as simple soldier, as noted earlier)
408.	8.33.21	A large number of soldiers	Roman (under Narses and John)

(cont.)

Numbers	Location	Usage	Type
409.	8.34.10	A few Roman soldiers	Roman (general—part of Gothic treachery on the part of Ragnaris)
410.	8.34.12	Recover his own soldiers	Roman (under Pakourios)
411.	SH 5.30	No one, either commander or soldier, cared to face the perils of war	Roman (dissatisfied after Solomon's death)
412.	5.34	Some few soldiers	Roman (under Solomon)
413.	6.3	Enrolled in the registers of soldiers	Roman (Zimarchus, Ditybistus, and Justin, farmers from Illyria, set off to Constantinople to become Roman soldiers)
414.	10.9	Nor did a single soldier	Roman (outraged enough by Theodora)
415.	11.2	The rolls of soldiers	Roman (reference to Justinian's reforms of the military and more)
416.	11.23	While many were being destroyed by the soldiers	Roman (wreaking havoc among some peasants)
417.	11.28	Engaged with the soldiers	Roman (up against the Samaritans)
418.	14.13	Practically all the soldiers ... were abandoning their proper posts	Roman (on garrison in the palace)
419.	18.8	Many of the soldiers too	Roman (perished during the war in Africa)
420.	18.11	Became a grievance to the soldiers	Roman (Justinian late in paying them)
421.	22.5	Enrolled among the soldiers of the prefect	Roman (soldiers of the praetorian prefect)
422.	23.12	Provisions for soldiers	Roman (in general—landowners to supply them)
423.	23.12	To the quartermasters of the soldiers	Roman (in general)

(*cont.*)

Numbers	Location	Usage	Type
424.	23.22	Had to house the soldiers	Roman (billeted by some civilians)
425.	24.1	His treatment of the soldiers	Roman (in general—part of his complaints on behalf of the soldiers)
426.	24.4	By continually promoting the soldiers	Roman (lower-ranking, regarding pay and promotion)
427.	24.6	For the surviving soldiers	Roman (manpower shortages regular)
428.	24.7	Kept grinding down the soldiers	Roman (ground down "as if to reward them in this way for the dangers they faced in war"; some called Greeklings, etc)
429.	24.8	The soldiers, broken in manifold ways	Roman (not those from the palatine guards"—includes being removed from the military rolls, and losing the will to fight in war)
430.	24.9	Lay these charges ... upon the soldiers	Roman (blamed for crimes they did not commit)
431.	24.10	Not only the soldiers oppressed	Roman (not only the soldiers oppressed by the *logothetai*, but officers too)
432.	24.12	Subject of the soldiers	Roman (in general)
433.	24.12	In earlier times stationed a very great multitude of soldiers at all points of the Empire's frontier in order to guard the boundaries of the Roman domain	Roman (this the comment on *limitanei*)
434.	24.14	The frontiers ... remained destitute of guards and the soldiers [suffered]	Roman (frontier, turned to charity to make ends meet)
435.	24.15	No less than 3,500 other soldiers ... *scholarii*	Roman (the *scholarii*)

(cont.)

Numbers	Location	Usage	Type
436.	24.27	Emperor should present to each one of the soldiers	Roman (in general, regarding donatives)
437.	24.28	Present five gold staters to each soldier	Roman (in general, regarding donatives)
438.	26.17	And the soldiers	Roman (suffered at the hands of Justinian, in a list of those wronged)
439.	26.33	He stationed soldiers there to the number of 2,000	Roman (frontier to be garrisoned at Thermopylae)
440.	26.33	These soldiers were to be maintained therefrom	Roman (frontier to be garrisoned at Thermopylae)
441.	29.31	A large number of soldiers	Roman (under Malthanes, a Cilician and *referendarius*, dispatched to Thrace)
442.	29.31	Sending the soldiers to the houses	Roman (under Malthanes, sent to billet in houses at Tarsus)
443.	30.16	The state had also been wont from ancient times to maintain a great number of camels, which followed the Roman army … nor did the soldiers find themselves in want of any of the necessities	Roman (given camels, probably frontier)
444.	Build. 1.1.11	He strengthened the Roman domain … by a multitude of soldiers	Roman (general, but possibly frontier)
445.	1.7.3	These … chanced to be Roman soldiers who served in the Twelfth Legion	Roman (legionaries who had been in the Twelfth Legion at Melitene in Armenia)
446.	2.3.26	He also built numerous barracks for the soldiers	Roman (at Dara, possibly frontier)

(cont.)

Numbers	Location	Usage	Type
447.	2.9.8	He established a garrison (φρουρὰν)[e] of soldiers	Roman (Sura, possibly frontier)
448.	2.11.12	A garrison (φυλακτηρίου)[f] of soldiers	Roman (Palmyra, possibly frontier)
449.	3.1.24	A Roman soldier ... never fought under ... the king	Roman (had never fought for Armenia)
450.	3.1.27	Soldiers however did not follow them as Romans	Roman/Armenian (satrap not in charge of Roman soldiers)
451.	3.1.29	A very large number of rolls of Roman soldiers	Roman (frontier, under dukes, for Armenia)
452.	3.3.6	Garrison (φρουρὰν) of soldiers	Roman (Pheison, possibly frontier)
453.	3.3.8	With a garrison (φρουρᾷ) of soldiers	Roman (Citharizon, frontier, under 1 of 2 dukes of Armenia)
454.	3.4.16	Unit of Roman soldiers ... the unit was called legion	Roman (Melitene, frontier)
455.	3.4.16	Barracks for the soldiers	Roman (Melitene, frontier)
456.	3.6.13	Strong garrisons (φρουροὺς) of Roman soldiers	Roman (Tzanica in general, frontier)
457.	3.6.17	Commander of soldiers	Roman (Horonon, frontier, under a duke)
458.	3.6.22	Sufficient garrison (φυλακτήριον) of Roman soldiers	Roman (Sisilisson, possibly frontier)
459.	3.6.26	Commander of soldiers	Roman (Schamalinichon and Tzanzacon, possibly frontier)
460.	4.1.6	Garrisons (φυλακτήρια) of soldiers	Roman (Balkans in general, possibly frontier)
461.	4.1.33	Garrisons (φυλακτήριά) of soldiers	Roman (all along the Danube, probably frontier)

e A φρουρά is a garrison in terms of a body of soldiers rather than the physical space where those soldiers might be based.

f A φυλακτήριον is a garrison that is a physical space where soldiers are based rather than the body of soldiers.

(cont.)

Numbers	Location	Usage	Type
462.	4.2.14	He established about 2,000 soldiers as guards (garrison - φρουρούς)	Roman (Thermopylae, possibly/probably frontier—as in *SH* 26.33)
463.	4.5.1	Garrisons (φυλακτηρίοις) of soldiers	Roman (Illyricum along the Danube, possibly frontier)
464.	4.6.37	Garrisons (φρουρὰς) of soldiers	Roman (Illyricum in general, possibly frontier)
465.	4.10.17	Rolls of soldiers	Roman (long walls of Chersonese, possibly frontier)
466.	4.10.23	The needs of the soldiers	Roman (long walls of Chersonese, possibly frontier)
467.	5.7.8	Garrison (φρουρὰν) of soldiers ... but not more than ten men	Roman (Mt Garizin, possibly frontier)
468.	5.7.13	Fearing the soldiers	Roman (Mt Garizin, possibly frontier)
469.	5.8.9	Garrison (φυλακτήριόν) of soldiers	Roman (Mt. Sinai, probably frontier)
470.	6.6.6[g]	Garrison (φρουρὰν) of soldiers	Roman (Adramytus, probably frontier)
471.	6.6.10	Where the soldiers were building their stockade	Roman (Caputvada, probably frontier)
472.	6.6.18	Trustworthy[h] garrisons (φρουροὺς) of soldiers	Roman (Aumetra, probably frontier)
473.	6.7.1	Fortifications of soldiers	Roman (Numidia in general, probably frontier)
474.	6.7.8	Sufficient garrisons (φυλακτήρια) of soldiers	Roman (cities around Mt. Aurasius, probably frontier)
475.	6.7.17	Garrisons (φυλακτηρίοις) of soldiers	Roman (in general, frontier likely)

[g] Surely the most devilish garrison of the lot.
[h] This is the only instance in which a garrison is called "trustworthy", ἐχέγγυος.

Bibliography

Adontz, N. 1970. *Armenia in the Period of Justinian.* Lisbon.

Adshead, K. 1996. "Procopius and the Samaritans," in P. Allen and E. Jeffreys (eds.), *The Sixth Century: End or Beginning?* Brisbane, 35–41.

Alofs, E. 2015a. "Studies on Mounted Warfare in Asia III," *War in History* 22: 132–154.

Alofs, E. 2015b. "Studies on Mounted Warfare in Asia IV," *War in History* 22: 275–297.

Alofs, E. 2014a. "Studies on Mounted Warfare in Asia I," *War in History* 21: 423–444.

Alofs, E. 2014b. "Studies on Mounted Warfare in Asia II," *War in History* 22: 4–27.

Amory, P. 1997. *People and Identity in Ostrogothic Italy.* Cambridge.

Arce, I. 2015. "Severan *Castra*, Tetrarchic *Quadriburgia*, Justinian *Coenobia*, and Ghassanid *Diyarat*: Patterns of Transformation of *Limes Arabicus* Forts During Late Antiquity," in R. Collins and M. Weber (eds.), *Roman Military Architecture on the Frontiers: Armies and Their Architecture in Late Antiquity.* Oxford, 98–122.

Arce, I. 2010. "Qasr Hallabat, Qasr Bshir and Deir el Kahf. Building Techniques, Architectural Typology and Change of Use of Three Quadriburgia from the Limes Arabicus. Interpretation and Significance." *Anejos de AEspA* 57: 455–481.

Arce, I. 2008. "Hallabat: Castellum, Coenobium, Praetorium, Qasr. The Construction of a Palatine Architecture under the Umayyads." In *Residences, Castles, Settlments—Transformation Processes from Late Antiquity to Early Islamic Times*, edited by K. Bartl and A. Moaz. Damascus, 153–182.

Arce, I. 2006. "Qasr Hallabat (Jordan) Revisited: Reassessment of the Material Evidence." In *Muslim Military Architecture in Greater Syria*, edited by H. Kennedy, Leiden, 26–44.

Arce, I., Feissel, D., Weber, T. 2014. *The Edict of Anastasius I (491–518 AD). An Interim Report.* Amman.

Arjava, A. 1996. *Women and Law in Late Antiquity.* Oxford.

Asdracha, C. 2003. *Inscriptions protobyzantines et Byzantines de la Thrace orientale et d'île d'imbros (IIIe–XVe Siècles): presentation et commentaire historique.* Athens.

Ayvazyan, A. 2012. *The Armenian Military in the Byzantine Empire: Conflict and Alliance Under Justinian and Maurice.* Alfortville.

Baldwin, B. 2006. "Aspects of the Suda," *Byzantion* 76: 11–31.

Ball, J. 2016. *Collecting the Field: A Methodological Reassessment of Greek and Roman Battlefield Archaeology.* PhD Thesis, University of Liverpool.

Banning, E. 1986. "Peasants, Pastoralists, and the *Pax Romana*." *BASOR* 261: 25–50.

Baragwanath, E. 2008. *Motivation and Narrative in Herodotus.* Oxford.

Barnish, S., Lee, D., and M. Whitby. 2000. "Government and Administration," in A. Cameron, B. Ward-Perkins, and M. Whitby (eds), *Cambridge Ancient History Volume XIV.* Cambridge, 164–206.

Basso, F. and G. Greatrex. 2017. "How to Interpret Procopius' Preface to the *Wars*," in Lillington-Martin and Turquois (2017), 59–72.

Batty, R. 2007. *Rome and the Nomads. The Pontic-Danubian Realm in Antiquity.* Oxford.

Beaucamp, J. 1990. *Le statut de la femme a Byzance.* Paris.

Bell, P. 2009. *Three Political Voices from the Age of Justinian.* Liverpool.

Bell, H. I., Martin, V., Turner, E. G., Van Berchem, D. 1962. *The Abinnaeus Archive.* Oxford.

Bellucci, N., and L. Bortolussi. 2016. "Thetati in the Roman Military Papyri: An Inquiry on Soldiers Killed in Battle," *Aegyptus* 94: 75–82.

Birkenmeier, J. W. 2002. *The Development of the Komnenian Army, 1081–1180.* Leiden.

Bivar 1972. "Cavalry equipment and tactics on Euphrates," *DOP* 26: 273–291.

Bond, S. 2016. *Trade and Taboo.* Ann Arbor.

Bondoc, D. 2011–2012. "A Germanic Grave inside the Late Roman Fortification of Sucidava-Celei," *Oltenia* 18–19: 133–142.

Bondoc, D., and M. Cojoc. 2014. "German Discoveries at Sucidava-Celei in the 6th Century," *Studia Academica Šumenensia* 1: 39–50.

Bonner, M. 2020. *The Last Empire of Iran.* London.

Bonner, M. 2011. *Three Neglected Sources of Sasanian History.* Paris.

Börm, H. 2008. "Es war allerdings nicht so, dass sie es im Sinne eines Tributes erhielten, wie viele meinten ...": Anlässe und Funktion der persischen Geldforderungen an die Römer (3. bis 6. Jh.)," *Historia* 57: 327–346.

Börm, H. 2007. *Prokop und die Perser: Untersuchungen zu den römischen-sasanidischen Kontakten in der ausgehenden Spätantike.* Stuttgart.

Bouvier, B. and C. Wherli. 1985. "Une affaire militaire," *ZPE* 59: 71–74.

Bowersock, G. 2013. *The Throne of Adulis. Red Sea Warson the Eve of Islam.* Oxford.

Bowersock, G. 1983. *Roman Arabia.* Cambridge, MA.

Brand, C. M. (trans.). 1976. *Deeds of John and Manuel Comnenus.* New York.

Brands, G. 2016. *Antiochia in der Spätantike.* Berlin.

Braun, H. 1886. *Procopius Caesariensis quatenus imitatus sit Thucydidem.* Erlangen.

Breccia, G. 2004. "L'*arco* e la spada. Procopio e il nuovo esercito bizantino," Rivista di ricerche bizantinistiche 1: 73–99.

Brennan, P. 2015. "Units in the *Notitia Dignitatum*," in Y. Le Bohec, G. Greatrex et al. (2015), 1049–1054.

Brennan, P. 2007. "Zosimos II. 34.1 and 'The Constantinian Reform': using Johannes Lydos to expose an insidious fabrication," in A. Lewin, P. Pellegrini, Z. Fiema, and S. Janniard (eds.), *The Late Roman Army in the Near East from Diocletian to the Arab Conquest.* Oxford, 211–218.

Brennan, P. 1998. "The User's Guide to the *Notitia Dignitatum*: the Case of the *Dux Armeniae (ND Or.* 38)." *Antichthon* 32: 34–49.

Brennan, P. 1996. "The *Notitia Dignitatum*," in *Les Littératures Techniques dans l'Antiquité Romaine.* Geneva, 147–178.

Brennan, P. 1980. "Combined legionary detachments as artillery units in late-Roman Danubian bridgehead dispositions," *Chiron* 10: 553–567.

Brodka, D. 2018. *Narses—Politik, Krieg und Historiographie im 6. Jahrhundert n. Chr.* Berlin.

Brodka, D. 2016. "Prokop von Kaisareia und seine Informanten. Ein Identifikationsversuch," *Historia* 65: 108–124.

Brodka, D. 2004. *Die Geschichtsphilosophie in der spätantiken Historiographie*. Frankfurt am Main.

Brown, A. 2010. "Justinian, Procopius, and deception: Literary lies, imperial politics, and the archaeology of sixth-century Greece," in A. Turner, J. Kim, O. Chong-Gossard, and F. Vervaet (eds.), *Private and public lies: The discourse of despotism and deceit in the Graeco-Roman world*. Leiden, 355–369.

Brubaker, L. 2005. "The age of Justinian: gender and society," in M. Maas (ed.), *The Cambridge Companion to the age of Justinian*. Cambridge, 427–447.

Brubaker, L. 2004. "Sex, Lies, and Textuality: The *Secret History* of Prokopios and the Rhetoric of Gender in Sixth-Century Byzantium," in Brubaker, L. and J. M. H. Smith (eds.), *Gender in the Early Medieval World, East and West, 300–900*. Cambridge, 83–101.

Brunt, P. 1971. *Roman Manpower*. Oxford.

Burckhardt, L. A. 1999. "Katalogos," in H. Cancik and H. Schneider (eds.), *Der neue Pauly*. Stuttgart, Volume 6, col. 337.

Burns, R. 2016. "Diocletian's Fortifications of Syria and Arabia," in S. Lieu and P. McKechnie (eds.), *Aspects of the Roman East, Volume II*. Turnhuot, 1–77.

Bury, J. B. 1923. *History of the Later Roman Empire from the Death of Theodosius I to the Death of Justinian*. London.

Butcher, K. 2018. "Zenobia (modern Halibiye, Syria)," in O. Nicholson (ed.), *Oxford Dictionary of Late Antiquity*. New York, 1608–1609.

Cameron, A. 2017. "Writing About Procopius Then and Now," in Lillington-Martin and Turquois (2017), 13–25.

Cameron, A. 1985. *Procopius and the Sixth Century*. London: Duckworth.

Campbell, B. 1994. *The Roman Army, 31 BC–AD 337: A Sourcebook*. London.

Campbell, B., and L. Tritle (eds.). 2013. *The Oxford Handbook to Warfare in the Classical World*.

Caner, D. 2010. *History and Hagiography from the Late Antique Sinai*. Liverpool.

Carandini, A., ed. 2017. *The Atlas of Ancient Rome*. Princeton.

Carafa, P. 2017. "The Aurelian Walls," in Carndini (2017), 85–89.

Carrié, J.-M. 2004. "La système de recrutement des armée romaines de Dioclétien aux Valentiniens," in Y. Le Bohec, and C. Wolff (eds.), *L'Armée Romaine de Dioclétien à Valentinien 1er*. Paris, 371–87.

Carrié, J.-M. 2002. "Fournitures militaires, recrutement et archéologie des fortifications," *AntTard* 10: 427–42.

Carrié, J.-M. 1995. "L'État à la recherche de nouveaux modes de fijinancement des armées (Rome et Byz- ance, IVe–VIIIe siècles)", in A. Cameron (ed.), *The Byzantine and Early Islamic Near East III: States, Resources and Armies*. Princeton, 31–53.

Casey, P. J. 1996. "Justinian, the *limitanei*, and Arab-Byzantine relations in the 6th c." *JRA* 9: 214–222.

Cesa, M. 1982. "Etnografia e geografia nella visione storica di Procopio di Cesarea," *SCO* 32: 189–215.

Cesa, M. 1981. "La politica di Guistiniano verso l'occidente nel guidizio di Procopio," *Athenaeum* 59: 389–409.

Cherf, W. 2011. "Procopius *De Aedificiis* 4.2.1–22 on the Thermopylae Frontier," *BZ* 104: 71–113.

Christ, M. 2001. "The Conscription of Athenian Hoplites," *CQ* 51: 398–422.

Clark, G. 1994. *Women in Late Antiquity*. Oxford.

Coello, T. 1996. *Unit Sizes in the Late Roman Army*. Oxford.

Collins, R. 2012. *Hadrian's Wall and the End of Empire*. London.

Colombo, M. 2009. "La forza numerica e la composizione degli eserciti campali durante l'alto impero: legion e *auxilia* da Cesare Augusto a Traiano," *Historia* 58: 96–117.

Colvin, I. 2013. "Reporting Battles and Understanding Campaigns in Procopius and Agathias: Classicising Historians' Use of Archived Documents as Sources," in A. Sarantis and N. Christie (2013), 571–597.

Conant, J. 2012. *Staying Roman: Conquest and Identity in Africa and the Mediterranean, 439–700*. Cambridge.

Cooper, K. 2016. "The Heroine and the Historian: Procopius of Caesarea on the Troubled Reign of Queen Amalasuentha," in J. Arnold, S. Bjornlie, and K. Sessa (eds.), *A Companion to Ostrogothic Italy*. Leiden, 296–315.

Cosmo, N. and M. Mass, eds. 2018. *Empires and Exchanges in Eurasian Late Antiquity*. Cambridge.

Coulston, J. 2003. "Tacitus, Historiae I.79 and the impact of Sarmatian warfare on the Roman empire," in von Carnap-Bornheim, C. (ed.), *Kontakt—Kooperation—Konflikt: Germanen und Sarmaten zwischen dem 1. und dem 4. Jahrhundert nach Christus*. Kiel, 415–433.

Coulston, J. 1986. "Roman, Parthian and Sassanid tactical developments," in Freeman, P. & Kennedy, D. (eds.), *The Defence of the Roman and Byzantine East*. Oxford, 59–75.

Croke, B. 2007. "Justinian under Justin: Reconfiguring a reign," *BZ* 100: 13–56.

Croke, B. 2001. *Count Marcellinus and His Chronicle*. Oxford.

Croke, B. and J. Crow. 1983. "Procopius and Dara," *JRS* 73: 143–159.

Crow, J. 2007. "Amida and Tropaeum Traiani: A Comparison of Late Antique Fortress Cities on the Lower Danube and Mesopotamia," in A. Poulter (ed.), *The Transition to Late Antiquity, on the Danube and Beyond*. Oxford, 435–455.

Crow, J. 1995. "The Long Walls of Thrace," in C. Mango and G. Dagron (eds.), *Constantinople and its Hinterland*. Aldershot, 109–124.

Crowley, J. 2012. *The Psychology of the Athenian Hoplite: the Culture of Combat in Classical Athens*. Cambridge.

Cunha, E., and A. M. Silva. 1997. "War Lesions from the Famous Portuguese Medieval Battle of Aljubarrota," *International Journal of Osteoarchaeology* 7: 595–599.

Cunliffe, B. 2015. *By Steppe, Desert, and Ocean*. Oxford.

Curry, A. and G. Foard. 2016. "Where Are the Dead of Medieval Battles? A Preliminary Survey," *Journal of Conflict Archaeology* 11: 61–77.

Curta, F. 2016. "Avar Blitzkrieg, Slavic and Bulgar raiders, and Roman special ops: mobile warriors in the sixth-century Balkans," in stván Zimonyi and Osman Karatay (eds.), *Central Eurasia in the Middle Ages. Studies in Honour of Peter B. Golden*. Weisbaden, 69–90.

Curta, F. 2001. *The Making of the Slavs*. Cambridge.

Daly, G. 2002. *Cannae*. London.

Debié, M. 2004. "Du Grec en Syriaque : La transmission du récit de la prise d'Amid (502) dans l'historiographie," *BZ* 96: 601–622.

Decker, M. 2013. *The Byzantine Art of War*. Yardley, Pennsylvania.

De Light, L. 2012. *Peasants, Citizens and Soldiers: Studies in the Demographic History of Roman Italy 225 BC–AD 100*. Cambridge.

De Vries, B. 1998. *Umm el-Jimal: A Frontier Town and its Landscape in Northern Jordan, Volume 1*. Portsmouth, RI.

Dey, H. 2011. *The Aurelian Wall and the Refashioning of Imperial Rome, AD 271–885*. Cambridge.

Diesner, H.-J. 1972. "Das Bucellariertum von Stilicho und Sarus bis auf Aetius (454/55)," *Klio* 54: 321–350.

Diethart, J. M., and P. Dintsis, 1984. "Die Leontoklibanarier Versuch einer archäologisch-papyrologischen Zusammenschau," in W. Hörandner, J. Koder, O. Kresten, E. Trapp (eds.), *Byzantios. Festschri für Herbert Hunger zum 70 Geburststag*. Vienna, 67–79.

Dijkstra, J. 2014. "'I, Silko, Came to Talmis and Taphis'. Interactions between the Peoples beyond the Egyptian Frontier and Rome in Late Antiquity." In Dijsktra and Fisher (2014), 299–330

Dijsksra, J. 2008. *Philae and the End of Ancient Egyptian Religion. A Regional Study of Religious Transformation (298–642 CE)*. Leuven.

Dijkstra, J., and G. Fisher, eds. 2014. *Inside and Out: Interactions between Rome and the Peoples on the Arabian and Egyptian Frontiers in Late Antiquity (200–800 CE)*. Leuven: Peeters.

Di Segni, L. 2004. "The Beersheba tax edict reconsidered in the light of a newly discovered fragment." *SCI* 23: 131–158.

Di Segni, L. 2004. "The Beersheba tax edict reconsidered in the light of a newly discovered fragment." *SCI* 23: 131–158.

Dmitriev, S. 2018. "John Lydus' Knowledge of Latin and language politics in sixth-century Constantinople," *Byz* 111: 55–70.

Dmitriev, S. 2010. "John Lydus and His Contemporaries on Identities and Cultures of Sixth-Century Byzantium," *DOP* 64: 27–42.

Dubuisson, M. and J. Schamp, eds. and trans. 2006. *Jean le Lydien*. Paris.

Duncan-Jones, R. 1990. *Sculpture and Scale in the Roman Economy*. Cambridge.

Du Picq, A. 1987. *Battle Studies*. Harrisburg, PA.

Durliat, J. 1981. *Les dédicaces d'ouvrages de défense dans l'Afrique byzantine*. Rome.

Eadie, J. W. 1967. "The development of Roman mailed cavalry," *JRS* 57: 161–173.

Earl, D. 1972. "The Prologue-form in Ancient Historiography," *ANRW* 1.2: 842–855.

Eckstein, A. 2006. *Mediterranean Anarchy, Interstate War, and the Rise of Rome*. Berkeley.

Edwell et al. 2015. "Arabs in the Conflict Between Rome and Persia, AD 491–630." In Fisher (2015), 214–275.

Effros, B. 2003. *Merovingian Mortuary Archaeology and the Making of the Early Middle Ages*. Berkeley.

Eisenberg, M. and L. Mordechai. 2019. "The Justinianic Plague: An Interdisciplinary Review," *BMGS* 43: 156–180.

Elton, H. 2007. "Military Forces [the Later Roman Empire]," in Sabin, P., Van Wees, H. and M. Whitby (2007), 270–309.

Elton, H. 1996. *Warfare and Roman Europe, AD 350–425*. Oxford.

Engen, R. 2009. *Canadians Under Fire*. Kingston/Montreal.

Evans, J. 2005. *The Emperor Justinian and the Byzantine Empire*. Westport, CT.

Evans, J. 1972. *Procopius*. New York.

Fan Chiang, Shih-Cong. 2018. "Between Facts, Contexts, and Traditions: Procopius' Description of Women's Suffering During Wartime," in Greatrex and Janniard (2018), 229–247.

Fan Chiang, Shih-Cong. 2015. *Urban Civilians' Experiences in the Romano-Persian Wars, 502–591 CE*. Unpublished PhD dissertation. Kings College London.

Farrokh, K. 2017. *The Armies of Ancient Persia: The Sassanians*. Barnsley.

Feissel, D. 2000. "Les édifices de Justinien au témoignage. De Procope et de l'épigraphie," *AntTard* 8: 81–104.

Ferrill, A. 1986. *The Fall of the Roman Empire: the Military Explanation*. London.

Fiema, Z. T. 2002. "Late-antique Petra and its Hinterland: Recent research and new interpretations", in J. H. Humphrey (ed.), *The Roman and Byzantine Near East vol. 3*. Portsmouth, RI, 191–252.

Feissel, D. 1983. *Recueil des inscriptions chrétiennes de Macédoine du IIIe au VIe siècle*. Paris.

Fisher, G., ed. 2015. *Arabs and Empires Before Islam*. Oxford: Oxford University Press.

Fisher, G. 2011. *Between Empires. Arabs, Romans and Sasanians in Late Antiquity*. Oxford.

Flower, M. 2012. *Xenophon's Anabasis or the Expedition of Cyrus*. New York.

Fornara, C. 1984. *The Nature of History in Ancient Greece and Rome*. Berkeley.

Forsdyke, S., Balot, P. and E. Foster, eds. 2017. *The Oxford Handbook of Thucydides*. Oxford.

Foss, C. 2002. "The Empress Theodora," *Byzantion* 72: 141–176.

Fowden, E. 1999. *The Barbarian Plain*. Berkeley.

Fotiou, A. 1988. "Recruitment shortages in sixth-century Byzantium," *Byz* 58: 65–77.

Frankopan, P. 2015. *The Silk Road*. London.

Fuhrmann, C. 2012. *Policing the Roman Empire: Soldiers, Administration, and Public Order*. New York.

Gascou, J. 1976. "L'institution des beccellaires," *BIAO* 76: 144–156.

Geber, J. 2015. "Comparative Study of Perimortem Weapon Trauma in Two Early Medieval Skeletal Populations (AD 400–1200) from Ireland," *International Journal of Osteoarchaeology* 25: 253–264.

Genequand, D. 2015. "The Archaeological Evidence for the Jafnids and the Nasrids." In Fisher (2015), 172–213.

Gilliver, C. M. 1999. *The Roman Art of War*. Stroud.

Gilmer, J. 2013. "Procopius of Caesarea: a Case Study in Imperial Criticism," *Byzantina Symmeikta* 23: 45–57.

Goffart, W. 2006. *Barbarian Tides*. Philadelphia.

Goldsworthy, A. 1996. *The Roman Army at War, 100 BC–AD 200*. Oxford.

Graf, D. 1989. "Rome and the Saracens: Reassessing the Nomadic Menace," in T. Fahd (ed.), *L'Arabie priislamique et son environnement historique*. Leiden, 341–400.

Graf, D. 1978. "The Saracens and the Defense of the Arabian Frontier." *BASOR* 229: 1–26.

Graff, D. 2016. *The Eurasian Way of War*. London.

Greatrex, G. 2020. "Procopius and the Plague in 2020," *Boletín de la Sociedad Española de Bizantinística* 35: 5–12.

Greatrex, G. 2018. "Procopius' Attitude Towards Barbarians," in G. Greatrex and S. Janniard (eds.), *The World of Procopius*. Paris, 327–354.

Greatrex, G. 2016. "Malalas and Procopius," in Meier, M., and Radtki, C., and F. Schulz (eds), *Die Weltchronik des Johannes Malalas*. Stuttgart, 169–185.

Greatrex, G. 2015. "Les Jafnides et al defense de l'empire au VIe s." In *Les Jafnides, Des rois arabes au service de Byzance*. Paris, 121–154.

Greatrex, G. 2014a. "Perceptions of Procopius in Recent Scholarship," *Histos* 8: 76–121.

Greatrex, G. 2014b. "Perceptions of Procopius in Recent Scholarship (*Addenda*)," *Histos* 8: 121a–e.

Greatrex, G. 2014c. "Procopius and the Roman Imperial Policy in the Arabian and Egyptian Frontier Zones." In Dijkstra and Fisher (2014), 249–264.

Greatrex, G. 2007a. "Roman frontiers and foreign policy in the East", in R. Alston and S. Lieu (eds.), *Aspects of the Roman East*. Turnhout, 103–173.

Greatrex, G. 2007b. "Dukes of the Eastern Frontier," in J. Drinkwater and B. Salway (eds.), *Wolf Liebeschuetz Reflected*. London, 87–98.

Greatrex, G. 1998. *Rome and Persia at War, AD 502–532*. Leeds.

Greatrex, G. 1995. "Procopius and Agathias on the Defences of the Thracian Chersonese," in C. Mango and G. Dagron (eds.), *Constantinople and its Hinterland*. Aldershot, 125–129.

Greatrex, G., Elton, H., and Burgess, R. 2005. "Urbicius' Epitedeuma: An Edition, Translation and Commentary," *BZ* 98: 35–74.

Greatrex, G. and Lieu, S., eds. 2002. *The Roman Eastern Frontier and the Persian Wars, Part II: AD 363–630*. London.

Greatrex, G. and S. Janniard, eds. 2018. *The World of Procopius/Le Monde de Procope*. Paris.

Gregory, S. 1997. *Roman Military Architecture on the Eastern Frontier*. Amsterdam.

Gregory, T. 2000. "Procopius on Greece," *AntTard* 8: 105–114.

Grosse, R. 1920. *Römische Militärgeschichte von Gallienus bis zum Beginn der byzantinischen Themenverfassung*. Berlin.

Grossman, D. 2004. *On Combat*. Millstadt, IL.

Grossman, D. 1995. *On Killing*. New York.

Haldon, J. et al. 2018. "Plagues, Climate Change, and the End of an Empire: A Response to Kyle Harper's The Fate of Rome (3): Disease, Agency, and Collapse," *History Compass* 16, e12507.

Haldon, J. 2002. "Some Aspects of Early Byzantine Arms and Armour," in D. Nicolle (ed.), *A Companion to Medieval Arms and Armour*. Woodbridge, 65–79.

Haldon, J. 1999. *Warfare, State and Society in the Byzantine World, 565–1204*. London.

Haldon, J. 1993. "Administrative Continuities and Structural Transformations in East Roman Military Organisation c. 580–640," in F. Vallett, and M. Kazanski (eds.), *L'Armée romaine et les barbares du 4e au 7e siècle*. Paris, 45–51.

Haldon, J. 1979. *Recruitment and Conscription in the Byzantine Army c. 550–950*. Vienna.

Haldon, J. 1975. "Some Aspects of Byzantine Military Technology from Sixth to the Tenth Centuries," *BMGS* 1: 11–47.

Handley, M. A. 2011. *Dying on Foreign Shores. Travel and Mobility in the Late-Antique West*. Portsmouth, RI.

Hanson, V. D. 2000. *The Western Way of War: Infantry Battle in Classical Greece*. 2nd edition. Berkeley.

Harl, O. 1996. "Die *Kataphraktarier* im römischen Heer—Panegyrik und Realität," *JRGZM* 43: 601–27.

Harries, J. 1999. *Law and Empire in Late Antiquity*. Cambridge.

Harper, K. 2018. "Integrating the Natural Sciences and Roman History: Challenges and Prospects," *History Compass* 16, e12520.

Harper, K. 2017. *The Fate of Rome: Climate, Disease, and the End of an Empire*. Princeton.

Harper, R. 1997. *Upper Zohar, an Early Byzantine Fort in Palaestina Tertia*. Oxford.
Haury, J., ed. 2001. *Procopii Caesariensis Opera Omnia*. Leipzig.
Hayes, G. 2016. "Sounds from a Silent Land," in S. Stevens and J. Conant (eds.), *North Africa under Byzantium and Early Islam*. Washington DC, 269–293.
Haynes, I. 2013. *Blood of the Provinces: The Roman Auxilia and the Making of Provincial Society from Augustus to the Severans*. Oxford.
Heather, P. 2018. *Rome Resurgent*. Oxford.
Heather, P. 1997. "Foedera and Foederati of the Fourth Century," in W. Pohl (ed.), *Kingdoms of the Empire: the Integration of Barbarians in Late Antiquity*. Leiden. 57–74.
Hebblewhite, M. 2016. "Sacramentum Militiae: Empty words in an Age of Chaos," in J. Armstrong (ed.), *Circum Mare: Themes in Ancient Warfare*. Leiden, 120–142.
Hebblewhite, M. and C. Whately. (eds.). Forthcoming. *A Companion to Bodyguards in the Ancient Mediterranean*. Leiden.
Hickey, T. 2012. *Wine, Wealth, and the State in Late Antique Egypt*. Ann Arbor.
Hildinger, E. 2013. "Steppe Nomadic Warfare," *Oxford Bibliographies Online*.
Hof, C. 2020. *Resafa 9,1. Resafa-Sergiupolis/Rusafat Hisham*. Wiesbaden.
Hoffmann, D. 1969/70. *Das spätrömische Bewegungsheer und die* Notitia Dignitatum. Dusseldorf.
Holder, P. 2003. "Auxiliary Deployment in the Reign of Hadrian," in J. J. Wilkes (ed.), *Documenting the Roman Army*. London, 101–145.
Holst, M. 2004. *Osteological Analysis, Heronbridge, Chester, Cheshire*. York, UK.
Honoré, T. 1978. *Tribonian*. London.
Hoogendijk, F. 1995. "Eine byzantinische Dialysis-Urkunde," *ZPE* 107: 105–112.
Howard-Johnston, J. 2013. "Military Infrastructure in the Roman Provinces North and South of the Armenian Taurus in Late Antiquity," in Sarantis and Christie (2013), 851–891.
Howard-Johnston, J. 2010. *Witness to a World Crisis*. Oxford.
Howard-Johnston, J. 2000. "The Education and Expertise of Procopius," *AntTard* 8: 19–30.
Howard-Johnston, J. 1996. "Anna Komnene and the *Alexiad*," in M. Mullett and D. Smythe (eds.), *Alexios I Komnenos Papers*. Belfast, 260–302.
Hoyland, R. 2015. *In God's Path*. Oxford.
Hunger, H. 1978. *Die hochsprachliche profane Literatur der Byzantiner*. Munich.
Hunger, H. 1976. "Thukydides bei Johannes Kantakuzenos Beobeachtungen zur Mimesis," *JÖB* 25: 181–93.
Hunt, P. 2007. "Military Forces," in Sabin et al. (2007). 108–146.
Intagliata, E. 2018. *Palmyra after Zenobia AD 273–750*. Oxford.
Isaac, B. 1990. *The Limits of Empire: the Roman Army in the East*. Oxford.
Isaac, B. 1988. "The Meaning of the Terms Limes and Limintanei," *JRS* 78: 125–47.
Jacobs, I. 2013. *Aesthetic Maintenance of Civic Space*. Leuven.

James, S. 2011. *Rome and the Sword*. London

James, S. 2006. "The impact of steppe peoples and the Partho-Sasanian world on the development of Roman military equipment and dress, 1st to 3rd centuries AD," in M. Mode, J. Tubach, and G. Sophia Vashalomidze (eds.), *Arms and armour as indicators of cultural transfer: the steppes and the ancient world from Hellenistic times to the early Middle Ages*. Weisbaden, 357–392.

James, S. 2004. *Excavations at Dura-Europos, Final Report VII, the Arms and Armour, and other Military Equipment*. London.

Janniard, S. 2015. "Les adaptations de l'armée romaine aux modes de combat des peuples des steppes (fin IVᵉ-début VIᵉ siècle apr. J.-C.)", in U. Roberto, L. Mecella (eds.), *Governare e riformare l'impero al momento della sua divisione: Oriente, Occidente, Illirico*. Rome, 1–34.

Janniard, S. 2011. *Les Transformations de l'Armée Romano-Byzantine (IIIᵉ–VIᵉ Siècles apr. J.-C.): Le Paradigme de la Bataille Rangée*. Unpublished PhD thesis, L'Atelier du Centre de Recherches Historiques.

Jones, A. H. M. 1964. *The Later Roman Empire, 284–602: A Social, Economic and Administrative Survey*. Oxford.

Kaegi, W. 1990. "Procopius the Military Historian," *BF* 15: 53–85.

Kaegi, W. 1981. *Byzantine Military Unrest, 471–843: An Interpretation*. Amsterdam.

Kaegi, W. 1965. "Arianism and the Byzantine Army in Africa," *Traditio* 21: 23–53.

Kagan, K. 2006a. *The Eye of Command*. Ann Arbor.

Kagan, K. 2006b. "Redefining Roman Grand Strategy." *JMH* 70: 333–362.

Kagan, D. and G. Viggiano, eds. 2013. *Men of Bronze*. Princeton.

Kaiser, A. M. 2015. "Egyptian Units and the Reliability of *Notitia Dignitatum*, Pars Orientis." *Historia* 64: 243–261.

Kaldellis, A. 2017. "How Perilous Was it to Write Political History in Late Antiquity?" *SLA* 1: 38–64.

Kaldellis, A. 2014. *The Wars of Justinian*. Indianapolis.

Kaldellis, A. 2013. *Ethnography After Antiquity*. Philadelphia.

Kaldellis, A. 2005. "The Works and Days of Hesychios the Illoustrios of Miletos," *GRBS* 45: 381–403.

Kaldellis, A. 2004a. *Procopius of Caesarea: Tryanny, History, and Philosophy at the End of Antiquity*. Philadelphia.

Kaldellis, A. 2004b. "Classicism, Barbarism, and Warfare: Prokopios and the Conservative Reaction to Later Roman Military Policy," *AJAH* 3: 189–218.

Kaldellis, A. 2004c. "Identifying Dissident Circles in Sixth-Century Byzantium: the Friendship of Prokopios and Ioannes Lydos," *Florilegium* 21: 1–17.

Kaldellis, A. 2003. "Things are not what they seem: Agathias Mythistoricus and the Last Laugh of Classical Culture," *CQ* 53: 295–300.

Kaldellis, A. 1999. "The Historical and Religious Views of Agathias: a Reinterpretation," *Byzantion* 69: 206–252.

Kaldellis, A. 1997. "Agathias on History and Poetry," *GRBS* 38: 295–305.

Kalli, M. 2004. *The Manuscript Tradition of Procopius' Gothic Wars*. Munich.

Karantabias, M. 2018. "The Projection of Imperial Power in Procopius," in Greatrex and Janniard (2018), 55–76.

Kazhdan, A. 1991 (2005). "Photios," in A. Kazhdan (ed.), *Oxford Dictionary of Byzantine*. Accessed via *Oxford Reference Online*.

Kazhdan, A. and A. Epstein. 1985. *Change in Byzantine Culture in the Eleventh and Twelfth Centuries*. Berkeley.

Keegan, J. 1976. *The Face of Battle*. London.

Keenan, J. 1990. "Evidence for the Byzantine Army in the Syene Papyri," *BASP* 27: 139–150.

Keenan, J. 1974. "The Names Flavius and Aurelius as Status Designations in Later Roman Egypt," *ZPE* 13 (1974): 283–304.

Keenan, J. 1973. "The Names Flavius and Aurelius as Status Designations in Later Roman Egypt," *ZPE* 11 (1973): 33–63.

Kelly, C. 2006. "John Lydus and the eastern Praetorian prefecture in the Sixth Century AD," *BZ* 98: 431–458.

Kelly C. 2004. *Ruling the Later Roman Empire*. Cambridge, MA.

Kelso, I. 2003. "Artillery as a Classicizing Digression," *Historia* 52: 122–125.

Kennedy, D. 2004. *The Roman Army in Jordan*. London: Council for British Research on the Levant.

Kennedy, D. and D. Riley. 1990. *Rome's Desert Frontier from the Air*. Austin.

Kennedy, H. 2001. *Armies of the Caliphs*. London.

Kim, H. Y. 2016. *The Huns*. London.

Kim, H. Y. 2013. *The Huns, Rome and the Birth of Europe*. Cambridge.

Koehn, C. 2018. *Justinian und die Armee des frühen Byzanz*. Boston/Berlin.

Konijnendijk, R. 2017. *Classical Greek Tactics: A Cultural History*. Leiden.

Kouroumali, M. 2013. "The Justinianic Reconquest of Italy: Imperial Campaigns and Local Responses," in Sarantis and Christie (2013), 969–999.

Kraemer C. J. 1958. *Excavations at Nessana, Vol. 3: The Non-Literary Papyri*. Princeton, NJ.

Kruse, M. 2018. "Economic Thought and Ideology in Procopius of Caesarea," in Greatrex and Janniard (2018), 39–54.

Kruse, M. 2017a. "Archery in the Preface to Procopius' *Wars*," *Studies in Late Antiquity* 1: 381–406.

Kruse, M. 2017b. "Justinian's Laws and Procopius' *Wars*," in Lillington-Martin and Turqouis (2017), 186–200.

Kucera, P. 2016. "al-Qasr: the Roman *Castrum* of Dakhleh Oasis," in R. Bagnall, P. Davoli, and C. Hope (eds.), *The Oasis Papers 6*. Oxford, 305–316.

Kulikowski, M. 2000. "The *Notitia Dignitatum* as a Historical Source." *Historia* 49: 358–377.

Laniado, A. 2015. *Ethnos et droit dans le monde protobyzantin*. Geneva.

Lauffray, J. 1983. *Halabiyya-Zenobia, place forte du limes oriental et la Haute-Mésopotamie au VIe siècle; v. 1 Les duchés frontaliers de Mésopotamie et les fortifications de Zenobia*. Paris.

Le Bohec, Y. 2007. "Limitanei et comitatenses. Critique de la thèse attribuée à Theodor Mommsen," *Latomus* 66: 659–672.

Le Bohec, Y. 2006. *L'armée romaine sous le Bas-Empire*. Paris.

Le Bohec, Y., G. Greatrex et al. (eds.). 2015. The *Encyclopedia of the Roman Army*. Malden, MA.

Lee, J. W. I. 2007. *A Greek Army on the March*. Cambridge.

Lee, A. D. 2011. "Military history in late antiquity: Changing perspectives and paradigms," in L. Brice and J. Roberts (eds.), *Recent Directions in the Military History of the Ancient World*. Claremont, CA, 145–166.

Lee, A. D. 2007a. *War in Late Antiquity: A Social History*. Oxford.

Lee, A. D. 2007b. "Warfare and the State [the Later Roman State]," in Sabin, Van Wees, and Whitby (2007b). 379–423.

Lee, A. D. 2005. "The Army at War," in M. Maas (ed.), *The Cambridge Companion to the Age of Justinian*. Cambridge. 113–133.

Lee, A. D. 1993. *Information and Frontiers*. Cambridge.

Lenski, N. 2009. "Schiavi armati e formazione di eserciti private nel mondo tardoantico," in G. P. Urso (ed.), *Ordine e disordine nel mondo Greco e romano*. Pisa, 145–175.

Lenski, N. 2007. "Two Sieges of Amida (AD 359 and 502–503) and the Experience of Combat in the Late Roman Near East," in Lewin, A. S. and P. Pellegrini (eds.), *The Late Roman Army in the Near East from Diocletian to the Arab Conquest*. Oxford, 219–236.

Lewin, A. 2015. "The 'Strategy of the Roman Empire' in Late Antiquity in the Near East. Did it Really Exist and Were the Jafnids a Part of it?" in *Les Jafnides, Des rois arabes au service de Byzance*. Paris, 155–192.

Lichtenberger, A. and R. Raja. 2016. "Jarash Northwest Quarter Project." In "Archaeology in Jordan, 2014 and 2015 Seasons." *AJA* 120: 643–645.

Liebeschuetz, W. 1996. "The Romans Demilitarised: the Evidence of Procopius," *SCI* 15: 230–239.

Liebeschuetz, W. 1993. "Ecclesiastical Historians on Their Own Times," *Studi Patristica* 24: 151–163.

Liebeschuetz, W. 1990. *Barbarians and Bishops*. Oxford.

Liebeschuetz W. 1977. "The Defences of Syria in the Sixth Century," in *Studien zu den Militärgrenzen II*. Köln, 487–499.

Lillington-Martin, C. 2017. "Procopius, *paredros/quaestor, Codex Justinianus*, 1.27 and Belisarius' Strategy in the Mediterranean," in Lillington-Martin and Turquois (2017), 157–185.

Lillington-Martin, C. 2013. "Procopius on the Struggle for Dara in 530 and Rome in 537–538: Reconciling Texts and Landscapes," in Sarantis and Christie (2013), 599–630.

Lillington, C. and E. Turquois, (eds.). 2017. *Procopius of Caesarea: Literary and Historical Interpretations*. London.

Little, L. K. (ed.). 2007. *Plague and the End of Antiquity: The Pandemic of 541–750*. Cambridge.

Littlewood, A. R., ed. 1995. *Originality in Byzantine Literature, Art, and Music*. Oxford.

Luttwak, E. 1976. *The Grand Strategy of the Roman Empire*. Baltimore.

Luce, T. J. 2002. *The Greek Historians*. London.

MacLennan, H. 1946. *Two Solitudes*. Toronto.

Maas, M., ed. 2015. *Cambridge Companion to the Age of Attila*. Cambridge.

Maas, M. 1992. *John Lydus and the Roman Past: Antiquarianism and Politics in the Age of Justinian*. London.

Macrides, R. 2000. "The Pen and the Sword. Who Wrote the *Alexiad*?" in T. Gouma-Peterson (ed.), *Anna Komnene and Her Times*. New York, 63–81.

Magness, J. 1999. "Redating the forts at Ein Boqeq, Upper Zohar, and other sites in SE Judea, and the implications for the nature of the *Limes Palaestinae*," in J. H. Humphries (ed.), *The Roman and Byzantine Near East*, vol. 2. Portsmouth, R, 189–206.

Mango, C. 1980. *Byzantium: the empire of New Rome*. London.

Mann, J. C. 1963. "The Role of the Frontier Zone in Army Recruitment," in *V Congressus Internationalis Limitis Romani Studiosorum*. Zagreb, 143–150.

Marincola, J. 1997. *Authority and Tradition in Ancient Historiography*. Cambridge.

Marshall, S. L. A. 1947. *Men Against Fire*. New York.

Martindale, J. 1992. *The Prosopography of the Later Roman Empire, Volume III, AD 527–641*. Cambridge.

Martindale, J. 1989. *The Prosopographay of the Later Roman Empire, Volume II, AD 395–527*. Cambridge.

Maspero, J. 1912. *Organisation militaire de l'Égypte Byzantine*. Paris.

McCormick, M. 2016. "Tracking Mass Death during the Fall of Rome's Empire (II): a First Inventory," *JRA* 29: 1008–1046.

McCormick, M. 2015. "Tracking Mass Death during the Fall of Rome's Empire (I)," *JRA* 28: 325–357.

McMahon, L. 2014. *The foederati, the phoideratoi, and the symmachoi of the late antique east (ca. A.D. 400–650)*. Unpublished M.A. Thesis, University of Ottawa.

Meier, M. 2020. "The 'Justinianic Plague': An 'Inconsequential Pandemic'? A Reply," *Medizinhistorisches Journal*, pre-print.

Meier, M. 2016. "The 'Justinianic Plague': The Economic Consequences of the Pandemic in the Eastern Roman Empire and Its Cultural and Religious Effects," *EME* 24: 267–292.

Meier, M. 2004. "Prokop, Agathias, die Pest und das 'Ende' der antiken Historiographie," HZ 278: 281–310.

Meier, M. 1999. "Beobachtungen zu den sogenannten Pestschilderungen bei Thukydides II 47–54 und bei Prokop, Bell. Pers. II 22–23," Tyche 14: 177–210.

Meyerson, P. 1988. "Justinian's Novel 103 and the Reorganization of Palestine," BASOR 269: 65–71.

Miller, T. S. 1976. "The Plague in John VI Cantacuzenus and Thucydides," GRBS 17: 385–95.

Mitchell, S. 2014. A History of the Later Roman Empire, AD 284–641, 2nd ed. Oxford.

Mitthof, F. 2001. Annona Militaris: Die Heeresversorgung im spätaniken Ägypten. Florence.

Modéran, Y. 2003. Les Maures et l'Afrique romaine (IVe–VIIe siècle). Rome.

Mommsen, T. 1889. "'Das römische Militärwesen seit Diocletian," Hermes 24: 195–279.

Modéran, Y. 1996. "La renaissance des cités dans l'Afrique du VIe siècle d'après une inscription récemment publiée," in C. Lepelly (ed.), La fin de la cité antique et les débuts de la cité médiévale. Bari, 85–114.

Mordechai, L. and M. Eisenberg. 2019. "Rejecting Catastrophe: The Case of the Justinianic Plague," P&P 244: 3–50.

Müller, A. 1912. "Das Heer Justinians nach Procop und Agathias", Philologus 71: 101–138.

Nechaeava, E. 2014. Embassies—Negotiations—Gifts: Systems of East Roman Diplomacy in Late Antiquity. Stuttgart.

Nicasie, M. J. 1998. Twilight of Empire: The Roman Army from the Reign of Diocletian until the Battle of Adrianople. Amsterdam.

Nilsson, I. 2006. "To Narrate Events of the Past: On Byzantine Historians, and Historians on Byzantium," in J. Burke (ed.), Byzantine Narrative. Papers in Honour of Roger Scott. Melbourne, 47–58.

Oliverio, G. 1936. Documenti Antichi dell'Africa Italiana II. Bergamo.

Onur, F. 2017. "The Anastasian Military Decree from Perge in Pamphylia: Revised 2nd Edition," Gephyra 14: 133–212.

Onur, F. 2014. Monumentum Pergense. Anastasios'un Ordu Fermani. Istanbul.

Onur, F. 2009. "The Roman Army in Pamphylia: From the Third to Sixth Centuries A.D.," Adalya 12: 299–318.

Parnell, D. 2017. Justinian's Men. London.

Parnell, D. 2015. "Barbarians and Brothers-in-Arms: Byzantines on Barbarian Soldiers in the Sixth Century," BZ 108: 809–826.

Parnell, D. 2012. "A Prosopographical Approach to Justinian's Army," Medieval Prosopography 27: 1–75.

Parnell, D. 2010. Justinian's Men: The Ethnic and Regional Origins of Byzantine Officers and Officials, ca. 518–610. Unpublished thesis. Saint Louis University.

Parker, S. T., ed. 2006. *The Roman Frontier in Central Jordan: Final report on the* Limes Arabicus *Project, 1980–1989*. Cambridge, MA.

Parker, S. T. 1986. *Romans and Saracens. A History of the Arabian Frontier*. Winona Lake.

Parker, H. M. D. 1933. "The Legions of Diocletian and Constantine," *JRS* 23: 175–189.

Pazdernik, C. 2006. "Xenophon's *Hellenica* in Procopius' *Wars*: Pharnabazus and Belisarius," *GRBS* 46: 175–206.

Pazdernik, C. 2000. "Procopius and Thucydides on the Labors of War: Belisarius and Brasidas in the Field," *TAPha* 130: 149–187.

Pearson, E. 2019. "Decimation and Unit Cohesion: Why Were Roman Legionaries Willing to Perform Decimation?" *JMH* 83: 665–688.

Petersen, L. R. 2013. *Siege Warfare and Military Organization in the Successor States (400–800 AD)*. Leiden.

Petitjean, M. 2014. "Classicisme, Barbarie, et Guerre Romaine", *AntTard* 22: 255–262.

Phang, S. 2007. "Military Documents, Languages, and Literacy," in P. Erdkamp (ed.), *A Companion to the Roman Army*. Malden, MA, 286–305.

Pickett, J. 2017. "Water and Empire in the *De aedificiis* of Procopius," *DOP* 71: 95–125

Pitcher, L. V. 2009. *Writing Ancient History*. London.

Pitcher, L. V. 2007. "Characterization in Ancient Historiography," in J. Marincola (ed.), *A Companion to Greek and Roman Historiography*. Oxford, 102–117.

Pollard, N. 2013. "*Imperatores castra dedicaverunt:* Security, Army Bases, and Military Dispositions in Later Roman Egypt (Late Third-Fourth Century)." *JLA* 6: 3–36.

Pollard, N. 2000. *Soldiers, Cities, and Civilians in Roman Syria*. Ann Arbor.

Porten, B. 1996. *The Elephantine Papyri in English*. Leiden.

Potter, D. 2015. *Theodora: Actress, Empress, Saint*. Oxford.

Poulter, A. 2007. "Interpreting Finds in Context: Nicopolis and Dichin Revisited", in *Objects in Context, Objects in Use*, edd. L. Lavan, E. Swift, T. Putzeys. Leiden, 685–705.

Pringle, D. 2001. *The Defence of Byzantine Africa from Justinian to the Arab Conquest (reprint of 1981 edition, slightly revised)*. Oxford.

Rance, P. 2007. "Battle [the Later Roman Empire]," in Sabin, Van Wees, and Whitby (2007), 342–378.

Rance, P. 2005. "Narses and the Battle of Taginae (Busta Gallorum): Procopius and Sixth-Century Warfare," *Historia* 54: 424–472.

Rance, P. 2004. "The *fulcum*, the Late Roman and Byzantine *testudo*. The Germanisation of Roman Infantry Tactics," *GRBS* 44: 265–326.

Ravegnani, G. 2005. "Le unità dell'esercito bizantino nel VI secolo tra continuità e innovazione," in S. Gasparri (ed.), *Alto Medioevo mediterraneo*. Florence, 185–205.

Ravegnani, G. 2004. *I Bizantini e la Guerra*. Rome.

Ravegnani, G. 1998. *Soldati di Bisanzio in età giustinianea*. Rome.

Richardot, P. 2005. *La Fin de l'Armée Romaine 284–476*. Paris: Economica, 2005.

Roberto, U. and L. Mecessa (eds.) (2015). *Governare e riformare l'impero al momento della sua divisione: Oriente, Occidente, Illirico*. Rome.

Rop, J. 2019. "The Phocian Betrayal at Thermopylae," *Historia* 68: 413–435.

Roques, D. 2000. "Histoire et rhétorique dans l'oeuvre de Procope de Césarée: Procope est-il un historien?" in Criscuolo, U. and R. Maisano (eds.), *Categorie linguistische e concettuali della storiografia bizantina*. Naples, 9–39.

Rosenstein, N. 2004. *Rome at War*. Chapel Hill.

Ross, A. 2017. "Narrator and Participant in Procopius' *Wars*," in Lillington-Martin and Turquois (2017), 73–90.

Roth, J. 1999. *The Logistics of the Roman Army at War (264 B.C.–A.D. 235)*. Leiden.

Roth, J. 1994. "The Size and Organization of the Roman Imperial Legion," *Historia* 43: 346–362.

Roxan, M. 1976. "Pre-Severan Auxilia Named in the Notitia Dignitatum," in R. Goodburn and P. Bartholomew (eds.), *Aspects of the Notita Dignitatum*. Oxford, 59–80.

Rubin, Z. 1995. "The Reforms of Khusro Anushirwan," in A. Cameron (ed.), *The Byzantine and Early Islamic Near East Volume III: States, Resources, and Armies*. Princeton, 227–297.

Ruffini, G. 2018. *Life in an Egyptian Village in Late Antiquity*. Cambridge.

Russell, D. 1998. "The Panegyrists and Their Teachers," in Ma. Whitby (ed.), *The Power of Propaganda. The Role of Panegyric in Late Antiquity*. Leiden, 17–50.

Sabin, P. 2000. "The Face of Roman Battle," *JRS* 90: 1–17.

Sabin, P., Van Wees, H. and M. Whitby, eds. 2007. *The Cambridge History of Greek and Roman Warfare Volume II: Rome from the late Republic to the late Empire*. Cambridge.

Salway, B. 2015. "Late Antiquity," in C. Bruun and J. Edmondson (eds.), *The Oxford Handbook of Roman Epigraphy*. New York, 364–393.

Sarantis, A. 2019. "Military Provisioning in the Sixth-Century Balkans," *JLA* 12: 329–379.

Sarantis, A. 2017a. "Roman or Barbarian? Ethnic identities and political loyalties in the Balkans according to Procopius," in Lillington-Martin and Turquois (2017), 217–237.

Sarantis, A. 2017b. "Justinian and Africa, 533–548," in M. Whitby and H. Sidebottom (eds.), *The Encyclopedia of Ancient Battles*. Chichester, 1214–1230.

Sarantis, A. 2016. *Justinian's Balkan Wars*. Cambridge.

Sarantis, A. 2013. "Military Equipment and Weaponry: A Bibliographic Essay," in Sarantis and Christie (2013), 153–175.

Sarantis, A. 2009. "War and diplomacy in Pannonia and the north-west Balkans during the reign of Justinian: the Gepid threat and imperial responses," *DOP* 63: 15–40.

Sarantis, A. and N. Christie, eds. 2013. *War and Warfare in Late Antiquity: Current Perspectives*. Leiden.

Sarris, P. 2017. "Landownership and Local Society in the Writings of Procopius," in Lillington-Martin and Turquois (2017), 238–250.

Sarris, P. 2007. "Bubonic Plague in Byzantium: The Evidence of Non-Literary Sources," in Little (2007), 119–134.

Sarris, P. 2006. *Economy and Society in the Age of Justinian*. Cambridge.
Sarris, P. 2002. "The Justinianic Plague: Origins and Effects," *Continuity and Change* 17: 169–182.
Sartres, M. 1982. *Trois études sur l'Arabie romaine et byzantine*. Brussels.
Scharf, R. 2001. *Foederati. Von der völkerrechtlichen Kategorie zur byzantinischen Truppengattung*. Vienna.
Schmitt, O. 2015. "Bucellarii, Buccellarii," in Le Bohec, Y, G. Greatrex et al. (2015), 120–121.
Schmitt, O. 2001. "Stärke, Struktur und Genese des comitatensischen Infanterienumerus," *BJ* 201: 93–111.
Schmitt, O. 1994. "Die buccellarii," *Tyche* 9: 147–174.
Scott, R. 2012. *Byzantine Chronicles and the Sixth Century*. Farnham.
Scott, R. 2006. "Narrating Justinian: from Malalas to Manasses," in J. Burke (ed.), *Byzantine Narrative. Papers in Honour of Roger Scott*. Melbourne, 29–46.
Scott, R. 1981. "The Classical Tradition in Byzantine Historiography," in Mullett, M. and R. Scott (eds.), *Byzantium and the Classical Tradition*. Birmingham, 61–74.
Shahîd, I. 2010. *Byzantium and the Arabs in the Sixth Century, Volume 2, Part 2*. Washington DC.
Shahîd, I. 2002. *Byzantium and the Arabs in the Sixth Century, Volume 2, Part 1*. Washington DC.
Shahîd, I. 1995b. *Byzantium and the Arabs in the Sixth Century, Volume 1, Part 2*. Washington DC.
Shahîd, I. 1995a. *Byzantium and the Arabs in the Sixth Century, Volume 1, Part 1*. Washington DC.
Shahîd, I. 1984. *Byzantium and the Arabs in the Fourth Century*. Washington: Dumbarton.
Shaw, B. 1984. "Latin Funerary Epigraphy and the Later Roman Empire," *Historia* 33: 457–497.
Shaw, B. 1982. "Easters of Flesh, Drinkers of Milk. The Ancient Mediterranean Ideology of the Pastoral Nomad." *AncSoc* 13/14: 5–31.
Sears, M. 2019. *Understanding Greek Warfare*. London.
Sessa, K. 2019. "The New Environmental Fall of Rome: A Methodological Consideration," *JLA* 12: 211–255.
Sidebottom, H. 2004. *Ancient Warfare*. Oxford.
Signes Codoñer, J. (trans.). 2000. *Historia Secreta—Procopio de Cesarea*. Madrid.
Sinclair, K. 2013. *War Writing in Middle Byzantine Historiography. Sources, Influences and Trends*. Unpublished PhD thesis. University of Birmingham.
Sivan, H. 2008. *Palestine in Late Antiquity*. Oxford.
Skeat, T. C. 1964. *The Chester Beatty Papyri*. Dublin.
Skinner, P. 2015. "Visible Prowess? Reading Men's Head and Face Wounds in Early Medieval Europe to 1000CE," in Tracy and DeVries (2015), 81–101.
Smith, M. 2017. *Mortal Wounds*. Barnsley, Yorkshire.
Southern, P. and K. R. Dixon. 1996. *The Late Roman Army*. New Haven.

Spaul, J. 2000. *Cohors2*. Oxford.

Spaul, J. 1994. *Ala2*. Andover.

Speidel, M. 1984. "Catafractarii, Clibanarii and the Rise of the Later Roman Mailed Cavalry," *Epigraphica Anatolica* 4: 151–156.

Stein, E. 1949. *Histoire du Bas Empire II: De la disparition de l'Empire d'Occident à la mort de Justinien*. Trans. J-R. Palanque. Paris.

Stewart, M. 2016. *The Soldier's Life*. Leeds.

Sutherland, T. 2000. "Recording the Grave," in Fiorato, V., Boylston, A., and C. Knüsel (eds.), *Blood Red Roses: The History, Archaeology and Anthropology of a Mass Grave from the Battle of Towton, AD 1461*. Oxford, 36–44.

Syvänne, I. 2015. "*foederati*," in Y. Le Bohec, G. Greatrex et al. (2015), 406–507.

Syvänne, I. 2004. *The Age of Hippotoxotai*. Tampere.

Talbot, A. M. and D. F. Sullivan (trans.). 2005. *The History of Leo the Deacon: Byzantine Military Expansion in the Tenth Century*. Washington DC.

Teall, J. 1965. "The Barbarians in Justinian's Armies," *Speculum* 40: 294–322.

Thompson, E. A. 1958. "Early Germanic Warfare," *P&P* 14: 2–27.

Tomlin, R. 2008. "Jones and the army of the 4th c.," in D. Gwynn (ed.), *A. H. M. Jones and the Later Roman Empire*. Leiden, 143–165.

Tomlin, R. 2000. "The legions in the late empire," in *Roman Frontiers and Their Fortresses*, ed. R. J. Brewer, 159–78. London/Cardiff: Society of Antiquaries of London.

Tomlin, R. 1972. "*Seniores-Iuniores* in the late Roman field army," *AJP* 93: 253–78.

Toynbee, A. 1973. *Constantine Porphyrogenitus and His World*. Oxford.

Traina, G. 2009. *428 AD. An Extraordinary Year at the End of the Empire*. Princeton.

Treadgold, W. 2007. *The Early Byzantine Historians*. London.

Treadgold, W. 2005. "Standardized Numbers in the Byzantine Army," *War in History* 12: 1–14.

Treadgold, W. 1995. *Byzantium and its Army, 284–1081*. Stanford.

Turquois, E. 2015. "Technical Writing, Genre and Aesthetic in Procopius," in G. Greatrex and H. Elton (eds.), Shifting Genres in Late Antiquity. Farnham, 219–231.

Van Berchem, D. 1952. *L'Armée de Dioclétien et la Réforme Constantinienne*. Paris.

Vannesse, M. 2010. *La défense de l'Occident romain pendant l'Antiquité tardive: recherches géostratégiques sur l'Italie de 284 à 410 ap. J.-C.* Brussels: Collection Latomus.

Ward, W. 2015. *Mirage of the Saracen*. Berkeley: University of California Press.

Whately, C. forthcoming a. "Looking for Unit Cohesion at the End of Antiquity," in J. Hall, G. Lee, and L. Rawlings (eds.), *Unit Cohesion in Antiquity* (title tbc). London.

Whately, C. forthcoming b. "Procopius, Soldiers, and Strategy on the Southeastern Frontier in the Age of Justinian," in C. Robin, C. and M. Wissa (eds.), *Aksum, Himyar, and Egypt: Merchants, trade, religion and the changing world of the cities from Justinian to 'Abd el-Malek* (title tbc). Edinburgh.

Whately, C. 2019. "Procopius on the Siege of Rome in AD 537/538," in J. Armstrong and M. Trundle (eds.), *Brill's Companion to Ancient Sieges*. Leiden, 265–284.

Whately, C. 2018. "Combat Motivation at the End of Antiquity", in G. Greatrex and S. Janniard (eds.), *The World of Procopius*. Paris, 185–203.

Whately, C. 2017a. "Thucydides and the Historians of the Later Roman Empire," in Forsdyke, Balot, and Foster (2017) 691–707.

Whately, C. 2017b. "Procopius and the Characterization of Bessas: Where History Meets Historiography", in E. Turquois & C. Lillington-Martin (2017), 123–136

Whately, C. 2016a. *Battles and Generals: Combat, Culture, and Didacticism in Procopius' Wars*. Leiden.

Whately, C. 2016b. "Some Observations on Procopius' Use of Numbers in Descriptions of Combat in Wars 1–7," *Phoenix* 69: 394–411.

Whately, C. 2016c. "Camels, Soldiers, and Pilgrims in Sixth Century Nessana", *Scripta Classica Israelica* 35: 121–135.

Whately, C. 2015a. "Making Sense of the Frontier Armies in Late Antiquity: an Historian's Perspective", in R. Collins and M. Weber (eds.), *Roman Military Architecture on the Frontiers: Armies and Their Architecture in Late Antiquity*. Oxford, 6–17.

Whately, C. 2015b. "Soldiers and Their Families on the Late Roman Frontier in Central Jordan", in G. Wrightson (ed.), *The Many Faces of War in the Ancient World*. Newcastle, 283–301.

Whately, C. 2014. "Arabs, Outsiders, and Stereotypes from Ammianus Marcellinus to Theophylact Simocatta." In Dijkstra and Fisher (2014), 215–233.

Whately, C. 2013a. Organisation and Life in the Military: A Bibliographic Essay," in Sarantis and Christie (2013), 209–238.

Whately, C. 2013b. "el-Lejjūn: Logistics anad Localisation on Rome's East Frontier in the 6th c.", in in Sarantis and Christie (2013), 893–924.

Whately, C. 2008. "Indiscipline in the Sixth Century Historiography of Generals," Bragg, E., Hau, L. I., and E. Macaulay-Lewis (eds.), *Beyond the Battlefield: New perspectives on warfare and society in the Graeco-Roman world*. Newcastle, 241–258.

Wheeler, E. 2016a. "Parthian Auxilia in the Roman Army Part I: From the Late Republic to c. 70 A.D.," in C. Wolff and P. Faure (eds.), *Les auxiliaires de l'armée romaine*. Paris, 171–222.

Wheeler, E. 2016b. "Parthian Auxilia in the Roman Army, Part II: From the Flavians to the Late Empire," *HIMA* 5: 103–137.

Wheeler, E. 2004a. "The Legion as Phalanx in the Late Empire (I)," in Le Bohec, Y. and C. Wolff (eds.), *L'armée romaine de Dioclétien á Valentinien 1er*. Paris. 309–358.

Wheeler, E. 2004b. "The Legion as Phalanx in the Late Empire (II)," in *Revue des Etudes Militaires Anciennes* 1: 147–175.

Wheeler, E. 1979. "The Legion as Phalanx," *Chrion* 9: 303–318.

Whitby, M. 2015. "Recruitment, Social and Geographic Aspects: Late Empire," in Y. Le Bohec, G. Greatrex et al. (2015), 817–820.

Whitby, M. 2013. "Siege Warfare and Counter-Siege Tactics in Late Antiquity (ca. 250–640)," in Sarantis and Christie (2013), 433–459.

Whitby, M. 2004. "Emperors and Armies, AD 235–395," in S. Swain and M. Edwards (eds.), *Approaching Late Antiquity*. Oxford, 156–186.

Whitby, M. 2000. "The Army, c. 420–602," in Cameron, A., Ward-Perkins, B., and M. Whitby (eds.), *The Cambridge Ancient History Volume XIV. Late Antiquity: Empire and Successors, A.D. 425–600*. Cambridge, 288–314.

Whitby, M. 1995. "Recruitment in Roman Armies from Justinian to Heraclius, ca. 565–615," in Cameron (ed.). 1995. *The Byzantine and Early Islamic Near East Volume III: States, Resources, and Armies*. Princeton. 61–124.

Whitby, M. 1992. "Greek Historical Writing after Procopius," in Cameron and Conrad (1992), 25–81.

Whitby, M. 1989. "Procopius and Antioch," in D. H. French and C. S. Lightfoot (eds.), *The Defence of the Roman and Byzantine East*. Oxford, 537–553.

Whitby, M. 1987. "Notes on Some Justinianic Constructions," *Byzantinisch-Neugriechischen Jahrbücher* 23: 91–112.

Whitby, M. 1986a. "Procopius and the Development of Roman Defences in Upper Mesopotamia," in Freeman, P. and D. Kennedy (eds.), *The Defence of the Roman and Byzantine East*. Oxford, 717–735.

Whitby, M. 1986b. "Procopius' Description of Dara (Buildings II.1–3.)," in Freeman, P. and D. Kennedy (eds.), *The Defence of the Roman and Byzantine East*. Oxford, 737–783.

Whitby, M. 1985. "Justinian's Bridge over the Sangarius and the Date of Procopius' de Aedificiis," *JHS* 105: 129–148.

Whitby, M. 1984. "Procopius' Description of Martyropolis (de Aedificiis III.2.10–14)," *Byzantinoslavica* 45: 177–182.

Whitby, Ma. and M. Whitby, eds. and trans. 1989. *Chronicon Paschale*. Liverpool.

Wiewiorowski, J. 2012. "The Defence of the Long Walls of Thrace under Justinian the Great (527–565 A.D.)," *Bulgaria Mediaevalis* 3: 235–247.

Wiseman, T. P. 1993. "Lying Historians: Seven Types of Mendacity," in Gill, C. and T. P. Wiseman (eds.), *Lies and Fiction in the Ancient World*. Exeter, 122–146.

Wood, P. 2013. *The Chronicle of Seert: Christian Historical Imagination in Late Antique Iraq*. Oxford.

Woosman-Savage, R. and K. DeVries. 2015. "Battle Trauma in Medieval Warfare: Wounds, Weapons and Armor," in Tracy and DeVries (2015), 27–56.

Yuretich, L., ed. and trans. 2018. *The Chronicle of Constantine Manasses*. Liverpool.

Zuckerman, C. 2004. *Du Village à l'Empire*. Paris.

Zuckerman, C. 1998. "Two Reforms of the 370s: Recruiting Soldiers and Senators in the Divided Empire," *REByz* 56: 79–139.

Zuckerman, C. 1988. "Legio V Macedonica in Egypt," *Tyche* 3: 279–287.

Index Locorum

The first figure is the passage number, the second one is the page number (in this book).

AE			Basil		
1990, 146		6	*Ennaratio in prophetam Isaiam*		
2002, 624		6	3.101		83
2005, 1730		123	*Homilia exhortatoria ad sanctum*		
2011, 1810		123	*baptisma*		
Agathias, *Histories*			31.440		83
1.4.4		75	*In Ebrosius*		
1.12.6		116	31.457		83
1.14.3		75	*Letters*		
1.15.1		116	351		66
1.19.4		116	BGU		
1.21.6		75	2.673		63
1.22.1		130	12.2137		202
1.22.2		75	12.2139		202
2.3.8		75	12.2141		70
2.4.10		213	12.2197		163, 202
2.5.4		119	19.2804		63
2.7.3–4		116			
2.10.7		50	Cassius Dio		
2.14.4		116	40.65.1		66
3.4.6		116	40.65.2		66
3.27.1		116	ChLA		
3.28.4		50	10.407		63
4.18.1		116	41.1193		63, 70
4.21.5		116	43.242		51
4.21.6		116	CIL		
5.14.3		76	3.14065		122
5.15.4		76	3.14149		142
5.15.7–8		213	5.6784		122
5.16.2–3		213	6.9898		116
5.22.8		119	8.4354		163
Ammianus Marcellinus			11.1693		6
15.1.1		42	11.5632		122
16.10.8		124	13.848		122
16.12.7		124	13.3493		122
18.9.3		58	13.3495		122
18.9.4		124	13.6238		122
29.5.20		124	*Codex Theodosianus*		
30.1.11		124	7.1.18		96
Aristophanes			7.4.22pr		96
Knights (eq.)			7.4.30		143
1369		65	7.13.7.3		96

Codex Theodosianus (cont.)

7.20.4pr	96
7.20.4.1	55
7.20.4.2	96
7.20.4.3	96
7.22.8	96
8.1.10	96

Corippus, *John Troglita*

1.426	108
4.472–563	108

Corpus Iuris Civilis
  Codex Justinianus

1.4.20	113
1.5.12.17	109, 114
1.27	176
1.27.1.16	164
1.27.1.18	164
1.27.1.21–42	164
1.27.2pr	164
1.27.2.2–3	164
1.27.2.4b	164
1.27.2.8	96, 98, 99, 160, 165, 195
1.27.2.14	166
1.27.2.20–34	165
1.27.5	176, 177
1.29	205
1.29.4	206
1.29.5	108, 205
1.31.4	49
1.31.5pr	190, 193
1.31.5.2	48, 55, 193
1.41	49
1.42	50
1.42.1	193
1.42.2	177, 219
1.46.4pr	193
1.46.4.2	166
2.50.1	217
2.50.3–7	218
2.50.8	218
2.51	218
2.53.5	220
3.23.2	218
3.28.37	218
4.61.5	12
4.52.4	218
4.65.35	12, 109, 168
5.4.21	221
5.5.1	222
5.9.3	221
5.11.7	222
5.14.11	222
5.16.2	222
5.17.7	217
5.16.27	220
6.21.7	217
6.21.16	50
6.40.3	222
6.62.2	96
7.35.1	218
7.35.6	220
9.9.15	217
9.9.19	217
9.12.10pr	115
9.12.10.1	115
9.41.8pr	12
11.60.1–3	166
11.60.3	166
12.17	190
12.23.7pr	97
12.23.7.18	97
12.27.13	219
12.27.19–35	219
12.35.14pr	166
12.35.14	63, 180
12.35.15	115
12.35.17	50, 160, 190, 192
12.35.18	160
12.37.8	63
12.42	84
12.42.1	63
12.42.2–3	218
12.59.8	193

Digest

49.3.16	194

Novels of Justinian

2	220
6	49
6.2–3	69
8	160
21	150
22	215, 220, 221
22.7	221
22.14	216
24	176
24.1	201
25	69
25.1	201

INDEX LOCORUM

26	176	5.33	115
28.5.1	115	7.46	115
30	176	Hesychius, *Lexicon*	
30.5.1	115	1249	66
31	150		
41	97, 98	IGLSyr	
50	97	13.1 9046	84
74	221	21.4 50	202
74.4.1–3	222	Isidore of Seville (*Etymologies*)	
85	115	1.24.1–2	52
102	68, 160, 169, 170		
103	98, 160, 162, 169	John Chrysostom, *Catecheses ad illuminandos*	
103.3.1	162	7.30	83
116	109	John of Ephesus, *HE*	
116.1	115, 214	3.13	198, 203
117	98, 214, 215, 221	3.25–26	114
117.8	221	3.26	203
117.11	109, 215	Jordanes	
118	214	*Getica*	
119	214	16.89	74, 109
120	214	21.112	74, 109
122	214	28.145	74, 109
123.25	69	32.165	109
140	220	36.191	74
147.2	109	38.197	74
148	68	60.312	36
148.2	109	*Romana*	
		155	74
Demosthenes		217	74
13.4	65	236	74
18.105	65	239	74
50.6	65	261	74
Dexippus, fragments		373–374	36
24.21	66	Josephus, *Jewish Antiquities*	
Dialogue on Political Science (anonymous)		12.47	83
4.12	35	Joshua (Pseudo) Stylites, *Chronicle*	
		51	155
Eunapius, *History*		56	155
1.1.6–94	42	310–313	199
Evagrius, *HE*			
5.14	114, 203–204	Libanius	
5.25	40	*Letters*	
6.1	64	17.1	83
6.11	195	*Orations*	
10.41	209	1.18.B	66
		1.29B	66
Herodotus		1.34C	66
3.139	115	1.48C	66
4.78	115		

Lives of the Pontiffs, *Liber Pontificalis*
   147–148   36
Lucian
  How to Write History
    49   43
  Navigium
    33   65
Lydus, John
  On the Magistrates
    1.9.5   77
    1.12   77
    1.16   77
    1.16.3   77
    1.46   76
    1.46.3–7   76
    1.48.2   77
    2.11.1   78
    2.18.1   78
    2.22.1   78
    2.24.3   78
    2.27.2   78
    3.2.2   83
    3.3.1   76
    3.3.2   77
    3.3.2–3   78
    3.3.1   78
    3.3.2   78
    3.3.6   77
    3.4.1   78
    3.4.2   78
    3.8.1   79
    3.9.1–2   77
    3.12.4   79
    3.22.1   79
    3.38.1   79
    3.34.1   77
    3.66.4   79
  On the Months
    1.27   79
    1.28   80
Lysias
  25.16   65

Malalas, John
  2.11   75
  2.16   75
  5.2   75
  12.10   75
  12.40   75
  12.40.4   167
  13.27   75
  14.22   109
  16.9   75
  18.2   75
  18.2.6   167
  18.5   75
  18.8.10   40
  18.10   108, 205
  18.14   198
  18.34   201
  18.60   46
  18.65   46
  18.71   199
  18.129   75
  18.141   109
MAMA
  1.68   5
Marcellinus, Count/Comes
  499.1   46
  529   73
  530   46
  535.1   73
  545.2   73
Maurice, *Strategikon*
  1.2   131
  1.3.8   61
  1.4   197
  1.5.2   197
  2.5.6   61
  2.13   35
  4.1   211
  7B.6   50
  8.2   123
  8.2.31   61
  12.B.4   61
Menander Protector
  1.4   67
  3.6   72
  3.232   67
  3.240   72
  3.243   67
  3.245   67
  3.285   67
  5.9   67
  8.87   72
  8.91   72

INDEX LOCORUM

13.43	67	37.31	146
23.18	67	37.32	146
31.15	67	37.33	146
		37.34	146, 147
Notitia Dignitatum		37.35	146
East (or.)		38.14	146
6	98	38.30	151
6.37	202	40.11–17	97
6.43	202	*West (occ.)*	
6.44	202	25.21	142
6.49	58	25.26	142
7.24	97, 104	26.13	142
7.27	202, 203	26.19	142
7.35	104		
7.38	97, 104	P. Apoll.	
7.48	104	37	69
9.6	105	87	69
9.18	105	P. Cair. Masp.	
9.21	105	1.67002	202
9.30	105	1.67009	63, 202
9.39	105	1.67056	163, 202
11.21	157	1.67057	202
31	192	1.67058	163, 202
31.23–24	202	1.67091	202
32.30	149	2.67126	63, 202
32.31	159	2.67151	67
33.26	149	2. 67168	69
33.28	149, 160	2.67200	67
34.24	171	3.67321	67, 106, 202
35.24	60, 148	P. Dip.	
35.31	148	122	202
36.28	148	P. Horak	
37.14	146	32	69
37.15	146	P. Ital.	
37.16	146	18–19	202
37.17	146	P. Laur.	
37.18	146	3.111	63
37.19	146	P. Lond.	
37.20	146, 147	4.1360	69
37.21	146	4.1379	69
37.22	146	4.1401	69
37.23	146	4.1406	69
37.25	146	4.1436	69
37.26	146	5.1663	67, 175, 176, 202
37.27	146	5.1722	63, 68
37.28	146	5.1723	63
37.29	146	5.1724	63
37.30	146	5.1728	63

P. Lond. (*cont.*)		Polyaenus	
5.1734	63	3.3	67
5.1855	63	Procopius[1]	
P. Muench.		*Buildings*	
1.1	195	1.2.19.2	64
1.2	50, 83, 190, 197	1.11.19	72
1.4	195	2.1.2	174
1.4+5V	63	2.1.4	147
1.8	63	2.1.7	174
1.9	63	2.1.8–10	175
1.11	63	2.1.11–27	174
1.15	63	2.2.10	150
1.16	63	2.2.20–21	175
1.16	63	2.2.26	175
P. Ness.		2.3.26	150
3.14	177	2.4.1	147
3.15	62, 177	2.4.10	175
3.16	177	2.4.14	175
3.17	177	2.4.21	175
3.18	177	2.6.2	147, 148
3.19	177	2.6.9	146, 148
3.20	177	2.6.14	147, 148
3.21	177	2.6.16	148
3.22	177	2.7.1	148
3.23	177	2.8.8	147
3.24	177	2.8.11	149
3.25	177	2.8.24	149
3.26	177	2.9.1	149
3.27	177	2.9.8	149
3.28	177	2.9.9	175
3.29	177	2.9.10	147, 150
3.30	177	2.9.11	175
3.35	162	2.9.18	148
3.37	48, 176	2.9.19	149
P. Oxy.		2.11.10	174
1.144	69	2.11.12	149
8.1108	69	3.1.9	99
9.1184	70	3.1.16	150
16.1913	69	3.1.24	150
72.4920	70	3.1.27	150
P. Pommersf.		3.1.28–29	150
1	83	3.1.29	150
P. Ross. Georg.		3.1.128	146
4.4	69		
5.30	63		
P.Ryl.			
4.609	196		
P. Worp.			
33	63		

---

1 In part to prevent this list from getting out of control, I have not included under Procopius those passages referred to in the book's tables and in the appendix.

INDEX LOCORUM

3.1.129	108	6.3.5	64
3.2.1	146	6.22	212
3.3.6	99, 145, 148, 150	7.10	130
3.3.7	148	7.31.2	72
3.3.8	145, 146, 150	10.9	12, 98
3.3.14	146, 150	11.2.4	64
3.4.15	148, 149	11.3–11	174
3.4.16	59, 71, 149	15.29	72
3.5.1	148, 150	18.25	174
3.6.9	150	18.44	212
3.6.13	150	24.1	40, 145
3.6.18	146	24.3.1	64
3.6.22	99, 148, 150	24.3–6	219
3.6.26	148, 150	24.5	215
4.1.6	150	24.5.2	64
4.1.33	150	24.5.5	64
4.2.14	152	24.7	190
4.2.28	148, 152	24.12	98, 174
4.3.15.3	64	24.12–14	143
4.4.1.4	64	24.13	144
4.4.3.1	64	24.15	98
4.5.1	152	24.18	196
4.5.4	152	24.19.2	64
4.6.37	152	24.25.1	72
4.9.11	148, 152	24.29	12, 145
4.10.17	148, 152	24.30.2	64
5.1.13	173	24.30.7	72
5.4.7	148, 152	*Wars*	
5.4.14	152	1.1.3	31
5.7.12	152	1.1.4	32
5.7.13	152	1.1.12	130
5.8.1	148	1.1.12–14	126
5.8.9	152, 174	1.1.13	130
6.2.2	148	1.15	32
6.4.1	101	1.1.6	32
6.4.11	101	1.4.14	41
6.5.14	101	1.4.16	41
6.5.1–15	101	1.4.20	41
6.6.2	152	1.4.21	41
6.6.8	152	1.4.22	41
6.6.10	153	1.4.39	41
6.6.18	148, 153	1.6.18	16, 102
6.7.1	101, 153	1.7.4	110
6.7.8	148, 153	1.7.8	126
6.7.8–11	101	1.8.2	72, 103
6.7.15	148, 153	1.8.4	41
6.7.17	153	1.8.19	41
Secret History		1.10.19	160
5.30	12	1.12.24	33
6.2–3	194–195	1.13.5	106, 155, 159

Wars (cont.)

1.13.9	53, 103	1.21.21–28	48
1.13.10	53	1.23.25	16
1.13.19	53, 119, 155	1.24.1–58	33
1.13.19–23	103	1.24.40	207
1.13.20	53, 54	1.24.44	12
1.13.21	53, 54	1.24.51	72
1.13.22	107, 116	1.25.25	41
1.13.23	118	1.26.5	17
1.13.24	119	2.1.7	40
1.13.27	119	2.3.14	40
1.13.29	72	2.5.3	178
1.13.30	12, 106	2.5.7	160
1.13.38	119	2.5.11	155
1.14.1	16, 102, 106	2.5.12	126
1.14.16	119	2.5.23	155
1.14.5	116	2.7.7	155
1.14.25	16, 118	2.7.12	156
1.14.28	106	2.8.2	157
1.14.31	59, 71	2.8.7	126
1.14.31–35	125	2.8.10	126
1.14.35	126	2.8.13	157
1.18.41–48	126	2.8.15	126
1.14.42	119	2.8.17	157
1.14.49	71	2.8.19	16
1.14.52	118	2.8.33	16
1.17.11	41	2.8.35	41
1.17.13	41	2.9.10	41
1.17.17	34	2.10.11	116
1.17.19	41	2.10.23	16
1.17.46	146	2.12.26	41
1.18.5	105, 118	2.12.32	41
1.18.5–7	200	2.12.33	41
1.18.6	119	2.13.16	156, 160
1.18.9	41	2.13–16–29	156
1.18.12	106	2.14.8	205
1.18.24	106	2.16.17	158
1.18.26	118, 119	2.17.4	156
1.18.30	119	2.17.14–15	126
1.18.31–35	126	2.18.8	16
1.18.36	119	2.18.13	16
1.18.39–40	200	2.19.10	200
1.18.42	119	2.19.15	17
1.18.45	118	2.19.23–25	198
1.18.52	16, 53, 102	2.19.33–34	158
1.18.53	16, 53	2.19.41	64
1.19.27–37	162	2.20.13	160
1.21.5	155	2.20.14	156
		2.20.14–16	160

INDEX LOCORUM

2.21.3	16, 110	3.11.5–6	111
2.21.4	127	3.11.6–9	112
2.21.7	126	3.11.7	17, 107
2.21.8	127	3.11.18	107
2.21.13–15	211	3.11.19	207
2.21.20	16, 211	3.12.2	188
2.21.34	211	3.12.3	34
2.22.14	64	3.13.24	188
2.23.1–2	209	3.14.3–6	34
2.23.12–13	51	3.14.7	34
2.24.1	211	3.14.11–13	34
2.24.12–16	211	3.14.15	34
2.24.14	160	3.14.39	34
2.25.5–35	212	3.15.8	42
2.25.14	72	3.15.10	42
2.26.7	156	3.15.15	42
2.26.25	156	3.15.24	42
2.26.26	156	3.15.35	34
2.26.28	126	3.15.36	127
2.28.32	16	3.19.11	188
3.1.27	205	3.19.23	116
3.2.25	41	3.20.1	188
3.2.26	41	3.21.21	41
3.2.27	41	3.23.13	119
3.3.32	41	3.23.5	116
3.4.5	41	3.25.1	198
3.4.30	41	4.3.8	59, 71, 72
3.4.35	41	4.4.15–25	116
3.5.5	41	4.5.2	98
3.5.18	59, 71	4.5.5	59, 71, 118
3.5.24	41	4.7.20	16, 101, 102
3.6.1	41	4.10.9	127
3.6.2	41	4.11.32	12
3.6.4	41	4.11.49	72
3.6.14	41	4.13.15	127
3.7.10	41	4.14.7	101
3.8.18	41	4.14.8	101
3.8.27	119, 126	4.14.12	102
3.10.29–31	187	4.14.12–15	113
3.10.32	187	4.14.17	198, 205
3.11.1–19	71, 187	4.14.18	16, 101, 102
3.11.1	107	4.14.40	102
3.11.2	17, 107, 112	4.14.41	34
3.11.2–3	113	4.14.42	102
3.11.2–12	111	4.16.3	40, 197, 229
3.11.3	110	4.17.5	59, 71
3.11.3–4	198	4.17.32	12
3.11.5	107, 205	4.18.2–9	213

Wars (cont.)

4.19.3	64, 102, 204	5.23.9	72
4.19.6	197	5.23.9–12	37
4.20.12	17	5.23.12	72
4.20.27	12	5.23.21	72
4.21.4	42	5.23.24–27	37
4.22.12–17	220	5.24.30	41
4.23.12	102	5.25.11	64
4.23.13	64	5.27.1	17, 198
4.23.17	220	5.27.4–5	127
4.24.11	127	5.27.6	37, 38
4.24.13	41	5.27.11	127
4.26.10–12	213	5.27.14	127
4.28.46	108	5.27.15	127
5.1.25	41	5.27.19	128
5.2.8	116	5.27.23	119
5.5.2	17	5.27.27–28	128
5.5.2–4	107, 112	5.28.1–18	126
5.5.5	207	5.28.13	128
5.5.16	127	5.28.19	119
5.7.26	198, 199	5.28.21	119, 126
5.9.2	40, 41	5.28.21–22	128
5.9.6	41	5.28.22	72, 119
5.9.7	41	5.28.24	119
5.11.2	41	5.29.14	119
5.11.3	33	5.29.16	16, 103
5.12.2	41	5.29.17	126, 128
5.12.21	102	5.29.21	119
5.12.51	16	5.29.22	128
5.14.1	117	5.29.37–38	126
5.14.3	42	5.29.38	119
5.14.9	42	5.29.41	128
5.16.1	19	5.29.42	126, 128
5.16.20	41	5.29.43	48
5.16.21	41	6.1.1	119
5.17.7	98	6.1.2	119
5.17.17	17, 111	6.1.9	128
5.18.4	12	6.1.11–19	37
5.18.18	119	6.1.20	37, 126
5.18.43	188	6.1.26–34	37
5.19.14	36	6.1.30	128
5.21.14–22	38	6.2.9–13	37
5.22.4	127	6.2.14–15	37
5.22.4–5	37	6.2.38	36
5.22.7	127	6.3.30	64
5.22.10	72, 119	6.4.1–2	34, 36
5.22.20	126	6.4.3–4	34
5.23.3	58, 117	6.4.6	188
		6.4.19	34

INDEX LOCORUM

6.4.20	36, 188	7.13.21–22	200
6.4.27	42	7.14.21	40
6.4.28	41	7.18.19	41
6.5.1	17	7.19.6	17
6.5.2	36	7.19.23	40
6.5.9	118	7.19.25	17
6.5.14–16	37	7.20.4	18
6.5.18–20	37, 118	7.21.4	16
6.5.20	118	7.27.3	116
6.7.14	188	7.27.17	41
6.7.12–15	36	7.30.3	188
6.9.14	72	7.33.13	17, 189
6.10.10	12	7.34.1–40	200
6.13.9	119	7.36.15	42
6.16.4	72	7.38.23	64
6.16.11	16, 102	7.39.8	102
6.17.10	34	7.39.16–20	200, 207, 223
6.20.30	41	7.39.17	189
6.23.23–28	33, 35	7.39.18	189
6.25.3	129	7.39.20	189
6.25.18	41	7.40.38	64
6.26.3–26	18	8.2.2	41
6.26.5	12	8.2.16	41, 65
6.29.32	33	8.3.5	41
6.29.34	64	8.3.10	41
7.1.8	12, 55, 128	8.5.7	41
7.1.20	207	8.5.13	17
7.1.21	116	8.5.23	41
7.3.10	198	8.6.2	41
7.4.21–30	126, 130	8.6.3	41
7.5.13	119	8.6.16–31	41
7.5.7–12	126	8.8.11	116
7.6.14	118	8.8.30–1	126
7.27.3	205	8.8.31	119
7.27.20	200	8.8.32	119
7.8.20	16, 64, 102	8.8.32–34	126
7.10.1	199	8.8.32–37	129
7.10.1–3	194, 198	8.8.29–30	129
7.11.12–18	194	8.8.31	129
7.11.15–16	199	8.9.5	156
7.11.16	194	8.9.21	72
7.12.3	199	8.11.8	41
7.12.3–5	190	8.12.17	16
7.12.4	188	8.13.4	126
7.12.9–10	190	8.13.8	156
7.12.16	41	8.14.1–44	156
7.13.19	40	8.14.11	129
7.13.21	187	8.14.14	156

Wars (cont.)

8.14.22	156
8.14.31	129
8.14.44	42
8.15.25	41
8.19.2	42
8.20.9	41
8.20.48	42
8.20.49	42
8.20.56	42
8.23.16	103
8.23.30	119, 129
8.23.32	129
8.23.34	129
8.23.35	119
8.25.14	42
8.26.5–6	188
8.26.10	199, 204
8.26.10–13	189
8.27.2	59
8.28.8	129
8.29.4	41
8.29.13	129
8.29.15	119
8.29.22	119
8.29.22–28	18, 129
8.29.23	126
8.31.1	119
8.31.3	17
8.31.5	119, 126, 129
8.31.8	16
8.32.2	16
8.32.4	72
8.32.5	129
8.32.9	129
8.32.32	41
8.32.34	12, 41, 119
8.33.10	117
8.35.18	59
8.35.19	119, 126
8.35.23	119

PSI

3.196	69
8.953	199
8.956	199

PUAES

2.171	170
3.18	161, 170

RMR

1	72
34	51
63	49

Rufinus, *Against Jerome*

2.36	51

SB

5.8028	63, 67, 175, 176
18.13127	175, 176
18.13321	63
18.13884	68, 69
20.14704	63
22.15801	63

SEG

9.356	81, 83, 175, 177, 203
9.356.1	83
9.356.5	81
9.356.7	49, 73, 81
9.356.14	81
9.356.26	62
31.1554	36, 62, 81, 83, 166
31.1554, 3	5
31.1554, 19	5
31.1554, 45	62
35.1360	166
45.850	109
45.856	115
51.921	109

Stud. Pal.

20.139	202

Suda

Λ, 549	143
Κ, 630, 1	66
Κ, 630, 2–4	66
Π, 2479	143

Theodoret, *Ecclesiastical History*

2.11	66

Theophanes

AM 6074	251

Theophylact Simocatta, *Historiae*

1.15.2	116
2.16.6	67
2.6.9	60, 67
3.10.1	67
3.11.7	67
3.12.4	203

4.2.9	67	Vegetius		
8.9.3	67	1.2	196	
Thucydides		1.7	196	
1.10.4	66	1.8	77	
1.22.1	33	2.18	50	
2.13	209	2.5	197	
2.14	209	3. Pr. 8	179	
2.34–46	209			
2.47.1–2.55.1	209	Xenophon		
2.65	209	*Anabasis*		
2.79.6	71	1.2.25	71	
3.87.3	71	1.8.8	71	
4.43.4	71	2.2.14	71	
5.67.1	71	3.4.22	71	
6.26.1	65	*Cyropaedia*		
6.26.2	66	2.2.10	115	
6.31.3	65, 66	7.5.84	115	
6.43	65	8.3.6	115	
6.43.1	66	*Hellenica*		
7.16.2	66	2.4.9	65	
7.20.2	66	*Memorabilia*		
8.24.3	66	3.4.1	67	
TM				
63877	70	Zachariah (Pseudo), *Ecclesiastical History*		
		7.4.g	155	
		7.5.a	155	

General Index

This index does not include references to items in the appendix.

Abandanes   210, 211
Ad Decimum, Battle of   116, 135, 137
Aelian   66
Aeschmanus   19, 22
Aetius   74
Africa   6, 17, 33, 34, 71, 73, 96, 99–104, 114, 142, 163–166, 176, 204
Agathias   6, 7, 50, 67, 72, 73, 75–76, 116, 213, 227
Aigan   13, 28, 53, 54, 55, 56, 104, 107
Aigisthus   34
Al-Hadid   171
al-Harith   40
al-Mundhir   42, 158
al-Quweira   172, 173
Alae (specific)
    Ala I Hamiorum Syrorum Sagitariorum   123,
    Ala I Pannoniorum et Gallorum   121–122
    Ala I Thracum Veteranorum sagittariorum   123, 146
    Ala Augusta Ituraeorum sagittariorum   123
    Ala Augusta Parthorum et Araborum Sagittaria   123
    Ala Nona Miliaria   146
    Ala Prima Nova Diocletiana   148
    Ala Prima Valentiana   146
    Ala Secunda Constantiana   146
    Ala Secunda Felix Valentiniana   146
    Ala Secunda Miliarensis   146
    Ala Sexta Hispanorum   146
    Ala Ulpia Contariorum   122
Alae (late antiquity)   142, 147, 169
Alamanni   49, 122
Alani   59, 74
Althias   13, 23, 111, 112, 114, 127
Amida   34, 41, 58, 75, 110, 122, 124, 154, 155, 175, 181, 227
Ammaedara   101
Ammianus Marcellinus   4, 34, 42, 49, 58, 122, 124, 227

Anastasius (and edicts)   5, 49, 50, 60, 61, 62, 73, 76, 80, 83, 97, 113, 160, 165, 166, 170, 175, 176, 196, 203, 213, 227
Andreas   14, 15
Anglon, Battle of   212
Anio   37
Ansilas   18, 19, 21, 129
Antae   93, 137, 138, 244
Antaiopolis   63
Antinoopolis   68, 70
Antioch   126, 156, 157, 178, 212
Antonina   36, 84, 145, 188
Antoninus Pius   122
Anush-Zad   211
Anzalas   21, 130
Aphrodito   7, 60, 195
Apokrisarios   46, 68, 69, 70
Aqaba   172
Aquilinus   21, 37, 118
Arab   27, 28, 30, 43, 123, 169, 180
Arabia   142, 143, 146, 168, 169, 173
Arborychi   15, 243
Archaeopolis   156
Archer   95, 109, 111, 117–131, 147, 201, 226
Areobindus   13, 23, 155, 242
Argek   22, 156
Arians   91, 102, 113
Aristophanes   66
Aristus   46
Arithmos   58, 59, 60, 61–64, 67, 68, 69, 70, 73, 77, 80, 81, 82, 83, 122, 167, 176, 192
Armeni (unit)   98
Armenian   23, 24, 25, 27, 30, 40, 43, 86, 87, 93, 107, 155, 200
Armenia   33, 103, 108, 111, 146, 150, 151, 205, 211
Artabanes   21, 88, 250
Artabanes 2, 13, 28, 103, 132
Artemis-in-Tauris   41
Arzes   22, 37
Ascan   28, 53, 54, 55, 104
Asia   152, 173

GENERAL INDEX 293

Asia Minor 186, 200
Athenodorus 21
Augustalis 83, 191
Augustus 121, 191, 221
Aumetra 148, 153
Aurelius Asclepiades 142, 171
Auxilia Palatina 58, 104, 105, 106
Auximum 34
Avars 130

Babas 23, 132, 156
Badias 101
Bagai 101
Bainobaudes 149
Balas 13, 28
Balkans 60, 97, 110, 145, 151, 154, 161, 178, 186, 198, 199, 200, 204
Barbarization 109, 131, 226
Barbation 21
Barbatus 13, 23, 107, 112
Baresmanas 55, 56
Basil 66, 83
Beersheba 62, 169, 170, 177
Belisarius 3, 6, 7, 8, 13, 14, 15, 19, 20, 23, 31, 32, 33, 34, 35, 36, 37, 38, 39, 40, 42, 43, 44, 45, 47, 53, 54, 60, 73, 75, 82, 87, 88, 98, 101, 104, 107, 110, 111, 112, 116, 117, 118, 126, 127, 128, 132, 138, 145, 158, 165, 176, 178, 187, 188, 189, 194, 198, 202, 204, 207, 210, 211, 212, 213, 229
Beroea 50, 155
Beros 28, 132, 160
Bessas 28, 103, 112, 128, 132, 155
Black Sea 41
Blemmyes 162
Bonus 23, 97
Boriades 13, 21
Bucellarii 10, 13, 19, 43, 54, 61, 71, 107, 108, 115, 116, 131, 186, 189, 204, 206, 207, 208, 222, 226
Bulgar 46, 47
Bulgaria 121
Buraido 100
Burcentius 12, 18, 20
Busta Gallorum, Battle of 117, 119, 129, 136, 139, 204
Buzes 13, 23, 53, 54, 55, 76, 103, 104, 132, 155, 156, 157, 158

Byzacium 15, 87

Caesarea (Cappadocia) 148, 152
Caesarea (Israel/Palestine) 176
Calama 101
Caligati milites 221
Caligula 123
Callinicum, Battle of 54, 56, 71, 75, 102, 105, 107, 118, 119, 126, 135, 137, 200, 213
Camel 161, 162, 175
Campidoctor 5
Candac 109
Cappadocia 34, 148, 152, 168, 176
Caria 97
Carthage 15, 40, 101, 135, 137, 197, 229
Casilinum, Battle of 6, 50, 75, 213
Cassiodorus 97
Cassius Dio 66
Castra Praetorii Mobeni 142, 143
Castrum Moenoenum 143
Catalaunian Plains, Battle of 73, 74
Cataphract 49, 121, 122, 124
Cavalry 6, 13, 17, 35, 53, 54, 56, 61, 65, 96, 105, 112, 117, 118, 119, 120, 121, 122, 123, 125, 129, 130, 131, 137, 138, 139, 142, 147, 164, 176, 189, 198, 200, 201, 212, 213, 226
Cenomani 212
China 120
Chorsomantis 128
Chorsomanus 19
Chronicle of Seert 211
Chronicon Paschale 47
Circesium 60, 67, 146, 147, 148, 178
Citharizon 145, 146, 148, 151, 160, 181
Clibanarius 63, 121, 122, 157
Coccas 21
Codex Justinianus 48, 55, 62, 63, 84, 96, 97, 108, 147, 175, 180, 187, 192, 193, 205, 221
Codex Theodosianus 143
Cohortes
  Cohors I Hispanorum Veterana 49
  Cohors III Dalmatae Equitata 159
  Cohors Milliaria Germanorum 151
  Cohors Octava Voluntaria 146
  Cohors Prima Miliaria Thracum 146
  Cohors Prima Thracum 146
  Cohors Tertia Alpinorum 146
  Cohors Tertia Felix Arabum 146, 147
  Cohors Tertia Asturum 142, 146

Comes
　Comes Africae   124, 142
　Comes Excubitorum   26, 27, 44
　Comes Foederatum   109, 114
　Comes Orientis   167
　Comes Pontica Shore   198
　Comes Tingitanae   142
Comitatenses   10, 16, 17, 59, 60, 71, 84, 95, 96, 97, 98, 99, 100, 101, 102, 103, 104, 105, 106, 107, 108, 109, 110, 111, 114, 115, 131, 141, 150, 162, 163, 164, 165, 166, 179, 180, 186, 193, 203, 205, 206, 225, 229
Comitatus   97
Conon   13, 23, 132
Conscription (recruitment)   66, 84, 194, 195, 208, 225
Constantianus 2   198, 200
Constantinople   16, 33, 46, 55, 60, 98, 115, 147, 148, 151, 152, 189, 198, 201, 203, 209, 210, 211, 212, 213, 223
Constantius II   23, 103, 132, 198, 200
Contus   122
Corippus   6, 107, 108
Corruption   99, 165, 186, 209, 213, 214, 218, 220, 222
Cornuti   49
Count Marcellinus   46, 47, 73, 75
Cululis   100
Cuneus   97
Cutilas   21
Cutzes   157, 158
Cyclades   97
Cyprian   111, 112
Cyprus   97
Cyrenaica   49, 62, 73, 81, 83, 175, 176
Cyril   13, 24, 53, 55, 104, 107, 111, 112, 114
Cyrillus   53, 104, 184

Dabusis   101, 148, 153
Daci   98, 201, 202
Dacia/Dacian   121, 159
Dalmatia   15
Danube   49, 151, 152, 198, 223
Dara   15, 86, 118, 126, 147, 150, 153, 155, 156, 160, 174, 175, 177
Dara, Battle of   14, 52, 53, 54, 56, 75, 102, 104, 105, 106, 119, 126, 155, 213
Dardania   49
Deir el-Kahf   171, 172

Demographics   10, 186, 208, 209, 210, 212, 214, 226
Dexippus   66
Dialogue on Political Science (anonymous)   35, 117
Dinawari   211
Diogenes   13, 21, 37, 116, 118
Diplomas (Roman Military)   122
Dody   108, 109
Dorotheus   13, 24, 53, 55, 104, 107, 111, 114, 133
Draconarius   5, 6
Dura Europos   52, 72
Dux   5, 18, 23, 24, 26, 27, 29, 30, 162, 170, 191, 216
　Dux Arabia   146
　Dux Foenicis   159
　Dux Libyae   203
　Dux Mesopotamiae   148, 149
　Dux Moesiae   97
　Dux Oshorene   148
　Dux Phoenice libanensis   53, 158, 159
　Dux Syriae   149
　Dux Thebaidos   83

Edessa   126, 156, 181, 236
Egypt   7, 19, 26, 48, 60, 62, 97, 100, 106, 122, 161, 162, 163, 164, 167, 173, 175, 176, 177, 190, 193, 195, 196, 199, 201, 202, 203, 214, 220
Einsiedlensis   38
El-Lejjūn   161, 169, 171, 173
El-Quweira   172, 173
Elephantine   83, 162, 190, 191
Emalac   115, 116
En-Boqeq   163, 170, 173
Ennes   24, 51
Equites   143, 147, 169
　Equites Dalmatae Illyriciani   142, 146, 159
　Equites Mauri Illyriciani   142, 146, 149
　Equites Mauri Scutarii   201, 202
　Equites Promoti Illyriciani   142, 146
　Equites Promoti Indigenae   146
　Equites Sagittarii Cordueni   124,
　Equites Sagittarii Indigenae   142, 146, 147, 148
　Equites Sagittarii Parthi   124
　Equites Scutarii Illyriciani   146
　Illyriciani   142
　Indigenae   142

GENERAL INDEX

Estotzas 108, 109
Etruscans 212
Eurasia 95, 120, 121, 130, 131, 226
Euripides 41
Eusebius 109, 169
Evagrius 40, 64, 114, 195, 203, 209
Exercitus 73, 97

Fabricae 156, 157
Felices Perso-Armenii 201, 202
Felices Theodosiani 98
Field Army
   African 71, 96, 98, 99, 100, 103, 131
   Armenian 103, 205
   Eastern 61, 103, 104, 105, 106, 108, 211
   Illyrian 61, 103, 105, 204
   Thracian 61, 103, 204
Flavius Patermouthis 7, 50, 83, 190, 191, 192, 197
Flavius Ziper 100
Foederati 10, 13, 14, 17, 54, 61, 71, 74, 87, 91, 95, 98, 102, 107, 108, 109, 110, 111, 112, 113, 114, 115, 131, 162, 180, 186, 189, 198, 200, 206, 214, 225

Gaeana 101, 148, 153
Gaiseric 71
Gallipoli 148
Gaul 49, 213
Gelimer 71, 187
George 44
George 2, 21
Germanus 01, 24, 40, 53, 133
Germanus 04, 40, 55, 59, 104, 117, 188, 189, 197, 207, 208, 222
Gezon 20
Ghassanid 27, 28, 169, 173, 178
Girgis 101
Goths 16, 17, 19, 28, 33, 35, 37, 38, 39, 74, 101, 102, 103, 109, 110, 111, 113, 127, 128, 129, 131, 188, 189, 198, 199, 203, 204
Gudilas 21

Hagia Sophia 1, 47, 147
Halabiye 149
Hamians 123
Hannibal 212
Hemerium 147, 150

Hephaestion 83
Hephthalites 102
Heraclius 47
Herdotus 31, 115
Hermogenes 53, 54, 104, 105
Hermopolis 73, 105, 106, 196
Heruls 13, 15, 17, 28, 29, 30, 53, 54, 55, 90, 92, 93, 104, 105, 106, 110, 111, 112, 113, 116, 119, 156, 160, 189, 199, 200
Hesychius 66
Hierocles 100, 163
Hippikos 65
Hippo Regius 100, 163
Hippotoxotai, Horse Archery 95, 120, 123, 124, 125, 126, 127, 128, 129, 130
Homer 6, 125
Honorius 38
Hoplites 118
Horobam (Aborrhas River) 148
Humayma 172
Huns 13, 29, 54, 55, 56, 90, 91, 107, 112, 128, 130, 131, 137, 156, 188, 189, 190, 194, 198, 199
Hunt's Pridianum 49, 51
Hypatius 41, 133, 155

Iaudas 127
Iberians 29, 112
Illyricum 15, 47, 103, 105, 132, 133, 134, 152
Illyrians 23, 26, 46, 61, 89, 93, 110, 139, 194, 198, 200, 204
Infantry 5, 6, 13, 17, 35, 54, 58, 59, 61, 65, 76, 78, 86, 87, 88, 89, 91, 93, 95, 104, 105, 112, 113, 117, 118, 119, 120, 121, 129, 131, 135, 136, 137, 142, 147, 164, 176, 192, 201, 212, 213, 2226, 229
Innocentius 24, 49, 88, 111, 112, 113
Isaurians 18, 24, 26, 27, 90, 91, 92, 105, 107, 112, 199, 200, 204
Israel 7, 60, 62, 173, 176
Italy 10, 33, 34, 40, 44, 50, 55, 96, 98, 101, 102, 103, 112, 114, 120, 129, 130, 178, 187, 188, 189, 190, 194, 198, 200, 201, 202, 204, 207, 210, 211, 212, 228
Ituraeans 123

John the Armenian 13, 116
John Lydus 76, 77, 78, 79, 83, 84

John 14 of Vitalian   103, 133
Jordan   7, 62, 80, 81, 142, 169, 170, 172, 173, 227
Jordanes   73, 74, 109, 227
Josephus   83
Joshua (Pseudo) Stylites   6, 155, 159, 199
Julian   66, 122, 124

Kalkriese   52
Katalogos   5, 10, 58, 59, 60, 64, 65, 66, 67, 68, 69, 70, 71, 72, 73, 77, 78, 79, 80, 82, 83, 84, 85, 86, 87, 88, 89, 95, 106, 107, 11, 118, 135, 197, 225
Kavadh   42, 154, 161, 189
Khirbet el-Fityan   171, 172
Khirbet el-Khalde   172
Khirbet er-Zona   171, 172
Khusro   110, 126, 160, 161, 175, 178, 210, 211, 212
Koutilas   37
Kutrigur   44

Laipso   49
Lanciarii   76
Laribus   101
Laterculus   79
Lazi   41, 89, 139, 156
Lazica   156
Lebanon, Phoenice Libanensis   15, 53, 155, 157, 158, 159, 203
Legions   5, 15, 35, 59, 60, 62, 66, 71, 74, 76, 77, 82, 96, 97, 98, 106, 146, 147, 149, 169, 172, 180, 202, 212, 227
   Legio I Illyricorum   149
   Legio IV Parthica   60, 148
   Legio V Macedonica   63, 202
   Legio XII Fulminata   149
   Legio XVI Flavia Firma   149
   Legiones Comitatenses   96, 97, 104, 105, 106, 180, 202
   Legion of Memphis   63
   Legion (Palatine)   97, 105
   Legion of Philae   63
   Legio Prima Adiutrix   76
   Legio Pseudocomitatenses   104, 105, 106
   Legio Quartae Martiae   146
Legion (Scythian)   202
Legion of Syene   63
Legio Tertiae Cyrenaicae   146
Leontoclibanarii/Leontoklibanarii   63, 70, 122

Lepcis Magna   101
Levant   60, 123
Libanius   66, 83
Liber Pontificalis   36
Libya   15, 80, 86, 97, 101, 152, 184, 201, 203
Libyes Iustiniani   201, 202, 203
Limitanei   10, 12, 13, 15, 17, 60, 62, 70, 75, 81, 96, 98, 99, 100, 101, 106, 108, 109, 114, 131, 141–185, 186, 192, 193, 204, 205, 206, 226, 228, 229
Lochos   59, 66, 118
Logothetes   85, 214, 218, 219
Lucian   43

Macedoni   201, 202
Madaba Map   169
Magister   18, 103, 193
   Magister Militum   53, 78, 80, 83, 103, 132–134
   Magister Militum per Africam   103
   Magister Militum per Armeniam   103, 108, 177, 178, 205
   Magister Militum per Illyricum   103
   Magister Officiorum   53, 155, 166
   Magister Militum per Orientem   53, 83, 103, 104, 205
   Magister Militum per Thracias   103
   Magister Militum praesantalis   58, 98, 202
   Magister Militum vacans   103
Malalas, John   1, 40, 46, 47, 48, 56, 61, 73, 75, 108, 109, 159, 163, 167, 198, 199, 201, 205
Marcellus (a few Marcelli)   13, 26, 44, 53, 55, 104, 111, 112, 114, 133
Marriage   7, 214, 215, 216, 217, 218, 220, 221
Martin   13, 26, 111, 112, 114, 156, 160, 198, 211
Martinianus   1, 20
Martyropolis   46, 48, 146, 155, 211
Mascula   100
Massagetae   19, 27, 28, 29, 30, 53, 90, 104, 105, 106, 111, 112, 203
Matricium/Matrix   50, 80, 83, 84, 196, 197, 225
Mauretania   123
Maurice, *Strategikon*   5, 6, 35, 50, 60, 61, 72, 105, 114, 117, 129, 130, 197, 211
Maximinus   21, 117, 142, 208
Meligedius   20
Melitene   59, 71, 148, 149, 150, 155

GENERAL INDEX

Menander Protector   65, 67, 72
Menochiae   142, 143
Mesopotamia   8, 15, 86, 148, 168, 175, 178
Milev   101
Mindes   20
Moesia   97, 121
Mohile   142
Molatzes   157, 159
Mons Lactarius   71
Moors   28, 45, 63, 70, 91, 107, 110, 112, 128, 198, 199, 220
Mt. Papua   127
Mundila   22, 37
Mundo   14

Naples   34, 36, 135, 136
Narses   7, 17, 19, 75, 89, 116, 129, 130, 134, 188, 189, 200, 204, 213
Negev   62
Neocaesarea   148, 149
Nessana   48, 60, 62, 163, 170, 175, 176, 177
Nicetas   104
North Africa   6, 33, 53, 73, 96, 98, 100, 124, 141, 142, 152, 163, 164, 166, 175, 176, 195, 219
Notitia Dignitatum   5, 6, 13, 58, 60, 61, 63, 97, 103, 104, 105, 122, 124, 142, 143, 146, 148, 149, 150, 151, 154, 157, 159, 160, 168, 169, 170, 192, 202
Novels of Justinian   60, 62, 64, 68, 97, 160, 166, 169, 176, 214, 215, 221
Numerus   9, 59, 60, 61, 63, 100, 163, 170
  Numerus bis Electorum   100, 163
  Numerus Hipponis Regii   100, 163
  Numidae Justiniani/Iustiniani   163
  Numerus Primi Felices Iustiniani   100, 163
Numidia   63, 67, 73, 87, 101, 153, 170

Obba   101
Odonachos   156
Oea   101, 105
Optiones   6, 12, 25, 68, 87, 168, 214
Orestes   33
Ortaias   45
Osimo   34, 136, 138
Ostia   34, 84

Palatini   98
Palermo   127
Palestina Secunda   162
Palestine   7, 15, 27, 142, 161, 162, 169, 173, 174, 176
Palmyra   53, 149, 159, 167, 174
Pamphylia   97
Pannonia   122, 123
Pappus   13, 26, 107, 112
Paraetonitae Iustiniani   203
Parthia, Parthians   60, 123
Paternus (*Tactics*)   27
Patricius   41, 155, 167
Paul (Pauls)   19, 21, 26, 129, 134, 159
Paul of Cilicia   44
Peloponnese   148
Peranius   29, 37, 112, 134, 156
Perge   5, 48, 60, 62, 80, 81, 82, 83, 97, 105, 106, 164, 165
Persarmenia   28, 29, 30, 211
Petra   126, 136, 138, 156, 170
Pezikos   65, 118
Phalanx   75, 77, 118, 119, 129, 135, 136
Pharas   13, 29, 53, 54, 55, 56, 104, 111, 119
Pheison   145, 148, 151
Philae   63
Philemouth   29, 134, 160
Phyle   66
Plague   10, 51, 179, 186, 209, 210, 211, 212, 213, 214, 215, 218, 222, 229
Polybius   212
Portugal   52
Praepositus limitis Zabensis   142
Praesantal (army, general)   58, 62, 132, 133, 134, 202, 204, 205
Pridiana   49, 51
Primicerius   5, 81, 192
Primi Felices Iustiniani   100, 163
Primi Theodosiani   6, 98
Probatoria   48, 50, 83, 161, 190, 192, 193
Pseudocomitatenses   96, 97, 104, 105, 106
Psidia   176

Qasr Bshir   142, 143, 171, 172
Qasr el-Azraq   171, 172
Qasr el-Hallabat   5, 62, 80, 81, 161, 166, 169, 170, 171, 173, 227

Qasr eth-Thuraiya   171, 172
Quartoparthoi   50, 60, 67

Raid   37, 48, 138, 174, 179, 194
Reges (Regii)   58, 117
Resafa/Sergiopolis   149
Rhabdios   147
Rhinocrura   62
River Hippis, Battle of   128, 136, 139
Rome
    Asinarian Gate   18
    Pinciana Gate   36, 37, 51, 128
    Salarian Gate   36, 37
Rufinus (Rufinues)   13, 26, 29 107, 112, 134
Rufinus (author)   51
Rujm es-Sadaqa   171
Rusguniae   100
Rusticus   116

Sabines   212
Sailors   90
Salones   15
Sangiban   74
Sarmatians   74, 121, 123
Sarmatization   121
Sarsinates   212
Scalae Veteres   71, 135, 137
Schamalinichon   148, 151
Scholae   12, 59, 71, 168
Scholares (Scholarii)   48, 98, 196
Scriniarii   81
Scrinium Laterculi (sacred bureau of the register for archiving)   48, 49
Scythae Iustiniani   201, 202
Scythia/Scythians   63, 97, 202, 203
Sea of Azov   41
Septum   148, 153
Severus Alexander   121
Sextodalmaticae/Sexto Dalmatae   63
Shahnameh   211
Shield Bearer (hypaspistes)   14, 16, 17, 19, 20, 21, 22, 42, 43, 56, 90, 91, 92, 93, 107, 112, 115, 116, 118, 190, 207, 223, 225, 227
Siccca Veneria   101
Sicily   34, 135, 137
Signiferi   76
Simmas   29, 53, 54, 55, 101
Sinai (Mt.)   148, 152, 174

Sinnion   13, 29, 44
Sisilisson   148, 151, 182
Sittas   30, 40, 134, 205
Slavs   105, 198, 199
Solomon   6, 7, 13, 27, 44, 102, 111, 114, 134, 204
Spatharius   116
Spearman (doryphoros)   19, 21, 22, 37, 116, 117, 197, 207
Stephanes   115
Steppes   37, 120, 121, 123, 124, 128, 130
Stotzas   22, 73, 91, 102, 108, 109, 127
Strasbourg, Battle of   49, 122, 124, 227
Strata Diocletiana   40, 148, 169
Stratiwtai (Soldiers – Greek)   66, 95, 98, 107, 110, 115
Stratiwtikos   65, 67, 68, 73, 83
Suda   7, 66, 143
Sunicas   30, 53, 54, 55, 56, 75, 104
Sura   126, 147, 149, 155
Syene   50, 63, 195
Symmachoi   13, 54, 61, 74, 95, 108, 114, 199
Synecdemus of Hierocles   100
Syracuse   34
Syria, Syrians   24, 50, 123, 149, 158, 163, 168, 172, 173, 174, 181, 199, 204

Tagma   61, 63, 72, 75, 77
Tapacae   101
Tertiodalmatae/Tertio Dalmatae   159
Thamugadi   101
Thannourioi   147, 148, 174
    Big Thannourios   148
    Thannurin   148
Thebaid   67, 83, 176, 191, 192, 196
Theodohad   40
Theodora   1, 98, 144, 145, 220
Theodoret   66
Theodosiopolis   148, 151, 160
Theophanes   47, 114, 196, 203
Theophylact Simocatta   5, 44, 49, 60, 67, 72, 116, 203, 227
Thermopylae   151, 152, 153
Theudimund   21
Thrace   15, 25, 44, 46, 88, 89, 112, 156, 157, 176, 188, 189, 194, 198, 200, 204, 223
Thracians   92, 110, 198, 200
Thucydides   4, 31, 33, 65, 66, 71, 209
Tiberius II   113, 163, 203

GENERAL INDEX

Tigisi 101
Tirones 77
Titlus 79
Totila 14, 16, 18, 103, 116, 188, 204
Towton, Battle of 52
Trajan (emperor) 65, 66, 89, 121
Trajan (spearman) 37, 118
Trajan's Column 121
Transtigritani 63
Tribunus (tribune) 142, 216
Tricamarum, Battle of 71, 119, 135, 137
Tzani 90, 93, 199, 200
Tzanica 151
Tzanzacon 148, 151

Udruh 171, 172
Uliaris 13, 22, 116
Ulifus 22, 116
Umm el-Jimal 62, 161, 170, 171, 173
Upper Zohar 163, 170, 173
Ursicinus 27, 58

Valens 124
Valerian 13, 27, 103, 111, 112, 114, 116, 134, 198
Vandals 16, 33, 34, 110, 187, 194, 198

Vegetius 35, 50, 77, 179, 196
Veii 76
Veneti 212
Vexillation 63, 76, 96, 97, 106, 196, 202
Vexillatio Comitatenses 96, 97, 104, 105, 106
Via Nova Traiana 169
Vimisdeon 148
Visby 52
Visigoths 74
Vittigis 18, 127, 128
Volunteers (recruitment) 66, 189, 194, 195, 198

Wadi Sirhan 170, 172
War of the Roses 52
Wills (soldiers') 217
Wives (military) 215, 216, 217, 220, 221, 222

Xenophon 4, 8, 9, 66, 71, 115, 230

Zachariah (Pseudo) 155, 159
Zarter 19, 22
Zenobia 147 149, 160
Zeugma 147, 149

Printed in the United States
by Baker & Taylor Publisher Services